RESEARCH IN COUNSELLING AND PSYCHOTHERAPY

Research in Counselling and Psychotherapy

Practical Applications

Edited by
WINDY DRYDEN

SAGE Publications
London • Thousand Oaks • New Delhi

First published 1996

SAGE Publications Ltd
6 Bonhill Street
London EC2A 4PU

SAGE Publications Inc
2455 Teller Road
Thousand Oaks, California 91320

SAGE Publications India Pvt Ltd
32, M-Block Market
Greater Kailash – I
New Delhi 110 048

British Library Cataloguing in Publication data

A catalogue record for this book is available from the British Library.

ISBN 0 8039 7840-5
ISBN 0 8039 7841-3 (pbk)

Library of Congress catalog record available

Typeset by Mayhew Typesetting, Rhayader, Powys
Printed in Great Britain by The Cromwell Press Ltd,
Broughton Gifford, Melksham, Wiltshire

Contents

List of Contributors

Windy Dryden is Professor of Counselling at Goldsmiths College, University of London. He has authored or edited over ninety books including *Facilitating Client Change in Rational Emotive Behaviour Therapy* (Whurr Publications, 1995) and *Daring to be Myself: A Case of Rational-Emotive Therapy*, written with Joseph Yankura (Open University Press, 1992). In addition, he edits 12 book series in the area of counselling and psychotherapy, including the *Brief Therapy and Counselling* series (Wiley) and *Developing Counselling* (Sage Publications). His major interests are in rational emotive behaviour therapy, eclecticism and integration in psychotherapy and, increasingly, writing short, accessible self-help books for the general public.

Michael Barkham, PhD, trained as a clinical psychologist and worked for 10 years at the Medical Research Council/Economic and Social Research Council (MRC/ESRC) Social and Applied Psychology Unit at the University of Sheffield and was involved in a series of psychotherapy studies investigating the processes and outcomes of time-limited therapies. In 1995 he took up post as Senior Lecturer in Clinical Psychology and Deputy Director of the Psychological Therapies Research Centre at the University of Leeds. He was the 1991 recipient of the May Davidson Award (Division of Clinical Psychology, BPS) and is currently UK Vice-President of the Society for Psychotherapy Research.

Donald H. Baucom, PhD, is a distinguished professor and Director of Clinical Psychology at the University of North Carolina. He has conducted a number of controlled treatment outcome studies validating the effectiveness of behavioral marital therapy, cognitive restructuring, and emotional expressiveness with maritally distressed couples. In recent years, he has worked in collaboration with Norman Epstein to study cognitive processes in couples, with a primary emphasis on couples' standards and attributions. Baucom and Epstein have co-authored *Cognitive Behavioral Marital Therapy*. In addition to his research efforts, he maintains an active clinical practice, and he has won several awards for excellence in undergraduate teaching.

Larry E. Beutler, PhD, is Professor and Director of the Counseling/Clinical/School Psychology Program at the University of California, Santa Barbara. He obtained his PhD from the University of Nebraska in 1970, and subsequently served on the faculties of Duke University Medical

School, Stephen F. Austin State University, Baylor College of Medicine and the University of Arizona. Dr Beutler is a diplomate of the American Board of Professional Psychology (ABPP) and a past international President of the Society for Psychotherapy Research (SPR). He is currently the Editor of the *Journal of Consulting and Clinical Psychology*. He is a Fellow of the American Psychological Association, the American Psychological Society and the International Fellowship of Eclectic Psychotherapists. He is the author of approximately two hundred scientific papers and chapters, and is the author, editor or co-author of 10 books on psychotherapy and psychopathology.

Frank W. Bond recently received his PhD in psychology from Goldsmiths College, University of London. His supervisor was Windy Dryden, with whom he continues to conduct research on cognitive-behavioural theories of psychopathology. Currently, Dr Bond is receiving further clinical training at the Cognitive-Behavioural Psychotherapy Unit, University College London School of Medicine.

Gillian Butler, PhD, is a consultant clinical psychologist working in Oxford. She has alternated working within the National Health Service and doing research in Oxford University's Department of Psychiatry on the development and evaluation of psychological treatments for more complex and persistent anxiety disorders. She is interested in making psychological ideas and research findings readily accessible, and has written booklets in which psychological treatments are explained in a simple and practical manner. Together with Tony Hope, she has also written *Manage Your Mind: The Mental Fitness Guide*, a book for the general public which explains a wide range of psychological ideas in practical and usable terms.

Norman Epstein is a Professor of Family Studies at the University of Maryland, in College Park, Maryland. He received his PhD in clinical psychology from the University of California at Los Angeles. He is a Fellow in the divisions of family psychology and psychotherapy of the American Psychological Association, as well as a clinical member of the American Association for Marriage and Family Therapy. In addition to his teaching, research and clinical training activities at the University of Maryland, he has a part-time private practice with individuals and couples. For over twenty years, his research, clinical work and publications have focused on the assessment and treatment of relationship problems, depression and anxiety.

Susan D. Field, PhD, read psychology at Southampton University and then carried out her doctoral research on the assimilation model at the Medical Research Council/Economic and Social Research Council (MRC/ESRC) Social and Applied Psychology Unit at the University of Sheffield. She is currently undertaking training in clinical psychology (D.Clin.Psy.) at the University of Leeds.

Marvin R. Goldfried is Professor of Psychology and Psychiatry at the State University of New York at Stony Brook. In addition to his teaching, clinical supervision and research, he maintains a limited practice of psychotherapy in New York City. He is a diplomate in clinical psychology, editorial board member of professional journals and author of several books. Dr Goldfried is co-founder of the Society for the Exploration of Psychotherapy Integration.

Rhonda Goldman, MA, is completing her PhD in clinical psychology at York University, Toronto. She is presently a clinical psychology intern at the Clarke Institute of Psychiatry in Toronto. Her dissertation research focuses on processes of change in psychotherapy.

Leslie S. Greenberg is Professor of Psychology at York University, Toronto, and Director of the Psychotherapy Research Centre. He is Past President of the Society for Psychotherapy Research. He is in private practice in couples and individual therapy in Toronto and trains therapists in emotionally focused approaches to treatment. He has written a number of books with colleagues on psychotherapy research and emotion in psychotherapy, the most recent of which is *Facilitating Emotional Change*, (Guilford, 1993) with L. Rice and R. Elliott. Books in press include *Working with Emotion* and two edited texts on the therapeutic alliance and emotion in marriage and marital therapy. He has published extensively on research on individual and couples therapy and is on the editorial board of a number of journals. He is currently conducting an NIMH-funded research project on the experiential change process in depression.

Gillian E. Hardy trained as a clinical and occupational psychologist and has worked both in the National Health Service and at the Medical Research Council/Economic and Social Research Council (MRC/ESRC) Social and Applied Psychology Unit at the University of Sheffield. Her research involvement has been investigating the processes and outcomes of time-limited psychotherapies. She is now at the University of Leeds.

Martin Heesacker, PhD, is Professor of Psychology at the University of Florida and a licensed psychologist. Having served on the psychology faculties of Ohio State University and Southern Illinois University, he received his doctorate from the University of Missouri in 1983. Author of nearly fifty journal articles and book chapters, he was a Fulbright Scholar, Eli Lilly Foundation Teaching Fellow, University of Florida Teaching Award recipient, recipient of the Early Career Award from the Counseling Psychology Division of the American Psychological Association (APA) and a Fellow of the APA.

Alvin R. Mahrer, PhD, is Professor at the School of Psychology, University of Ottawa. A Fellow of the American Psychological Association and former President of one of its divisions, he is one of 12 psychotherapists included in the APA's Psychotherapy Videotape Series. He is author of 11 books and approximately two hundred chapters, articles and studies on psychotherapy, especially his experiential psychotherapy. As a working clinician and practitioner, he is involved in theorising, teaching, philosophising and researching, and was the recipient of the University of Ottawa Award for Excellence in Research in 1992. He wants to discover the secrets of psychotherapy, and become a fine therapist.

Shelley McMain, PhD, is a staff psychologist at the Addiction Research Foundation in Toronto. She conducts research on the processes of change in psychotherapy and is currently interested in studying psychotherapeutic processes with an opiate-dependent population.

Cristina Mejia-Millan is a doctoral student in the Counseling Psychology Program at the University of Florida. An honours baccalaureate graduate of the University of Florida, Ms Mejia-Millan was a member of Golden Key Honor Society, the honour society Phi Kappa Phi and Omicrom Delta Kappa Leadership Honorary. She serves as a Care Team Associate at the Alachua County, Florida Crisis Center. Her research interests include attitude change processes and their relationships to counselling psychology, as well as the interface of social psychology and counselling psychology more broadly.

Patrick J. Raue earned his BA from the Catholic University of America and his MA and PhD in clinical psychology from the State University of New York at Stony Brook. He is involved in clinical and research activities and has published in the area of the therapeutic alliance and psychotherapy integration.

William B. Stiles is a Professor in the Department of Psychology at Miami University in Oxford, Ohio. Since 1984, he has frequently visited the United Kingdom to collaborate with the Medical Research Council/ Economic and Social Research Council (MRC/ESRC) Social and Applied Psychology Unit at the University of Sheffield on various psychotherapy studies.

Shaké G. Toukmanian, PhD (University of Utah), is Associate Professor of Psychology and the past Director of Clinical Training at York University in Toronto. She has held academic positions at Bishop's and McGill Universities in Quebec. She is the co-editor with D.L. Rennie of *Psychotherapy Process Research: Paradigmatic and Narrative Approaches* (Sage Publications, 1992). A member of the York University Psychotherapy Research Centre, her present focus is on the application of relevant concepts and research findings in the cognitive sciences to the study of change processes in experiential psychotherapies.

Douglas A. Vakoch is a doctoral candidate in clinical psychology at the State University of New York at Stony Brook. He is trained primarily in cognitive-behavioural therapy, and his research focuses on therapists' perceptions of patients' interpersonal issues. He is especially interested in how these perceptions are influenced by therapists' epistemological style, theoretical orientation and level of experience. Prior to his clinical work, he received an MA in the history and philosophy of science from the University of Notre Dame for his studies in continental philosophies of psychology and psychoanalysis.

Rebecca E. Williams, MA, M.Ed, is currently completing her doctorate in clinical psychology in the Counseling/Clinical/School Psychology Program at the University of California, Santa Barbara. She received her BA from Williams College, her M.Ed. from Harvard University and her MA from the University of California, Santa Barbara. Ms Williams has published a number of articles and chapters in the areas of alcohol and drug abuse, childhood sexual abuse, integrative and eclectic psychotherapy, and bridging the gap between psychotherapy research and practice. Ms Williams is a psychology intern at the University of California, San Diego Department of Psychiatry and the La Jolla Veterans Administration.

Susan L. Wiser received a BA from the Pennsylvania State University, and an MA and PhD in clinical psychology from the State University of New York at Stony Brook. She left New York for the mountains of Montana, where she provided clinical services at the Montana State University Counseling Center and at the Crow Indian Reservation. She has taken a 'sabbatical' to travel the western United States and Asia, and then intends to settle in the mountains of the West and engage in clinical, teaching and research activities.

Heidi A. Zetzer, PhD, obtained a Master's Degree in counseling psychology from the Ohio State University in 1986 and a PhD in counseling psychology from the University of California, Santa Barbara, in 1990. She is currently a licensed psychologist and Project Coordinator of the Psychotherapy Research Project in the Graduate School of Education at UCSB. In addition, she is an adjunct faculty member of Antioch University, Santa Barbara. Research and clinical interests include: alcohol and drug abuse; child sexual abuse; eating disorders; psychology of women; and psychotherapy process and outcome.

Preface

The main purpose of this book is to help bridge the gap that currently exists between research and practice in counselling and psychotherapy. Many researchers are suspicious of the pronouncements of counselling and psychotherapy practitioners because these are not backed up by research, and practitioners tend to ignore research findings because they consider that these findings have little relevance for their clinical practice. While research articles often contain a section on 'implications for practice', these are frequently very brief and are too general to be practically applied.

Consequently, I invited a number of researchers to describe their research programmes and to spell out the practical applications of their findings. I urged contributors to be concise in their description of their research and expansive in their speculations concerning how their findings can inform the practice of counselling and psychotherapy. Virtually all contributors had difficulty with this task. In their first draft most of them spent more time describing their research than considering the practical applications of their findings. While their final drafts do reflect the brief that they were originally set, it seemed to me that addressing the basic question that I had set them did not come at all easily to the authors. Many admitted this in letters to me. This is not a deficiency in those whose work appears in these pages. Rather, it probably reflects a problem in the way that counsellors and psychotherapists are trained. If the research–practice divide is to be traversed, then research, skills training and supervised clinical practice need to be far more closely integrated on training courses than they are at present.

Having said all this, I want to thank my contributors for taking on such a challenging task and for shedding some light on the relevance that their research studies have for practitioners. While this light is still dimmer than I had hoped, it does point the way towards the integration of research and practice. The present book should be viewed against this backdrop.

Finally, please note that when case studies are referred to, all identifiable material has been changed and pseudonyms used to safeguard client anonymity.

Windy Dryden

Acknowledgement

I wish to thank Jean Male for her assistance in preparing this manuscript for publication.

1

The Assimilation Model: Theory, Research and Practical Guidelines

Michael Barkham, William B. Stiles, Gillian E. Hardy and Susan D. Field

Background

This chapter summarises a programme of research investigating an integrative theory of psychotherapeutic change that we call the *assimilation model* (Stiles et al., 1990). First, we describe the model. Then, we present research findings, largely by using clinical material. And finally, we suggest a range of practice implications for researchers, counsellors and psychotherapists. The work has been carried out mainly at two research centres: the Department of Psychology at Miami University, Ohio, USA (Stiles, Sloan, Meshot & Anderson, 1991); and the MRC/ESRC Social and Applied Psychology Unit at Sheffield University, UK (Shapiro et al., 1991). In 1995, this latter group moved to the Psychological Therapies Research Centre, University of Leeds, UK, where the work continues.

Theory

The assimilation model proposes that clients in successful psychotherapy follow a specific sequence in processing their problematic or painful experiences as these are assimilated into schemata during the therapeutic interaction. The main components of the model comprise (a) schema, (b) problematic experience and (c) the complementary processes of assimilation and accommodation. A schema is a familiar pattern of ideas or a way of thinking about something to which new experiences can become assimilated. It 'must apply to the client's personal experience and behavior; it cannot be a purely abstract construction' (Stiles et al., 1990, p. 412). A problematic experience is 'a perception, intention, impulse, attitude, wish, fantasy or idea that causes psychological discomfort when brought to awareness or put into action' (Stiles et al., 1990, p. 412). As the client assimilates an experience, a schema gradually changes to accommodate it and integrates it, incorporating it into its system of associations.

The assimilation model posits eight stages, which are contained within the Assimilation of Problematic Experiences Scale (APES; Stiles, Morrison, et al., 1991) and have been named warded off, unwanted thoughts, vague awareness/emergence, problem statement/clarification, understanding/ insight, application/working through, problem solution, and mastery. These eight stages began with Elliott's list of immediate therapeutic impacts, which he derived from clients' open-ended descriptions of helpful and unhelpful events within therapy sessions (Elliott, 1985; Elliott, James, Reimschuessel, Cislo & Sack, 1985; see also Elliott & Wexler, 1994). They have been elaborated and ordered in the assimilation model as a way of describing developmental changes in clients' experiences. The APES stages listed in Table 1.1 represent our current understanding of how this development proceeds.

In some respects, this sequence resembles that adopted in the *stages of change* model (McConnaughy, DiClemente, Prochaska & Velicer, 1989; Prochaska & DiClemente, 1984), in which clients move from the stages of 'pre-contemplation' and 'contemplation' to 'action' and subsequently 'maintenance'. Like the stages of change model, the assimilation model is concerned with specific problematic experiences; clients may come to therapy with problems at different stages, and they may address each problem at different times during therapy.

The assimilation model seeks to describe change processes that are common to most or all psychotherapies, and it does not prescribe a particular therapeutic approach. Nevertheless, by describing the process of change at a relatively detailed level, it may help clinicians conceptualise what their clients are experiencing, and it may suggest guidelines for when particular types of therapeutic interventions will be most effective.

Different psychotherapeutic approaches appear to focus on different ranges along the assimilation continuum shown in Table 1.1 (Shapiro, Barkham, Reynolds, Hardy & Stiles, 1992; Stiles, Barkham, Shapiro & Firth-Cozens, 1992; Stiles et al., 1990, cf. Prochaska & DiClemente, 1984). In psychodynamic, experiential and interpersonal psychotherapies, therapists often consider a client's presenting complaints as reflecting problematic experiences that are currently inaccessible (APES stage 0) or actively avoided (APES stage 1), and they may begin by exploring the client's feelings and background to expose the underlying experiences (APES stage 2). By contrast, in cognitive and behavioural therapies, therapists seem more likely to take a client's presenting complaints at face value (APES stage 3) and proceed to negotiate a contract about targets for change. With the target problems defined, they move on to data-gathering, analysis and reformulation in terms of rational and behavioural principles (APES stage 4), followed by a programme designed to apply the new understanding (APES stage 5). Thus, the model suggests that relatively well-assimilated problems might do better in cognitive or behavioural treatments, whereas poorly assimilated problems might do better in a psychodynamic, experiential or interpersonal approach. This division is not absolute, of course; probably most therapies can work at many levels to some degree.

Table 1.1   *Assimilation of Problematic Experiences Scale (APES)*

0   *Warded off*
Content is unformed; client is unaware of the problem. Affect may be minimal, reflecting successful avoidance.

1   *Unwanted thoughts*
Content reflects emergence of thoughts associated with discomfort. Client prefers not to think about it; topics are raised by therapist or external circumstances. Affect (which is often more salient than the content) involves strong or overwhelming negative feelings – anxiety, fear, sadness. Despite the feelings' intensity, they may be unfocused and their connection with the content may be unclear.

2   *Vague awareness/emergence*
Client acknowledges the existence of a problematic experience, and describes uncomfortable associated thoughts, but cannot formulate the problem clearly. Affect includes acute psychological pain or panic clearly associated with the problematic thoughts and experiences.

3   *Problem statement/clarification*
Content includes a clear statement of a problem – something that could be worked on. Affect is negative but manageable, not panicky.

4   *Understanding/insight*
The problematic experience is placed into a schema, formulated, understood, with clear connective links. Affect may be mixed, with some unpleasant recognitions, but with curiosity or even pleasant surprise of the 'aha' sort.

5   *Application/working through*
The understanding is used to work on a problem; there is reference to specific problem-solving efforts, though without complete success. Client may describe considering alternatives or systematically selecting courses of action. Affective tone is positive, business-like, optimistic.

6   *Problem solution*
Client achieves a successful solution for a specific problem. Affect is positive, satisfied, proud of accomplishment.

7   *Mastery*
Client successfully uses solutions in new situations; this generalising is largely automatic, not salient. Affect is positive when the topic is raised, but otherwise neutral (that is, this is no longer something to get excited about).

Contextual background to research studies

The studies we review in this chapter, like most of the published research on the assimilation model, have drawn on a series of research projects undertaken by the Sheffield psychotherapy research group. Each of these projects has concerned the processes and outcomes of two contrasting psychosocial treatments for depression: a cognitive-behavioural therapy (CB, also called 'prescriptive therapy') and a psychodynamic-interpersonal therapy (PI, also called 'exploratory therapy'). The objectives, strategy and techniques of both treatments were set out in separate manuals which therapists used during their initial training and subsequently to guide and monitor treatment delivery (Firth & Shapiro, 1985; Shapiro & Firth, 1985). The CB therapy was multi-modal, offering cognitive and behavioural strategies for application by the client including anxiety-control training, self-management procedures and cognitive restructuring. PI therapy was based on Hobson's conversational model (Hobson, 1985). Using psychodynamic, interpersonal and experiential concepts, it focuses on the client–therapist relationship as a vehicle for understanding and modifying interpersonal difficulties. In each project, clients have been assessed before and after treatment with a battery of self-report and structured interview measures, including the Beck Depression Inventory (BDI; Beck, Ward, Mendelson, Mock & Erbaugh, 1961). In addition, they have regularly (at least weekly) rated the intensity of their main symptoms using variants of the personal questionnaire method (PQ; Barkham, Stiles & Shapiro, 1993; Phillips, 1986). PQs are an idiographic measure enabling clients to express their own problems in their own words.

The first Sheffield Psychotherapy Project (SPP1; Shapiro & Firth, 1987) used a cross-over design in which 40 clients were randomly assigned to either 8 sessions of CB followed by 8 sessions of PI or to 8 sessions of PI followed by 8 sessions of CB, with the same therapist throughout. Based on the rationale that the relatively successful cases are more likely to show evidence of assimilation, four good outcome SPP1 cases were selected, based on pre–post differences on the BDI. These four cases were studied intensively using a qualitative approach to identity problematic experiences that seemed to have been assimilated and to track the experiences across sessions (Stiles, Morrison et al., 1991; Stiles, Shapiro & Harper, 1994; Stiles, Shapiro, Harper & Morrison, 1995). A portion of one of the cases is described later in this chapter. SPP1 clients' PQ ratings were the basis for an assimilation model-based quantitative comparison of thematic continuity in the two treatment orders (PI–CB versus CB–PI; Stiles, Barkham, Shapiro & Firth-Cozens, 1992), which is also summarised later.

The second Sheffield Psychotherapy Project (SPP2; Shapiro, Barkham, Hardy & Morrison, 1990; Shapiro et al., 1994; Shapiro et al., 1995) compared two durations (8 or 16 weekly sessions) of the two treatments (PI or CB therapy) for clients (total $N = 117$) who met criteria for a diagnosis of major depressive episode. Change on the BDI was again used to select cases that were used in a project to develop psychometrically sound quantitative methods for assessing degree of assimilation (Field, Barkham, Shapiro & Stiles, 1994; Field, Stiles, Barkham & Shapiro, 1995). We later summarise one of these cases.

The Sheffield Integrative Project (SIP; Shapiro et al., 1992) comprised a panel of 12 clients seen in an integrative form of CB and PI therapy, in which we combined CB and PI treatments using the assimilation model as an integrating framework. We later describe a part of a single case study from this panel.

Case Studies

In this section, to provide clinically based accounts of the assimilation process, we summarise three single case studies, one derived from each of the three Sheffield projects outlined above. These three cases provide a bridge between research and practice. We have focused on clinical material to show how the work is grounded in the therapy process and followed this with a clinical commentary to highlight potential implications for practitioners. Hence, while these case studies draw upon a research perspective, they are also presented as examples of practice.

A qualitative method approach: The case of Jane Davis

In the first study (Stiles et al., 1995), particular problematic experiences were identified and tracked qualitatively across therapy sessions. Assimilation was assessed by a team of researchers who discussed the target passages and their context, rather than attempting independent ratings.

Jane Davis was a 34-year-old woman referred to therapy for panic attacks and depression. She was assigned to the PI–CB treatment order within SPP1. The BDI pre–post therapy change scores were 24 to 3. Jane had difficulty expressing feelings, and this difficulty appeared to be an aspect of her depression. This was manifest in the use of objectifying language (for example, using the third person when referring to herself). This was apparent in the initial session, in which the therapist raised the issue of her use of objectifying language on at least five occasions: For example:

> *Therapist*: So that adds a dimension of hopelessness [to being lonely]. You're stuck with it because no one would live with you; no one would love you enough.
> *Jane*: I think that's fair, yeah [*Therapist*: But, er –] which I suppose is sometimes, you know again, why one puts up the front, [*Therapist*: Yes.] but fronts can also be equally off-putting.
> *Therapist*: And even now again the language: Why 'one'? You know, why one puts up the front. We're dealing, you know, we're –
> *Jane*: [Over *Therapist*] Sorry, that's just me. [*Therapist*: Yes, but –] though, yeah, OK [*laughs*], it is important.

In her first speaking turn, Jane's use of 'one' implied that she was distracted from the feeling (APES stage 0: warded off), and her expression 'that's just me' had a dismissing effect (APES stage 1: unwanted thoughts). However, her subsequent utterance 'yeah, OK, it is important' intimated an awareness (APES stage 2: vague awareness/emergence).

In a later example, towards the end of session 1, Jane was talking about her panic attacks and how these had motivated her to seek therapy:

> *Jane*: Perhaps I would have been able to trundle on, but I, again as you say, I've got the language. I've read enough books and seen enough people [*Therapist*: Um.] to think 'well, no, Davis, it would have got you sometime in some form or other, I think'.

> *Therapist*: Yeah, you've several times done this internal dialogue with yourself as 'Davis', your surname.
>
> *Jane*: Yes, that's very much a ritualised thing among me and my friends, actually.
>
> *Therapist*: You and your friends use your surname?
>
> *Jane*: We tend to talk to each other in surnames.
>
> *Therapist*: Umm. Well, are you, yes, maybe this makes you feel picked up on or under the microscope, but I cannot help having a feeling that is kind of, is somehow less intimate, less personal.
>
> *Jane*: [*change of tone, whispers*] What does that mean?
>
> *Therapist*: The, the, that using surname is a [*Jane*: Oh.] less intimate way of talking about yourself and . . .
>
> *Jane*: What, now?
>
> *Therapist*: No, using your surname is a less intimate and personal way of talking about yourself. That's how it strikes me. [*Jane*: Yeah.] And I get the feeling that somehow you do objectify yourself, not as a person but as a name on a list.
>
> *Jane*: Yes, put like that.
>
> *Therapist*: As a name, a cipher somehow, an object.
>
> *Jane*: Yes, yes. I think there's something in that.

The objectifying language theme appeared warded off at first ('well, no Davis, it would have got you sometime'; APES stage 0). Eventually, in response to the therapist's disclosure of his own reaction to the use of the surname, Jane admitted the issue to awareness ('I think there's something in that'; APES stage 2).

Towards the middle of session 5, there is evidence of an understanding of Jane's use of objectifying language:

> *Jane*: I think the risk bit . . . in a situation is how the other person is going to respond. [*Therapist*: Mm-hm.] . . . Quite often, I am with people, perhaps, who all need to come and see you for this same treatment, who all function in the same way. . . . We all operate in very much the same way.
>
> *Therapist*: . . . The whole lifestyle shores you up, and you c-, you could carry on like that for years. . . . I think what you're saying is you can do without these people shoring up your defences. So the implication [*Jane*: Yes.] for choice of friends is somehow to try and get away from that pattern of –
>
> *Jane*: Which I think is beginning to happen, slightly, um, slowly.
>
> *Therapist*: Mm. People that relate to you in other ways are coming into your life.
>
> *Jane*: Um, yes. And th- people who are more naturally demonstrative, et cetera, et cetera [*Therapist*: Mm.] than, than some of the others. . . . Just 'cause one's been going slightly different places, um, over the past few months, which, believe it or not, you know, frees me up more. . . . So all I'm saying, I think, is: it is slowly changing.

Here Jane expressed an understanding of the protective function of her objectifying language ('the risk . . . is how the other person is going to respond'; APES stage 4). The therapist's exploratory reflections identified her wish for greater intimacy and brought Jane to describe how she could apply her understanding (for example, choosing friends 'who are more naturally demonstrative').

Jane's progress in treatment – her assimilation of the objectifying language strand of her difficulty in identifying feelings – can be seen in the following extract from session 15:

Jane: I think, I think perhaps I have been trying to extend that. For example, last week, over the argument with a friend, [*Therapist*: Right.] that there I was certainly trying to, um, to operate more openly. And I suppose also more honestly.

Therapist: So how does that work out in practice? What does it involve saying that's different?

Jane: It's really one thing: just being much more personal, um, even in terms of language. Like, I know, and I use it frequently: I use 'one' when I mean 'me' or 'I'. Ahm. Which may sound little. But, you know, consciously trying to emphasise that [*Therapist*: Right.] it is, it is me [*Therapist*: Right.] the person, as opposed to 'one does this' and 'one does that'. [*Therapist*: Yes, yes.] And so you keep it over there. [*Therapist*: Right.] Um, so I mean, small things like that, and, and where necessary – it hasn't been anything very dramatic so far – but saying 'Well, look, look, no stop, I want to say this', or 'This may surprise you'. Which was what went on with that altercation with some – the friend. Um, so, starting to rewrite, and say look, I would like to rewrite, some of the assumptions that are fed back [by others].

Thus, Jane had applied her understanding to the specific problem of being more open with others, communicating her needs and dealing with conflict. The progress appeared, to the authors at least, consistent with the APES sequence described in Table 1.1.

Clinical commentary

How does this research inform therapists? The assimilation model attempts to provide a framework for understanding what is happening. It does not necessarily prescribe how the therapist should respond. This will be shaped variously by a range of factors, including the therapeutic approach being used, in response to client requirements.

The assimilation model directs the therapist's attention toward moving particular problematic experiences from one stage to the next. That is, the model dissects the generic treatment goal (symptomatic improvement) into a series of subgoals corresponding to the assimilation stages shown in Table 1.1. As an illustration, in the passage from session 1 of Jane's treatment, the therapist drew attention to Jane's use of objectifying language, empathically acknowledged her feelings of loneliness and disclosed his own reaction to her use of surnames. This use of the therapeutic relationship was consistent with the PI therapeutic approach and appeared to help move the objectifying language strand of Jane's difficulty in expressing feelings from an unwanted thoughts stage toward vague awareness/ emergence.

It seems to us that clinical evidence of the vague awareness/emergence stage is a marker indicating a client's readiness to pursue focused therapeutic work on a particular topic. The emergence stage of the assimilation model represents a transition from avoidance toward a potential for active therapeutic engagement by the client. The case of Jane shows this by her initial investment in distancing and non-engaging activities through the use of objectifying language. The assimilation model helps with testing whether the client is open to such emerging thoughts (stage 2) or retracts due to the unpleasant thoughts (stage 1) into a warded off state (stage 0).

A quantitative method approach: The case of Marie

Results from qualitative studies of cases like Jane's appear consistent with the assimilation model's hypothesis that successful resolution of a particular problematic experience proceeds by movement through the stages shown in Table 1.1 (Stiles, Meshot, et al., 1992; Stiles, Morrison, et al., 1991; Stiles et al., 1995). The assimilation ratings in these case studies, however, were made by investigators who arrived at consensus decisions after discussing case transcripts with each other. Although a consensual approach has high clinical plausibility, three methodological objections arise from the complexity of the rating task. First, the rating process involves more than a single task and the raters can become less reliable when asked to perform multiple decisions. Second, in discussing particular passages, raters might be unduly swayed by the view of one individual. And third, although contextual information is often essential for understanding a particular passage, raters' knowledge of a passage's location in the transcripts and familiarity with the model opens the possibility of an expectation-confirming bias in their ratings. What happens when a more objective methodology is used to test the prediction concerning progression through stages?

From the SPP2 data pool, we (Field et al., 1994) selected a client, Marie, who (1) had been randomly assigned to PI treatment of the shorter (8-session) duration; (2) had returned relatively stable BDI scores across three pre-treatment assessments (29, 25 and 27), indicating no marked pre-therapy improvement; and (3) showed clinically significant change across therapy. Marie's post-treatment BDI scores were well within the normal range (2 at termination, 4 at three-month follow-up and 5 at one-year follow-up) and her improvement on other assessment measures was comparable. This degree of change meets the most stringent criterion for clinical significance offered by Jacobson and Truax (1991), so we expected to be able to find evidence of successful assimilation.

Assimilation was assessed in three phases by independent groups of raters. First, a clinically prominent content domain was identified and relevant passages were excerpted from session transcripts by two raters. Second, statements of central problematic experiences were constructed by three further raters. Third, the selected passages were presented in random order, and the level of assimilation of each problematic experience was rated independently by six further raters. In each phase of analysis, raters indicated their confidence in their judgements, and only high-confidence data were used in subsequent analyses. Our intent was to develop a systematic procedure for extracting the essence of the assimilation process while reducing contextual information that might engender bias in the final rating.

To test whether there was increasing assimilation across successive excerpts, assimilation ratings based on the median ratings for the most salient and reliably identified problematic experience were plotted against the sequence of 17 selected client speaking turns. Figure 1.1 presents the plot which suggests a positive progression across therapy. Across the 17 speaking turns, Kendall's $\tau = .68$, $N = 17$, $p < .01$.

The client, Marie, was 42 years old and married, with an adult son. Marie's immediate family unit included her mother, who had lived with the family for the past 17 years. Marie's mother was suffering from senile dementia and was in and out of the hospital during the time Marie was attending therapy. Marie was a white-collar employee, responsible for the running of an office and the supervision of eight people. She heard about the research clinic from a friend at work and applied for therapy, complaining of lack of concentration and worries about making correct decisions. One of her major concerns was that she would have to stay off work because of 'illness' (that is, depression). Marie had been on anxiolytic and anti-depressant medication for eight months before applying to the clinic for treatment.

The main target set of 17 excerpts (technically, speaking turns) concerned Marie's 'coming to terms with feeling guilty about letting go of her mother'. Arranged in their temporal sequence, these provide a clinical account of Marie assimilating this central problematic experience. We present a selection. The initial number in parenthesis following the extract denotes the corresponding therapy excerpt in Figure 1.1, while the APES ratings are the medians of those obtained in the third phase of the procedure (cf. Table 1.2).

In session 1, Marie began with her guilt between the levels of unwanted thoughts and awareness:

> My mum lives with us and she's 84. . . . She's lived with us for 17 years. . . . She has senile dementia and I finally made the decision last week for her to go into permanent care because I can't cope any more. . . . I wish she'd die before I have to send her in. (1: APES rating = 1.6)

But later in the session, she showed more awareness of the impending loss:

> I suppose it bothers me really. . . . I am afraid of someone close to me dying. (2: APES rating = 1.9)

The issue appeared again in session 5, where it became a major theme:

> When I go to see her I feel very guilty that perhaps I ought to carry on and try and keep her at home and look after her. I'm not sure what that involves. . . . I suppose giving up my job. . . . It's just so muddled up. (3: APES rating = 2.0)

In the same turn, Marie also talked about being under pressure to take more responsibility at work and about blocking her thinking about this:

> I don't feel anything about that at the moment. It seems to be second, until I get this sorted out.

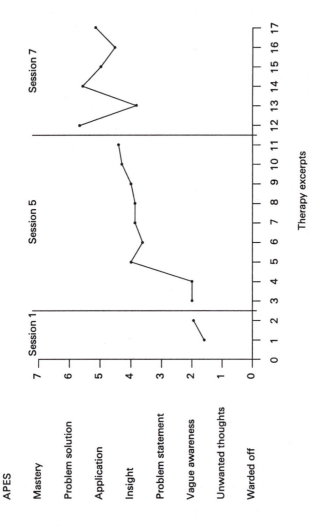

Figure 1.1 *The median Assimilation of Problematic Experiences Scale (APES) ratings for the problematic experience statement, 'the client coming to terms with feeling guilty about letting go of her mother.'*

Source: Journal of Counseling Psychology (1994), *41*, 403.

Her major concern was to understand her history of depressions:

> But their [the medical profession's] suggestion is, that I would have another breakdown, become ill, or have a depression, whatever or whatever you want to call it. And that sets me off thinking, why, again. I'm back to the same old question, why, why does it make any difference? Are we saying that depressions are as a result of extra work? Extra pressure? . . . But it's just my mind isn't it? (4: APES rating = 2.0)

Later in session 5, Marie began to clarify the problem and see her particular role in it.

> I can't cope with her at home, and in truth I don't want to cope with her at home anymore, because I've had enough, and I want to, have a better life, have a better way of life, nothing drastic by any means, just be free from that one particular pressure, once I admit that I feel guilty. Why can't I simply accept that, that that's not a bad thing to feel? That it's a reasonable thing to feel? (5: APES rating = 4.0)

And in the same turn, she began to show an understanding of the cause of her depressions:

> So why don't I forget about it? Why don't I let it go? Why do I have to keep reaping it all up with my own mind? That's what causes the depressions isn't it? Going over old ground, remembering all the bad things I've done.

This advance was then consolidated:

> And facing the fact that it's not wrong to feel guilty, and it doesn't hurt to cry about it when I come out from seeing her, and when I go and see her, and she says, 'have you come to take me home?' the knife doesn't twist as much now. . . . I'm not shirking it, I'm not covering it up like I was doing a few weeks ago, I'm not pretending. . . . She has moments when she seems more lucid than others, but it still doesn't make any difference, I still can't go back on the decision I've made for me. (10: APES rating = 4.4)

And finally, she concluded:

> Yeah, and it's, it's great really to know that I've made a decision, to know that I can go home, and to look at that bedroom and say 'right, it's going to be stripped, and it's going to be used for something else, and none of that is particularly hurting me mum, she's going to be taken care of, and I'm still going to go and visit her, and I'm still going to go and see her. But now I'll get on with my life.' (11: APES rating = 4.5)

By session 7, Marie's mother had gone into a nursing home:

> I can go and see her without feeling guilty. . . . She's going to die I suppose in the not too distant future, and already as far as I'm concerned, she's gone, you know I'll visit her, but she's gone. (12: APES rating = 5.6)

Marie made a statement about her mother but flagged a potential awareness of new feelings:

> I've let my mum go and I feel different. (13: APES rating = 3.8)

However, she was able to resolve her previously hidden resentment towards her mother with her current feelings of relief.

> It's my life now. . . . I think I resented having to give her so much. . . . I was never given that much as a child and now it's gone and I like her a lot more too. (14: APES rating = 5.5)

She was able to summarise her feelings about the relationship between her mother going and her own feelings about her past and about her ability to let go of her bad feelings from her past:

> I know that, now my mum's gone, a lot of badness has gone with it. . . . People looking on would say 'that's simply because I haven't got to look after her', the physical side of it again. . . . But I know it's not that. . . . It's letting go of everything that was ever bad when I was young. . . . And I didn't know until she went; somehow she reminded me of all those things. (16: APES rating = 4.2)

The ratings signalled that much of the assimilation took place in session 5 (see Figure 1.1). They suggest that the issue of 'coming to terms with feeling guilty about letting go of her mother' was not worked on until client and therapist were ready. It was not addressed immediately when it was first raised in session 1. The findings suggest that the assimilation of this problematic experience proceeded at quite irregular rates within this treatment. The pattern of progress in a specific domain being made mainly in one session has been replicated in a further case study (Field et al., 1995).

Clinical commentary

What is particularly interesting from this research case is that it confirms the transitional position of the vague awareness/emergence stage, as discussed in relation to the earlier case. Only when Marie was operating at the stage of emergence at the beginning of session 5 did the therapeutic work begin to make rapid, substantial progress in relation to the theme in question. However, again we are wary of prescribing what a therapist should do other than to state that monitoring by the therapist using the assimilation model may well help in selecting a topic which the client is ready to work on.

An integrative therapy approach: The case of Ms M

The third case we summarise draws on our attempts to use the assimilation model as an integrative theory for employing combinations of the PI and CB therapies (Shapiro et al., 1992). The principle underlying the integration was the theoretical hypothesis that a PI approach would be relatively more effective with poorly assimilated problematic experiences (APES stages 0–2), whereas a CB approach would be relatively more effective with better-assimilated material (at or above APES stage 3).

Our design of this integrative therapy used an eight-session format. The first session was conceptualised as mainly an assessment, in which the therapist's task was to convey the principles of the two treatment approaches and to identify the client's main problem domains and the extent to which the problematic experiences were assimilated. The orientation of each following session was to be either CB or PI – the decision to be based on constraints derived from a combination of research and clinical considerations. One constraint was that there should be no more than two consecutive sessions employing the same orientation. A further constraint was that the two final sessions (that is, sessions 7 and 8) should be in the sequence PI followed by CB. The treatment orientation decision was to be taken after a review of work during the initial 10 minutes of each session.

Once the orientation of the session was decided, the treatment method was to be a relatively 'pure' version of PI or CB. Hence, much rested on the negotiation between client and therapist at the beginning of the session in terms of (1) deciding which approach to use and (2) obtaining the client's commitment to working within the chosen approach.

Ms M, a 40-year-old divorced woman with two children, was referred to the research clinic by her family doctor and presented with physical symptoms of palpitations and panic attacks. She had to care for two children and her mother and the running of the house. Following the initial therapy session, which was conceptualised as an assessment, the therapist identified four areas of work (problematic experiences). The first two areas were physical symptoms and fears of letting people down, which were to be addressed using anxiety management techniques and cognitive techniques respectively. The other two areas, her ambivalent relationship with her mother and her own needs for autonomy and freedom, were domains which were deemed to be less well assimilated and therefore required more 'exploratory', PI therapy.

In the following session the client and therapist began work on the client's latter two problems using a PI focus. The client described having unwanted conflictual thoughts about whether her children should stay at home in the holidays to help her move, or go to see their father.

We use the next (third) session, when either a CB or PI orientation could have been chosen, to illustrate client–therapist negotiation about which treatment to use. At the beginning of the session, the client reported a powerful emotional reaction resulting from the previous session:

Ms M: I went away and felt I was [aged] 105. . . . I was just totally wiped out really, lots of palpitations and feeling shaky and not wanting to do very much.
Therapist: This was like your body in turmoil and your mind like numb in some way . . .
Ms M: And then over the weekend I felt a lot better . . . everybody's being very supportive and Mum's being very good. . . . I'm not getting all the niggly little demands . . .
Therapist: She's responding to what is happening here.
Ms M: Yes, I think since then [last week] there's been a marked difference . . .

The therapist then noted the improvement in feeling as well as behavioural changes in her relationship with her mother. The client then produced cognitive evidence of problem clarification (APES stage 3):

> *Ms M*: When thinking about last week I suddenly felt that I've always been trapped between somebody or other . . . and I've never positively realised it clearly, perhaps only felt it emotionally.

The therapist used this material to negotiate a CB focus on steps required to develop her own personal space. The client took up this suggestion:

> *Ms M*: Right. I feel that would be very positive. Yes, I feel the need to do something positive.

As one measure of Ms M's progress in therapy, we used the Therapy Session Topic Review (TSTR; Barkham, Stiles & Rigsby, 1989 – see Appendix). The TSTR seeks to measure the process of assimilation within a specific theme or problem domain, as seen from the client's perspective. It supplies definitions of seven of the eight assimilation model (excluding warded off, which is, by definition, inaccessible) and asks the client to briefly describe any in-session event that corresponded to each definition. In the Sheffield Integrative Project, the TSTR was completed by clients after each therapy session. We also used the Therapy Inter-session Topic Review (TISTR; Barkham et al., 1989), which was completed immediately *prior* to each session. The TISTR is identical to the TSTR, except that it asks for descriptions of events in relation to each of the stages which occurred during the week since the last therapy session.

On the TSTR and TISTR, Ms M provided a total of 40 statements during her eight-session treatment. These were typed and listed in random order, without identifying the assimilation stage to which Ms M had assigned them. A rater who was unfamiliar with the case but familiar with the assimilation model then classified each of these statements as belonging to one of three themes that seemed prominent in Ms M's therapy. For the purposes of illustration, we will focus on just one theme here: *equality*, which dealt with crediting her own needs and developing her own personal space. The eight statements identified as relating to equality are shown in Table 1.2.

Comparing the results from the TSTR with those from the TISTR suggests that, from the client's perspective, the process of assimilation occurred between sessions as much as within sessions. Progress on this particular problem ('equality') was concentrated in four sessions (that is, sessions 2–5), which included both PI and CB approaches. The progress of this theme through the assimilation stages followed the predicted sequence reasonably closely (compare Table 1.2 with Table 1.1).

Clinical commentary

This third case provides an example in which the assimilation model was used to assess the client's level of operating in particular problem domains and to suggest possible therapeutic routes which the therapist might take. Here the assimilation model is being used as a therapeutic assessment to

Table 1.2 *Ms M's topic reviews of equality theme*

Session	Mode	Assimilation level	Client's TSTR/TISTR statement
2(I)	PI	Unwanted thoughts	About the summer holidays (school) and about the children going to see their father when I need their support for moving house. Feeling guilty for depriving them, but really needing to put myself first.
3	CB	Problem statement/ clarification	The problem of putting myself first or at least on a par with my children.
3(I)	CB	Problem statement/ clarification	The basic problem is one of being unable to put myself first or at least on a par with others, financially and in house and friendship situations. I have made good progress in last 10 days with good results.
3(I)	CB	Understanding/insight	My understanding relates to the problem already stated. I realise it is *my* problem and that if I put myself first others will comply. Hard to do, certainly makes me uneasy and elated at the same time.
3(I)	CB	Application/working through	I understand now that it was easier to efface myself in favour of others' needs than to risk unpleasantness, though it made me discontent and stressed. I have applied this realisation to my problems at home and stated clearly what I need.
4	PI	Problem solution	Anxiety about depriving my children of a visit to their father this summer because I need them here. Worried about their reaction. Simply discussed it with them and was surprised at the positive outcome.
5	CB	Problem solution	The problem was tackling my children on plans for the summer which put my needs before theirs – without feeling awful about it. I quietly spoke to both of them separately and stated the pros and cons. They have both accepted this quite well and I think I will feel much easier dealing with a similar situation in future.
5	CB	Mastery	I had been practising putting myself first financially and had for the first time put money into my deposit account. An emergency arose but I found an alternative solution and did *not* touch the money I had put aside.

Note: (I) = Inter-session material reported on TISTR form completed immediately prior to the following session; all other statements recorded on TSTR forms immediately after the session.

inform the therapist about therapeutic strategy at the session level. Importantly, data from the case of Ms M suggest that assimilation can be seen as a quasi-autonomous client process, open to influence by the therapist's interventions, but not necessarily determined by the therapist.

The session strategy of first assessing the assimilation level of the client's most salient problem and then deciding which theoretical approach to take represents a novel approach to an integrated treatment. It offers the advantage of a larger therapeutic repertoire – making use of two (or, potentially, more) different theoretical approaches – while maintaining conceptual coherence of the approach being used within any one session. The research goals in this case introduced some constraints (for example, no more than two consecutive sessions using the same approach) that might not be necessary in a clinical application.

Group contrast design: Treatment order and continuity

The cross-over design of SPP1 (eight sessions of one treatment followed by eight sessions of the other) provided a unique base from which to explore the suggestion that the PI and CB approaches tend to focus on problems at different levels of assimilation. In a quantitative, group contrast design, we tested the hypothesis that progress *on particular problems* would be relatively smooth and steady for clients who received treatment in the PI–CB order, whereas progress would tend to follow a relatively curved or discontinuous course for clients in the CB–PI order (Stiles, Barkham et al., 1992). Insofar as most clients bring a variety of problems to treatment, most should find some benefit in both treatments and both orders, so expectation is consistent with the generally equivalent overall outcomes of the two treatment orders (Shapiro & Firth, 1987).

The differential-smoothness hypothesis rested on the assumption that therapeutic progress on a particular problem depends on whether its degree of assimilation matches that presumed by the treatment approach. In the PI–CB order, work was expected to focus first on becoming aware of, formulating and understanding of unassimilated experiences. If this was successful, the client could enter the second period with these problems more-or-less formulated and accessible to the pursuit of rational solutions in practical situations, as fostered by CB treatment. Thus, the same problems can be dealt with throughout the two treatments, resulting in relatively smooth and steady progress with respect to problems considered individually. By contrast, in the CB–PI order, work was expected to focus first on problems sufficiently assimilated to be stated clearly. Then, to the extent that CB work was successful, these problems would be understood and rational solutions applied by the midpoint of treatment, so that these clients would be likely to require a change in problem focus at mid-treatment. Thus, considered on a per problem basis, progress in the CB–PI order should be more likely to be relatively curved or discontinuous: the initially more assimilated problems should show early improvement in response to CB treatment and later relative stagnation as they are neglected during the PI period, whereas the less assimilated problems should show early stagnation during the CB period, followed by later improvement when they are addressed in PI treatment.

Testing this hypothesis required regular measurement of the intensity of each of a client's problems. Using the PQ procedure (Phillips, 1986), 39 of the 40 SPP1 clients (one failed to complete sufficient forms) recorded the intensity of each of 10 individualised problems times a week across an average of 182 days, before and during the course of their treatment (Barkham et al., 1993). We plotted each problem's intensity against time and measured the degree of curve in each plot (technically, the improvement in fit achieved by using a quadratic rather than a linear approximation). Using a numerical criterion for determining whether a plot was curved or not, we then classified the plot of each problem ($N = 390$) as 'not curved', 'positively (U-shaped) curved', or 'negatively (inverted-U) curved'.

Consistent with the hypothesis that progress would be relatively discontinuous in the CB–PI order, 41.5 per cent of the CB–PI clients' plots were classified as curved (either positive or negative), whereas only 15.8 per cent of the PI–CB clients' plots were so classified. Looked at another way, clients' mean degree of curve was significantly greater in the CB–PI order ($M = 0.128$) than in the PI–CB order ($M = 0.047$), $t(37) = 3.07$, $p < .01$. The effect size (mean difference divided by mean standard deviation) was 1.0, a large effect. Twelve of the 20 clients in the CB–PI order had a mean curve index greater than 0.100, whereas only 2 of the 19 clients in the PI–CB order had a mean curve index greater than 0.100 (Stiles, Barkham, et al., 1992). These results supported the hypothesis that problem intensity would tend to decline relatively steadily in the PI–CB treatment order, whereas the rate of improvement would tend to change from earlier to later phases in the CB–PI order. Indirectly, they also supported the suggestion that PI and CB therapies tend to focus on problems at different levels of assimilation.

Practical guidelines

The assimilation model is a conceptualisation of the process of therapeutic change, not a prescription of treatment method. Its goal is integrative. Acknowledging that very diverse psychotherapeutic approaches appear more or less equivalently effective (Lambert & Bergin, 1994; Luborsky, Singer & Luborsky, 1975; Smith, Glass & Miller, 1980; Stiles, Shapiro & Elliott, 1986), the assimilation model seeks to accommodate the technical diversity and understand the equivalence. The process of assimilation and the sequence of cognitive/emotional stages outlined in Table 1.1 are advanced as common to most or all successful therapies. On the other hand, understanding can and should guide practice.

Intervention strategies and tactics

We have suggested that the assimilation model can contribute to psychotherapeutic decision-making at two levels, which we'll call strategy and tactics – the choice of treatment and the implementation of treatment.

At a strategic level, the assimilation model suggests that two broad classes of extant therapies – the psychodynamic, interpersonal and experiential therapies, on the one hand, represented in the Sheffield projects by PI, and the cognitive and behavioural therapies on the other, represented in the Sheffield projects by CB – may be best suited for problems at different levels of assimilation. PI-type therapies may be best suited for relatively unassimilated problems, whereas CB-type therapies may be best suited for somewhat better assimilated (that is, formulated) problems.

Importantly, this suitability is based mainly on convergence of the conceptualisations. Whether PI techniques differentially aid emergence and expression of problematic experiences and CB techniques differentially aid reformulation and application is an unanswered empirical question. The results of the continuity study described in the preceding section offer some indirect support but are far from conclusive. Furthermore, there is currently no formal, reliable method for assessing the degree of assimilation of clients' presenting problems. Thus, a good deal more work will be required before firm assimilation-based clinical recommendations about treatment assignment are justified.

At a tactical level, the assimilation model draws attention to the process of psychotherapeutic change, specifically, to (a) problem domains within the broader presenting picture and (b) developmental features of the change process (systematic stages of assimilation). This provides a basis for a 'process diagnosis' (cf. Greenberg, Rice & Elliott, 1993). Some problems are more easily talked about than others, and this may reflect their differing levels of assimilation. Informed by the model, a clinician might identify the client's currently central problematic experience and informally assess its stage of assimilation. For example, if the client cannot grasp what the problem is, or is vague, then the problematic experience may be considered as not having reached the problem statement/clarification stage (APES stage 3, Table 1.1). If the client also exhibits intense negative affect, this points toward vague awareness/emergence (APES stage 2), whereas if the client exhibits active avoidance, this points toward unwanted thoughts (APES stage 1). On the other hand, if the client can generally state the problem in a psychologically meaningful way, then the therapist can proceed up the scale by testing the client's current understanding of his or her problem. A practical aid to this is to use the Therapy Session Topic Review (TSTR; Barkham et al., 1989) form, which is described later and appears in the Appendix, as a framework to identify problems at particular stages in the assimilation model.

The model suggests subgoals of therapy corresponding to the APES levels (Table 1.1). An appropriate therapist response, then, is one that facilitates movement from one stage to the next. Such subgoals, which are cast with respect to a particular problematic experience, can realistically be achieved within a single session or even within a single episode. As presently formulated, the model does not prescribe which intervention works best at which assimilation stage. For example, in many psycho-dynamic approaches, when resistance is evident in response to questions concerning a client's relationship with a significant other, it may signal that the level of assimilation is low and that a relatively gentle exploratory approach is indicated. Different clinicians might intervene differently, however, depending on their theoretical formulation, the content of the problematic experience, the client's and their own personality, and so forth. The assimilation model thus tends to move treatment decisions to a micro-problem level, rather than leaving them at the level of diagnostic criteria or broad assessments such as 'obsessional behaviours' or 'interpersonal difficulties'.

Evaluation: Using the TSTR

The assimilation model suggests that therapeutic change might be con-sidered as a series of mini-outcomes reflecting movement from one stage to another. The TSTR and TISTR offer an approach to evaluating this movement that has some advantages for clinical as well as research use. The TSTR is included as an Appendix to this chapter. It is not copyrighted, so readers may use it freely in their practice and research (though we'd appreciate hearing about applications and results).

The TSTR offers a novel assessment strategy that allows clients to describe their experiences in their own words in response to any of the stages which are relevant to them, while also yielding a direct quantitative scaling. By contrast, items in conventional measures, such as the BDI, describe symptoms and experiences (for example, headaches, anxiety, guilt) in an invariant format and ask clients to endorse or rate them. The usual alternatives to this rigid structure are thoroughly qualitative measures using open-ended formats, such as Llewelyn's Helpful Aspects of Therapy questionnaire (Llewelyn, Elliott, Shapiro, Hardy & Firth-Cozens, 1988), which ask clients to describe helpful or hindering aspects of sessions in their own words. Scaling of responses to such qualitative responses must be done later by raters.

In the TSTR, clients are given the scale's anchor points (that is, the APES stages) and invited to provide the scale content (their unique experience). Thus, where conventional measures present pre-packaged problems and ask clients to rate them, the TSTR asks clients to nominate a salient problem and map it onto the most appropriate stage of the assimilation model. By subsequently sorting clients' stated experiences according to a particular theme (as was done in constructing Table 1.2), it becomes possible to track the change of a salient problem domain in terms of the assimilation model.

In addition, the quality of the response may in itself be a useful indicator. For example, a client who has completed the form minimally but then fills in meaningful responses may mirror a process of engagement in the therapeutic task.

Although our research protocols have required that clients' forms are not seen by the researchers and clinicians until after the course of therapy has been completed, in less constrained settings TSTR responses might be used to inform the ongoing process of therapy. For example, we can imagine a situation in which a client completes the inter-session form (that is, the TISTR) immediately prior to a session, and the form is passed to the therapist at the beginning of the session. This might help identify the major impacts for the client over the past week and assist in shaping the focus for the therapeutic work. Of course, the form might show no impact, and this would also be of use.

In comparison with asking the client at the beginning of the session, using the TISTR allows the client time to focus on the impact of the previous session in the absence of the therapist. The TISTR provides the client with a framework for viewing how he or she is responding to problems which may be particularly useful to him or her. One aim of therapy is to enable clients to act independently and not be dependent on the therapist. And of course, because it is framed in terms of the assimilation model, the TISTR offers the therapist a direct link to a theoretical conceptualisation of the current status of the case.

Conclusion

Overall, the assimilation model provides the therapist with a trans-theoretical framework for seeing what is happening in relation to clients' experiences of particular problematic experiences. It can be used as a guiding assessment procedure as well as for evaluating the impacts of therapy across time.

Appendix

THERAPY SESSION TOPIC REVIEW

Client No. _____   Date _____

Please think about today's therapy session as you read the questions below. We aren't looking for 'right' or 'wrong' answers to the questions. We're just trying to find out how therapy works for various people. We appreciate your help.

Please remember that your therapist will not see any of your answers until all your therapy sessions are finished. You are free to talk or not talk with your therapist about any thoughts or feelings you have as a result of answering these questions.

1 Unwanted thoughts

During your session today, did you or your therapist discuss anything that you would have rather avoided? (For example, maybe the therapist said something that led to your feeling sad or angry or anxious or afraid.)

Please circle one of the following:　　　　Yes　　No

If you answered 'yes', please state briefly what it was that you or your therapist said that made you feel uncomfortable.

What were your feelings about this topic?

2 Vague awareness

During your session today, did you clearly feel discomfort (anxiety, fear, anger, sadness) about an important topic but not feel able to clearly express the basic problem in words? (If this happened, you may have found yourself struggling to express the issue that you sensed was underneath the discomfort.)

Please circle one of the following:　　　　Yes　　No

If you answered 'yes', please state the topic (as well as you can) and describe briefly the feelings you were having about the topic. If you can say why you were having those feelings, please explain briefly.

3 Problem recognition

During your session today, did you become aware of a problem, manage to define it clearly, and feel that you now will be able to start working on it?

Please circle one of the following:　　　　Yes　　No

If you answered 'yes', please briefly describe the problem you defined in the session.

4 Understanding/Insight

During your session today, did you discuss some clearer understanding about yourself or about a problem you have been having. If this happened, you may feel that the problem now makes sense to you, or you can see how the problem came about. (This understanding may have felt partly painful, but you also may have felt satisfaction at seeing a connection.)

Please circle one of the following: Yes   No

If you answered 'yes', please state briefly the understanding that you achieved or discussed today.

5   Application of understanding

During your session today, did you use some new way of understanding yourself to work on a specific problem? Or, did you describe a recent instance outside the session in which you used some new understanding in this way? (Examples of working on a specific problem include figuring out which alternatives are available to you in facing the problem, or choosing a particular course of action to help you deal with the problem.)

Please circle one of the following: Yes   No

If you answered 'yes', please state briefly the new way of understanding yourself that was involved and the specific problem to which you applied that new understanding.

6   Problem solution

During your session today, did you discuss or report a successful solution for a specific problem (or part of a problem) in your life? (For example, did you discuss an event in which you successfully overcame some personal difficulty that you had worked on in previous sessions?)

Please circle one of the following: Yes   No

If you answered 'yes', please briefly describe the problem you faced, and the successful solution you achieved.

7   Mastery

During your session today, did you mention or discuss any topic or issue that used to be a problem for you, but which is no longer a problem. (You may have automatically applied a solution to a new situation without getting excited about it at the time.) Your overcoming this problem may or may not be a result of applying solutions developed in therapy.

Please circle one of the following: Yes   No

If you answered 'yes', please state the topic or issue and describe briefly why it is no longer a problem.

References

Barkham, M., Stiles, W.B., & Rigsby, R.K. (1989). *The Therapy Session Topic Review Forms* (Memo No. 159). Psychological Therapies Research Centre, University of Leeds, Leeds LS2 9JT, UK.

Barkham, M., Stiles, W.B., & Shapiro, D.A. (1993). The shape of change in psychotherapy: A longitudinal assessment of personal problems. *Journal of Consulting and Clinical Psychology, 61,* 667–677.

Beck, A.T., Ward, C.H., Mendelson, M., Mock, J., & Erbaugh, J. (1961). An inventory for measuring depression. *Archives of General Psychiatry, 4,* 561–571.

Elliott, R. (1985). Helpful and nonhelpful events in brief counseling interviews: An empirical taxonomy. *Journal of Counseling Psychology, 32,* 307–322.

Elliott, R., James, E., Reimschuessel, C., Cislo, D., & Sack, N. (1985). Significant events and the analysis of immediate therapeutic impacts. *Psychotherapy, 22,* 620–630.

Elliott, R., & Wexler, M.M. (1994). Measuring the impact of sessions in process-experiential therapy of depression: The Session Impacts Scale. *Journal of Counseling Psychology, 41,* 166–174.

Field, S.D., Barkham, M., Shapiro, D.A., & Stiles, W.B. (1994). Assessment of assimilation in psychotherapy: A quantitative case study of problematic experiences with a significant other. *Journal of Counseling Psychology, 41,* 397–406.

Field, S.D., Stiles, W.B., Barkham, M., & Shapiro, D.A. (1995, June). *Quantitative assessment of assimilation in two cases of psychodynamic-interpersonal psychotherapy.* Paper presented at the International Meeting of the Society for Psychotherapy Research, Vancouver.

Firth, J., & Shapiro, D.A. (1985). *Prescriptive therapy manual for the Sheffield Psychotherapy Project* (Memo No. 58). Psychological Therapies Research Centre, University of Leeds, Leeds LS2 9JT, UK.

Greenberg, L.S., Rice, L.N., & Elliott, R. (1993). *Facilitating emotional change: The moment-by-moment process.* New York: Guilford.

Hobson, R.F. (1985). *Forms of feeling: The heart of psychotherapy.* London: Tavistock Press.

Jacobson, N.S., & Truax, P. (1991). Clinical significance: A statistical approach to defining meaningful change in psychotherapy research. *Journal of Consulting and Clinical Psychology, 59,* 12–19.

Lambert, M.J., & Bergin, A.E. (1994). The effectiveness of psychotherapy. In A.E. Bergin & S.L. Garfield (Eds.), *Handbook of psychotherapy and behavior change* (4th ed., pp. 143–189). New York: Wiley.

Llewelyn, S.P., Elliott, R., Shapiro, D.A., Hardy, G., & Firth-Cozens, J. (1988). Client perceptions of significant events in prescriptive and exploratory periods of individual therapy. *British Journal of Clinical Psychology, 27,* 105–114.

Luborsky, L., Singer, B., & Luborsky, L. (1975). Comparative studies of psychotherapies. *Archives of General Psychiatry, 32,* 995–1008.

McConnaughy, E.A., DiClemente, C.C., Prochaska, J.O., & Velicer, W.F. (1989). Stages of change in psychotherapy: A follow-up report. *Psychotherapy, 26,* 494–503.

Phillips, J.P.N. (1986). Shapiro Personal Questionnaire and generalized personal questionnaire techniques: A repeated measures individualized outcome measurement. In L.S. Greenberg & W.M. Pinsof (Eds.), *The psychotherapeutic process: A research handbook* (pp. 557–589). New York: Guilford.

Prochaska, J.O., & DiClemente, C.C. (1984). *The transtheoretical approach: Crossing the boundaries of therapy.* Homewood, IL: Dow Jones-Irwin.

Shapiro, D.A., Barkham, M., Hardy, G.E., & Morrison, L.A. (1990). The Second Sheffield Psychotherapy Project: Rationale, design, and preliminary outcome data. *British Journal of Medical Psychology, 63,* 97–108.

Shapiro, D.A., Barkham, M., Hardy, G.E., Morrison, L.A., Reynolds, S., Startup, M., & Harper, H. (1991). University of Sheffield Psychotherapy Research Program: Medical Research Council–Economic and Social Research Council Social and Applied Psychology

Unit. In L.E. Beutler & M. Crago (Eds.), *Psychotherapy research: An international review of programmatic studies* (pp. 234–242). Washington, DC: American Psychological Association.

Shapiro, D.A., Barkham, M., Rees, A., Hardy, G.E., Reynolds, S., & Startup, M. (1994). Effects of treatment duration and severity of depression on the effectiveness of cognitive-behavioral and psychodynamic-interpersonal psychotherapy. *Journal of Consulting and Clinical Psychology, 62,* 522–534.

Shapiro, D.A., Barkham, M., Reynolds, S., Hardy, G., & Stiles, W.B. (1992). Prescriptive and exploratory psychotherapies: Toward an integration based on the assimilation model. *Journal of Psychotherapy Integration, 2,* 253–272.

Shapiro, D.A., & Firth, J. (1985). *Exploratory therapy manual for the Sheffield Psychotherapy Project* (SAPU Memo No. 57). Psychological Therapies Research Centre, University of Leeds, Leeds LS2 9JT, UK.

Shapiro, D.A., & Firth, J. (1987). Prescriptive vs exploratory psychotherapy: Outcome of the Sheffield Psychotherapy Project. *British Journal of Psychiatry, 151,* 790–799.

Shapiro, D.A., Rees, A., Barkham, M., Hardy, G., Reynolds, S., & Startup, M. (1995). Effects of treatment duration and severity of depression on the maintenance of gains following cognitive-behavioral and psychodynamic-interpersonal psychotherapy. *Journal of Consulting and Clinical Psychology, 63,* 378–387.

Smith, M.L., Glass, G.V., & Miller, T.I. (1980). *The benefits of psychotherapy.* Baltimore, MD: Johns Hopkins University Press.

Stiles, W.B., Barkham, M., Shapiro, D.A., & Firth-Cozens, J. (1992). Treatment order and thematic continuity between contrasting psychotherapies: Exploring an implication of the assimilation model. *Psychotherapy Research, 2,* 112–124.

Stiles, W.B., Elliott, R., Llewelyn, S.P., Firth-Cozens, J.A., Margison, F.R., Shapiro, D.A., & Hardy, G.E. (1990). Assimilation of problematic experiences by clients in psychotherapy. *Psychotherapy, 27,* 411–420.

Stiles, W.B., Meshot, C.M., Anderson, T.M., Sloan, W.W., Jr (1992). Assimilation of problematic experiences: The case of John Jones. *Psychotherapy Research, 2,* 81–101.

Stiles, W.B., Morrison, L.A., Haw, S.K., Harper, H., Shapiro, D.A., & Firth-Cozens, J. (1991). Longitudinal study of assimilation in exploratory psychotherapy. *Psychotherapy, 38,* 195–206.

Stiles, W.B., Shapiro, D.A., & Elliott, R. (1986). 'Are all psychotherapies equivalent?' *American Psychologist, 41,* 165–180.

Stiles, W.B., Shapiro, D.A., & Harper, H. (1994). Finding the way from process to outcome: Blind alleys and unmarked trails. In R.L. Russell (Ed.), *Psychotherapy research: Assessing and redirecting the tradition* (pp. 36–64). New York: Guilford.

Stiles, W.B., Shapiro, D.A., Harper, H., & Morrison, L.A. (1995). Therapist contributions to psychotherapeutic assimilation: An alternative to the drug metaphor. *British Journal of Medical Psychology, 68,* 1–13.

Stiles, W.B., Sloan, W.W., Jr, Meshot, C.M., & Anderson, T.M. (1991). Taking a closer look: Psychotherapy research at Miami University. In L.E. Beutler & M. Crago (Eds.), *Psychotherapy research: An international review of programmatic studies* (pp. 290–293). Washington, DC: American Psychological Association.

2

Research Applications of Prescriptive Therapy

Larry E. Beutler, Heidi A. Zetzer and Rebecca E. Williams

'Prescriptive psychotherapy' identifies a collection of clinical approaches that are bound together by their commitment to research evidence, rather than clinical theories, as the foundation for developing treatment programs and plans. 'Technical eclecticism', 'systematic eclecticism', 'technical integration' and 'strategic integration' are synonymous terms that frequently are used to describe these approaches. 'Prescriptive' approaches are cross-cutting in that they draw from a variety of different theories; they are empirical, in that they embrace research evidence as the basis for treatment selection; and they are systematic, in that they present consistent and clear decisional rules for selecting and applying treatments.

The better known prescriptive approaches to treatment planning are multi-modal psychotherapy (Lazarus, 1976), transtheoretical psychotherapy (Prochaska & DiClemente, 1986) and systematic treatment selection (STS; Beutler & Clarkin, 1990). These approaches differ from one another in two ways. First, they each identify a different array of patient factors that serve as indicators for assigning therapeutic activities, and, second, they work from different levels of abstraction when prescribing treatment plans. Multi-modal therapy, for example, identifies a menu of specific techniques that can be matched to patient indicators, while STS and transtheoretical psychotherapy fit psychotherapeutic strategies to various patient indicators. At a more abstract level, some approaches to psychotherapy develop theoretically guided postulates and constructs by combining principles from two or more theories. Because they are far removed from the level of practice, these latter formulations are not usually considered to be 'prescriptive', and are conventionally referred to as 'theoretical integrations' (Norcross, 1986).

The fact that different patient variables and treatment dimensions are matched in these different prescriptive models is understandable given the several hundred patient variables, therapist characteristics and treatment dimensions identified as potentially valuable in prior clinical research (Beutler, 1991a, 1991b). Because it has not yet been determined either how many of these variables are truly distinct from one another or which of them are most closely related to treatment outcomes, practitioners of each prescriptive model have been left to their own devices to determine which variables to use to make treatment decisions. More often than not, these decisions reflect the private theories and preferred philosophies that may be associated with different theoretical brands or models. But these differences belie basic similarities that exist at a more basic level. Prescriptive practitioners share a common, profound respect for the crucible of clinical research to make the ultimate determination of the dimensions that are most viable.

Among the various prescriptive approaches, systematic treatment selection (Beutler & Clarkin, 1990) has been considered by many (for example, Birk, 1991; Mahalik, 1990; Norcross & Goldfried, 1992) to be the most comprehensive and well integrated. The comprehensiveness of this approach derives from a systematic effort to extract guiding principles not only from traditional theories, but also from other integrative models. Beginning with the two independent, eclectic approaches originally developed by the authors themselves (Beutler, 1983; Frances, Clarkin & Perry, 1984), empirically derived principles were incorporated from a variety of eclectic models (for example, Beitman, 1987; Garfield, 1980; Prochaska & DiClemente, 1986). The most empirically sound indicators and contra-indicators for assigning a broad array of treatment aspects were identified and incorporated from these different models of treatment selection to provide a comprehensive model with which to make empirically valid treatment decisions.

These integrative efforts resulted in a model of clinical decision-making that embodies three key strengths: (1) the dimensions selected to comprise the model were each founded on empirical evidence of efficacy; (2) the model outlines a series of proposed relationships that can be subjected to prospective tests; and (3) these proposed relationships cover the full range of treatment decisions that face the clinician.

Beutler and Clarkin (1990) outline four domains that comprise the sequence of clinical decision-making. Within each of these domains, there are classes and subclasses of more specific dimensions, each of which were initially included because of the existence of promising empirical literature that indicated the nature of effective treatment. The first domain, *patient predisposing characteristics*, is central to all the others and is comprised of three more specific subclasses, each of which embodies an aspect of functioning: (1) problem areas are comprised of specific diagnostic variables and associated problem types; (2) environmental variables are comprised of social networks, support systems and areas of social functioning; and (3) personal characteristics are comprised of specific variables that encompass situational states (for example, treatment expectations, levels of distress, etc.), trait-like patterns (for example, coping styles, interpersonal patterns, etc.) and residual problem characteristics (for example, complexity, severity of impairment, patient demographic characteristics, etc.).

Based upon available empirical information, patient predisposing variables are used to construct recommendations for a strategic and tailored treatment plan. The elements of this plan reflect the subcategories of the other three domains:

1   *Treatment context factors*. Variations in planned treatment include permutations of the treatment setting, the intensity (that is, frequency and length) of treatment, the nature of the treatment modality to be applied (that is, medical versus psychosocial or some combination) and the treatment format (that is, individual, multi-person therapy, class of medication, etc.) to be used.

2   *Relationship qualities*. Variations of the plan embody selective treatment in two areas – the fit of therapist and patient personality and belief styles and the nature of pre-therapy preparation that may best be administered.

3   *Selection of treatment strategies*. Specific treatment strategies vary with respect to the nature of the treatment goals (that is, symptom change versus conflict change), the level of experience addressed by the intervention (that is, unconscious motivations, emotional recognition, cognitions or overt behavior) and the level of direction required by the therapist (for example, use of homework, balancing the therapist's role as teacher and collaborator, etc.).

While the systematic treatment selection model is a relatively recent innovation, it is a product of an ongoing, foundational research program initiated and maintained by the first author and his colleagues for nearly three decades (Beutler, Engle, Shoham-Salomon et al., 1991). Since its inception in 1970, the research program has produced over a hundred empirical papers, an equal number of theoretical and methodological treatises, 10 books and numerous presentations. These works have been devoted to addressing interrelationships among patient predisposing characteristics and each of the other three domains of the model.

Two of the domains comprising STS, relationship qualities and specific psychotherapy strategies have received the largest amount of attention in our own research on patient differential predictors of treatment efficacy. We have directed relatively less attention to determining how and if treatment context factors, such as setting, intensity, mode and format, enhance treatment fit with patients. Thus, it has been advantageous to look to the findings of other research programs to supplement the dimensions and domains of the model. This reliance on other research programs to supplement and extend our efforts is illustrated in the recent collaborative work with Drs John Clarkin (Beutler & Clarkin, 1990), Bruce Bongar (Bongar & Beutler, 1994) and Kenneth I. Howard (Kopta, Howard, Lowry & Beutler, 1994).

The research conducted between 1970 and 1980, when our first technical eclectic model was formulated, was largely focused on the domain that we came to identify as 'relationship qualities'. This research identified the variables that related to effective patient–therapist matching and to enhancing effective therapeutic communication. Beginning in the early

1980s, our research efforts turned to a closer scrutiny of the fourth domain – the fit between specific treatment strategies and identified patient qualities. The temporal split between these two phases of the research program has never been complete; throughout each period, some of our work has addressed all four of the domains as well as some of the subdimensions within the model.

In the following pages we will summarize some of the major findings of our research program that have served to help define and support the viability of the STS model of treatment planning.

Research on relationship qualities

The first stepping stone of the STS model was the identification of matching patient and therapist qualities that comprised compatible and persuasive working relationships. From the beginning, the first author was intrigued with the observation that patients' values and beliefs seemed to move closer to those of their therapists during the process of successful, but not during unsuccessful, psychotherapy (Beutler, 1972, 1973b). This observation formed the basis of a series of studies, largely during the 1970s, that focused on the nature of patient–therapist matching that might lead to enhanced outcomes (for example, Beutler, 1971a, 1971b; Beutler, Johnson, Neville, Elkins & Jobe, 1975; Beutler, Johnson, Neville & Workman, 1972a, 1972b, 1973). While the major focus of this research was on individual therapy, some studies extended the work to group therapy (Beutler, Jobe & Elkins, 1974), while others focused on marital therapy (Beutler, 1971a), and still others (Beutler, 1979b) compared several treatment formats with one another. Other studies extended the matching dimensions to alternative patient samples, including a variety of outpatient (Beutler, Pollack & Jobe, 1978) and inpatient (for example, Beutler, Jobe & Elkins, 1974; Johnson, Beutler & Neville, 1978a, 1978b) settings and samples.

While much of the early research was devoted to exploring attitude and value similarities and dissimilarities, demographic matches, especially with reference to patient–therapist sexual similarity, were also explored (Johnson et al., 1978a, 1978b). Likewise, a variety of psychological variables were explored as potential mediators of attitude similarity effects. One's regional or perceived distance from a treatment source, rather than the actual number of miles, for example, was found to enhance patient perceptions of treatment credibility (Beutler, Johnson et al., 1972a) while patient persuadability (Beutler, Arizmendi, Crago, Shanfield & Hagaman, 1983) was found to only modestly enhance the power of patient–therapist attitude compatibility to effect change (Kolb, Beutler, Davis, Crago & Shanfield, 1985).

While most of the foregoing work focused on how we might directly impact therapeutic outcome by constructing a good match between patient and therapist initial attitudes and backgrounds, we also explored indirect ways of facilitating the production of good outcomes. These studies focused on ways to enhance the therapeutic relationship and associated therapeutic processes, constituting an effort to identify ways in which the problems of incompatible matches could be overcome by the therapist. In this research, we explored the role of therapist facilitative skills and perceived credibility as an expert in enhancing both attitudinal compatible and incompatible patient–therapist dyads (for example, Beutler, Johnson et al., 1972b; Beutler, Johnson, Neville & Workman, 1973), and went on to identify the role of these enhanced relationships in therapeutic outcome (Beutler, Johnson et al., 1972a; Beutler, Johnson, Neville, Workman & Elkins, 1973; Lafferty, Beutler & Crago, 1989).

Collectively, the research in this area (see reviews by Beutler 1979b, 1981; Beutler, Clarkin, Crago & Bergan, 1991) consistently revealed that: (1) effective therapy was accompanied by convergence of patient beliefs and values on those of the therapist; and (2) the amount of attitude/value convergence was predicted by a complex pattern of initial similarities and differences between patients and therapists, with outcome being most strongly associated with levels of initial attitude/value differences. To some degree, these findings are consistent with what would be predicted by established theories of persuasion. In recent years, however, we have become dissatisfied with the accuracy of predictions made from general theories of persuasion and we have developed predictive models that are specific to the psychotherapy relationship (Beutler & Bergan, 1991).

Combining our research findings with those of others (Beutler, Crago & Arizmendi, 1986; Beutler, Machado & Neufeldt, 1994), we have come to believe that relationship quality is enhanced by a patient–therapist match in which the participants are demographically similar (for example, Johnson et al., 1978a, 1978b) but attitudinally dissimilar, particularly in regards to attitudes about attachment and intimacy (for example, Arizmendi, Beutler, Shanfield & Crago, 1985; Beutler, Arizmendi et al., 1983). The STS model incorporated these findings and conclusions by advocating that patients be assigned to therapists who are demographically similar and attitudinally disparate, to the degree that this is possible and feasible. Additionally, our research on the contributors to effective attitudinal matching (Beutler, 1971b; Beutler, Johnson et al., 1972a), as well as on the mediating roles that location (Beutler, Johnson et al., 1972b) and patient personality traits (Kolb et al., 1985; Stansell, Beutler, Neville & Johnson, 1975) play on therapist process and relationship qualities (Salvio, Beutler, Engle & Wood, 1993) led to the incorporation, in STS, of suggestions for overcoming the constraining and limiting effects of incompatible matches (Beutler, 1983; Beutler & Clarkin, 1990).

Selection of specific therapy contexts and strategies

The question of which treatment procedures, under what conditions, and independent of any particular therapist, work best for which patient remains of central interest to researchers and clinicians alike (Whiston & Sexton, 1993). Psychotherapy is comprised of a set of complex tasks, and practitioners need comprehensive knowledge of how different processes used in psychotherapy interact with patient characteristics in order to make treatment decisions that will maximize and optimize therapeutic power. Not all relevant patient characteristics are immutable; many are changing and dynamic as they interact with therapist personalities and attitudes. Thus, it is insufficient to study only initial patient qualities with static assignment of therapists or therapy types. Our research on the selection of specific strategies that differentially fit a variety of patients at different points in the therapeutic endeavor began quite unobtrusively, and has consisted of several interdigitated phases.

Overview

The first phase of this research arose from a few exploratory and naturalistic investigations of the relative efficacy of different formats of treatment delivery (Beutler, 1979b). Like many, if not most, of such studies, few main effect differences were noted. However, some suggestive patterns appeared through post-hoc analyses of how therapy and patient characteristics interacted. From these observations, we initiated comprehensive searches of the extant literature in an effort to identify patient characteristics that had been found in other research to interact with various aspects of treatment. We began with obvious characteristics of patients and treatments, such as the interaction between patient diagnoses and the brand of therapy (for example, cognitive therapy, psychoanalytic therapy, etc.). Unlike others who had reviewed comparative psychotherapy outcome studies and found that therapy outcomes were largely indistinguishable (for example, Luborsky, Singer & Luborsky, 1975), we cross-tabulated treatment effects with various characteristics of the patient samples used in the identified studies (Beutler, 1979b, 1983). We reasoned that the null effects found by others may have reflected inordinate heterogeneity among patient types.

Our concern that heterogeneous patient samples may have obscured differential efficacy rates among different treatments became greater with the initiation of the NIMH Collaborative Study of Depression (Elkin, Parloff, Hadley & Autry, 1985; Elkin et al., 1989). We feared that the use of diagnosis and general severity of symptoms, as the primary mediating patient variables, would not yield either clear or clinically meaningful indicators for making differential treatment decisions (see Beutler, 1991a; Beutler & Crago, 1987). Thus, we embarked on the task of discovering what patient and treatment variables were sufficiently specific to allow differential outcome effects to emerge, if these effects were indeed present when patients were matched to treatments.

Selecting the most promising patient and treatment matching variables is not an easy task given the exceedingly large number of constructs that have been incorporated into various theories or subjected to empirical scrutiny

(Beutler, 1991a). Selective reviews of the literature allowed us to reduce the number of promising variables by combining similar constructs, but the list remained cumbersome and excessively long. For example, the systematic treatment selection model outlined by Beutler and Clarkin (1990) was able to reduce the hundreds of potential variables to approximately forty different treatment matching dimensions, using rational methods. However, this is still an unmanageable number of variables for most clinicians to employ.

Hence, we initiated a second phase of this research devoted to manualizing and validating the efficacies of a variety of treatments. These treatments were selected and their corresponding manuals were designed to embody contrasting characteristics that were assumed to be operative in effective prescriptive treatment planning. The first three manuals developed were based on principles of cognitive therapy (CT; Yost, Beutler, Corbishley & Allender, 1986), experiential therapy (FEP; Daldrup, Beutler, Engle & Greenberg, 1988) and non-directive, self-guided therapy (S/SDT; Beutler, 1973a; Scogin, Hamblin & Beutler, 1987). These manuals were developed in order to facilitate comparisons of different combinations of patient and therapy qualities. We also developed training and compliance assessment procedures for each of the models.

So that our efforts would be compatible with the NIMH Collaborative Study and other similar research programs, each of the treatment manuals we developed was then validated and confirmed to be effective. We tested the overall efficacy of these manualized treatments by comparing them either to therapy as usual (Beutler, Frank, Scheiber, Calvert & Gaines, 1984), or to various prescribed (Beutler, Scogin et al., 1987) and non-prescribed (Shisslak et al., 1985) drug treatments. Finally, the efficacy of each treatment was validated in a comparison to a minimal treatment condition (CT; Beutler, Scogin et al., 1987; FEP: Beutler, Daldrup et al., 1987; S/SDT: Jobe, Beutler & Green, 1976; Scogin et al., 1987).

This validational phase set the stage for the third and current phase of our research. In this phase, the objectives have been to concentrate on a few, relatively promising matching dimensions and to establish their roles as indicators and contra-indicators for the contrasting dimensions of treatment embodied in the treatment manuals. By a process of rational analysis and exploratory research (Beutler & Consoli, 1992; Beutler, Consoli & Williams, 1994; Beutler & Hodgson, 1993; Gaw & Beutler, 1995), we identified five of the more promising variables for directing differential treatment decisions, and have organized our efforts to refine the concepts originally presented by Beutler and Clarkin (1990) around these variables. The five variables are as follows:

1   *Functional problem severity.* Severity, as indexed by diminished social functioning, loss of social support systems and diminished work and family functioning, suggests the need for restrictive treatment environments, for long-term or frequent treatment sessions, and for the

use of pharmacotherapy. Less severe impairments are associated with less intensive and restrictive treatment needs.

2   *Subjective distress.* High levels of self-attributed, personal distress suggest the use of procedures to reduce stress and reattribute sources of anxiety. Very low levels of distress indicate the desirability of confronting the patient and challenging the patient's perceptions of his or her role in creating and maintaining problems. In addition, other procedures that increase arousal and personal ownership of distressful reactions might be introduced. These postulates assume that an optimal level of self-attributed distress is desirable or necessary to support psychotherapeutic movement.

3   *Problem complexity.* Complexity is indicated by a history of recurrence, indicators of chronicity, the presence of personality disorders and indicators of wide-ranging symptoms or multiple diagnoses. Complexity is assumed to relate to the breadth of desirable treatment goals. The more complex the problem, the more the optimal treatment objectives are thought to include changes at the systemic and conflictual levels. Problems of lesser complexity indicate correspondingly less need to extend treatment beyond the goals of symptom removal.

4   *Coping style.* Acting out, projection, impulsivity and direct avoidance all comprise 'externalizing' methods of coping with anxiety. Self-reflection, self-criticism, emotional restriction and social withdrawal all reflect 'internalizing' coping methods. Externalization is postulated as an indicator for the use of behavioral control and cognitive change procedures, while internalization is thought to indicate the need for insight-oriented change procedures.

5   *Resistance potential.* It is assumed that patients vary widely in their need to maintain freedom from authoritative and external control.[1] Resistance against loss of personal control is manifest in both trait-like and state-like behaviors. This variability indicates the need to vary therapist confrontational and directive methods in correspondence to these patient resistance levels. During periods of high resistance, non-directive or paradoxical interventions are thought to be indicated, while directive and educational procedures are indicated during periods of low resistance.

The third phase of our research has explored the validity of each of these matching dimensions independently (see Beutler, 1983; Beutler & Clarkin, 1990). A fourth phase of research is planned and now being initiated even while the third phase is still in process. This fourth phase will test the hypothesis that treatment efficacy can be improved by combining interventions from different theories into a single, comprehensive treatment package. This combination would entail the matching of patients and therapies along several dimensions at once. Thus, the treatment may combine elements that are behavioral (for example, exposure and homework), insight-oriented (for example, interpretation), experiential (for example, imagery for inducing arousal) and cognitive (for example, cognitive rehearsal, identification of automatic thoughts) in order optimally to fit or match with corresponding patient dimensions. When implemented with all five patient–therapy matching dimensions under current investigation, this will be the refining test of STS.

Summary of major findings

In phase three of our research program, we have concentrated on exploring the predictive validity of three of the five dimensions speculated to be intimately involved in treatment selection. While all five dimensions have been the focus of continuing theoretical and conceptual research, we have focused on these three variables because they are the most difficult to measure and the least understood. These variables include *subjective distress, coping style* and *resistance potential.*

Phase three of our research was actually initiated by an early naturalistic study that inspected the differential impact of various therapeutic activities on depressed and anxious patients (Beutler & Mitchell, 1981). This study revealed systematic interaction effects between patient coping style and treatment type that cut across diagnoses. The demonstration that insight-oriented procedures exerted their greatest effects among internalizing patients, the group for whom behavioral interventions exerted the poorest effects, led us to initiate our first randomized clinical trial study of selected, manualized treatments, which proved to be a keystone in the Arizona Psychotherapy Research Program (Beutler, Engle, Shoham-Salomon et al., 1991).

This first study (Beutler, Frank et al., 1984) compared three models of group psychotherapy with one another and with a treatment-as-usual control condition. The sample was comprised of acutely disturbed psychiatric inpatients who presented for short-term inpatient care with mixed symptoms and diagnoses. The three treatment models were cognitive-behavioral therapy, experiential-gestalt therapy and an interactive supportive therapy, selected to represent models that varied in level of directive support provided and emotion aroused. The baseline treatment components provided to all patients included individual therapy, ward milieu and recreational therapy. Outcome was assessed by three independent sources: therapist discharge ratings of global improvement; pre- and post-treatment patient ratings on a standardized symptom index; and nurses ratings of ward behavior at the beginning and end of treatment.

While the results failed to show strong effects of group treatments, they did indicate that insight-oriented, abreactive group treatment was associated with a mean worsening of condition in this acutely disturbed population. This finding, along with indications of positive effects associated with individual therapy, led us to look much more specifically at the characteristics of patients and how well they fit with the nature of their individual treatments. A follow-up naturalistic analysis was undertaken of

108 of these patients in order to determine if various degrees of match and mismatch between patient resistance and therapy directiveness, on the one hand, and patient coping style and therapy insight versus behavioral focus, on the other, were related to improvement (Calvert, Beutler & Crago, 1988).

The results of this study confirmed the importance of patient internalization as an indicator for insight-oriented therapies and of patient externalization as an indicator for behavioral and cognitively oriented therapies. Unreliable measurement impeded the effort to assess the role of patient resistance potential in directive and non-directive therapies, and reinforced the view that stronger measurement procedures for this dimension were needed. The study also provided post-hoc support for the suggestion that level of distress and functional impairment contra-indicated the use of experiential, abreactive and confrontational procedures.

To pursue these results further, three more systematically controlled, randomized clinical trials studies have been initiated in order to look specifically at all three patient dimensions as predictors of beneficial outcomes in therapies that varied in corresponding ways. In the most extensive of these studies, we (Beutler, Engle, Mohr et al., 1991) randomly assigned depressed outpatients who varied on both resistance potential and coping style (trait-like dimensions) to one of three treatments. The treatments were manualized, pre-tested and designed to vary in level of therapist directiveness, focus on insight versus behavioral change, and the degree to which therapy worked to increase or decrease proximal arousal. Cognitive therapy (CT; Yost et al., 1986) was therapist-directed, non-insight-oriented and designed directly to temper emotional arousal. Focused experiential therapy (FEP; Daldrup et al., 1988) was therapist-directed, insight/awareness-focused and designed to increase focused patient arousal. Supportive self-directed therapy (S/SDT; Scogin et al., 1987) was non-directive, insight-focused and designed to exert little direct impact on proximal arousal states.

At the end of a 20-week course of treatment, it was determined that the insight-oriented treatments were most effective among internalizing patients; behavioral/symptom-oriented therapies were most effective among externalizing patients; directive therapies were most effective among non-resistant patients; non-directive therapies were most effective among resistant patients (Beutler, Engle, Mohr et al., 1991); subjective distress was an indicator for risk of deterioration (Mohr et al., 1990); emotion-arousing therapies among low aroused patients were associated with positive outcomes (Burgoon et al., 1994); and non-verbal cues were more consistent indicators of patient arousal levels than verbal content (Mohr, Shoham-Salomon, Engle & Beutler, 1991).

A further test of the power of these matching dimensions is to be found in the degree to which effects are maintained during the months following treatment. In a one-year follow-up of patients in the foregoing study, those who were mismatched for treatment (that is, internalizers in symptom-focused therapy and resistant patients in directive procedures) did not show the degree of continued improvement during follow-up period that was evident among those who were matched for treatment (Beutler, Machado, Engle & Mohr, 1993). This finding confirms the value of both matching dimensions for allaying relapse and facilitating continuing post-therapy improvement.

The second study explored the cross-cultural transportability of these findings in a sample of patients from the Bern Psychotherapy Research Program (Beutler, Mohr, Grawe, Engle & MacDonald, 1991). This study confirmed the validity of several measures of resistance potential and coping style as predictors of positive outcomes when patients were exposed to directive versus non-directive and insight versus behaviorally focused treatments, respectively.

The third study (Beutler, Patterson et al., 1993) in this series is currently underway. The Couples Alcoholism Treatment (CAT) Project was initiated in 1990 and is now in its final year of data-gathering. It is a study of the relative efficacy of cognitive-behavioral and family systems therapies for alcoholics who are randomly matched and mismatched to treatment according to their scores on measures of coping style and resistance potential (frequently referred to as 'interpersonal reactance'). The two treatments to which patients are randomly assigned are administered in a couples format, and vary in degree of therapist directiveness and demand as well as in the degree of behavioral-symptom focus.

The cognitive-behavioral therapy (Wakefield, Yost, Williams & Patterson, in press) is symptom-focused, defines the patient's problem as a behavior (drinking), and requires compliance with a non-drinking participation contract. The family systems therapy (Rohrbaugh, Shoham, Spungen & Steinglass, 1994), on the other hand, focuses on changing family and couple interactions, identifies system patterns and conflicts as the problem rather than drinking, and defines a consultation rather than treatment role for the therapist in order to allow participants to make their own decision regarding alcohol cessation.

It is predicted that internalizing drinkers who receive family systems therapy (insight-oriented and non-directive) will show greater improvement than internalizing drinkers who are 'mismatched' and randomly assigned to the cognitive therapy (task-oriented and directive). Likewise, the externalizing drinkers assigned to cognitive therapy are expected to show greater improvement on the outcome variables than those assigned to family systems therapy. Furthermore, it is predicted that drinkers who are highly interpersonally reactant will benefit more from the non-directive nature of systems therapy than from the directive, cognitive therapy. Conversely, drinkers low in interpersonal reactance are expected to show greater improvement in a directive form of treatment (cognitive therapy) (Beutler, Patterson et al., 1993).

Outcome results for this study are not yet available. Preliminary results have confirmed the discriminant validity of coping style and resistance potential, and have provided evidence of the efficacy of the treatments. As we evaluate differential outcomes, we hope to determine which of the treatment and patient combinations are most closely associated with the cessation of alcohol use and the maintenance of sobriety.

In addition to the foregoing studies, several of past and current colleagues and collaborators have gone on to explore the role that patient reactance levels (that is, extreme resistance potential – the likelihood that patients will do the *opposite* of that advocated by a therapist) play in differential treatment efficacy (for example, Shoham-Salomon, Avner & Neeman, 1989). These studies suggest that highly reactant patients are candidates for the use of paradoxical interventions, and lend support to the view that matching the therapy approach to patient resistance levels improves outcome.

Crossing the bridge from research to practice

As a whole, results from the third phase of our research program demonstrate the practicality of considering patient–therapy interaction effects in the prediction of psychotherapy outcome. Our research suggests that therapists will do well to consider more than either the major symptoms, the patient diagnosis or the theoretical leanings of the therapist when planning treatment (see Beutler, 1989, 1991a, 1991b). A psychotherapist applying STS methods uses the assessment of patient and therapist characteristics to guide the development of a treatment plan that addresses three domains: (a) treatment contexts, (b) therapist assignment and other relationship enhancement procedures, and (c) treatment strategies and techniques (Beutler, Consoli & Williams, 1994). Practitioners of prescriptive psychotherapy cross the bridge between research and practice repeatedly, as they systematically assess their patients, make empirically based treatment decisions, re-evaluate these decisions in light of patient progress and adjust the administration of their techniques or therapeutic stance to fit guiding principles or strategies (Goldfried, Castonguay & Safran, 1992).

Following an explicit set of decisional criteria (Gaw & Beutler, 1995), the STS therapist pursues the following steps. First, the therapist selects the appropriate treatment contexts, keeping open the question of whether treatment is required at all. If severity of function impairment is indicative of treatment, a decision is made about an optimal treatment location or setting (community, inpatient or outpatient), a combination of treatment formats (for example, balance of individual, group and family involvement), the integration of psychosocial and medical modes of intervention, and the anticipated intensity (that is, duration and frequency) of treatment contacts (Beutler, Consoli & Williams, 1994). These decisions reflect initial assessments of the severity of patient impairment, including the number of life-functioning areas affected, the availability of social support systems and the chronicity of the condition (Gaw & Beutler, 1995).

Second, the therapist plans the nature and quality of the therapist–patient relationship. As observed in our early research (Beutler, 1981, 1989; Beutler, Johnson, Neville, Workman & Elkins, 1973), the integrity and strength of the therapeutic alliance may be fortified by assigning therapists to patients with similar demographic backgrounds, sex, age and ethnicity. In addition, the outcome of treatment can be enhanced if patients and therapists are somewhat dissimilar in the degree to which they value autonomy and intimacy in interpersonal relationships (Beutler, 1971a, 1971b; Johnson, Neville & Beutler, 1973).

When making less than desirable 'fits' in the assignment of therapists, role induction techniques can be a useful method for teaching patients about the process of psychotherapy and the roles that the patient and therapist may adopt. Patients who lack familiarity with psychotherapy may benefit from an informed understanding of what to expect in treatment (Beutler, Crago & Arizmendi, 1986).

Therapists also may work to create a more comfortable environment for patients who are agitated or distressed by self-disclosure, which is an essential part of the psychotherapeutic process, by managing their own in-session behavior. Enhancing the smoothness of therapeutic communication, altering the level of confrontation and varying the depth of the session are procedures extracted from experiential therapy (Daldrup et al., 1988) to manage patient distress levels and to facilitate patient participation and self-exploration. These strategies also help the patient alter dependency patterns and increase levels of experiencing within sessions, all of which have been related to positive outcomes (Hill, Beutler & Daldrup, 1989).

Once the therapist has determined the setting in which to provide treatment, the mode and format through which to deliver it, the objectives to pursue and the therapeutic contract to establish initially, he or she uses this information to direct the focus of treatment either toward achieving insight or toward symptom removal (Beutler, Consoli & Williams, 1994). The selection of the treatment outcome objectives and the within-session work is guided by the chronicity and generality of the patient's problem (a dimension we have called 'complexity'), the patient's coping style and the individual's anticipated level of interpersonal resistance.

Generally speaking, our research (Beutler, Engle, Mohr et al., 1991; Beutler, Mohr et al., 1991) indicates that patients who favor internalizing coping strategies will achieve the greatest benefit from treatment techniques that foster the experience and expression of emotion and personal insight. Those who favor externalizing coping strategies, in contrast, tend to do better with task-oriented, symptom-focused techniques that foster personal responsibility, teach self-management and encourage the containment of highly charged affect. Furthermore, highly reactant patients are expected to resist therapist directives to perform specific tasks like homework assignments. Therefore, non-directive, supportive or self-directed techniques are likely to achieve greater compliance with treatment and so may lead to better outcomes for resistant patients. Patients low in reactance are expected to do well with either directive or non-directive techniques.

The cases presented below are drawn from two sources and non-essential details were modified to reduce recognizability. Consent for using material obtained for research and teaching purposes was obtained in both cases. The first case is an example of a drinker and partner who were randomly assigned to family systems treatment as part of the CAT Project (Beutler, Patterson et al., 1993). In many ways, this case represents the status of the treatment field: clients seek treatment with an agency and then are assigned to an established or 'set' treatment that is designed for the patient's diagnostic problems. This 'one-size-fits-all' approach to treatment produces a variety of outcomes. Our first case is a demonstration of a poor fit between client characteristics and treatment mode, which, in turn, led to a negative outcome.

The second case presented here is an example of the systematic application of prescriptive psychotherapy to a case of clinical depression. The case represents an effort to adapt the treatments to the patient's predisposing characteristics, following the STS model. This case represents a positive outcome.

Case example: A mismatch

At the time of intake, Al was a 35-year-old Caucasian male married to a 30-year-old Filipino-American woman, named Pat. They had been married for 10 years and had three children, aged 3, 5 and 8. Al was trained in a technical field, but was fired from his workplace six months earlier for drinking on the job. Pat was an elementary-school teacher and had held the same job for the last eight years. Al was seeking treatment for his 'alcohol problem', which he reported had worsened in the last three years. The symptoms associated with his alcohol use fulfilled the DSM-IV criteria (American Psychiatric Association, 1994) for alcohol dependence (he evidenced both alcohol tolerance and withdrawal).

Al also reported that he was hospitalized for a suicide attempt and severe depression two years ago. He denied current suicidal feelings, and indicated that his depression had not been 'that bad' since the hospitalization. Al's MacAndrew Alcoholism Scale score was 65 (MacAndrew, 1965) and his Michigan Alcohol Screening Test (MAST) (Selzer, 1971) score was 30; both indicated at least moderate abuse. His Beck Depression Inventory score (BDI) (Beck, 1990) was 13 (mild). His average alcohol consumption over the last three months was 20 ounces of hard liquor per day (14 standard drinks), usually after work. He consumed the same amount of alcohol on weekends, but started drinking early in the afternoon. Al reported that he needed to drink to relax and feel 'refreshed' in the morning. He also reported that while he had never been treated for his 'alcohol addiction', he did experience great success with a cognitive-behavioral treatment program for smoking cessation several years earlier.

Pat reported that she suffered from migraine headaches, which prevented her from completing her lesson plans. The headaches had disabled her five to six times in the past six months. She also reported feeling depressed and tired. Pat's BDI score was seven (within normal limits). Her reasons for seeking treatment included complaints about Al's behavior when he was intoxicated. She reported that he became argumentative and belligerent at those times.

Al and Pat were randomly assigned to work with an experienced family systems therapist who was born in Southeast Asia and trained in the United States. If the therapist had been able to assess the clients' characteristics in accordance with the STS model, she might have determined first that the degree of demographic dissimilarity of the therapist and drinker was substantial; they were not well matched, suggesting that a good working relationship was unlikely to develop (Beutler, 1979a, 1979c; Beutler, Johnson et al., 1975). The therapist's demographic fit (similarity) with the patient's wife was more conducive to developing an alliance. As this analysis might have predicted, Al remarked repeatedly during treatment that he believed that his real motives and feelings could not be understood by a foreign-born therapist. Pat, who was ethnically more similar to the therapist than Al, seemed to feel greater affinity for the therapist, but this stimulated controversy and prevented Pat from optimally benefiting from her work with the therapist.

The therapist was not using the STS model and so did not rely on relevant patient indicators (for example, Gaw & Beutler, 1995) as a technical guide to building the therapeutic relationship. For example, Al did not seem to know what to expect from family systems psychotherapy and might have benefited from participation in behavior role induction procedures. Instead of offering these techniques, the therapist did her best to improve the relationship by eliciting and reflecting Al's view of himself and his world. This approach might work well for some clients, but failed to solidify a working alliance with Al.

In other ways as well, the patients' assignment to family systems therapy resulted in a consistent mismatch with other prescriptive recommendations for specific techniques and strategies that would have arisen from following STS guidelines. For example, the *functional severity* of Al's problem was moderate, not so high that inpatient care would be recommended, but high enough so that long-term intervention, rather than the time-limited treatment offered, would probably have been indicated by STS (Beutler, Consoli & Williams, 1994). The length of the patient's drinking history suggested risks of relapse and invoked the desirability of an ongoing intervention beyond time-limited treatment. Like most contemporary, 'one-size-fits-all' manualized and managed care treatments, time limits were imposed by the treatment model independent of these considerations.

The *complexity* of Al's presenting problem also was moderately mismatched to treatment. His problem was more isolated and constricted than was indicated by the family system therapy's focus on systemic themes and persistent patterns. The reported depression, work problems, chronicity and marital problems appeared to have been secondary reactions to and inseparable from his prolonged alcohol use. This view fit the client's treatment goal, which was simply to stop drinking. Al believed that alcoholism was 'just something that happened to you'. Even though Pat complained about Al's alcohol use, she attributed all co-existent problems to his drinking problem. She presumed that once he was sober and she was less stressed, her headaches would subside.

Subjective distress was judged to be low, a condition that argued for the use of procedures that confronted fears and provoked enough personalized distress to motivate change (Burgoon et al., 1994; Hill et al., 1989). Both partners reported a great deal of discomfort with their situation, but expressed this as blame on each other and on alcohol rather than as evidence of personal responsibility for their problems. They expressed a high degree of hostility toward one another, but neither one demonstrated a willingness to accept responsibility for changing their relationship patterns.

The foregoing patient predisposing variables were not specifically used to adjust the treatment applications of either of the two treatments used in the CAT Project. The two treatments were designed to contrast on the level of 'fit' with two other patient dimensions: *coping style* and *resistance potential*. These latter dimensions were assessed for both Al and Pat, via the MMPI-2 (Butcher, Dahlstrom, Graham, Tellegen & Kaemmer, 1989) as per prior research (Beutler, Engle, Mohr et al., 1991).

Al's MMPI-2, two-point code was 4–3 (Pd = 67 and Hy = 59). Both of these scales (psychopathic and hystrionic) reflected an externalizing coping style. Two other MMPI-2 methods that were used to indicate coping style in this study confirmed this view. Respondents with this configuration are typically extroverted and sociable; they act impulsively and sometimes aggressively as a way of avoiding anxiety, and their relationships tend to be superficial. They frequently have problems with authority and perceive themselves to be the victims of other people or of uncontrollable, external forces (Butcher, 1989; Graham, 1993).

Pat's two-point code was 6–3 (Pa = 74 and Hy = 73) (paranoia and hystrionic); though mixed on this index, her other MMPI-2 indices confirmed that she also had an externalizing coping style. Clients with her particular configuration tend to display long-term psychological maladjustment. They frequently report somatic complaints and feel as though others are insensitive to their needs and unconcerned about their welfare. Respondents with this code may also report feeling lonely, victimized and isolated (Butcher, 1989), and usually fail to recognize or acknowledge their own role in these interpersonal problems (Graham, 1993).

Given these indices, the treatment prescribed by STS would be a cognitive-behavioral intervention rather than the family systems intervention that they received. Perhaps this accounts for the couple's premature termination after completing 15 of the scheduled 20 sessions.

Only the couple's high potential for interpersonal resistance was consistent with the treatment characteristics provided by the family system's therapy, in this case the level of directiveness provided. This resistance potential was evident in their interactions with each other and confirmed on both of their MMPI-2s. Al resisted Pat's efforts to modify his behavior by accusing her of being overly critical. He, in turn, tried to control her behavior through barter and intimidation. For example, he refused to work toward sobriety until Pat agreed to work on alleviating her stress-induced migraine headaches. The cognitive therapy model used in the CAT Project was designed to behaviorally address both of these patterns through redirecting reinforcement contingencies and establishing behavioral exchange programs.

Family systems therapy, as we have developed it (Rohrbaugh et al., 1994), utilizes non-directive, non-authoritarian and paradoxical procedures that are well fit to patients with high levels of resistance potential. The therapist began family systems therapy assuming the benign role of a consultant rather than a treatment provider. For example, Al and Pat were asked to explore how Al's alcohol use harmed and benefited the family, but they were not encouraged to do anything about it initially. These strategies seemed to work well in the beginning. The therapist's stance was affirming and the techniques employed were, for the most part, very non-directive.

After a few sessions, the treatment team presented its opinion about the couple's strengths and weaknesses and offered Pat and Al 'treatment' to transcend the 'evaluation' that had thus far organized the goals of their conjoint contacts. As the therapist adopted more of an authoritative, 'treater' role, resistance increased. Some directive techniques that were part of the standard manualized presentation (for example, family sculpting or notifying others about his plan to avoid alcohol) provoked resistance from Al, who described them as too intrusive or revealing. Al's request for behavioral procedures to help with symptoms of craving would have been a logical recommendation in STS. However, utilizing a single model of therapy restricted the range of interventions available to the therapist. She accommodated his wishes within the limits allowed by the theoretical model but ultimately redirected the focus of treatment to a search for family themes.

Al managed to abstain from alcohol use for the first three weeks of the family system's treatment phase. He later lapsed, abstained, lapsed again and finally resumed his usual level of alcohol use for the duration of treatment. When treatment ended prematurely, few treatment gains were noted by either the clients or the therapist. Al reported that he started on antabuse immediately after leaving the CAT Project. This approach failed him after two weeks time and he again resumed drinking. A few months after that he learned about a self-directed program for sobriety and has been abstinent for two months.

Case study: A match.

At the time of intake, Dee was a 45-year-old divorced woman who was seeking therapy two weeks after being discharged from a psychiatric hospital. Her admission to the hospital three weeks prior was precipitated by a serious suicide attempt that had been preceded by the termination of her employment and a divorce. She had a history of periodic drinking binges, usually elicited by a significant loss. She had made one previous suicide attempt, had a 10-year history of treatment for recurrent depression, had lost several jobs and presented with a diagnosis of both recurrent major depression and borderline personality disorder. The patient was evaluated for treatment suitability by the first author and was entered into STS-guided therapy.

Following the STS model, an initial 'dyadic' evaluation (Beutler, 1973b) was made to define the degree of patient–therapist match. This analysis revealed that Dee's demographic background was compatible with that of the therapist. While patient and therapist sex differed, Dee expressed preference for a male therapist, and her ethnic, religious, age and socio-economic background factors were all similar to those of the therapist. This 'fit' suggested that there was a basis for the development of a good working relationship (Beutler, Johnson et al., 1975; Stansell et al., 1975). In addition, consideration was given to the five specific variables noted in the foregoing pages in outlining a treatment plan.

The *functional severity* of the problem was moderate, based upon her psychiatric history, the lack of social support resources, and a mental status evaluation. She reported only one friendship, and this individual had refused to see her since her suicide attempt. Her inability to function adequately in work, marital and parental roles suggested the need for long-term treatment. On the positive side, she was willing to make a no-suicide contract, which, coupled with the recommendations of the referring psychiatrist, formed sufficient evidence that she was suitable for outpatient care (Beutler & Clarkin, 1990; Gaw & Beutler, 1995).

Problem complexity was judged to be high, based upon chronicity, the multiplicity of symptoms, the wide range of life functions affected and the presence of a personality disorder diagnosis. Hence, the outcome goals selected were to go beyond the reduction of depressive symptoms to alter patterns of recurrent interpersonal conflict, the structure of her social network and precipitating internal conflicts (Beutler, Consoli & Williams, 1994). Based upon considerations of both functional severity and complexity (Beutler & Clarkin, 1990), a contract for 20 initial sessions was negotiated with the indication that this might relieve some symptoms and provide a basis for a second and more extended contract that would work more directly on recurrent personal and interpersonal problems.

Subjective distress was measured with a variety of standard anxiety scales (Gaw & Beutler, 1995). She scored in the upper 10 per cent of psychiatric outpatients and at the same time was self-blaming and despondent over what she perceived as her own inability to get along with others. This level of distress indicated an immediate need to reduce levels of arousal by providing support and structure, while attempting to increase the availability of social supports to moderate her distress. Daily activity logs, relaxation and exercise training, structured activities to increase social contact, a program of behavioral and cognitive monitoring and readings on the topic of self-esteem were assigned during the first 20 sessions in order to provide structure and direction.

Dee's *coping style* was assessed by administration of the MMPI-2 (see Gaw & Beutler, 1995; Beutler, Engle et al., 1991). Elevations were in the upper 10 per cent for most clinical scales, confirming the complexity and severity of the problems. In addition, the two-point profile was 2–4 (D, Pd, both > 80), followed closely by scale 6 (Pa). This profile suggested a combination of both internalizing and externalizing features (Beutler, Engle et al., 1991). Two formal indices of internalization–externalization favored the dominance of an externalizing pattern. Based upon her MMPI-2 profile, such individuals are often described as depressed, irritable and moody. They often exhibit a recurrent pattern of self-defeating behaviors characterized by impulsive and often passive-aggressive acts. They have difficulty maintaining intimacy, and often establish excessively dependent relationships with sudden changes of feelings and attachments (Butcher et al., 1989).

These externalizing patterns suggest the susceptibility of response to behavioral structuring (for example, Calvert et al., 1988) and for identifying and changing the automatic thought patterns that are associated with or precede impulsive acts. The concomitant internalizing qualities of self-blame and self-criticism also suggest the desirability of some form of insight-oriented interventions. We elected to work toward the identification of cognitive schema, addressing these in the same cognitive-behavioral way as was to be used to defuse the automatic thoughts associated with her impulsive behaviors. Additionally, we decided to use the behavioral homework assignments described earlier to support the behavioral changes needed to reduce risk of suicidal and other impulsive acts.

Resistance potential was assessed by the Therapeutic Reactance Scale (Dowd, Milne & Wise, 1991). The scores revealed her to be one standard deviation below the mean, indicating at least a superficially cooperative attitude with therapy and the ability to benefit from directive procedures (Beutler, Mohr et al., 1991). This view was supported by observing her compliant response to homework assignments. Accordingly, this evaluation indicated the probable success of therapist-directed procedures and home-work assignments. The therapist provided direct suggestions for structuring her environment and coping with stress. Additionally, interpretations of transference, reflecting on the similarities between her idealized and ambivalent therapist attachment and the nature of her attachment to other men, were also adopted as procedures that would fit both the insight-oriented goals of therapy and her level of resistance potential.

With this background, Dee's psychotherapy unfolded smoothly. Her anxious and depressive symptoms gradually declined, and within the first 25 sessions she returned to the high normal range. Treatment continued for 20 months, and on two occasions sudden reduction in depressive symptoms or improved interpersonal contact occurred only to be immediately followed by a job or family crisis. These events invariably threw her into a period of depression and suicidal ideation. The pattern was so noticeable that early on it was possible for the therapist to predict aloud that her crisis response would occur when work and relationships started to improve. As she has begun to explore the schematic structures associated with this recurrent pattern, she discovered that she had a basic belief of being unworthy of happiness. This schema was used to organize treatment goals as indicated by the complexity of the problems presented (Beutler & Clarkin, 1990).

After the first year of therapy, the patient finally agreed to a change in her therapy contract, moving toward the goal of 'living' rather than simply 'not killing' herself. This terminology implied a willingness to accept an improved quality of life, one that was inconsistent with the pattern of chronic unemployment and job failure to which she had become accustomed. By the time of termination, she had obtained stable employment, had developed a network of friendships, had lost 20 pounds of unwanted weight, and was exploring the feasibility of developing another love relationship. She terminated with the acknowledgment that her delay in getting better was associated with a fear of giving up dependency on the support and direction of the therapist.

Notes

Work on this paper was partially supported by research grant No. AA 08970 to the first author. Co-Principle Investigators include Professors Varda Shoham and Theodore Jacob.

1. Originally, this dimension was described as 'reactance', a term that evolved from social psychology research. Reactance describes a state-like tendency of an individual to behave in a manner that is *opposite* to that advocated by an authority when there is no obvious choice given. As such, reactance only describes an extreme example of a more general resistance trait, a propensity to respond in a manner that ranges from static restraint to open opposition when faced with authoritatively imposed choices. The more general trait of 'resistance', as well as its state manifestations, seem to us to have more relevance to the clinician than the narrow range of oppositional and situational behavior described by the term 'reactance'.

References

American Psychiatric Association (1994). *Diagnostic and Statistical Manual of Mental Disorders* (4th ed.). Washington, DC: APA.

Arizmendi, T.G., Beutler, L.E., Shanfield, S.B., & Crago, M. (1985). Client–therapist value similarity and psychotherapy outcome: A microscopic approach. *Psychotherapy: Theory, Research and Practice*, *22*, 16–21.

Beck, A.T. (1990). *The Beck Depression Inventory*. Minneapolis: National Computer Systems.

Beitman, B.D. (1987). *The structure of individual psychotherapy.* New York: Guilford.

Beutler, L.E. (1971a). Attitude similarity in marital therapy. *Journal of Consulting and Clinical Psychology, 37,* 298–301.

Beutler, L.E. (1971b). Predicting outcomes of psychotherapy: A comparison of predictions from two attitude theories. *Journal of Consulting and Clinical Psychology, 37,* 411–416.

Beutler, L.E. (1972). Value and attitude changes in psychotherapy: A case for dyadic assessment. *Psychotherapy: Theory, Research and Practice, 9,* 362–367.

Beutler, L.E. (1973a). A self-directed approach to treating a complex neurosis. *Journal of Clinical Psychology, 29,* 106–108.

Beutler, L.E. (1973b). The therapy dyad: Yet another look at diagnostic assessment. *Journal of Personality Assessment, 37,* 393–408.

Beutler, L.E. (1979a, December). Individual, group, and family therapy modes: Patient–therapist value compatibility and treatment effectiveness. *Journal of Counseling and Psychotherapy.* pp. 43–59.

Beutler, L.E. (1979b). Toward specific psychological therapies for specific conditions. *Journal of Consulting and Clinical Psychology, 47,* 882–897.

Beutler, L.E. (1979c). Values, beliefs, religion and the persuasive influence of psychotherapy. *Psychotherapy: Theory, Research and Practice, 16,* 432–440.

Beutler, L.E. (1981). Convergence in counseling and psychotherapy: A current look. *Clinical Psychology Review, 1,* 79–101.

Beutler, L.E. (1983). *Eclectic psychotherapy: A systemic approach.* New York: Pergamon.

Beutler, L.E. (1989). Differential treatment selection: The role of diagnosis in psychotherapy. *Psychotherapy, 26,* 271–281.

Beutler, L.E. (1991a). Have all won and must all have prizes? Revisiting Luborsky et al.'s verdict. *Journal of Consulting and Clinical Psychology, 59,* 226–232.

Beutler, L.E. (1991b). Selective treatment matching: Systematic eclectic psychotherapy. *Psychotherapy, 28,* 457–462.

Beutler, L.E., Arizmendi, T.G., Crago, M., Shanfield, S., & Hagaman, R. (1983). The effects of value similarity and client persuasability on value convergence and psychotherapy improvement. *Journal of Social and Clinical Psychology, 1,* 231–245.

Beutler, L.E., & Bergan, J. (1991). Value change in counseling and psychotherapy. *Journal of Counseling Psychology, 38,* 16–24.

Beutler, L.E., & Clarkin, J. (1990). *Systematic treatment selection: Toward targeted therapeutic interventions.* New York: Brunner/Mazel.

Beutler, L.E., Clarkin, J., Crago, M., & Bergan, J. (1991). Client–therapist matching. In C.R. Snyder & D.R. Forsyth (Eds.), *Handbook of social and clinical psychology: The health perspective* (pp. 699–716). New York: Pergamon.

Beutler, L.E., & Consoli, A.J. (1992). Systemic eclectic psychotherapy. In J.C. Norcross & M.R. Goldfried (Eds.), *Handbook of psychotherapy integration* (pp. 264–299). New York: Basic Books.

Beutler, L.E., Consoli, A.J., & Williams, R.E. (1995). Integrative and eclectic therapies in practice. In B. Bongar & L.E. Beutler (Eds.), *Comprehensive textbook of psychotherapy* (pp. 274–292). New York: Oxford University Press.

Beutler, L.E., & Crago, M. (1987). Strategies and techniques of psychotherapeutic intervention. *Annual Review, 6,* 378–397.

Beutler, L.E., Crago, M., & Arizmendi, T.G. (1986). Therapist variables in psychotherapy process and outcome. In S.L. Garfield & A.E. Bergin (Eds.), *Handbook of psychotherapy and behavior change* (3rd ed., pp. 257–310). New York: Wiley.

Beutler, L.E., Daldrup, R.J., Engle, D., Oro'-Beutler, M.E., Meredith, K., & Boyer, J.T. (1987). Effects of therapeutically induced affect arousal on depressive symptoms, pain, and beta-endorphins among rheumatoid arthritis patients. *Pain, 29,* 325–334.

Beutler, L.E., Engle, D., Mohr, D., Daldrup, R.J., Bergan, J., Meredith, K., & Merry, W. (1991). Predictors of differential response to cognitive, experiential, and self-directed psychotherapeutic techniques. *Journal of Consulting and Clinical Psychology, 59,* 333–340.

Beutler, L.E., Engle, D., Shoham-Salomon, V., Mohr, D.C., Dean, J.C., & Bernat, E.M.

(1991). University of Arizona: Searching for differential treatments. In L.E. Beutler & M. Crago (Eds.), *Psychotherapy research: An international review of programmatic studies* (pp. 90–97). Washington, DC: American Psychological Association.

Beutler, L.E., Frank, M., Scheiber, S.C., Calvert, S., & Gaines, J. (1984). Comparative effects of group psychotherapies in a short-term inpatient setting: An experience with deterioration effects. *Psychiatry, 47*, 66–76.

Beutler, L.E., & Hodgson, A.B. (1993). Prescriptive psychotherapy. In G. Stricker & J.R. Gold (Eds.), *Comprehensive handbook of psychotherapy integration* (pp. 151–163). New York: Plenum Press.

Beutler, L.E., Jobe, A.M., & Elkins, D. (1974). Outcomes in group psychotherapy: Using persuasion theory to increase treatment efficiency. *Journal of Consulting and Clinical Psychology, 42*, 547–553.

Beutler, L.E., Johnson, D.T., Neville, C.W., Jr, Elkins, D., & Jobe, A.M. (1975). Attitude similarity and therapist credibility as predictors of attitude change and improvement in psychotherapy. *Journal of Consulting and Clinical Psychology, 43*, 90–91.

Beutler, L.E., Johnson, D.T., Neville, C.W., Jr, & Workman, S.N. (1972a). 'Accurate empathy' and the A–B dichotomy. *Journal of Consulting and Clinical Psychology, 38*, 372–375.

Beutler, L.E., Johnson, D.T., Neville, C.W., Jr, & Workman, S.N. (1972b). Effort expended as a determiner of treatment evaluation and outcome: The honor of a prophet in his own country. *Journal of Consulting and Clinical Psychology, 39*, 495–500.

Beutler, L.E., Johnson, D.T., Neville, C.W., Jr, & Workman, S.N. (1973). Some sources of variance in 'Accurate empathy' ratings. *Journal of Consulting and Clinical Psychology, 40*, 167–169.

Beutler, L.E., Johnson, D.T., Neville, C.W., Jr, Workman, S.N., & Elkins, D. (1973). The A–B therapy type distinction, accurate empathy, nonpossessive warmth and genuineness in psychotherapy. *Journal of Abnormal Psychology, 32*, 273–277.

Beutler, L.E., Machado, P.P.P., Engle, D., & Mohr, D. (1993). Differential patient × treatment maintenance among cognitive, experiential, and self-directed psychotherapies. *Journal of Psychotherapy Integration, 3*, 15–31.

Beutler, L.E., Machado, P.P.P., & Neufeldt, S. (1994). Therapist variables. In S.L. Garfield & A.E. Bergin (Eds.), *Handbook of psychotherapy and behavior change* (4th ed.; pp. 229–269). New York: Wiley.

Beutler, L.E., & Mitchell, R. (1981). Differential psychotherapy outcome among depressed and impulsive patients as a function of analytic and experiential treatment procedures. *Psychiatry, 44*, 297–306.

Beutler, L.E., Mohr, D.C., Grawe, K., Engle, D., & MacDonald, R. (1991). Looking for differential treatment effects: Cross-cultural predictors of differential psychotherapy efficacy. *Journal of Psychotherapy Integration, 1*(2), 121–141.

Beutler, L.E., Patterson, K.M., Jacob, T., Shoham, V., Yost, E., & Rohrbaugh, M. (1993). Matching treatment to alcoholism subtype. *Psychotherapy, 30*, 463–472.

Beutler, L.E., Pollack, S., & Jobe, A.M. (1978). 'Acceptance,' values and therapeutic change. *Journal of Consulting and Clinical Psychology, 46*, 198–199.

Beutler, L.E., Scogin, F., Kirkish, P., Schretlen, D., Corbishley, M.A., Hamblin, D., Meredith, K., Potter, R., Bamford, C.R., & Levenson, A.I. (1987). Group cognitive therapy and Alprazolam in the treatment of depression in older adults. *Journal of Consulting and Clinical Psychology, 55*, 550–556.

Birk, L. (1991). Systematic Treatment Selection [Preview of L.E. Beutler & J.F. Clarkin, *Systematic Treatment Selection: Toward targeted therapeutic intervention*]. *Journal of Psychotherapy Integration, 1*, 77–80.

Bongar, B., & Beutler, L.E. (Eds.). (1994). *Comprehensive textbook of psychotherapy.* New York: Oxford University Press.

Burgoon, J.K., Beutler, L.E., Le Poire, B.A., Engle, D., Bergan, J., Salvio, M.A., & Mohr, D.C. (1994). Nonverbal indices of arousal in group psychotherapy. *Psychotherapy, 30*, 616–624.

Butcher, J.N. (1989). *The Minnesota report: Adult clinical system interpretive report.* Minneapolis: National Computer Systems.

Butcher, J.N., Dahlstrom, W.G., Graham, J.R., Tellegen, A., & Kaemmer, B. (1989). *Minnesota Multiphasic Personality Inventory-2 (MMPI-2): Manual for administration and scoring.* Minneapolis: University of Minnesota Press.

Calvert, S.J., Beutler, L.E., & Crago, M. (1988). Psychotherapy outcome as a function of therapist–patient matching on selected variables. *Journal of Social and Clinical Psychology, 6,* 104–117.

Daldrup, R.J., Beutler, L.E., Engle, D., & Greenberg, L.S. (1988). *Focused expressive psychotherapy: Freeing the overcontrolled patient.* New York: Guilford.

Dowd, E.T., Milne, C.R., & Wise, S.L. (1991). The Therapeutic Reactance Scale: A measure of psychological reactance. *Journal of Counseling and Development, 69,* 541–545.

Elkin, I., Parloff, M.B., Hadley, S.W., & Autry, J.H. (1985). NIMH treatment of depression collaborative research program. *Archives of General Psychiatry, 42,* 304–316.

Elkin, I., Shea, T., Watkins, J.T., Imber, S.D., Sotsky, S.M., Collins, J.F., Glass, D.R., Pilkonis, P.A., Leber, W.R., Docherty, J.P., Feister, S.J., & Parloff, M.B. (1989). National Institute of Mental Health treatment of depression collaborative research program. *Archives of General Psychiatry, 46,* 971–982.

Frances, A., Clarkin, J., & Perry, S. (1984). *Differential therapeutics in psychiatry.* New York: Brunner/Mazel.

Garfield, S.L. (1980). *Psychotherapy: An eclectic approach.* New York: Wiley.

Gaw, K.F., & Beutler, L.E. (1995). Integrating treatment recommendations. In L.E. Beutler & M. Berren (Eds.), *Integrative assessment of adult personality* (pp. 280–319). New York: Guilford.

Goldfried, M.R., Castonguay, L.G., & Safran, J.D. (1992). Core issues and future directions on psychotherapy integration. In J.C. Norcross & M.R. Goldfried (Eds.), *Handbook of psychotherapy integration* (pp. 593–616). New York: Basic Books.

Graham, J.R. (1993). *MMPI-2: Assessing personality and psychopathology* (2nd ed.). New York: Oxford University Press.

Hill, D.C., Beutler, L.E., & Daldrup, R. (1989). The relationship of process to outcome in brief experiential psychotherapy for chronic pain. *Journal of Clinical Psychology, 45,* 951–956.

Jobe, A.M., Beutler, L.E., & Green, G. (1976). A comparative analysis of the therapist's importance in implosive therapy. *Psychotherapy: Theory, Research and Practice, 12,* 392–396.

Johnson, D.T., Beutler, L.E., & Neville, C.W., Jr. (1978a). Effects of therapist sex and patient sex on treatment outcome and duration. *JJAS Catalog of Selected Documents in Psychology, 8,* 87.

Johnson, D.T., Beutler, L.E., & Neville, C.W., Jr. (1978b). Effects of therapist sex, patient sex, and time on AMA discharge rates of psychiatric inpatients. *JJAS Catalog of Selected Documents in Psychology, 8,* 88.

Johnson, D.T., Neville, C.W., Jr, & Beutler, L.E. (1973). A–B therapy scale norms: An initial effort to standardize criterion group election. *Catalog of Selected Documents in Psychology, 3,* 13–14.

Kolb, D.L., Beutler, L.E., Davis, C.S., Crago, M., & Shanfield, S.B. (1985). Patient and therapy process variables to dropout and change on psychotherapy. *Psychotherapy, 22,* 702–710.

Kopta, S.M., Howard, K.I., Lowry, J.L., & Beutler, L.E. (1994). The psychotherapy dosage model and clinical significance: A comparison of treatment response rates over time for psychological symptoms. *Journal of Consulting and Clinical Psychology, 62,* 1009–1016.

Lafferty, P., Beutler, L.E., & Crago, M. (1989). Differences between more and less effective psychotherapists: A study of select therapist variables. *Journal of Consulting and Clinical Psychology, 57,* 76–80.

Lazarus, A.A. (1976). *Multimodal behavior therapy.* New York: Springer.

Luborsky, L., Singer, B., & Luborsky, L. (1975). Comparative studies of psychotherapies. *Archives of General Psychiatry, 32*, 995–1008.

MacAndrew, C. (1965). The differentiation of alcoholic out-patients from nonalcoholic psychiatric patients by means of the MMPI. *Quarterly Journal of the Studies on Alcohol, 26*, 238–246.

Mahalik, J.R. (1990). Systematic eclectic models. *The Counseling Psychologist, 18*, 655–679.

Mohr, D.C., Beutler, L.E., Engle, D., Shoham-Salomon, V., Bergan, J., Kaszniak, A.W., & Yost, E. (1990). Identification of patients at risk for non-response and negative outcome in psychotherapy. *Journal of Consulting and Clinical Psychology, 58*, 622–628.

Mohr, D.C., Shoham-Salomon, V., Engle, D., & Beutler, L.E. (1991). The expression of anger in psychotherapy for depression: Its role and measurement. *Psychotherapy Research, 1*, 125–135.

Norcross, J.C. (1986). Eclectic psychotherapy: An introduction and overview. In J.C. Norcross (Ed.), *Handbook of eclectic psychotherapy* (pp. 3–24). New York: Brunner/Mazel.

Norcross, J.C., & Goldfried, M.R. (Eds.). (1992) *Handbook of psychotherapy integration* (pp. 264–299). New York: Basic Books.

Prochaska, J.O., & DiClemente, C.C. (1986). The transtheoretical approach. In J.C. Norcross (Ed.), *Handbook of eclectic psychotherapy* (pp. 163–200). New York: Brunner/Mazel.

Rohrbaugh, M., Shoham, V., Spungen, C., & Steinglass, P. (1994). Family systems therapy in practice: A systemic couples therapy for problem drinking. In B. Bongar & L.E. Beutler (Eds.), *Comprehensive textbook of psychotherapy* (pp. 228–253). New York: Oxford University Press.

Salvio, M., Beutler, L.E., Engle, D., & Wood, J.M. (1992). The strength of therapeutic alliance in three treatments for depression. *Psychotherapy Research, 2*, 31–36.

Scogin, F., Hamblin, D., & Beutler, L.E. (1987). Bibliotherapy for depressed older adults: A self-help alternative. *The Gerontologist, 27*, 383–387.

Selzer, M.L. (1971). The Michigan Alcohol Screening Test: The quest for a new diagnostic instrument. *American Journal of Psychiatry, 127*, 1653–1658.

Shisslak, C.M., Beutler, L.E., Scheiber, S., Gaines, J.A., Lawall, J., & Crago, M. (1985). Patterns of caffeine use and prescribed medications in psychiatric inpatients. *Psychological Reports, 57*, 39–42.

Shoham-Salomon, V., Avner, R., & Neeman, K. (1989). 'You are changed if you do and changed if you don't': Mechanisms underlying paradoxical interventions. *Journal of Consulting and Clinical Psychology, 57*, 590–598.

Stansell, V., Beutler, L.E., Neville, C.W., Jr, & Johnson, D.T. (1975). MMPI correlations of extreme field-independence and field-dependence in a psychiatric population. *Journal of Perceptual and Motor Skills, 40*, 539–544.

Wakefield, P., Yost, E., Williams, R.E., & Patterson, K.M. (in press). *Cognitive–behavioral therapy of alcoholic couples*. New York: Guilford.

Whiston, S.C., & Sexton, T.L. (1993). An overview of psychotherapy outcome research: Implications for practice. *Professional Psychology: Research and Practice, 24*(1), 43–51.

Yost, E., Beutler, L.E., Corbishley, A., & Allender, J. (1986). *Group cognitive therapy: A treatment approach for depressed older adults*. New York: Pergamon.

3

A Research Program on Attitude Change Processes and Their Applications to Counseling

Martin Heesacker and Cristina Mejia-Millan

The purpose of this chapter is to highlight the applications to counseling of a 14-year research program on attitude change processes. This research program has explored basic attitude change processes (for example, Heesacker, Petty & Cacioppo, 1984; Petty, Cacioppo & Heesacker, 1981; Petty, Wells, Heesacker, Brock & Cacioppo, 1983), as well as the validity of Strong's (1968) early theory of counseling social influence processes (for example, Heppner & Heesacker, 1982, 1983; Heesacker and Heppner, 1983). Finally, this research program has evaluated the utility of Petty and Cacioppo's elaboration likelihood model of attitude change (1986; ELM) from conceptual (Cacioppo, Claiborn, Petty & Heesacker, 1991; Heesacker, 1985a, 1986b, 1991; Heesacker, Conner & Prichard, 1994; Petty, Cacioppo & Heesacker, 1984), empirical (for example, Ernst & Heesacker, 1993; Gilbert, Heesacker & Gannon, 1991; Heesacker, 1986a; Rosenthal, Heesacker & Neimeyer, 1995) and practical (for example, Heesacker, 1989; Heesacker & Harris, 1993; Petty, Heesacker & Hughes, in press) perspectives.

Several key issues have dominated the focus of research and thought in this field, a field that has been of central importance to counseling researchers (Wampold & White, 1985). These issues have evolved over time, starting in the 1960s, with the focus on simply conceptualizing counseling and psychotherapeutically relevant processes as occasions of social influence or attitude change (for example, Frank, 1961; Strong, 1968).

The second focus in this literature was driven by Strong's seminal 1968 article, in which he emphasized client perceptions of counselor expertness, attractiveness and trustworthiness as keys to counselors influencing clients. Over a hundred empirical studies have been devoted to varying aspects of these issues, although the primary emphasis of this literature has been on determining what specific stimuli subjects regard as indicative of expertness, attractiveness and trustworthiness. In a later section of this chapter we will describe reviews of this body of literature.

The third major focus, though generating much less empirical research, involved assessing the degree to which Strong's model fit with the behavior of actual clients. Several papers revealed that Strong's (1968) model failed to explain actual client influence behavior adequately. In a later section of this chapter we will describe three of these studies and their practical implications for counseling.

As a consequence of this work, the focus shifted again, this time to alternate conceptual models for explaining influence processes in counseling. Several new conceptual models were advanced, most of them by Strong, himself, and his colleagues, who recognized the limitations of his earlier formulation even before empirical investigations showing those limitations were published. Work by Strong and Claiborn (1982), Strong and Matriss (1973) and, most recently, Strong, Hills, Kilmartin and DeVries (1968) each represent important conceptual advances over Strong's 1968 paper.

Perhaps the most influential of these recent conceptual advances was the development by Petty and Cacioppo (1986) of their elaboration likelihood model of attitude change (ELM). The most recent shift in this literature has been toward evaluating the utility of the ELM in understanding counseling as an attitude change process. The ELM has stimulated empirical work in the field in the same way that Strong's (1968) model was a catalyst for empirical research on the counseling influence process in the 1970s and 1980s. In later sections of this chapter, the ELM will be described, both basic and applied research on the ELM will be outlined, reviews of the ELM–counseling literature will be summarized and non-empirical, application-oriented articles and chapters will also be described.

Classic counseling social influence research

One important aspect of this program of research is the attempt to validate the prevailing model with actual counseling clients. Up until the time of these studies, the prevailing model was validated almost exclusively with studies on non-client college students. A series of studies to be described next fails to provide support for the prevailing model. This failure was the major impetus for the research applying Petty and Cacioppo's ELM to counseling contexts.

Studies on the validity of Early Theory

Heppner & Heesacker (1982) In their 1982 study, Heppner and Heesacker examined (1) the interpersonal influence process in a real-life counseling context over eight sessions; (2) whether perceptions of counselor expertness, attractiveness and trustworthiness were affected by the client characteristic need for counseling; and (3) the influence process in the advanced stages of a client–counselor relationship. Clients in the study were students who were seeking counseling through the university, and beginning or advanced practicum students or doctoral level interns served as counselors. Clients and counselors completed questionnaires at both the beginning and the end of the eight counseling sessions. Experience level did not affect the way the counselors were viewed. Finally, perceptions of counselor expertness, attractiveness and trustworthiness did change over time, but for half the counselors the initial rating was moderate and grew more negative. For the other half, the initial rating was moderate and grew more positive over time, with almost no counselor rating staying the same.

Heppner & Heesacker (1983)   The study by Heppner and Heesacker (1983) also investigated the interpersonal influence process within counseling. The specific aspect examined included (1) three perceived counselor characteristics (expertness, attractiveness and trustworthiness) and their relationship with client satisfaction; (2) the relationship between specific expectations on the three perceived counselor characteristics and satisfaction; and (3) the effects of actual counselor experience level on the three characteristics and client satisfaction. Practicum students, interns and senior staff of a university counseling center served as counselors in this study of responses by counseling center clients. Clients completed questionnaires prior to counseling, as well as after several weeks of counseling. Results indicated that pre-counseling expectations were not highly correlated with ratings of client satisfaction, and, most importantly for this chapter, differing counselor experience levels did not significantly affect clients' perceptions of counselor expertness, attractiveness, trustworthiness or satisfaction.

Heesacker & Heppner (1983)   The Counselor Rating Form (CRF) is the most widely used measure of counselor expertness, attractiveness and trustworthiness in interpersonal influence research. Heesacker and Heppner (1983) evaluated its factor structure and factor loadings with a clinical sample, because the scale originally had been developed on college student non-client samples and had been used with these samples for the most part. In this study, clients of a university counseling center were asked to complete the CRF after seven counseling sessions. Unlike the factor data from the college-student sample, these results indicated that only a single factor was operating in clients' perceptions of counselors. A second analysis showed that, at the end of counseling, clients' ratings of counselor expertness, attractiveness and trustworthiness did not significantly differ. In other words, it appears as though clients simply did not make the distinctions between these seemingly different evaluative categories. So, with actual clients, the CRF appears to function as a one-factor instrument, not as the three-factor instrument it was designed to be. Instead, clients seemed to just make global 'good counselor–bad counselor' evaluations.

Practice implications

Taken together, these three Heppner–Heesacker articles seriously call into question the validity of Strong's (1968) interpersonal influence model.

Counselors could easily be fooled into believing that the 100+ studies on counselor expertness, attractiveness and trustworthiness that used college student subjects clearly show the importance of these factors in effective counseling. However, these three studies indicate that, unlike college student behavior, actual client behavior departs markedly from Strong's model. Actual client ratings did not discriminate very novice, intermediate and very expert counselors (Heppner & Heesacker, 1982, 1983), suggesting that clients may devote relatively little attention to counselor expertness, attractiveness and trustworthiness, variables thought by Strong (1968) to be so important in the influence process. The finding by Heesacker and Heppner (1983) that clients also fail to discriminate *among* these three dimensions of expertness, attractiveness and trustworthiness further undermines Strong's (1968) theory. The practical implication for counselors is that focusing effort on trying to appear to clients as an expert, attractive and trustworthy counselor may be ineffective in the influence process.

Introduction to the ELM

The elaboration likelihood model of attitude change (ELM) and research evaluating the ELM will be discussed next. The ELM provides important insight regarding why Strong's model is limited in its application to actual clients and provides effective alternatives to Strong's (1968) focus on counselor characteristics.

What is the ELM?

The ELM (Petty & Cacioppo, 1986) is a theory of attitude change in which attitude change is viewed as occurring along a continuum, with the central route of cognitive processing at one end and the peripheral route at the other. The dimension underlying this continuum is the likelihood that one will cognitively elaborate on (or carefully think about) an attitude topic or persuasive message. The probability of high elaboration likelihood is influenced by four factors: (1) the person's ability to elaborate; (2) the person's motivation to elaborate; (3) whether favorable or unfavorable thoughts predominate in the person's mind; and (4) whether these thoughts are stored into long-term memory.

For the sake of clarity of presentation, Petty and Cacioppo have divided the elaboration likelihood continuum into two discrete routes of persuasion: central (high elaboration likelihood) and peripheral (low elaboration likelihood). Central route attitude change is so named because of the relatively central role that effortful thinking plays in the attitude change process. Central route persuasion occurs when all these factors are present: people have the ability and motivation to elaborate (or think about) the topic when either their favorable or unfavorable thoughts predominate, and when those thoughts are consolidated into their long-term memory. Central route attitude change is associated with enduring attitude change that is difficult to reverse and that influences behavior.

If all of these conditions are not present, then attitude change will not occur via the central route, but may still occur via the peripheral route. Peripheral route attitude change is so named because effortful thinking plays only a peripheral role in the attitude change process. In peripheral route change, either simple decision rules (such as a long message is a good message) or simple associative cues (such as an attractive fashion model associated with a product) serve to influence attitudes. Peripheral route attitude change is associated with short-lived attitude change that is easy to reverse and that has relatively little influence on behavior (see Figure 3.1).

Sometimes attitude change is the function of the interaction of central and peripheral route elements. This point underscores the importance of viewing elaboration likelihood as a continuum and these two routes as convenient simplification. For example, in cases where motivation to cognitively process is moderate, rather than low or high, a peripheral route cue, such as whether the speaker has high or low credibility, may determine whether people process the attitude topic centrally or peripherally (for example, Harris, 1988). Studies by Heesacker et al., (1984) and Heesacker (1986a), which will be discussed later, serve as good examples of moderate motivation and the interaction of central and peripheral route elements.

This brief description, while technically accurate and straightforward, by no means details fully the rich body of theory and research associated with the ELM. Readers are referred to Petty and Cacioppo's (1986) monograph about the ELM, as well as to descriptions of other advances in the basic research on the ELM (for example, Harkins & Petty, 1983; Petty, Cacioppo & Kasmer, 1988; Petty, Cacioppo, Sedikides & Strathman, 1988; Petty, Gleicher & Baker, 1991; Petty, Kasmer, Haugtvedt & Cacioppo, 1987).

The case of Dave

To demonstrate more clearly how the ELM might apply to a counseling situation, what follows is a description of a case in which the first author was the counselor and used the ELM to enhance treatment (from Heesacker, 1989). A client the first author worked with will serve as an example of how the ELM can be used with clients. Dave was a 35-year-old white, male graduate student, who came into counselling because he felt depressed at the recent break-up of his marriage of some 10 years and his new, and perhaps distant, relationship with his three children. Dave was working the evening shift at a local hospital, in addition to attending school full-time. Tapes of the sessions were not retained, so the case has been reconstructed from notes and memory, both of which are only approximate, and surely kinder to the counselor than verbatim transcripts would be.

Counseling with Date can be divided, for the sake of brevity, into three segments. Only in the third segment was the ELM employed, because until

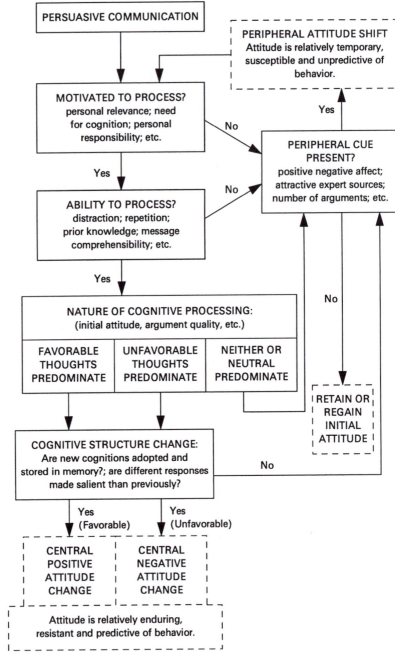

Figure 3.1   *Central and peripheral routes to persuasion, which serve as the two endpoints along the elaboration likelihood continuum.* (From R.E. Petty & J.T. Cacioppo, *Communication and persuasion: Central and peripheral routes to attitude change,* New York: Springer-Verlag, 1986, p. 4. Reprinted by permission of the authors.)

then it was not clear to the counselor what was an appropriate direction for influence.

Segment one   In the first segment, Dave and the counselor established their relationship and Dave ventilated all the thoughts and feelings that resulted from the marriage break-up. In addition, he was able to associate this life crisis with others, with the result that he established the theme of good versus evil as one that typified his sense of self.

Although the work Dave did was intense, difficult and somewhat helpful, the counselor never felt completely sure about Dave's psychological processes or about the appropriate diagnosis. Because he was not sure what an appropriate intervention would be, the counselor chose to make no specific influence attempts, except for those about the counseling process, such as focusing on both feelings and thoughts.

Segment two   In segment two, Dave's life worsened considerably. He lost his job, stopped paying child support, was then denied access to his children, wrecked his car, started doing poorly in and eventually quit school, lost his place to live, and so on. During this period, he went through similar depressive responses and ventilation as before, but the counselor was beginning to see a pattern in Dave's behavior. What had, in the past, seemed like innocuous comments about drinking and substance abuse took on new meaning. Dave told the counselor that his father was an alcoholic. Dave was able to associate drinking and drug use with each of the losses he had reported earlier. The counselor was able to recognize Dave's pattern of loss, depression and inability to cope as a common substance abuse pattern. Using the DSM-III criteria (American Psychiatric Association, 1980), Dave had a substance abuse disorder. According to the counselor's theoretical position regarding substance abuse, this needed to be treated successfully before psychological concerns, if there were any, could be assessed and treated appropriately. The substance abuse literature suggested to the counselor that inpatient treatment, associated with a specialized support group like Alcoholic or Narcotics Anonymous, was the treatment of choice. So, the goal of the influence attempt was to have Dave join inpatient treatment and a support group.

It is important to distinguish here between conformity and attitude change as two ways to influence people's behavior. In conformity, people engage in the behavior because they feel coerced or pressured to do so from outside sources, for example joining a treatment program because the counselor expects it. In attitude change, people engage in the behavior because they feel the desire to do so from within. Research suggests that people will persist in conformity behavior only as long as they feel external pressure. Conformity would not have been a good influence strategy for Dave, because long after the counselor was gone, Dave would have to stay in the treatment program and attend support group meetings. In general, effective social influence in counseling must be based on attitude change, not conformity, because the changes desired in counseling typically need to generalize beyond the counseling session. Sometimes counselor expertness, attractiveness and trustworthiness may serve to increase conformity and not central route attitude change. Counselors need to be careful not to mistake conformity for attitude change.

Segment three The counselor's first intervention was simply to tell Dave that he thought Dave was a substance abuser. Perhaps Dave needed no attitude change on this topic, in which case he would agree and would, perhaps happily, check in for treatment. Given the denial typically associated with substance abuse, this did not seem likely and, in fact, did not happen. Making this assertion to Dave also could help the counselor assess Dave's motivation and ability to think about the intervention and to help develop the persuasive interventions that the counselor would make in the future. Dave denied being a substance abuser, saying that he knew that the counselor meant well, but was simply misinformed. This was Dave's attempt at counter-persuasion. What the counselor learned from Dave's response was that he was not yet influenced, but was motivated and able to think about the topic of his substance abuse. This was encouraging from an ELM viewpoint. If the counselor presented points that Dave could understand and respond to favorably, he would be likely to engage in central route attitude change, leading to the desired behavior of joining treatment and a support group.

The key at this point was to accurately assess the kind of arguments that Dave would find convincing. The first clues came from the counselor's general knowledge of Dave. Dave was intellectual and he liked hard evidence. In addition, Dave often would say in earlier sessions things like, 'You really don't know me very well, yet', which implied that he valued highly knowledge of himself, and that perhaps he felt vulnerable to someone who did not know him. The counselor used these two clues of hard evidence and personal knowledge, coupled with Dave's counter-argument of incorrect diagnosis, to make his first attempt at attitude change. The counselor said something like, 'OK, if my diagnosis is wrong, I'll be glad to change it, but let's go through a list of the characteristics of a substance abuser to check out my accuracy.'

This intervention would provide hard facts about substance abuse. Fitting the counselor's knowledge of Dave with the list would, it was hoped, indicate that the counselor knew Dave well. Demonstrating that the counselor's diagnosis was based on fitting Dave's personal situation to standard criteria might convince Dave that the misdiagnosis was Dave's, not the counselor's. Going through each of the criteria, slowly and out loud, improved the chances that Dave could and would think about each point. The counselor was almost stunned at Dave's reaction at the completion of the procedure. Dave sat back in his chair and said something similar to, 'I don't believe it: I'm a damned alcoholic.' Attitude change had occurred!

As knowledge of the typical substance abuser in treatment would suggest, the process of attitude change was far from over. First, admitting you are a substance abuser is different from being convinced to go into treatment. Second, although Dave's first wave of cognitive responses to the counselor's intervention had been predominantly favorable, as Dave realized the implications of this attitude, he might well have become motivated to generate counter-arguments and change his attitude again.

At the next session, Dave was angry with the counselor and detailed various proofs that he was not a substance abuser. His final proof was that he had started to partially abstain from drinking and drug use. He urgently wanted the counselor to believe this, and appeared frail as he looked for approval. The counselor suggested that attempts to abstain were symptoms of substance abuse, not evidence against it.

Then Dave changed approaches. He began to wonder out loud why the counselor was out to hurt him. The counselor acknowledged that Dave must have felt hurt when confronted, but that it was a deep caring for Dave, and not a desire to hurt, that forced him to make these painful points. The counselor shared that it was stressful and unpleasant to make these confrontations, and that he would not have done so if he were not convinced that they had to be made. The counselor pointed out that he had invested a lot of time and energy in Dave that year, so why would he want to hurt Dave now? The goal of this intervention was simply to provide ideas that Dave would find convincing about the counselor's motivation to make the substance abuse diagnosis. To increase the probability that Dave would really think about the counselor's lack of motivation to hurt, he asked Dave to take time to think of any reason why the counselor would want to hurt him. After several minutes of thinking and discarding reasons, Dave seemed convinced that the counselor was not trying to hurt him.

Next, the counselor pointed out that even if his motivation had been to hurt Dave, the truth of the points was still the same. What hurt was that Dave felt it to be true. The counselor thought that Dave's hard evidence side would respond well to this point.

Dave then simply rejected the diagnosis, saying something like, 'I just know I'm not a substance abuser.' To which the counselor responded with something like, 'Tell me how you know that. I've told you how I know you are, now tell me how you know you're not.' The purpose of this intervention was to have Dave demonstrate to himself that, using his criteria of self-knowledge and hard evidence, the substance abuse conclusion made more sense than the opposite conclusion.

These intellectual arguments work well in the laboratory and worked well with Dave, but with other clients they may not. People differ in what they find convincing. The thoughts that form the basis of central route attitudes can range from cold, dispassionate ones to very emotionally intense ones.

For the remainder of that session and for a few following, Dave wanted to discuss his real psychological problems and to ignore their difference of opinion about his substance abuse. Next, they discussed the issue of what should be treated first, substance abuse or the psychological problems that Dave thought caused substance abuse. This was very encouraging to the counselor, because Dave was implicitly acknowledging his substance abuse. Dave's reluctance to attend an inpatient treatment program was unchanged, but his reluctance to admit that he was a substance abuser was diminishing. The counselor pointed out instances in Dave's recent life where he seemed unable to cope with change and difficulties, because of the effects of his substance abuse. Likewise, important psychological changes Dave might need to make would be impossible while he was still an active substance abuser. The counselor also pointed out that substance abuse often triggers psychological dysfunction, such as depression, so without substance abuse controlled, it would be impossible to accurately determine what psychological problems needed to be dealt with. With these remarks, all of the counselor's major points had been presented in a way Dave appeared to find convincing, as had the counselor's responses to Dave's major objections. Dave left the fourth session in this third segment convinced that he was a substance abuser, but not yet willing to seek treatment.

Dave failed to return for counseling for several weeks following this session. When he did return, it was following a low ebb in his life. He said that he had been unable to abstain from alcohol and drugs, and that he was convinced his life-style would soon kill him. When the counselor brought up specific treatment programs, Dave resisted. He was still not committed to treatment! His proposal was that he see the counselor as his treatment for substance abuse. The counselor pointed out that outpatient substance abuse treatment is generally less successful than inpatient, and that, in any case, the counselor was not adequately prepared to do so.

At this point, the counselor realized that he did not really understand the nature of Dave's resistance to joining an inpatient treatment program. Without knowing more about Dave's objections, the counselor could not make effective and influential interventions. They spent the rest of the session exploring and understanding Dave's objections. At the core of Dave's resistance was his conflict about being good versus being evil. He thought good people could control their drinking and drug use, bad people could not. Going to a treatment program was admitting to himself and others that he was a bad person. In addition, Dave had never forgiven his father for the difficulty his drinking had brought to Dave and the rest of his family. Dave had always thought that his father's entry into alcohol treatment was too easy an absolution of the father's wrongdoing. Likewise, Dave thought his own entry into a treatment program would be too easy an absolution of his own wrongdoing, as well as a tacit admission of how, like his father, he was a bad person. This exploration was stressful for both Dave and the counselor and they stopped for the day.

At the next session, the counselor directly addressed these issues of resistances to going to treatment. The counselor suggested that substance abuse and its treatment are not really issues of good versus evil, anymore than any other physical or psychological disorder, such as heart disease or schizophrenia. He told Dave that the only evil was that a treatable life-threatening disorder was going untreated. The counselor suggested that the similarities between Dave and his father existed whether or not Dave sought treatment. It was at this point, after weeks of careful work, that Dave actually agreed to seek inpatient substance abuse treatment. They set up an appointment for him immediately.

Epilogue In this particular case example, the focus was on (1) the counselor attempting to provide subjectively perceived strong arguments to influence the client to accept inpatient substance abuse treatment, and on (2) the counselor responding to the client's counter-arguments to inpatient treatment and to the idea that he was a substance abuser. With other clients, a counselor might have to spend time ensuring that the client has the optimum motivation and ability required to think about the content of the counselor's influence attempts. A counselor might also take time to facilitate the client's consolidation into memory of his or her own relevant cognitions that support the target attitude (in this case, a favorable attitude toward joining inpatient substance abuse treatment). In retrospect it appears that such a tragedy of memory consolidation could have been helpful in this case in ensuring long-term attitude change.

Important reviews of the literature

This section will serve as a brief guide to the five reviews of the counseling social influence literature that have been published in major journals over the last 15 years. This guide will serve as a survey of the major research-based conclusions in this literature, as well as a quick reference for readers wanting resources for more comprehensive and detailed information. For a comprehensive review of the basic, non-applied ELM research up to 1986, readers are referred to Petty and Cacioppo's (1986) monograph. We are not aware of a published comprehensive review of basic ELM research since 1986.

Corrigan, Dell, Lewis & Schmidt (1980); Heppner & Dixon (1981) These two reviews were published very close together and not surprisingly they both reflect the dominant position of Strong's (1968) interpersonal influence model in the empirical work on the social influence process done until that time. They focus on the many studies done regarding how college-student subjects perceived counselor cues associated with counselor expertness, attractiveness and trustworthiness, with primary emphasis on expertness and trustworthiness, the so-called 'credibility dyad'. A typical study would assess the degree to which a counselor with diplomas on the wall and other accoutrements of expertise was perceived relative to a counselor whose office was bare of such cues. Both of these reviews indicate that relatively less attention was paid in this literature to the impact of such cues on actual attitude change. Corrigan et al. (1980) is more detailed and the Heppner–Dixon (1981) article is more accessible. These reviews are likely to be useful to scholars in this area, but they may not be of as much utility to practicing counselors. This is because of subsequent research indicating that cues such as counselor expertness, attractiveness and trustworthiness have a limited role, and certainly not a simple and direct role, in enduring and behavior-related attitude change. What role they might play in moderate motivation or moderate elaboration likelihood conditions is only described in work reviewed later.

Heppner & Claiborn (1989)   The Heppner and Claiborn review serves as an update to reviews by Corrigan et al. (1980) and Heppner and Dixon (1981), and generally follows the framework of those two earlier reviews. There are two important structural additions to this review. First, there is a section with a critical analysis and set of recommendations regarding methodological issues in this research literature. Second, there is a section detailing theoretical limitations of prior research, as well as important theoretical advances that need additional research attention. In the theory section, Heppner and Claiborn described two major advances, McGuire's (1985) input–output persuasive communication matrix and Petty and Cacioppo's ELM (1986). They viewed these two conceptual models as important to future advances in the application of attitude change theory to psychotherapeutic settings.

McNeill & Stoltenberg (1989)   The published literature that applied the ELM to counseling situations is the exclusive focus of McNeill and Stoltenberg's (1989) review. Their enthusiasm after carefully reviewing that literature was more tempered than Heppner and Claiborn's: 'the relevance of the ELM for counseling has yet to be adequately tested. Much work remains to be done before we can unequivocally conclude that the ELM unifies the conflicting findings regarding the social influence process in counselling' (p. 29).

Strong, Welsch, Corcoran & Hoyt (1992)   Selected as a commemoration of the centennial of the American Psychological Association, this paper has the historical breadth and conceptual depth of the seminal contribution that it was intended to be. With the sweeping perspective gleaned from decades of involvement with this area, including arguably its earliest important empirical contribution, Strong and his colleagues have provided an outstanding description of the intellectual context for the field. While the McNeill–Stoltenberg paper represents the most focused of the reviews on the ELM and counseling, this paper represents the broadest and grandest review, one that shows the niche occupied by the ELM–counseling work within the larger historical and conceptual scheme.

Conceptual articles and chapters that apply the ELM to counseling

Heesacker and his colleagues have written a number of conceptual and practical application pieces that complement ELM applied and basic research. We will briefly outline the most practice-relevant of these pieces and will reference the rest, so that the reader can know where to access more detailed information (Heesacker, 1985a, 1986b, 1989, 1991; Cacioppo et al., 1991; Petty et al., in press).

Petty, Cacioppo & Heesacker (1984)   The first of these pieces, by Petty et al. (1984), was among the earliest writings about the application of the ELM to counseling. In addition to providing an easy-to-understand overview of the ELM and of the research testing it, this chapter provides a clear explanation of the conflicting findings in the literature regarding the effect of counselor expertness on attitude change. In essence, the notion of moderate motivation is detailed as the primary reason why sometimes counselors and other sources high in expertise facilitate increased attitude change, sometimes led to no attitude change, and sometimes led to attitude change in the opposite direction to that desired by the counselor. This chapter also details the importance of the attitude change route (central or peripheral) on attitude change duration and the influence of attitudes on subsequent behavior. The key points for practitioners are (1) without knowing clients' motivation-to-process level, the effect of being perceived by clients as an expert counselor will have an unknown and sometimes negative effect on attitude change; (2) if counselor expertness triggers decreased motivation and reduced cognitive processing, attitude change will be short-term and not very influential on subsequent behavior; and (3) if, however, counselor expertness triggers increased motivation, and if predominantly favorable cognitive processing results, attitude change will be enduring and will influence subsequent behavior.

Heesacker, Conner & Prichard (1995)   This paper reviews the literature on the ELM–counseling interface and identifies two waves of this work. In the second wave that the authors identify, studies were undertaken with less slavish adherence to basic research paradigms and with greater sensitivity to the counseling context than were those in the first wave. Results from these studies, they argue, provide clearer support for the utility of the ELM than first-wave studies. Based on their analysis, they also provide a research agenda for future research in this area. Of more direct relevance to counselors, Heesacker et al. (1995) also provides a list of practice-relevant conclusions from this literature. These include:

1. Therapeutically-relevant change is central route change. Although peripheral route change is easy to achieve, it does not lead to enduring, durable, behavior-oriented changes. The central route change does lead to these changes, so the attitude change focus in counseling should be on central route change.
2. The central–peripheral distinction means that the focus on counselor expertness, attractiveness, and trustworthiness is probably misguided. These

counselor characteristics serve almost exclusively as peripheral route cues. Central route change is influenced very little by these counselor characteristics, so the focus should be shifted away from them.

3. Inept attempts at attitude change can do more harm than good. In some cases these inept attempts lead to clients developing enduring and durable attitudes that are *opposite* to treatment-facilitative attitudes. If client motivation and ability to think about the attitude topic are high and if the counselor's points are easy for the client to generate thoughts against (or counterargue), then the client is likely to develop a central route attitude opposed to the counselor's position. This process could well be the source of a great deal of client oppositional behavior that heretofore has been blamed on client recalcitrance rather than counselor lack of skill.

4. Regardless of how expert, attractive, and trustworthy the counselor is perceived by the client, enduring attitude change will only take place to the extent that the counselor understands how to motivate and enable the client to engage in topic-favorable thinking. This motivation and this ability are rather narrow, only referring to motivation and ability to think about the attitude topic, for example joining a therapy group. Motivational problems can occur in two ways. Consistent with the Yerkes–Dodson (1908) curve, clients can be either too concerned or not concerned enough about the topic to think carefully about it (Harris, Heesacker, & Majia-Millan, 1994). Regarding ability, counselor comments are most influential when the client can think about them easily. Familiar language, for example, will make it easier for the client to think about the points the counselor is trying to make.

5. Understanding the idiosyncratic thoughts and thought processes of counseling clients is crucial to effective central route attitude change because it increases the likelihood that points to be raised by the counselor will elicit mostly favorable thoughts from the client. Not all clients find concrete examples compelling, and not all find statistics compelling. Arguing from within a client's core belief system may be far more effective than arguing against or outside it. Without understanding the client's unique thought content and processes counselors run the risk of being either ineffective in the change process or even counterproductive, facilitating attitudes opposed to the counseling goals rather than in favor of them.

6. Some attitudes are functionally unchangeable, at that particular point in time, so expending additional resources on them is not beneficial. On some issues a particular client arrives with a very enduring and durable attitude that is incompatible with some treatment goals. Change in the desired direction is not possible if a particular attitude was thoughtfully derived or if the client's motivation or ability to think about the issue are only in the direction of sustaining the original attitude (called biased processing). A savvy counselor will recognize this condition, shifting time and resources away from what is likely to be, at that moment, a fruitless influence attempt. Perhaps at a different time or after undergoing additional life experiences the client will be open to central route attitude change.

7. The ELM approach to counseling can be generalized beyond traditional face-to-face counseling, to include counseling consultation and outreach. In fact, several papers have already addressed the feasibility of such applications, with encouraging results (see, for example, Gilbert et al., 1991; Petty, Heesacker, & Hughes, in press; Pierce & Stoltenberg, 1990). (Heesacker et al., 1995)

Heesacker (1989)   Heesacker (1989) describes the application of the ELM to the case of Dave, described earlier, to clarify and demonstrate its clinical usefulness. Heesacker (1989) also discusses the important implications of the ELM for the social influence process in counseling. One of these implications is that to be most effective counselors should use the central route for attitude change. In using the central route, counselors should remember to focus on the four necessary components (client motivation, client ability, client favorable cognitive responses and consolidation of cognitive responses into client memory). Clients should also be motivated to consider carefully the meaning of the counselor's remarks. In order for the remarks to be considered thoughtfully, these remarks must be said in ways that are clearly understandable to the client. Finally, the client must have the ability to think about the content of these remarks, and for central route attitude change to occur, the client must find these remarks convincing by responding to them with a preponderance of favorable cognitions.

Heesacker & Harris (1993) Heesacker and Harris (1993) describe a practical decision tree that counselors can use to respond to clients who do not engage in the therapeutically relevant behaviors that the counselor believes are necessary. These failures to engage in the target behaviors may arise, according to this decision tree, in one of three broad areas: attitudes, instruction and correspondence. The model asks counselors to address three issues: (1) whether the client needs additional instruction; (2) whether the client needs attitude change; and (3) whether the client and/or counselor needs more accurate correspondence between his or her own thoughts and behavior or improved understanding of the thoughts and behavior of the other member of the counseling dyad. By working through a series of questions at each step of the decision tree, counselors can apply the lessons from the ELM and two other conceptual models to facilitate effective counselor–client interactions in the face of counseling difficulties.

In its most elemental form the decision tree asks the counselor three questions, corresponding to the three components of Martin and Hiebert's (1985) instructional counseling, the ELM and Martin's (1987) cognitive mediational counseling. From instructional counseling, the essential question is: 'Does the client have adequate knowledge to change? From the ELM, the essential question is: 'Does the client show (attitudinal) resistance?' Finally from cognitive mediational counseling, the essential question counselors ask themselves is: 'Is there correspondence between client and counselor cognitions and behavior?' Counselors whose clients are not responding as desired can work their way through each of these essential questions and the actions suggested in response to 'no' answers to these questions, to increase the degree to which clients ultimately are successful in the counseling process. Preliminary data from practicing counselors support the decision tree's utility.

ELM–counseling interface empirical articles

The confluence of two major factors led to the interest of Heesacker and his associates in the interface of the ELM and counseling. The first major factor was the research described earlier that demonstrated the limitations of Strong's (1968) theory in accounting for the responses of real clients. The second major factor was the basic ELM work just described, including research on the effects of rhetorical questions on attitude change (Petty et al., 1981), the effect of message recipients' body posture (Petty et al., 1983) and the influence of the individual difference variable field dependence/field independence on persuasive message processing (Heesacker et al., 1984). As is often the case in science, at about the same time other scholars were also starting to think about and do research on this interface (see the review of literature by McNeill & Stoltenberg, 1989).

Heesacker (1986a)

Study   Heesacker (1986a) applied the ELM to counseling in a study of undergraduates who either had or did not have a counseling-relevant problem of career concerns or dating and social skills concerns. The reasoning was that subjects with these concerns would have high motivation to process and therefore high elaboration likelihood, while subjects without these concerns would have low motivation to process and therefore low elaboration likelihood. Subjects heard a strong or weak pre-treatment intervention about joining either a social skills or career counseling group given by a source of high or low credibility (a counselor versus a student). The experimental hypotheses included: (1) subjects in need of counseling should show greater differentiation between strong and weak interventions; (2) subjects not in need of counseling should base attitude change on counselor credibility; (3) of all subjects with positive attitudes toward the counseling group, those with high need for counseling should show higher intent to participate, as well as actual participation; and (4) subjects with a need for counseling should have central route attitudes. The study failed to support these specific hypotheses; however, overall support was found for the ELM, because the results were explainable using the ELM and difficult to explain using Strong's (1968) model.

It appeared that the reason that the study failed to support the hypotheses was that elaboration likelihood levels were neither clearly high nor clearly low. The degree to which subjects' attitudes were affected by argument quality was influenced by counselor credibility. The low-credibility speaker triggered greater elaboration likelihood, thus the strong message was more convincing and the weak message less convincing when given by the low-credibility speaker than when given by the high-credibility speaker. The more moderate level of elaboration likelihood that appears to have occurred was similar to that discovered earlier in basic research on field dependence and field independence by Heesacker et al. (1984). In addition, Heesacker (1986a) found that as motivation increased and as intervention quality improved, more favorable attitudes toward the counselor occurred, consistent with the ELM.

Practice implications   The practice implications of the Heesacker (1986a) paper are, first, that there is empirical support for viewing counseling issues from the ELM perspective. This was the first study published in the *Journal of Counseling Psychology* relating the ELM to counseling and the second published on the ELM in any psychotherapy journal, after Stoltenberg and McNeil (1984). Second, these data underscore the limitations of Strong's (1968) model and describe the power of the ELM in understanding counseling-relevant influence processes. In particular, the two-way interaction of low versus high counselor credibility and strong versus weak argument quality would be difficult, if not impossible, to explain with Strong's (1968) model, but easy to explain using the ELM. These data show clearly that credibility per se does not influence thought-based, enduring attitude change. Instead credibility appears only to have an indirect influence, through its power to cause participants to think more or less about intervention content. Based on this study, counselors would do well to focus their efforts on developing arguments that elicit predominantly favorable cognitive responses in clients and reduce their efforts at appearing highly credible. Based on Heesacker (1986a), it appears that the most effective counselor would be one who comes across as relatively inexpert, but who, nonetheless, makes compelling points to which the client responds with predominantly favorable cognitive responses.

Gilbert, Heesacker & Gannon (1991) and Rosenthal, Heesacker & Neimeyer (in press)

Studies   The study by Gilbert et al (1991) sought to use an ELM-based intervention to change sexual aggression-supportive attitudes of men. A group of college men was divided into two groups, only one of which heard the psychoeducational intervention. This intervention was based on the central route requirements of motivation, ability and predominantly favorable cognitive responses. Motivation was achieved by presenting the material in an interesting format and by having participants role-play vignettes, rather than just reading or listening to a message. Ability was achieved by use of simple vocabulary and uncomplex message structure, by repeating the key points, and by summarizing the content at the end. Predominantly favorable responses were achieved by focusing on two key perspectives on the topic of attitudes that support sexual aggression. The first perspective was about the negative, intrapsychic consequences to the participants of accepting these beliefs. The second was about the societal sanctions that participants could experience for holding these attitudes. This approach provided a set of arguments that participants at different levels of moral development could embrace and respond to favorably.

Results indicated that men receiving the intervention changed their attitudes more than the control group. Also, one month later, in a different setting, this attitude change persisted among intervention subjects. Finally, measures of three ELM variables (motivation, ability and thought favorability) significantly predicted attitude change. Results indicated that the ELM served as a useful framework for designing preventive psycho-educational interventions.

The Rosenthal et al. (in press) study replicated Gilbert et al. and tested whether their psychoeducational intervention (described earlier) could influence rape-supportive attitudes of both traditional and non-traditional men and women. Male and female undergraduates were found to be either traditional or non-traditional in their attitudes about sex roles. These subjects were then put into the control group or received the psycho-educational intervention on rape. The results indicated that the intervention was effective for both men and women, and for both traditional and non-traditional subjects. The intervention subjects exhibited fewer rape-supportive attitudes and less support for rape myths than the control group. On later phone appeals that were ostensibly unrelated to the study, intervention subjects showed significantly less rape-supportive behavior than control subjects.

Practice implications These two studies have important implications for prevention, psychoeducation and structured-group interventions, rather than for more traditional one-to-one counseling. These studies document the utility of the ELM in developing an effective psychoeducational program designed to prevent sexual assault. In addition, they document that program effectiveness endured over time and that program-induced attitude change manifested itself in settings quite different from the original setting, thus ruling out social conformity pressures as an explanation for participants' attitude change. Finally, these studies suggest that topics such as men's attitudes toward women, which have been viewed by many counselors as difficult to change and as ripe for creating client defensiveness, can be powerfully influenced by ELM-based interventions. Although the focus of these programs was sexual assault prevention, we are confident that the principles that guided these efforts can be used successfully with other counseling topics that lend themselves to a structured, psycho-educational format, such as eating and body image, conflict resolution or coping with a dysfunctional family.

Ernst and Heesacker (1993)

Study In Ernst and Heesacker's (1993) work, assertiveness workshops based on the ELM were compared with typical assertiveness-training workshops. The subjects (college students) participated in one of the two types of assertiveness workshops and completed post-tests on the workshop attended. In the ELM-based workshop, motivation was enhanced by asking participants to think of times when failing to act assertively hurt them. Ability and consolidation of thoughts into memory were enhanced by asking participants near the end of the workshop to recall the favorable thoughts they had regarding engaging in assertive behavior. Favorable cognitive responses were enhanced by selecting from a large group of arguments the four arguments receiving the most favorable response in a pilot test of similar people.

Results indicated that as hypothesised the ELM-based workshop participants (1) developed more favorable attitudes regarding asserting themselves, (2) had a more positive evaluation of message quality, (3) expressed greater intention to act assertively and (4) reported greater ability to think about the topic than participants in the typical workshop. Most importantly, two weeks later, participants in the ELM-based workshop exhibited more assertive behavior, as reported by their roommates.

Practice implications The main practice implication of this study is that an *existing* counseling intervention, such as the assertiveness-training group that was the focus of this investigation, can be made significantly more effective by strategic changes based on the ELM. These changes need not radically alter the existing intervention. In fact, only a few key changes in the intervention itself were responsible for both immediate and more enduring improvements over the original intervention. In particular, the original workshop was improved by facilitating (1) central route processing, through increasing motivation and ability, and (2) favorable cognitive responding, by presenting persuasive arguments pilot-tested for their effectiveness. This study can serve as a model to counselors who want to enhance the effectiveness of group psychotherapy interventions without radically altering the content and focus.

A general approach to applying the ELM to counseling

As a way of facilitating the use of the ELM in specific counseling applications, we want to provide a general approach, which should be broadly applicable across a wide array of counseling situations. This general approach is based on the ELM, but distinguishes itself because of its practical focus. If the goal of the counselor is understanding, not influence, only the first two steps of this general approach will be needed. If the counselor's goal is attitude change, all the steps will be important.

An example

To begin the process of describing this general model and to help readers understand more fully the utility of the ELM, we next give an imaginary example of how this general approach might operate in a typical counseling psychology situation. Jimmy is a 13-year-old African-American male who lives in poverty. He is part of the 15 per cent of students from his school who ride buses to school.

Jimmy has an older brother, Robert, who has recently dropped out of school. He reported that when Robert dropped out, more arguments started to break out in his family, which consists of the two boys, a 2-year-old sister Carla, and the mother. Typically a below-average student, Jimmy has been a riddle to his teachers because he appeared, until lately, to make clear scholastic efforts, regularly doing his homework, paying attention in class and attending school regularly.

Lately, however, Jimmy has been doing even more poorly in his classes, making failing grades. Jimmy's homeroom and mathematics teacher, Mrs Ross, has reported to the guidance counselor that he is more sullen and withdrawn, although he has always been somewhat shy and detached in school. Jimmy has gotten into several arguments and fights with school-mates recently, as well, according to Mrs Ross, who has started conversing with Jimmy's other teachers informally about Jimmy.

Mrs Ross is typical of the teachers at Williams Middle school: 30 years old, Caucasian, middle-class, the spouse of a physician and the mother of two children in elementary school. The school was built 12 years ago in a predominantly Caucasian, upper-middle-class bedroom community of a larger Midwestern American community. The racial make-up of the school is 90 per cent Caucasian, 8 per cent African-American, 2 per cent other racial/ethnic groups.

The counselor is first asked to assess Jimmy's cognitive ability, because his teachers have expressed concern to his guidance counselor regarding whether placement in regular-track classes is appropriate or whether remedial classes would be better. Jimmy was brought in for a battery of cognitive ability tests. Jimmy failed to come to school on the first two of the three days when the school psychologist, Dr Craig, had scheduled the assessment. Finally, a call from the Principal's office to Jimmy's mother resulted in Jimmy arriving for the third appointment.

Jimmy exhibited many signs of resistance: lateness for the appointment, an averted gaze, slumped posture, minimal answers to questions, a long latency between questions and answers, and some sarcasm. Dr Craig realized that results of these cognitive ability tests would not be valid if Jimmy was not performing at his best level. So, he began the general approach by informally assessing Jimmy's attitude about taking the tests (Step 1 in the general approach to applying the ELM to school psychology). He asked Jimmy, 'So far, what do you think about what we are doing today? You won't get in trouble for answering honestly.' Jimmy said, 'Not much.' So, Dr Craig confirmed that Jimmy's attitude was negative, but he also wanted to know about Jimmy's attitude elaboration (Step 2), that is, was this a central or peripheral route attitude? So, he responded, 'What led you to think this way about what we are doing? Again, you can speak honestly here.' Jimmy indicated that he never did like tests much and never did very well. He said he thought that the school was just going to use this against him because he had been getting into trouble and they wanted a reason to throw him out, like they had thrown out his brother. Clearly, in Dr Craig's eyes, Jimmy had a negative and probably central route attitude, because clearly he had thought about what the testing meant for him and his future.

Dr Craig's next step was to clarify for himself what was his desired attitudinal position for Jimmy (Step 3). That didn't take long: he wanted Jimmy to have a positive attitude about the testing, about him doing his best, and about the test being beneficial, rather than harmful, to him. The desired route (Step 4) was central because he was trying to change a central route attitude and because he wanted Jimmy's test-taking behavior to be influenced.

His evaluation of route component needs (Step 5) took some time of talking with Jimmy and involved a certain amount of guesswork. However, he decided that Jimmy was sufficiently motivated to think about the issues and that, if the vocabulary and arguments were kept appropriate for a 13-year-old, ability would not be a concern. Dr Craig's primary concern in achieving central route change is eliciting predominantly favorable cognitive responses.

In preparing what he would say to Jimmy about trying his best on the testing (Step 6), Dr Craig tried to keep in mind the ways that he had heard Jimmy frame issues in his conversation with him. When he started talking to Jimmy he worked to say things that fit Jimmy's frame of reference, such as using examples and metaphors familiar to Jimmy. He also tried to use the kind of arguments that he had observed Jimmy to find persuasive. For example, Jimmy often seemed to be persuaded by people's heartfelt testimonials, so Dr Craig relied on testimonials as part of his overall message.

Because he was doing this face to face, Dr Craig started the reassessment of Jimmy's attitude (Step 7) even while he was talking, by watching Jimmy's expressions and listening to his spontaneous comments. Dr Craig could actually adjust his comments 'on line' by seeing how Jimmy responded to his points.

By the end of this conversation, Jimmy was actually participating in the conversation actively and generating statements that supported him doing his best on the tests. For example, Jimmy said that he never did like doing anything less than his best. Because of this and other comments Jimmy made, Dr Craig realized that he did not need to focus on Steps 8 to 11, at least not this time.

The final attitude evaluation came from observing Jimmy's test-taking behavior. Jimmy appeared to persevere on each of the tasks, even difficult ones. Interestingly, a large discrepancy between Jimmy's verbal and performance IQ scores along with some unusual Bender-Gestalt responses suggested to Dr Craig the possibility of neurological impairment, and Jimmy was referred to a neuropsychologist for additional evaluation. In addition, through gathering all the information for Jimmy's testing referral, Dr Craig became concerned about Jimmy's life stress and home issues, and saw Jimmy in short-term individual therapy.

Next, we describe in some detail the steps referred to in Dr Craig's work with Jimmy.

1. Assess attitudes

This can be done formally, through published assessment instruments, such as the Counselor Evaluation Inventory (Linden, Stone & Shertzer, 1965) or the Modern Racism Scale (McConahay, 1986). A second formal attitude assessment route involves developing an attitude measure, based on one of the standard procedures. These include Guttman, Thurstone, Likert and Osgood's semantic differential scales (see Cafferty, 1992, and McIver & Carmines, 1981, for reviews of these techniques), as well as unobtrusive measures (Webb, Campbell, Schwartz & Sechrest, 1966).

An alternative to formal attitude assessment is informal assessment. In informal assessment, the counselor asks about the attitude topic directly or indirectly, or observes people's attitude-relevant behaviors. Although much easier to use and more flexible than formal measures, these informal attempts could result in demand characteristics or reactivity by the person whose attitudes are being assessed, interpretation biases by the counselor and relatively insensitive and imprecise measurement of attitudes. We prefer to rely on formal assessment, but when situations do not allow formal assessment, informal assessment may be useful, as long as the pitfalls we have described are avoided as much as possible.

2. Assess attitude elaboration

Assessing attitude elaboration is similar to assessing attitudes, except that the counselor is looking at whether the attitude just assessed is a central or peripheral route attitude. Recall that the degree to which attitudes endure, guide behavior and are readily changeable differs for central and peripheral route attitudes. Central route attitudes are harder to change than peripheral route attitudes, because people resist additional careful thought that is required to change central route attitudes, and because central route attitudes often lead to biased cognitive responses to new information.

How do you assess for attitude elaboration? Again, this can be done both formally and informally. Formally, the thought-listing technique (Cacioppo & Petty, 1981) has been used to assess people's cognitive responses to attitude topics and to persuasive communications. The thought-listing technique typically involves instructing people to list the thoughts and ideas that came to mind while they were listening to the persuasive communication. These thought lists are then usually rated either by trained judges or by the persons themselves as reflecting either positively, negatively or neutrally on the attitude topic. Correlations between the overall positivity of people's thoughts and their attitudes, as measured by formal attitude measures, provide an estimate of the degree to which their attitudes are central route attitudes. Moderate to large correlations between thoughts and attitudes suggest central route attitudes and low correlations suggest peripheral route attitudes.

Informal assessment of attitude route involves either asking the person directly or observing indirect indicators regarding the degree to which the attitude is thought-based. The cautions regarding attitude measurement apply here as well. In addition, care must be taken not to create central route attitudes in the direction opposite to that desired, by asking people what the thoughts were that supported their attitude positions. Questions that ask people to report thoughts they had may actually induce new thinking and also may serve as memory rehearsal of prior thoughts.

This concludes the two sections important for attitude *understanding*. While these two sections are important for both understanding and influence, the remaining sections are primarily important when the goal is to influence attitudes.

3. Determine desired attitude position

Now the focus shifts from evaluating the other person or people to the counselor evaluating him- or herself. The counselor needs, at this point, to decide what attitude he or she would like the others to hold. This desired attitude position should be based on his or her evaluation of all relevant information, coupled with his or her technological background as a professional. One important suggestion about choosing the desired attitude position comes from the work of Fishbein and Ajzen (1974), who showed that specific attitudes predict specific behaviors and general attitudes predict a more general set of behaviors. A general attitude would be 'I like reading'. A specific attitude would be one that specifies target, action, context and time, according to Fishbein and Ajzen. For example, I like reading (action) my literature anthology (target) at home (context) when I return from counseling (time). General attitudes may affect a wide array of behaviors, but not necessarily any one specific behavior of interest. Specific attitudes may influence specific, particular behaviors more powerfully, without necessarily affecting more generally related behaviors.

4. Determine desired attitude route

The counselor needs to determine not only the attitude he or she wishes to change, but also whether it will be a central route or peripheral route. Central route changes last longer and influence behavior, which makes them desirable, but they are more difficult to create or change than peripheral route changes. On the other hand, peripheral route attitudes are relatively easy to change, but they do not endure or have much influence on behavior, especially behavior at anything but the lowest level of personal cost. Route is determined by two issues: (1) What route is the to-be-changed attitude?, and (2) Does the attitude need to endure or influence behavior? If the to-be-changed attitude is a central route attitude, then only central route change is likely to change it. If the attitude needs to endure or influence behavior, then central route change is required. Otherwise, peripheral route attitude change is indicated. For virtually every counseling context, central route change is required, because of the emphasis on enduring attitude change and real-world behavior change.

5. Evaluate route component needs

If you have selected the central route, you must next assess whether the components required for this change are present. Components that are not present will have to be facilitated in the person for central route change to occur. Motivation, ability, cognitive responses and memory consolidation are all necessary for central route change.

Formal assessment of motivation is available using both a trait perspective and a state perspective. The Need for Cognition Scale (NCS; Cacioppo & Petty, 1982; see review by Heesacker, 1985b) measures people's trait motivation to engage in effortful thought. People high in the need for cognition are likely to be highly motivated to think about the topic and persuasive message. State motivation can be measured by using one or more rating-scale items that ask people the degree to which the topic is important to them, relevant to them or will affect them personally (see Petty & Cacioppo, 1986, Chapter 2 for additional details).

Ability also can be formally evaluated from both trait and state perspectives. From a trait perspective, cognitive ability tests (CATs) may be useful in determining whether people have the basic intellectual ability to understand the message of a persuasive communication and the ability to respond with thoughts about it. State motivation can be measured by using one or more rating-scale items that ask the degree to which people feel distracted from thinking about the topic, have had sufficient time to think about topic-relevant issues or feel capable of thinking carefully about the issues (see Petty & Cacioppo, 1986, Chapter 2 for additional details).

Formal assessment of cognitive responses can be undertaken with the thought-listing technique (Cacioppo & Petty, 1981). This time, instead of focusing only on the positivity of thoughts, counselors should also focus on the types of thoughts. For example, do the thoughts betray a preference for anecdotal evidence? Do they betray some type of schematic knowledge, for example a particular religious or cultural orientation? Such patterns can be very useful in developing future message points that are likely to be persuasive. The style of argument that someone has found convincing in the past is likely to be convincing in the future. For example, someone who has been persuaded by anecdotes is likely to again be persuaded by them. Also, arguments framed to correspond to a person's well-developed schema (for example, a particular religious schema) have been shown to be more persuasive than arguments that ignore the schema (for example, Cacioppo, Petty & Sidera, 1982).

Finally, consolidation of thoughts into memory can be formally evaluated by asking people to recall their thoughts not only initially, but after some delay as well. The degree of accuracy of thought recall can serve as an index of consolidation, with greater accuracy indicating greater consolidation.

Counselors can also engage in informal assessment of motivation, ability, cognitive responses and consolidation. Again, conversations and observations can serve as informal information sources and, again, while more flexible than formal strategies, they also can result in biased and insensitive measurement, if care is not taken by the counselor.

On the peripheral route, the key components are (a) cue valence and (b) cue association. Cue valence refers to whether the cue is positive, such as an attractive person associated with the attitude object, or whether it is negative, such as a disliked person associated with the attitude object. Cue association refers to the link between the cue and the attitude object.' So, the degree to which John Major is viewed positively or negatively is valence. The degree to which he is associated with Britain as an attitude object is cue association. If John Major were viewed very positively and were closely associated with Britain in people's minds, then he would serve to enhance peripheral route attitudes in favor of Britain.

As yet, there are no formal measures of cue valence and cue association. However, informally, what counselors want to evaluate is what strongly positive or strongly negative symbols or simple decision rules are associated with the attitude topic, for the person targeted for persuasion, and how strongly that symbol or decision rule is associated with that topic. We will not detail these issues much further, because peripheral route change is relatively unlikely to be desired by counselors in the course of their typical work. Suffice it to say that the positivity of cues and how strongly cues are associated with the topic are crucial determinants of peripheral route change.

6. Prepare and give persuasive communication

As unusual as it may sound, we suggest that counselors prepare what they plan to say to a person whose attitude they wish to change. What one plans to say should reflect all of the prior five steps. There may be no chance to change the attitudes of the persons with whom you are working, but building your remarks based on this process will lead to an increased likelihood of effecting attitude change over more 'seat of the pants' strategies. The persuasive communication that you give may be a speech given all at once, but not necessarily. Counselors often have access to people over a prolonged period of time and perhaps across both formal and informal settings. It might be that a counselor's persuasive message transcends any single setting or time.

7. Reassess attitudes

This is a matter of redoing what was done in Step 1 above, but the counselor needs to approach this situation with added sensitivity because too immediate a measure may be biased by people's need to appear consistent to others (see Fiske & Taylor, 1991).

8. If the attitudes do not correspond to target attitudes, reassess route components

If a counselor's first attitude change attempt does not succeed, he or she must explore the reasons why that might be. Was the first measure accurate? Was the second? Was the assessment of whether the attitude was central or peripheral accurate? Was your evaluation of the components' presence and absence accurate? Was your intervention regarding the components effective? Was your persuasive communication persuasive? Did you allow enough time between attitude measures for consistency motives to dissipate? As just demonstrated, there are several places in which persuasive communication can go awry. To put this in perspective, however, it is probably no more complex than the problems solved by your neighborhood automotive mechanic!

9. Reprepare persuasive communication and give modified persuasive communication

As W.E. Hickson said, 'If at first you don't succeed, try, try again.' Based on all that was determined in Step 8, the counselor should modify the persuasive communication.

10. Reassess attitudes

This is the same process as Step 7, but the counselor should proceed with even more caution about consistency motivation, as well as about other kinds of reactivity by the person. This might be a good place to shift from formal to informal assessment or from informal to formal assessment.

11. Determine whether further persuasive communication is either needed or likely to be useful

This is the place where the counselor decides whether one more influence attempt is likely to lead to attitude change. Hickson had it amazingly right when he said 'try, try again', because after approximately three repetitions of a message, research has shown that people tire of it and actually grow more negative toward the persuasion topic (Cacioppo & Petty, 1979). So three attempts may be enough, unless the persuasive message was clearly different from the earlier one.

As we wrote earlier, one limitation of the ELM is that on some issues, at some times, and for some people, attitude change is not possible. While from a persuasion perspective this is a limitation, from a larger human perspective this reflects the strength of the human spirit. It should not be the case that one human can always change another. From a larger perspective, perhaps what the counselor is advocating should not occur, or at least should not occur then or for that person. In any event, there are real limits to attitude change and recognizing when you have reached those limits is important.

Also, there comes a point where additional attempts at persuasion may not only fail to be effective but may actually be counter-productive, resulting in attitudes in the direction *opposite* to that desired (called 'boomerang' in attitudes research).

Conclusions

We have reviewed empirical, theoretical and practical application articles and chapters emanating from the research of Heesacker and his associates on the application of the psychology of attitude change to counseling. The special emphasis of this chapter has been on the practical applications of this and related work. This chapter has moved from an initial focus on research testing the validity of Strong's (1968) classic article, through a discussion of Petty and Cacioppo's elaboration likelihood model of attitude change, to articles applying the ELM to counseling contexts, a review of application-relevant conceptual articles by Heesacker and his associates, brief overviews of the published reviews of this and related research, and finally concluding with a practical and general approach that counselors can use to apply the ELM to their own counseling practice.

We hope that we have portrayed this field the way that we view it, as a practical and useful one, based on historical and ever-evolving theoretical and empirical roots, yet with a vibrant present and a future filled with optimism. Likewise, we hope we have conveyed this research program accurately, as one continually evolving, but always focused on assessing theoretically powerful ideas regarding attitude change processes for the ways in which they can importantly inform and improve the work that counselors do.

Note

We wish to thank Romy Cawood, Jamie Nelson, and Mary Smith for their comments on earlier drafts of this chapter.

References

American Psychiatric Association. (1980). *Diagnostic and statistical manual of mental disorders.* Washington, DC: Author.

Cacioppo, J.T., Claiborn, C.D., Petty, R.E., & Heesacker, M. (1991). A general framework for the study of attitude change in psychotherapy. In C.R. Snyder and D.R. Forsyth (Eds.), *Handbook of social and clinical psychology: A health perspective* (pp. 523–539). Hillsdale, NJ: Erlbaum.

Cacioppo, J.T., & Petty, R.E. (1979). Effects of message repetition and position of cognitive responses, recall, and persuasion. *Journal of Personality and Social Psychology, 51,* 1032–1043.

Cacioppo, J.T., & Petty, R.E. (1981). Social psychological procedures for cognitive response assessment: The thought listing technique. In T. Merluzzi, C. Glass & M. Genest (Eds.), *Cognitive assessment* (pp. 309–342). New York: Guilford.

Cacioppo, J.T., & Petty, R.E. (1982). The need for cognition. *Journal of Personality and Social Psychology, 42*, 116–131.

Cacioppo, J.T., Petty, R.E., & Sidera, J. (1982). The effects of salient self-schema on the evaluation of proattitudinal editorials: Top-down versus bottom-up processing. *Journal of Experimental Social Psychology, 18*, 324–338.

Cafferty, T.P. (1992). Measuring and changing attitude in educational contexts. In F.J. Medway & T.P. Cafferty (Eds), *School psychology: A social psychological perspective* (pp. 25–46). Hillsdale, NJ: Erlbaum.

Corrigan, J.D., Dell, D.M., Lewis, K.N., & Schmidt, L.D. (1980). Counseling as a social influence process: A review. *Journal of Counseling Psychology, 27*, 395–441.

Ernst, J.M., & Heesacker, M. (1992). Application of the elaboration of likelihood model of attitude change to assertion training. *Journal of Counseling Psychology, 40*, 37–45.

Fishbein, M., & Ajzen, I. (1974). Attitudes toward objects as predictors of single and multiple behavioral criteria. *Psychological Review, 81*, 59–74.

Fiske, S.T., & Taylor, S.E. (1991). *Social cognition* (2nd ed.). New York: McGraw-Hill.

Frank, J.D. (1961). *Persuasion and healing.* Baltimore, MD: Johns Hopkins University Press.

Gilbert, G.J., Heesacker, M., & Gannon, L.J. (1991). Changing the sexual-aggression supportive attitudes of men: A psychoeducational intervention. *Journal of Counseling Psychology, 38*, 197–203.

Harkins, S.G., & Petty, R.E. (1983). Social context effects in persuasion: The effects of multiple sources and multiple targets. In P. Paulus (Ed.), *Basic group processes.* (pp. 149–175). New York: Springer.

Harris, J.E. (1988). *Moderate involvement and the elaboration likelihood model of attitude change.* Unpublished master's thesis, Southern Illinois University, Carbondale.

Harris, J.E., Heesacker, M., & Mejia-Millan, C. (1995). Does social anxiety hinder counseling-relevant attitude change processes? Manuscript submitted for publication.

Heesacker, M. (1985a). Applying attitude change theory to counseling. *Contemporary Social Psychology, 11*, 209–213.

Heesacker, M. (1985b). Need for Cognition Scale [Review of the Need for Cognition Scale]. In D.J. Keyser & R.C. Sweetland (Eds.), *Test critiques* (Vol. 3, pp. 466–474). Kansas City, MO: Test Corporation of America.

Heesacker, M. (1986a). Counseling pretreatment and the elaboration likelihood model of attitude change. *Journal of Counseling Psychology, 33*, 107–114.

Heesacker, M. (1986b). Extrapolating from the elaboration likelihood model of attitude change to counseling. In F.J. Dorn (Ed.), *The social influence process in counseling and psychotherapy* (pp. 43–53). Springfield, IL: Charles C. Thomas.

Heesacker, M. (1989). Counseling and the elaboration likelihood model of attitude change. In J.F. Cruz, R.A. Goncalves & P.P. Machado (Eds), *Psychology and education: Investigations and interventions* (pp. 39–52). Oporto, Portugal: Portuguese Psychological Association.

Heesacker, M. (1991). Attitudes and direct experience versus persuasive communication: A comment on Johnson. *Contemporary Social Psychology, 15*, 86–87.

Heesacker, M., Conner, K., & Prichard, S. (1995). Individual counseling and psychotherapy: Applications from the social psychology of attitude change. *The Counseling Psychologist, 23*, 611–632.

Heesacker, M., & Harris, J.E. (1993). Cognitive processes in counseling: A decision tree integrating two theoretical approaches. *The Counseling Psychologist, 20*, 687–711.

Heesacker, M., & Heppner, P.P. (1983). Using real-client perceptions to examine psychometric properties of the counselor rating form. *Journal of Counseling Psychology, 30*, 180–187.

Heesacker, M., Petty, R.E., & Cacioppo, J.T. (1984). Field dependence and attitude change: Source credibility can alter persuasion by affecting message-relevant thinking. *Journal of Personality, 51*, 653–666.

Heppner, P.P., & Claiborn, C.D. (1989). Social influence research in counseling: A review and critique. *Journal of Counseling Psychology, 36*, 365–387.

Heppner, P.P., & Dixon, D.N. (1981). A review of the interpersonal influence process in counseling. *Personnel and Guidance Journal, 59*, 542–550.

Heppner, P.P., & Heesacker, M. (1982). Interpersonal influence process in real-life counseling: Investigating client perceptions, counselor experience level, and counselor power over time. *Journal of Counseling Psychology, 29*, 215–223.

Heppner, P.P., & Heesacker, M. (1983). Perceived counselor characteristics, client expectations, and client satisfaction with counseling. *Journal of Counseling Psychology, 30*, 31–39.

Linden, J.D., Stone, S.C., & Shertzer, B. (1965). Development and evaluation of an inventory for rating counseling. *Personnel and Guidance Journal, 44*, 267–276.

Martin, J. (1987). *Cognitive instructional counseling*. London, Ontario, Canada: Althouse.

Martin, J., & Hiebert, B.A. (1985). *Instructional counseling: A method for counselors*. Pittsburgh, PA: University of Pittsburgh.

McConahay, J.B. (1986). Modern racism, ambivalence, and the Modern Racism Scale. In J.F. Dovidio & S.L. Gaertner (Eds.), *Prejudice, discrimination, and racism* (pp. 91–125). Orlando, FL: Academic Press.

McGuire, W.J. (1985). Attitudes and attitude change. In G. Lindzey & E. Aronson (Eds.), *Handbook of social psychology* (3rd ed., Vol. 2, pp. 233–346). New York: Random House.

McIver, J.P., & Carmines, E.G. (1981). *Unidimensional scaling*. Beverly Hills, CA: Sage.

McNeill, B.W., & Stoltenberg, J.W. (1989). Reconceptualizing social influence in counseling: The elaboration likelihood model. *Journal of Counseling Psychology, 36*, 24–33.

Petty, R.E., & Cacioppo, J.T. (1986). *Communication and persuasion: Central and peripheral routes to attitude change*. New York: Springer.

Petty, R.E., Cacioppo, J.T., & Heesacker, M. (1981). Effects of rhetorical questions on persuasion: A cognitive response analysis. *Journal of Personality and Social Psychology, 40*, 432–440.

Petty, R.E., Cacioppo, J.T., & Heesacker, M. (1984). Central and peripheral routes to persuasion: Application to counseling. In R.P. McGlynn, J.E. Maddux, C.D. Stoltenberg & J.H. Harvey (Eds.), *Social perception in clinical and counseling psychology* (pp. 59–89). Lubbock: Texas Tech Press.

Petty, R.E., Cacioppo, J.T., & Kasmer, J.A. (1988). The role of affect in the elaboration likelihood model of persuasion. In L. Donohew, H.E. Sypher, E.T. Higgins (Eds.), *Communication, social cognition, and affect* (pp. 117–146). Hillsdale, NJ: Erlbaum.

Petty, R.E., Cacioppo, J.T., Sedikides, C., & Strathman, A.J. (1988). Affect and persuasion: A contemporary perspective. *American Behavioral Scientist, 31*, 355–371.

Petty, R.E., Gleicher, F., & Baker, S.M. (1991). Multiple roles for affect in persuasion. In J. Forgas (Ed.), *Emotion and social judgments* (pp. 181–200). Oxford: Pergamon.

Petty, R.E., Heesacker, M., & Hughes, J.N. (in press). School psychology and the elaboration likelihood model of attitude change. Article invited by and under review at *Journal of School Psychology*.

Petty, R.E., Kasmer, J.A., Haugtvedt, C.P., & Cacioppo, J.T. (1987). Source and message factors in persuasion: A reply to Stiffs and Boster. *Communications Monographs, 54*, 257–263.

Petty, R.E., Wells, G.L., Heesacker, M., Brock, T.C., & Cacioppo, J.T. (1983). The effects of recipient posture on persuasion: A cognitive response analysis. *Personality and Social Psychology Bulletin, 9*, 209–222.

Pierce, R.A., & Stoltenberg, C.D. (1990). Increasing program persistence in professional weight loss programs involving cognitive self-persuasion. *Professional Psychology: Research and Practice, 21*, 210–215.

Rosenthal, E.H., Heesacker, M., & Neimeyer, G.J. (1995). Changing the rape supportive attitudes of traditional and nontraditional males and females. *Journal of Counseling Psychology, 42*, 171–177.

Stoltenberg, C.D., & McNeill, B.W. (1984). Effects of expertise and issue involvement on perceptions of counseling. *Journal of Social and Clinical Psychology, 2*, 314–325.

Strong, S.R. (1968). Counseling: An interpersonal influence process. *Journal of Counseling Psychology, 15,* 215–224.

Strong, S.R., & Claiborn, C.D. (1982). *Change through interaction: Social psychological processes of counseling and psychotherapy.* New York: Wiley.

Strong, S.R., Hills, H.I., Kilmartin, C.T., & DeVries, H. (1988). The dynamic relations among interpersonal behaviors: A test of complementarity and anticomplementarity. *Journal of Personality and Social Psychology, 54,* 798–810.

Strong, S.R., & Matross, R.P. (1973). Change processes in counseling and psychotherapy. *Journal of Counseling Psychology, 20,* 25–37.

Strong, S.R., Welsch, J.A., Corcoran, J.L., & Hoyt, W.T. (1992). Social psychology and counseling psychology: The history, products and promise of an interface. *Journal of Counseling Psychology, 39,* 139–157.

Wampold, B.E., & White, T.B. (1985). Research themes in counseling psychology: A cluster analysis of citations in the Process and Outcomes section of the *Journal of Counseling Psychology, 32,* 123–126.

Webb, E.J., Campbell, D.T., Schwartz, R.D., & Sechrest, L. (1966). *Unobtrusive measures.* Skokie, IL: Rand McNally.

Yerkes, R.M., & Dodson, J.D. (1908). The relation of strength of stimulus to rapidity of habit formation. *Journal of Comparative and Neurological Psychology, 18,* 459–482.

4

Research and Practice in the Treatment of Complex Anxiety Disorders: Developing More Effective Treatments

Gillian Butler

The series of research studies described in this chapter has contributed both to the development and to the evaluation of psychological treatments for more complex anxiety disorders. Two research threads have been constantly intertwined. One of them focuses on finding out more about cognitive processes in anxiety states and the other on evaluating specific methods of treating anxiety. The two are closely related to each other, and the findings of each inform the other, the results of every study providing new information as well as a source of new hypotheses to test, either in clinical practice or using more exploratory and experimental investigations.

As it takes much longer to evaluate a method of psychological treatment than it does to complete experimental investigations, there have been forced discontinuities in the research. It has taken place over a total time-span of 15 years, as a small thread in a constantly changing and developing field which has continuously influenced the form and content of the studies. In this chapter the connecting threads between the studies made by myself and my colleagues will be clarified and relatively little reference will be made to their changing theoretical and practical context. Of course this process of clarification comes with the benefit of hindsight and in response to the need to tell a relatively tidy and coherent story set in terms of progress along a path toward a goal. However, it is worth remembering that the way forward was not visible from the start, so each research step marked a new exploratory venture. The questions posed at each stage arose out of previous findings, and were questions to which those of us involved in the research at the time did not know the answers. We were not, therefore, setting out with a clear view of what was already waiting to be found, making an attempt to prove that a particular way of understanding anxiety or of treating it was 'right', but were attempting to find answers to questions that puzzled us and solutions to problems that were both intellectually challenging and a source of distress to our patients.

As indeed might be expected, the story did not always take one in expected directions, and both the clinical and the experimental investigations produced some unexpected findings. And the story has not ended.

There are always more questions to answer and it is certainly still possible to improve upon our methods for treating complex and long-standing anxiety disorders. This chapter is not intended to provide conclusive answers, but to explore the implications of the research for practice at this particular stage.

Starting points

By the end of the 1970s it had been demonstrated that exposure provides a simple, powerful and quick way to treat phobias. If you learn, by degrees, to face the situation that you fear, then there is an excellent chance that the fear will rapidly diminish, and if you do not allow avoidance to creep back again the fear will also be unlikely to return. Avoidance keeps anxiety going, and using graded exposure to reverse the avoidance reduces anxiety. The practical applications of these findings still provide the basis for the treatment of simple phobias.

A marked shift in attitude toward psychological treatment had also occurred during the 1970s, reflecting a move away from the assumption that the therapist's main job is to 'make people better', toward the view that patients benefit most from learning how to solve their own problems. Treatments such as exposure were therefore presented as methods of self-help which involved learning and practising new skills, and the skills were supposedly specific to the particular presenting problem. When we tested this assumption by comparing two methods for treating agoraphobia: exposure versus problem-solving (Cullington, Butler, Hibbert & Gelder, 1984), we found that the self-help problem-solving treatment, which taught people generic skills, was less effective than the self-help specific method of graded exposure, which involved repeatedly and frequently entering the situations that each person found alarming. Shifting the interaction between therapist and patient toward enabling people to use their own resources to solve problems was not as helpful as teaching them specific skills, how to practise them and how to apply them. The findings from this work with agoraphobics suggested that it was important to combine a self-help approach with specific instructions – in this case about how to reduce avoidance. In order to help people to overcome more complex anxiety states, we need to learn more about how to mobilise people's own coping resources and how to provide them with specific skills that could be targeted at clearly defined features of their anxiety.

The three main sources of specific skills, consistent with Lang's (1979) theory that emotion is a complex of three separate components, are behaviours, physiological sensations and subjective experiences (thoughts or cognitions). Historically speaking, two of these sources – the behavioural and the physiological ones – were tapped before the other. Specific methods for controlling physiological aspects of anxiety pharmacologically have always been important, despite problems with dependence and unwanted side-effects of the drugs. Psychological methods involve using relaxation, forms of meditation or biofeedback, and these methods were combined with the specific behavioural method of exposure in the treatment of anxiety partly because doing so has obvious face validity, and partly because the fear experienced when facing feared situations is genuine, alarming and distressing. It makes sense to combine self-help methods for managing fear with exposure, provided that doing so does not attenuate the effects of exposure. Much of the work on the development of treatments for anxiety states 15 years ago was focused on investigating this type of question – on clarifying our understanding of the parameters that determine the relative effectiveness of exposure; on unravelling the processes involved in exposure; and, for instance, finding out whether teaching people how to manage their anxiety also develops their coping skills and is therefore valuable, or prevents them engaging fully with the source of their fear and is therefore unhelpful.

This line of research is most readily pursued using simple phobias, and, as already mentioned, by the end of the 1970s patients with simple phobias already stood a good chance of 'solving their problems' using exposure, even though in practice strategies for managing anxiety were most often combined with exposure. One of the pressing, unanswered questions at this time, therefore, concerned how to treat those anxiety states in which avoidance appeared to play no part. Patients with generalised forms of anxiety suffer from anxiety apparently unpredictably. They feel at the mercy of events beyond their control as symptoms may overwhelm them 'out of the blue'. There was little reason to suppose that the treatments developed up to this stage could be adapted to help these people. Being unable to identify precise triggers for their symptoms meant that it was neither possible to build up a programme of counter-avoidance nor easy to mobilise personal self-management skills in advance. Indeed the failure of psychological treatments for these people was well recognised (Barrios & Shigetomi, 1979; Rachman & Wilson, 1980). The question that set in train the series of studies described below was therefore a very general one about how to apply what we already knew about the treatment of anxiety, especially concerning exposure and self-management skills, to solve the problems posed by generalised anxiety disorder (GAD). This chapter will describe the ways in which answers to this general question have been sought, dividing the research up into five main logical stages, and disregarding the fact that some of the investigations were conducted simultaneously rather than successively.

Stage 1: Can exposure be used to treat more complex anxiety states?

In 1979, when this series of investigations began, we supposed that it would not be possible to provide answers to this question working with patients suffering from GAD, which is a non-situational form of anxiety supposedly without avoidance. It would not be possible to use exposure and we did not know enough about the precise form of the anxiety or the details of its many aspects to be able to predict which of the many possible strategies for managing anxiety could provide specific help. We chose instead to focus on social anxiety, a complex but relatively specific type of anxiety in which avoidance is still present, but is supposedly less frequent and less consistent than in simple phobias, and we designed a study to find out whether exposure alone provides a more effective treatment than the combination of exposure and anxiety management (Butler, Cullington, Munby, Amies & Gelder, 1984). This strategy provided us with an opportunity to think about how to apply exposure when avoidance is less central and to start to develop a coherent version of anxiety management with potential for use in varied, unpredictable situations.

There are many reasons why social phobia presents special difficulties: it is defined not only in terms of a precise set of situations which is feared and avoided, but also in cognitive terms. Its main feature is 'fear of negative evaluation', whether or not that is real or perceived. Attempting to avoid negative evaluation may be rather like attempting to avoid a phantom – it is hard to know when you have succeeded. Another reason is that it is difficult successfully to avoid social contact of the kind that *might* provoke fear. This is partly because so many aspects of our lives necessarily involve interactions with others and partly because other people do things that provoke distress in social phobics unpredictably, and often, despite the spreading social awkwardness that follows, without understanding what they have done. The main research challenges at this stage were therefore to find out whether the supposedly powerful specific treatment for phobias, exposure, involving graduated, frequent and repeated contact with specific feared situations, could be applied to this more complex problem, and to define the content of anxiety management.

Design of the study

Two treatments were compared. The first of these was a pure form of exposure, without any of the additions that had become standard clinical practice, and that made both therapists and patients feel more comfortable in its application: advice about how to manage distressing symptoms of anxiety during exposure or in anticipation of it. Using pure exposure would provide a stringent test of the best available specific treatment for phobias and would highlight the difficulties in applying the principles of exposure in a complex situation. It would be impossible for therapists, when exposure produced sudden and severe levels of distress, to do anything but repeat the message about how avoidance maintains the problem and how facing the difficulty, however distressing at the time, breaks this vicious circle and is the only way of overcoming it.

This treatment was compared with a combination of exposure and anxiety management. At the time the research was planned, ideas about how to manage anxiety were expanding fast, but they had not been adequately evaluated. There was therefore much debate about the anxiety management part of the package. The main points of interest now concern both the form of this aspect of the treatment and its content. Ideas about anxiety management run the risk of being very disparate and providing the patient with a smorgasbord of suggestions from which to choose. Presenting too many ideas makes it hard for patients to learn and to practise specific methods and difficult for researchers to know which methods patients actually use and/or find helpful. In this case patients were provided with general information concerning how to identify the signs of anxiety early and use them as a cue to managing their symptoms, employing three specific techniques: relaxation, distraction and 'rational self-talk'. Relaxation was the best known, best developed and best evaluated method of managing symptoms available, but on its own had not been shown to have substantial effects. Distraction was included as it is the 'lowest common denominator' of all other methods. Asking patients to do something different when they feel anxious has the minimum effect of turning their attention away from their symptoms onto something else. Rational self-talk was a simple method of identifying and re-evaluating each person's specific anxiety-related thoughts, such as those concerning fear of negative evaluation. Patients learned all three methods, starting with relaxation, and specialised, if they wished, in the method they found most helpful.

The way in which the two treatments were given was precisely specified. The first half of each session was devoted to exposure alone. The second half of the session was then devoted to anxiety management in the first group, and to a 'filler' treatment called 'associative therapy', already shown to be credible and to have no known positive or negative effects, in the second group. Associative therapy involved 'learning how to stand back from your problem so that you can look at it clearly and objectively'. Using a particular event or situation of their own choosing, patients allowed related thoughts and memories to come freely to mind while the therapists listened attentively. Therapists were allowed to comment on recurring themes and to ask for elaboration or clarification, but were not allowed to make suggestions, and they answered any questions about overcoming social anxiety by emphasising the crucial importance of exposure.

Findings and their practical implications

First, it was clear that a treatment based purely on exposure could be used to treat social phobia. Both groups did equally well in the short run. In the second place we found that it was rarely possible to apply exposure in the recommended way using a graduated series of repeated and prolonged tasks (see Butler, 1985). Three of the problems were as follows: (1) graduated series of tasks can more easily be imagined than controlled or planned for social phobics, as other people, who trigger the anxiety, may unwittingly do threatening things, like ask for your opinion or focus their, and others', attention upon you; (2) no two social situations are exactly the same, so they cannot be repeated without running the risk of provoking different levels of anxiety, and recognising this may leave people feeling perpetually apprehensive rather than building up their social confidence; and (3) many social interactions are brief and self-limiting (greeting or thanking someone; making introductions; answering a question), so exposure to them cannot be prolonged until the anxiety they provoke dies away.

In practice we found that, rather than following the 'rules' of exposure, it was more important to encourage patients generally to approach rather than to avoid situations that they found difficult, explaining and demonstrating, using material relevant to each person, how the circular relationship between fear and avoidance maintains phobic anxiety and how exposure breaks the vicious circle. Then, when unable to predict what other people will do and how alarming a situation will become, or when unable to control social situations sufficiently to be able to attempt easier ones before moving up to harder ones, patients were able to create and take advantage of opportunities to practise as they arose. Once the theory and the rationale for exposure had been made explicit, patients could be encouraged to adopt an attitude of approach, and to use the wish to avoid as a cue to try to do the opposite, to the extent that they felt able at the time.

The third finding with useful practical implications was that many social phobics developed ways of disengaging themselves from difficult situations when they became too uncomfortable, for example by not giving them their full attention, or by finding that their attention was dominated by a sense of their own social incompetence or inadequacy. Helping these patients to recognise these forms of disengagement and to counteract them by focusing their attention on relevant features of the social situation outside themselves seemed to enable them to benefit from the exposure. For many social phobics this distressing form of self-consciousness interferes with their ability to interact with others. For these people, focusing on external features of the social situation and engaging themselves fully in the interaction was especially helpful and appeared to make them feel better about their social performance.

We were able to adapt exposure for use with social phobics by exploring during treatment the precise form that the avoidance took, and these explorations revealed that there are many subtle forms of avoidance in addition to the obvious ones like not going to pubs or parties. Subtle avoidance includes things like not talking about feelings, not expressing opinions or stating disagreements, not accepting a challenge, keeping in the background when with a group, and dressing so as to fade into the background. In adapting exposure for social phobics, we discovered how exposure could be used to counteract avoidance even when it does not take conventional forms.

Until this time it had been supposed that, for exposure to be effective, it was necessary to remain in the feared situation until the fear began to subside. But we found that many of the situations that social phobics find difficult are brief or time-limited, like introducing yourself or disagreeing with someone's opinion, and exposure to these situations was still useful. This was especially clear for the patients who had anxiety management as they used the cognitive strategies to identify their fears more precisely and could then use the situation to find out whether specific expectations were confirmed.

However, perhaps the most important set of findings, with the most widely accepted practical implications, concerned the added value of anxiety management. Only about two and a half hours altogether, spread over seven treatment sessions, was spent discussing anxiety management, yet six months after the end of treatment a clear advantage for the combination of exposure and anxiety management was found on four out of six measures of social anxiety and on two out of six more general measures. There were consistent trends favouring this treatment on every measure and none of the patients in this group requested further treatment during the following year, while 40 per cent of the patients in the group receiving exposure alone made such requests. This suggested that the added advantage of the anxiety management component increases over time.

More specifically, some of the data also suggested that the cognitive component of anxiety management was especially valuable. Immediately after treatment the fear of negative evaluation was significantly decreased for those who received anxiety management, and unchanged in the others. Before treatment most of the patients reported trying to manage their anxiety, and most of them used their own versions of the methods we suggested. However, few of them could use these methods successfully before treatment. Six months after the end of treatment, 86 per cent of those patients who received anxiety management found the methods they used effective, compared with 14 per cent of those who received exposure alone, and while their use of relaxation and distraction had doubled, the use of rational self-talk had increased more than five times. We speculated at the time that it was natural, and indeed only sensible, to try to manage anxiety when it occurs, and that most people use as their first line of defence some form of distraction. Therapists need to be aware, therefore, of the strategies that people are already using when they introduce anxiety management. They need to encourage people to continue using the methods that are likely to be helpful and to work out why these methods have not already been effective. Often this is because the strategies are only applied once anxiety is high, or they are inconsistently applied, or applied in an unskilled way. Much of the time people have the right idea but do not know how to put it into effect. If so, then it is especially important to think both about how to mobilise people's resources for coping when they are anxious and about how to use these resources in the most effective way. They may need as much help in adapting the methods they already use, and learning how to apply them at awkward moments or before they feel too anxious, as they do in learning new methods. In summary, the two main findings of practical value concerned the ways in which exposure could be adapted for use in more complex anxiety states and the value of mobilising people's own resources for managing their anxiety, particularly using cognitive methods. Whether or not anxiety management could be developed into an effective treatment for GAD was as yet unclear. However, it is useful, first, to consider questions about the cognitive aspects of anxiety.

Stage 2: What is the nature of thinking in anxiety?

The clinical value of understanding better the relationships between thoughts and moods was demonstrable in the case of depression at this stage, and it had provided the background and impetus to the development of cognitive therapy for depression (Beck, Rush, Shaw & Emery, 1979). But very little was known about the nature of thinking in anxiety. It is easy to accept that thoughts affect anxious mood ('They might have had an accident', 'I'm going to make a mess of this'), and also that when feeling anxious it is only too easy to think things like 'something will go wrong'. But we need to know more than this in order to be able to target specific features of anxious thinking in such a way as to help people feel better.

An exploratory investigation was followed by a series of more detailed studies (Butler, 1990). It was clear from the start that thoughts about threats or dangers predominate in anxious thinking (Beck, Laude & Bohnert, 1974), which is focused on the future and not, like depressive thinking, on the past. The distressing events about which people are concerned when they are anxious have not yet happened, but are anticipated or threatening to happen (Finlay-Jones & Brown, 1981). Three related hypotheses were explored in order to find out more about the specifics of anxious thinking. The first was that anxiety is associated with a bias in the interpretation of ambiguous material. We already knew that, in general, judgements about the meaning of ambiguous material are influenced by the presence or availability of relevant information, and it seemed likely that anxious people would have more threat-related information accessible to them, whether this was because they worried about such things or because they had increased experience of threats or dangers. The second hypothesis was that anxiety would be associated, for similar reasons, with a raised subjective probability for threatening events. The risk of unpleasant events happening would seem to be higher for people who were anxious than it would be for those who were not anxious. The third hypothesis was that anxiety would be associated with a tendency to rate the occurrence of threatening events as more harmful. The subjective cost of an unpleasant event, such as becoming ill or having an accident, would seem higher for anxious people than for others.

Three separate questionnaires were developed for the preliminary investigation and given to groups of patients who were generally anxious and to groups of control subjects. There was clear support for all three hypotheses (Butler & Mathews, 1983). Anxious patients were more likely than others to interpret ambiguous material as threatening, and they also rated the subjective cost of threatening events as higher than did controls. Both group differences suggest that threatening information has a greater impact on anxious people than on others. The subjective probability questionnaire allowed for more detailed analysis as it included subsets of questions referring to the probability of positive as well as negative events, and to the probability of events occurring to oneself as opposed to someone else. Anxious people rated the risk of threatening events as higher than others, and this difference was enhanced for threats to the self. So two effects seemed to be combined: a general increase in risk estimates and, superimposed upon this, a more specific increase in estimates of personal subjective risk. There were no differences in the ratings of the likelihood of positive, non-threatening events.

Subsequent studies showed that the tendency to overestimate risk is lower in patients who have improved after treatment for GAD and absent in patients who have recovered, and that those who have recovered also make similar estimates of the likelihood of unpleasant events happening to themselves and to other people. Subjective probabilities also change most in patients who receive a more effective treatment for persistent and severe GAD, change less in those who receive a less effective treatment, and do not change in patients who receive no treatment. In the latter study (Butler, Fennell, Robson & Gelder, 1991), it was found that changes in mood ratings were highly correlated with changes in subjective probabilities for negative events, indicating a close relationship between mood ratings and this measure of anxious thinking. In none of these studies were there consistent variations in estimates of the likelihood of positive events.

Ratings of subjective probability reflect one aspect of cognition in anxiety. Worry, the main defining feature of GAD, is another, more obvious cognitive component of anxiety. Although at this stage it had attracted little specific attention from clinical or experimental researchers, and therefore little was known about the process or about its precise effects, it seemed likely that tendencies to worry and to overestimate risk might be related. Worry seems to involve a specific focus on negative possibilities and uncertainties – on the unpleasant and distressing things that might happen. Worry should therefore both increase the availability of relevant information in memory and increase anxious mood, both of which are likely to be associated with higher subjective probability ratings. Indeed, questionnaire-based studies showed, as predicted, that risk estimates and worry were closely related in anxious patients as well as in non-anxious control subjects, in individuals as well as in groups, and when rating domains of concern as well as when rating specific items. The higher the trait anxiety score the wider the range of things that people worried about.

Altogether these findings suggest that the relationship between risk estimates and mood depends both on the amount of worrying and on the level of anxiety, especially on the enduring nature of that anxiety. Further work on worry is described in the last section of this chapter.

The relationship between risk estimates and mood may also depend on the particular concerns of each person. In a final study in this series (Butler & Mathews, 1987) we tested the predictions that anxiety arising from anticipation of a stressful examination would be associated with inflated judgements of the risk of negative events related to one's own performance in the examination, and that people with higher trait anxiety scores would show inflated risk estimates over a wider range of concerns. The subjective probability of pleasant and unpleasant events was rated on two occasions, one month and one day before the examination date. Increases in anticipatory anxiety as the examination approached were associated with increased subjective risk of examination failure, while the more stable personality trait of anxiety was associated with increases in perceived risk of all self-referred negative events, whether or not they related to examinations.

Altogether this series of studies showed that estimates of subjective risk and measures of anxious mood are consistently and significantly related to each other. This relationship varied according to (a) the level of anxiety, (b) the amount of worry, (c) the enduring nature of anxiety, or trait anxiety, and (d) a person's predominant concerns, in particular concerns about threats to the self. At the same time anxious people were found consistently to interpret ambiguous material as threatening, indicating that anxiety and thinking are likely to be related in more ways than one.

Practical implications

People who are worried or anxious are also pessimistic: they tend to think that unpleasant things are more likely to happen, and more likely to happen to them than to others. Regardless of the accuracy of the risk estimate, this suggests that if they were able to become less pessimistic they would be likely to worry less and to feel better. Breaking the connection between pessimism of this kind and other aspects of anxiety should be effective even if the relationship is circular, and works in the other direction as well. Specific cognitive methods for doing this have now been developed which involve helping anxious people to identify the predictions they are making, to recognise the liability of those predictions, and to develop skills for evaluating, and if possible disconfirming, the expectations to which they give rise. One way of doing this has been described in Butler (1989, p. 102). A meticulous but unforthcoming businessman felt anxious before attending a brief training course. On previous occasions he had struggled through such events 'by the skin of his teeth' and came away thinking that he had had a narrow escape. The cognitive strategies of identifying, examining and testing his particular expectations on that occasion were explained to him and he made two specific predictions: that he would not be able to speak up and that he would not be selected as a small group leader. After the first part of the course he thought about his participation thus far and judged the first prediction to be unfounded. The cognitive exercise alerted him to further predictions, such as 'I will not be able to argue my case clearly'. Testing out this prediction in practice resulted in his selection as a group leader. So a specific cognitive strategy was used in combination with traditional exposure and found, on this occasion, to be useful. This patient in fact remarked that the combination of strategies both reduced anxiety at the time and reduced anticipatory anxiety about future courses in a way that exposure without the cognitive intervention had previously failed to do.

In applying this method it is crucial for people to identify their specific prediction, and to accept the possibility that the prediction might not be accurate. The research findings suggest that strategies for helping them to do this include asking people to make predictions in different mood states or before and after a bout of worrying, so that they can see how the predictions fluctuate, or by asking them to predict the likelihood of the unpleasant event happening to someone else rather than to themselves.

As a therapist it is also helpful to remember that the stronger the trait of anxiety the more global the pessimistic predictions are likely to be. Therefore, if someone with a high trait anxiety score, for instance someone with long-standing GAD, has a specific reason to be anxious, such as hearing a rumour about redundancy, they will not only worry about the possibility of losing their job, but they will also worry about other things that concern them, like their relationships, local traffic congestion or even the weather. Each of these concerns can be dealt with separately in therapy, but it should be most useful to identify the core, or trigger, worry and deal with that first, and to help people recognise the global pattern of thinking so that they can recognise its relationship with anxiety and not be misled into believing that the predictions made in the midst of worry are accurate. The reason why all their concerns seem to be activated at once appears to be related to internal factors – to cognitive factors and to the level of trait anxiety – and not to external factors. If external factors become the main focus, treatment can get very side-tracked.

When cognitive methods of treatment were being developed it was often supposed that their purpose was to help people think more positively. The findings outlined above suggest that there may be little to be gained from working on optimism rather than pessimism in anxious populations (though see Seligman, 1991). Regardless of their level of anxiety, or how much they worry, anxious people appear to remain equally optimistic. Attempting to increase positive thinking is therefore most unlikely to be helpful when people are feeling anxious. It will be far more helpful – that is, far more likely to change their mood and help them to worry less – if they work on the negative aspects of their thinking in such a way as to re-evaluate the conclusions to which they have been drawn, for instance about the likelihood of unpleasant events.

Findings concerning the tendency to misinterpret ambiguous information in terms of threat have also been of practical value. This tendency may be a general feature of anxiety, and is clearly particularly important in the maintenance of panic disorder. Treatment aimed purely and specifically at reducing catastrophic misinterpretation of bodily sensations has been shown to be an effective treatment for panic (Clark et al., 1994). It also plays a valuable part in the treatment of other anxiety disorders such as GAD and hypochondriasis. Reports have now shown that response to treatment for panic disorder and to GAD can be predicted using versions of the original Interpretations Questionnaire developed for the research described above (Butler, 1993; Clark et al., 1994). In both cases those patients who started with the greatest tendency to interpret ambiguous information in terms of threat responded less well to treatment.

This suggests that the more entrenched the tendency to interpret ambiguous events (such as receiving an urgent message to ring home) as threatening or alarming, the harder it is to treat the anxiety. And this tendency is easily overlooked during treatment, partly because many ambiguous situations are quickly resolved and are not therefore brought up for discussion during therapy sessions, and partly because the misinterpretation is accepted by the patient as an accurate judgement that is not open to questioning and is never therefore revealed to be a misinterpretation. Therapists should watch out for examples of such misinterpretations, and provide patients with as much practice in re-evaluating them as possible, helping them to recognise when they are jumping to the sorts of conclusions that maintain anxiety symptoms.

When anxious, people tend to become preoccupied with themselves, self-aware and self-conscious. There is a strong temptation to attend to, and dwell upon, internal sensations of anxiety and this may also be associated with the finding described above concerning the tendency to make higher estimates of risk for oneself than for others. The practical value of this finding is that it suggests useful interventions such as asking anxious patients to contrast the predictions they make for other people with those they make for themselves, or asking them to think about what it is about themselves that makes them more likely to be subject to unpleasant occurrences. Often this leads to a discussion of a more deep-rooted sense of vulnerability that may be maintained as much by repeated experience of anxiety as by perceived failures and weaknesses – as if the internal sensations were themselves evidence about the external world ('because I feel anxious, that means something dreadful is going to happen'). In our experience this type of discussion is especially fruitful, and helps to build confidence and a more robust sense of being able to cope with whatever the future brings.

Stage 3: Can we devise a form of anxiety management that is effective for GAD?

Finding out more about how to treat social phobia, and about the nature of anxious cognitions, provided the information needed to construct a version of anxiety management that should have a good change of helping people with GAD. The most important points available at the time this stage of the research started were that (1) exposure can be modified for use when avoidance is relatively inconsistent and subtle; (2) anxiety management appears to contribute something useful to the treatment of social phobia; (3) the cognitive aspect of anxiety management may be particularly valuable; (4) cognitive aspects of social anxiety appear not to change without anxiety management; and (5) anxious thinking is typified by over-estimates of personal risk and a strong tendency to interpret ambiguous information in terms of threat. The next steps involved deciding exactly what form anxiety management for GAD should take, and how best to evaluate it.

Evaluating anxiety management as a treatment for GAD

The content of the anxiety management package evaluated by Butler, Cullington, Hibbert, Klimes and Gelder (1987) was influenced by pilot work conducted with patients suffering from GAD as well as by the research results available in 1984 when the project began. The pilot work convinced us of three points: (1) psychological treatments based on the self-help model can be more confusing than helpful if they are not held together by a coherent rationale – in our case a vicious circle model of anxiety that explains that anxiety can be controlled if the factors that maintain it are identified, and the vicious circles interrupted; (2) avoidance is probably present in GAD but takes unusual forms; and (3) patients with GAD often become demoralised and unconfident as well as anxious. The strategies included in anxiety management were adapted accordingly. They were presented as methods for breaking the vicious circles that otherwise maintain anxiety, and the main message (put into words by one patient as 'there *is* something you can do') was designed to reduce demoralisation and build confidence by mobilising people's resources for coping with their symptoms. The final package contained four relatively well-known pro-cedures for reducing symptoms – relaxation, distraction, controlling upsetting thoughts and panic management – and two procedures that had not previously been systematically employed in the treatment of generalised anxiety – graded practice (or exposure) to reduce avoidance and procedures to increase self-confidence and reduce demoralisation. The treatment was presented in a self-help booklet which has since been recommended by a Consensus Conference in their 'Guidelines for the Management of Patients with Generalised Anxiety' (1992).

As so little was known about GAD, anxiety management was compared with a waiting-list control group. It proved to have substantial effects not only on measures of anxiety, but also on those of depression and the frequency of panic attacks. These changes were replicated almost exactly when patients in the waiting-list group completed treatment. At the time that these results were presented, the size of the effects was considerably larger than had previously been reported, and the gains persisted un-changed for the following six months. Of course it is not possible from these results alone to know which components of anxiety management contributed most to its effectiveness. The following ideas about their practical implications are based on data from standard measures, structured interviews, informal observations and subsequent research findings (see also Butler, Gelder, Hibbert, Cullington & Klimes, 1987).

Practical implications

At variance with other reports in the literature, 80 per cent of the generally anxious patients reported experiencing situational anxiety and 64 per cent of them reported situational avoidance in addition to more subtle kinds of avoidance. Overall, their feared situations were varied, more diffuse and less focused than for phobic patients, and examples of more subtle forms of avoidance included not thinking about problems, avoiding doing anything that might provoke or exacerbate symptoms, and not doing something that might upset, anger or irritate other people. Simple exposure instructions, presented in the context of the vicious circle model of anxiety, were sufficient to reverse this avoidance and may be necessary if avoidance otherwise maintains anxiety. The message is that patients do not always need to progress up carefully specified hierarchies in order to benefit from exposure. If the theory is explained clearly to them, they can, with reminders from their therapists, apply it appropriately by themselves.

Distraction was found to be an ambiguous strategy. If used as a way of turning attention away from distressing symptoms of anxiety so as to be able better to engage in other tasks, it was helpful. However, as many patients pointed out, it could also be used as a way of avoiding something alarming, especially if keeping busy and occupied became a substitute for recognising and thinking about problems and how to deal with them. Patients were well able to understand its dangers, especially once they understood more about the effects of avoidance, and once these were explained they were also able to make use of distraction in a way that was apparently helpful. It therefore seems a pity to discourage the use of this strategy, as many clinicians now do, and more important to be explicit about its advantages and disadvantages so as to help patients use it appropriately.

Patients with major depressive disorder as well as GAD were excluded from this study if the depression was their primary problem. However, if GAD was thought to be primary, in that it had started first and associated depression was a secondary consequence (an understandable reaction to being faced with a chronic, apparently insoluble problem), then the depression was resolved when the anxiety was treated. In addition, there was a tendency for patients who were depressed as well as anxious to improve more than those who were not depressed. Indeed informal observations suggested that anxiety management helped people to recognise and make use of their own resources for coping generally, and that the realisation that they could do this was one of the factors that helped to dissipate the depression.

Demoralisation, defined as a non-depressed kind of hopelessness, is obviously related to depression, and the hypothesis that demoralisation interfered with patients' abilities to use their own resources received some support from this study. A predictive analysis carried out afterwards (Butler & Anastasiades, 1988) showed that those patients who were most demoralised responded least well. The strategies used to build confidence, especially taking up enjoyable activities, together with cognitive strategies directed at self-assessments, appeared to be especially effective in reducing demoralisation, although it is also important to mention that patients' reports about what they found helpful suggested that they were also greatly encouraged by the underlying simple rationale for treatment: 'nobody can cure your anxiety, but you can learn to control it'. Overall the general and specific elements of the treatment were reported to be equally effective (Butler, Cullington, Hibbert, Klimes & Gelder, 1987).

Before treatment started, the majority of patients had tried to control their anxiety using strategies similar to those used in anxiety management, including the cognitive ones (defined for the purposes of a structured interview as 'trying to change anxious thinking by saying something to yourself'). However, none of these strategies had proved effective at that stage, while the potentially counter-productive strategies of avoidance, taking tranquillisers or drinking alcohol were rated as more effective. It must therefore be important to identify all the strategies that people spontaneously try out to control their anxiety (and other reactions to it like smoking or drinking caffeine-laden drinks), as some of these could, in the long term, do more harm than good. At the same time, more than half the patients said that they found it helpful to take exercise, which is not likely to be counter-productive and might therefore usefully be included as part of treatment.

Stage 4: How can we make treatments for GAD more effective?

Although we had demonstrated that anxiety management was effective as a treatment for generalised anxiety, many questions remained unanswered. Despite the good results, about a third of the patients improved relatively little, and a few of these seemed quite resistant to treatment. Other researchers have also reported relatively high rates of failure to respond (for example, Borkovec & Mathews, 1988; Durham & Turvey, 1987), suggesting that none of the available treatments for GAD are yet as effective as psychological treatments for simpler anxiety states such as phobias and panic disorder. The task of the next stage was to compare two different treatments, both theoretically likely to be helpful, in an attempt to find out more about what factors contribute to effectiveness.

A behavioural treatment (BT) was compared with a cognitive-behavioural treatment (CBT) and with a waiting-list control group (Butler et al., 1991). BT included exposure, relaxation and practical procedures for building confidence and was presented with the vicious circle rationale used for anxiety management. CBT was given in the way described by Beck, Emery and Greenberg (1985), and the rationale explained how thoughts and feelings are related and how anxiety is maintained both by anxious thoughts and by thoughts about lack of confidence. The main steps involved were identifying, re-examining and testing out anxiety-related thoughts, during which stage behavioural tasks were used as appropriate. Patients were provided with booklets describing the treatment, which emphasised the need to develop both self-management skills and self-reliance through regular practice outside the treatment sessions. The treatments also contained other common elements: a simple rationale which provided the basis for individual formulations and was used to facilitate application of the rationale to each case, and emphasis on self-help, which provided a stimulus for a summary of treatment made by patients at the end, or 'blueprint' (see also Butler & Booth, 1991), which they could subsequently use as a reminder, and which helped to mobilise their resources for coping.

Findings and their practical implications

The findings show a consistent pattern of change supporting the superiority of CBT over BT, and this was greater at six months follow-up than immediately after treatment. This cannot be taken to suggest that BT is not an effective treatment for GAD, as patients in this group improved significantly during treatment on all but one measure of anxiety and maintained this improvement for the following six months. However, it does indicate some of the limitations of BT as a treatment for GAD. Two patients had to be withdrawn when they became increasingly depressed, and three more dropped out of treatment. There was no such attrition in the CBT group, and therapists' observations suggest that it was not possible, using BT, to deal adequately with patients' feelings of hope-lessness about being able to change, or with any reservations they might have about treatment, while these topics could readily be discussed and dealt with using CBT.

The advantage of CBT was perhaps most evident in measures of clinically significant change, which showed that six months after treatment had ended 42 per cent of the patients who received CBT met operationally defined criteria for a 'good outcome' compared with 5 per cent of those who received BT. Reports from patients collected by an independent assessor at this time showed that the cognitive intervention had apparently done more to bring about a change of attitude in the way patients looked at their problems and their resources. They showed a larger degree of cognitive change, reflected in such statements as, 'I found a way of dealing with it [anxiety] by myself', and 'It puts things in perspective'. During CBT it was also possible to discuss underlying beliefs and assumptions in such a way as (theoretically) to make people less susceptible to future anxiety states (an illustrative case example has been described in Butler, 1994a). Doing this may both make anxious people feel less vulnerable and threatened and also help to deal with beliefs about themselves which relate to low self-esteem and poor self-confidence. If these two problems are not tackled it is to be expected that, when faced with new events that provoke anxiety, it will be harder to mobilise the resources necessary to cope with them.

The observation that avoidance is present in GAD was confirmed in this study, and indeed therapists were able to adapt conventional methods of exposure to tackle this problem during BT. Avoidance was not ignored when doing CBT, but tackled in a more cognitive way. So patients were helped to identify the thoughts that prevented them approaching difficult situations, or the thoughts that made them wish to withdraw or avoid, and to re-examine these thoughts. Of course many times alternative thoughts could only successfully be re-evaluated using behavioural experiments, and these involved approaching rather than avoiding difficulties. So exposure also formed part of CBT, and it was most effective when carried out in such a way as to provide information relevant to specific fears, or to disconfirm clearly identified expectations.

Two general implications of these findings are also of practical value. First, those patients who readily adopted the self-help approach, and were able to respond actively rather than passively to their problem, were also better able to engage in treatment. As anxiety is a normal part of experience it will recur, and the only viable treatment option is to learn better how to manage it. It is therefore important for therapists to set up appropriate expectations in their patients, to dispel any beliefs that others can solve the problem for them, and to foster a belief in each person's potential for controlling his or her symptoms. If reservations and doubts about this message are not discussed, they may continue to interfere with progress.

Second, patients with GAD are often confused by the unpredictable and apparently uncontrollable nature of their symptoms. Presenting a clear rationale, and using an explicit formulation to fit this carefully to the specific form of each person's problem, reduces confusion and directs efforts to change along more fruitful channels. Relying on a unifying rationale also facilitates clear structuring of treatment sessions, which in turn provides a model for constructive problem-solving. Demonstrating and summarising the problem-solving method helps patients to become more skilled in their use of it, especially if during treatment they practise it outside the session and take responsibility for starting to work on aspects of the problem not yet focused on during therapy.

The complexity of GAD poses many problems for the therapist. Before this study began the new definition of GAD (DSM-III-R; American

Psychiatric Association, 1987), with its clear focus on the essential feature of 'anxious expectation' or worry, had just become available, and this definition has done much to help therapists recognise the importance of the cognitive aspect of the problem. It has, however, had the effect of focusing attention on worry while paying less attention to the secondary aspects of GAD, which include social anxiety, depression, panic, demoralisation, lack of confidence and low self-esteem. The practical value of delineating secondary aspects of the problem is inestimable. It helps to clarify to the patient what is going on, to focus attention on the process of worry rather than on its content, and to select specific aspects of the problem or difficulty to focus on. However, social anxiety and depression, in particular, can hold progress up, and therefore may need to be tackled directly. In this study we found, as predicted on the basis of the earlier one, that CBT would reduce depression as well as anxiety in patients who had both types of symptoms. One reason for this may be that the rationale for CBT, and the specific strategies for dealing with thoughts, can readily be applied to thoughts associated with feelings other than anxiety, in particular to thoughts associated with depression and with social anxiety, both of which involve negative self-evaluations. Whether or not they are also well suited for dealing with worry itself, which has been thought of as a rather unfocused cognitive, rather than affective, activity, is not so clear.

Stage 5: Finding out more about worry

If worry is the central problem in GAD, then we need to learn how to treat it. The assumption often made by people who use cognitive forms of treatment is that worry is another form of thinking and therefore the strategies for dealing with negative automatic thoughts, or underlying beliefs, can readily be applied to the treatment of worry. Unfortunately this assumption seems not to be wholly correct. In our clinical experience cognitive strategies are only of limited value when working with chronic worriers – with people with severe and long-standing forms of GAD. Of course worriers do misconstrue the evidence, and they get things out of proportion. They over-generalise or jump to unwarranted conclusions, and these 'errors of judgement' can be identified, re-evaluated and tested out in practice using standard cognitive methods. But worrisome thinking is not always so clearly specified. It often involves a form of ruminative speculation about the future during which patients ask themselves (and others) questions like 'what if . . .' and 'supposing that . . .', or they describe being subject to a stream of rather vague and distressing thoughts which skirt round all manner of distressing possibilities. If they pick on one for a short time, then another seems to replace it as soon as that one is dealt with. It is often difficult for worriers to specify exactly what it is that they are worried about in a way that makes the worry amenable to cognitive therapy, as if the worry was more like a sense of dread, or that something bad might happen, or the feeling of being faced with un-manageable difficulties or the fear of being overwhelmed. When standard cognitive strategies are applied, they may only be temporarily successful, and the worrisome activity, or worrisome state, re-emerges despite apparently successful re-evaluations.

Clearly it is important to find out more about worry, and about how to treat it. We started to do this by testing hypotheses that followed from Borkovec's theory that worry may be an avoidance reaction to distressing affective material (Borkovec & Hu, 1990; Borkovec & Inz, 1990; Borkovec, Shaddick & Hopkins, 1991). The main idea is that people worry, or become involved in conceptual activity, because this prevents them becoming overwhelmed with affect, or with images that provoke affect. If someone is late arriving home, it is less distressing, even though it still feels bad, to worry about what might have happened to him or her, in a rather vague and non-specific way, than to be subject to vivid images of a horrifying and gruesome accident. If so, then worrying has advantages that are likely to maintain the activity, and it should be associated with lower anxiety than imagery which provides no opportunity for avoiding confronting fear and distress.

However, if this account is accurate, worrying may have an unwanted side-effect. It may perpetuate anxiety in the longer run, as the fear and anxiety associated with distressing events has been avoided and avoidance maintains anxiety. If worry suppresses emotional activation, it may also interfere with emotional processing (Foa & Kozak, 1986; Rachman, 1980), which suggests that both the immediate and the delayed effects of worrying (for example, after a distressing event) should differ from the effects of engaging in imagery. In the short term, imagery should maintain anxiety while worry should not do so, or should do so less. In the longer term, worry should be a less successful way of reducing anxiety than imagery, and should be followed by a greater number of intrusive cognitions (indicating the relative failure of emotional processing).

These hypotheses were tested by Butler, Wells and Dewick (1995) using a sample of normal control subjects. First they filled in questionnaires concerning their mood state and tendency to worry or to use images. Then they watched a short video of an industrial accident that actually happened (made for training in safety at work). They re-rated their mood before engaging in a brief period of worry or imagery about the video. The questionnaires were repeated after this experimental manipulation and subjects kept diaries of worry, imagery and thoughts about the video for the following week.

Findings and their practical implications

The main findings, which still need replication, were consistent with the hypotheses. They showed that watching the video increased anxiety in all subjects, and that worrying reduced this anxiety significantly whereas imagery did not. Information from the diaries showed that worrying also led to significantly more intrusions during the following three days than did imagery. Although worry feels bad, it seems that it still feels less bad than something else, which more directly evokes distressing affect, and that it may therefore be self-maintaining. It could be maintaining either because success in avoiding distressing affect is reinforcing or because the failure to complete emotional processing leads to repeated experience of intrusive thoughts.

Relatively little is known about worry, even though the subject is now attracting much research interest (Davey & Tallis, 1994), so it may be premature to speculate about the practical implications of these findings. At least they suggest that exposure to distressing imagery may be helpful to worriers if they are able to specify what they are most afraid of, and to allow their imaginations to 'run away with them' sufficiently to be able to form relevant images. Further ideas about how to develop a range of strategies for treating worry, which have not yet been evaluated as treatments for GAD, are to be found in Butler (1994b). Worry is an especially interesting topic for future research both because of the opportunities it provides to learn more about the relationships between cognition and emotion and because anxious people so often describe it as one of their long-standing characteristics. Learning more about worry may help us to extend the treatments for GAD so as to make them more helpful to the most chronic patients, many of whom also fulfil criteria for one of the personality disorders.

Concluding ideas

There are a number of themes running through this chapter, which has primarily focused on a series of research studies aimed at improving the psychological treatments available for people with GAD. First, it appears that avoidance may well play an important part in the maintenance of GAD as well as in other forms of anxiety, and therefore that exposure can form a valuable part of the treatment for GAD. It may also be useful as a specific strategy for dealing with worry, if it can be used to help people confront the fears and images about the future that they find most alarming. Second, self-help treatments, in which patients have to play an active part, appear to be particularly well adapted for those cases in which anxiety triggers are hard to specify. Explaining the rationale for treatment, and helping patients to understand the principles of the proposed interventions, for example by using the collaborative methods that have been especially well developed by proponents of cognitive treatments, enables them creatively to apply the methods in situations which vary unpredictably. In the third place we have found repeatedly that both the general and the specific aspects of the treatments used appear to be valuable. This suggests that the way a treatment is presented, its 'delivery', is important, and that it is also important to devise, and evaluate, specific strategies for dealing with the different kinds of anxiety. Without careful research, for example into the nature of cognitions (and worries) in anxiety, or into the ways in which exposure can be applied in more complex situations, the development of more effective treatments would have been slower.

References

American Psychiatric Association. (1987). *Diagnostic and statistical manual of mental disorders* (3rd ed., rev.). Washington, DC: Author.

Barrios, B.S., & Shigetomi, C.C. (1979). Coping-skills training for the management of anxiety: A critical review. *Behavior Therapy, 10,* 491–522.

Beck, A.T., Emery, G., & Greenberg, R. (1985). *Anxiety disorders and phobias: A cognitive perspective.* New York: Guilford.

Beck, A.T., Laude, R., & Bohnert, M. (1974). Ideational components of anxiety neurosis. *Archives of General Psychiatry, 31,* 319–325.

Beck, A.T., Rush, A.J., Shaw, B.F., & Emery, G. (1979). *Cognitive Therapy of Depression.* New York: Guilford.

Borkovec, T.D., & Hu, S. (1990). The effect of worry on cardiovascular response to phobic imagery. *Behaviour Research and Therapy, 28,* 69–73.

Borkovec, T.D., & Inz, J. (1990). The nature of worry in generalized anxiety disorder: A predominance of thought activity. *Behaviour Research and Therapy, 28,* 153–158.

Borkovec, T.D., & Mathews, A.M. (1988). Treatment of nonphobic anxiety: A comparison of nondirective, cognitive and coping desensitization therapy. *Journal of Consulting and Clinical Psychology, 56,* 877–884.

Borkovec, T.D., Shaddick, R.N., & Hopkins, M. (1991). The nature of normal and pathological worry. In R. Rapee & D.H. Barlow (Eds.), *Chronic anxiety and mixed anxiety–depression* (pp. 29–51). New York: Guilford.

Butler, G. (1985). Exposure as a treatment for social phobia: Some instructive difficulties. *Behaviour Research and Therapy, 23,* 651–657.

Butler, G. (1989). Issues in the application of cognitive and behavioural strategies for the treatment of social phobia. *Clinical Psychology Review, 9,* 91–106.

Butler, G. (1990). *Anxiety and subjective risk.* PhD thesis, Open University, UK.

Butler, G. (1993). Predicting outcome after treatment for GAD. *Behaviour Research and Therapy, 31,* 211–213.

Butler, G. (1994a). Generalised anxiety disorder. In C. Last & M. Hersen (Eds.), *Adult behavior therapy casebook* (pp. 153–169). New York: Plenum.

Butler, G. (1994b). Treatment of worry in generalised anxiety disorder. In G.C.L. Davey & F. Tallis (Eds.), *Worrying: Perspectives on theory, assessment and treatment* (pp. 209–228). London: Wiley.

Butler, G., & Anastasiades, P. (1988). Predicting response to anxiety management in patients with generalised anxiety disorder. *Behaviour Research and Therapy, 26,* 531–534.

Butler, G., Cullington, A., Hibbert, G., Klimes, I., & Gelder, M. (1987). Anxiety management for persistent generalised anxiety. *British Journal of Psychiatry, 151,* 535–542.

Butler, G., Cullington, A., Munby, M., Amies, P., & Gelder, M. (1984). Exposure and anxiety management in the treatment of social phobia. *Journal of Consulting and Clinical Psychology, 52,* 642–650.

Butler, G., Fennell, M., Robson, P., & Gelder, M. (1991). A comparison of behavior therapy and cognitive behavior therapy in the treatment of generalised anxiety disorder. *Journal of Consulting and Clinical Psychology, 59,* 167–175.

Butler, G., Gelder, M., Hibbert, G., Cullington, A., & Klimes, I. (1987). Anxiety management: Developing effective strategies. *Behavior Research and Therapy, 25,* 517–522.

Butler, G., & Mathews, A. (1983). Cognitive processes in anxiety. *Advances in Behaviour Therapy and Research, 5,* 51–62.

Butler, G., & Mathews, A. (1987). Anticipatory anxiety and risk perception. *Cognitive Therapy and Research, 11,* 551–565.

Butler, G., Wells, A., & Dewick, H. (1995). Differential effects of worry and imagery after exposure to a stressful stimulus. *Behavioural and Cognitive Psychotherapy, 25,* 45–56.

Clark, D.M., Salkovskis, P.M., Hackmann, A., Middleton, H., Anastasiades, P., & Gelder, M. (1994). A comparison of cognitive therapy, applied relaxation and imipramine in the treatment of panic disorder. *British Journal of Psychiatry, 164,* 759–769.

Cullington, A., Butler, G., Hibbert, G., & Gelder, M. (1984). Problem solving: Not a treatment for agoraphobia. *Behavior Therapy, 15,* 280–286.

Davey, G.C.L., & Tallis, F. (1994). *Worrying: Perspectives on theory, assessment and treatment.* London: Wiley.

Durham, R.C., & Turvey, A.A. (1987). Cognitive therapy vs behaviour therapy in the treatment of chronic general anxiety: Outcome at discharge and at six month follow-up. *Behaviour Research and Therapy, 25,* 229–234.

Finlay-Jones, R.A., & Brown, G.W. (1981). Types of stressful life-event and the onset of anxiety and depressive disorders. *Psychological Medicine, 11,* 803–815.

Foa, E.B., & Kozak, M.J. (1985). Treatment of anxiety disorders: implications for psychopathology. In A.H. Tuma & J. Maser (Eds.), *Anxiety and the Anxiety Disorders,* Hillsdale, NJ: Erlbaum.

Guidelines for the management of patients with generalised anxiety. (1992). *Psychiatric Bulletin, 16,* 560–565.

Lang, P.J. (1979). A bio-informational theory of emotional imagery. *Psychophysiology, 16,* 495–512.

Rachman, S. (1980). Emotional processing. *Behaviour Research and Therapy, 18,* 51–60.

Rachman, S., & Wilson, T. (1980). *The effects of psychological therapies.* Oxford: Pergamon.

Seligman, M.E.P. (1991). *Learned optimism.* New York: Knopf.

5

Cognitive-Behavioral and Psychodynamic Therapies: A Comparison of Change Processes

Susan L. Wiser, Marvin R. Goldfried, Patrick J. Raue and Douglas A. Vakoch

In a recent conversation we had with a physician, the comparison was drawn between medicine and psychotherapy. Upon hearing us lament about the disagreement among psychotherapists as to the relative effectiveness of different forms of therapy and the mechanisms of change, he responded by stating 'What do you expect? After all, psychotherapy is an infant science.' We found his comment to be quite disconcerting, especially since the field of psychotherapy has been in existence for over a century (Freedheim, 1992). Given the countless hours spent by thousands of professionals in practice, research and theory, one would have hoped that some consensus could have been reached by now.

There has always been an essential tension between practice and research in psychotherapy. Clinicians lament that psychotherapy research is overly simplified by its methodological constraints and not directly relevant to what they do in practice. In turn, therapy researchers accuse practicing therapists of failing to attend to the research literature. Moreover, researchers and clinicians live in vastly different worlds. Practicing therapists succeed by virtue of their ability to maintain and establish a good therapeutic alliance, demonstrate clinical effectiveness and have a reliable source of referrals. The professional lives of psychotherapy researchers are governed by research grants, publications in prestigious journals and professional recognition.

The gap between research and practice has been further accentuated in recent years by virtue of the fact that current methodology used to study the effectiveness of psychotherapy has borrowed from the field of drug research. Thus, these 'clinical trials' involve manual-driven interventions for the treatment of individuals who have been categorized as having particular clinical disorders. Whereas the practicing therapist carefully formulates a case and selects the most appropriate intervention, such clinical trials require that the therapist adhere to a theory-driven manual in the treatment of a randomly assigned patient.

Although outcome research has made some important inroads in working with specific clinical problems such as anxiety disorders, the vast majority of comparative outcome studies have failed to yield any overall differences across varying therapy orientations. This failure to find consistent differences in outcome research has led an increasing number of researchers to become involved in studying the process of change (Dahl, Kaechele & Thoma, 1988; Greenberg & Pinsof, 1986). The goal of such process research is to better understand the change mechanisms associated with various interventions. What is of particular importance is that contemporary psychotherapy process research deals with issues that are of concern to the practicing therapist. The basic question addressed by such process research is: 'What did the therapist do to facilitate or impede change in the client?' As such, it directly addresses the question that practicing clinicians continually ask *themselves*, namely: 'What can I do to facilitate and avoid impeding change in this client?'

Different therapy orientations have provided varying explanations of the change processes that guide the clinical work within that school. Until recently, relatively few attempts had been made to delineate commonalities in the process of change that may exist across orientations. We believe that a study of the existing commonalities across orientations can provide the practicing therapist with invaluable information on both similar as well as unique mechanisms associated with different schools of thought.

If we set aside the theoretical jargon associated with different therapeutic orientations, it is possible to highlight what appear to be agreed-upon principles of change (Goldfried & Padawer, 1982). Thus, the change process may be seen as being initially facilitated by clients' *expectation of help* upon entering therapy. Originally discussed by Frank (1961) as a common factor shared by all healing practices, psychotherapy included, it continues to be accepted as an influential mechanism of initial change.

Another significant common mechanism of change is the *therapeutic relationship*. The therapeutic interaction provides the client with a warm, empathic and validating partner, an experience that in itself may bring about change. But additionally, the therapeutic relationship or alliance implicitly and/or explicitly encourages the client to risk new ways of behaving, both within and outside the therapy session. Perhaps breaking a history of problematic interpersonal patterns, such new behavior may include expressing a range of emotions, voicing rights or needs, or establishing trust with another individual.

Therapists of varying orientations also attempt to provide clients with *an alternate way of understanding themselves and their environment*. Clients enter therapy with a host of distorted views of themselves, current and past situations, and other individuals in their lives. All therapies have the common aim of aiding them in clarifying these views, either by interpretation, Socratic questioning or reformulation. Regardless of the specific method, the common mechanism is providing clients with feedback about their perceptions in an effort to establish a new and more adaptive awareness.

This new awareness often leads to what may be considered as a core change mechanism, namely the *corrective experience*. Originally formulated by Alexander and French (1946), this change principle aims to help clients engage in some new experience that will function to change perceptions, thoughts or feelings about themselves and others. In psychodynamic therapy, it might be the expression of anger toward the therapist, or having the experience of being understood rather than criticized. In behavior therapy, the corrective experience might consist of confronting a feared object, situation or person that had been previously avoided, with no harm ensuing. In experiential therapy, it could be the experience of telling a parent (perhaps symbolized by an empty chair), with a strong, firm voice rather than a choked, frightened one, how hurt and angry they were about how they were cared for as a child.

Finally, much of the therapeutic change process involves providing clients with ongoing *reality-testing*, which involves providing both an increased awareness (insight) and associated risk-taking (action) that results in corrective experiences.

In our own work on studying the therapeutic change process, we begin with the assumption that these common principles reflect robust phenomena, particularly since they may be found to play an important role in different schools of therapy. Consequently, we assume that these principles help us by delineating important arenas within which process research can take place, both to study the similarities and differences across different schools of thought, as well as to determine the parameters of such common change mechanisms that may result in differential therapeutic outcomes.

In an effort to uncover and highlight common and unique facets of these schools, our research group has focused predominantly on process comparisons of cognitive-behavioral and psychodynamic therapies. In the remainder of this chapter, we discuss the results of our empirical efforts to date, highlighting its relevance to clinical practice. The change processes we have studied involve the therapeutic relationship and clinical attempts at facilitating awareness. In addition, we have investigated clients' emotional experiencing in sessions, as it is believed to play an important role in a variety of different therapies (Greenberg & Safran, 1987; Guidano & Liotti, 1983; Mahoney, 1991).

The Stony Brook Research Program

In their work, clinicians split their focus between helping clients to explore, gain awareness of and better master both their intrapersonal and their interpersonal functioning. By intrapersonal functioning, we mean the internal aspects of the self: thoughts, feelings, fears, wishes, recollections, hopes, goals, judgments, memories, physiological states and moods. By interpersonal functioning, we mean the dynamics of clients' relations with others: what lies behind or accounts for the problematic interactions that they have with others, as well as what stops them from more effective and rewarding interpersonal relationships. Although intrapersonal and interpersonal dimensions of functioning clearly are closely intertwined, we find it useful to separate the two to facilitate a more cogent and clear clinical discussion of the ways in which therapists focus upon these issues in therapy.

With the bulk of outcome research demonstrating equivalent outcomes for various therapies with various client populations, questions about what specifically accounts for therapeutic efficacy arise. Such questions have guided our research efforts to date. We have been interested not only in how specific treatments facilitate change, but also in comparisons across different theoretical schools, to examine whether (1) similar patient changes are brought about through different therapeutic means in different treatments; (2) change is a function not of the specific effects of various therapies, but rather of underlying factors common to all forms of psychotherapy; or (3) therapists do not, in fact, practice therapy as differently from one another as theory might lead us to expect. As with most questions where multiple possible answers are posed, the truest and most complete answer is probably 'all of the above, and then some'. This response, true as it may be, is also terribly non-specific, offering no concrete and useful information to practicing clinicians.

In the section that follows, we offer findings garnered from comparative process and outcome studies in which our research group has attempted to address the question of what accounts for therapeutic change in small but specific ways. Admittedly, the overall puzzle of how different types of therapists actually practice therapy, and which methods used by which therapists with which clients are most effective, remains largely unsolved. Our findings, however, provide some small but concrete puzzle pieces that may be useful clinically, and may spur further specific research questions in the area.

Our research to date has included studies of Beck's cognitive therapy, cognitive-behavior therapy and psychodynamic therapy. As the studies make use of different types of therapy datasets, we will first describe the parameters of the various datasets used, and will then discuss our findings.

Datasets

Two of the datasets that we will be discussing are exclusively *process* datasets: they are sessions of therapy used for intensive analysis of in-session process, with no post-therapy outcome data available. They are used to compare process across theoretical schools, as well as to point to those processes that may be implicated in outcome, and thus could be looked at in future research from a process-outcome framework. The first dataset, which we will call the *demonstration* dataset, contains demonstration sessions of cognitive therapy (CT; Aaron Beck), cognitive-behavior therapy (CBT; Donald Meichenbaum) and psychodynamic therapy (PDT;

Hans Strupp) with the same depressed patient, Richard. These single-session demonstrations (see Shostrom, 1986), although limited in their potential generalizability to other therapists and to a full course of therapy, nonetheless provide a prototypic sample of each of these orientations, while at the same time controlling for client variables.

The second dataset used for comparative process purposes is referred to as the *change session* dataset. It contains 31 different therapist–client pairs (all therapists were multiply nominated by experts in their orientation as particularly competent therapists), each of whom contributed a single, clinically significant change session taken from the middle phase of their patient's ongoing outpatient course of psychotherapy. Each of these 31 therapists who participated in the study targeted one of their clients who presented with depressed and/or anxious symptomatology, and where interpersonal issues were an important focus in treatment. When a significant audiotaped change session occurred in the course of treatment (the client dealt with an interpersonal theme central to his or her difficulties and there was observable impact on the client both during the session and in the subsequent session or two), that one session was submitted for the study. This process eventuated in a dataset of 18 CBT change sessions and 13 PDT change sessions.

We also have examined two datasets that include post-therapy outcome measures. The first is a study of short-term CT with 30 depressed clients who underwent a course of approximately 15 sessions of cognitive psychotherapy (Hollon et al., 1992). For each of the 30 clients, one session was randomly chosen from the first half of the therapy (after the first three sessions) for examination, as 90 per cent of patients' improvement took place by this treatment midpoint. Standardized excerpts from these sessions were analyzed with various coding procedures. This dataset will hereafter be referred to as the *CT-outcome* dataset.

The second dataset for which outcome data were available is a comparison between 13 courses of short-term PDT and 13 courses of short-term CBT (8-session treatment) of patients presenting with depression and/or anxiety in Sheffield, England (Sheffield I; Shapiro & Firth, 1987). Two sessions (excluding session 1) were randomly selected from each case; within these two sessions, random segments were then selected for coding and analysis. This dataset will be termed the *comparative-outcome* dataset in the following discussion.

Comparative process findings: Intrapersonal aspects

An intrapersonal focus in treatment may serve a variety of purposes, including attempting to enhance a client's knowledge of self, elucidate explicit or implicit belief systems, or facilitate awareness of emotional states. While such purposes are shared by therapists schooled in a variety of therapeutic traditions, each underlying theoretical framework points therapists of that school to focus more or less upon particular aspects of their clients' intrapersonal functioning. For instance, it would be reasonable to expect that behavior therapists would demonstrate a greater focus upon the actions of their clients, cognitive therapists would evidence more work with their clients' thinking, and psychodynamic therapists would display more attention to their clients' fantasies for self and others. This would presumably be the case because each school has somewhat unique theoretical beliefs about the areas of client functioning that are most directly connected to psychological change.

Our first aim was to explore the similar and unique ways that various orientations of therapists practiced in order to determine the disparity between the practice, rather than the theory of psychotherapy.

Cognitive therapy versus cognitive-behavioral therapy A first comparison, drawn from the demonstration dataset, lies between the practice of CT (by Beck) and CBT (Meichenbaum). These two forms of therapy are often discussed interchangeably, but perhaps falsely so. We gathered preliminary evidence to show that, despite the strong theoretical cognitive emphasis in both of these treatments, a far greater proportion of the therapeutic hour was spent addressing client cognitive processes within a CT framework than was spent within a CBT framework. Specifically, there was a greater focus in CT on self-evaluations, expectations and general thoughts relative to the cognitive-behavioral demonstration. CT also placed more emphasis upon challenging the client's beliefs about reality, and upon highlighting the client's fantasy of the reaction he anticipated receiving from others. By contrast, there was a greater focus upon client emotion and behavior in CBT, relative to the focus paid to these two aspects within a CT framework.

The following summary examples are offered in the spirit of clinically illustrating the differing focus that was found statistically:

In CT: Richard, the client, explains that he is extremely lonely, and is depressed because he feels that he will remain lonely and alone forever. The therapist focuses on helping Richard to change his expectation of perpetual loneliness to a more hopeful expectation, by helping him to define positive aspects of self that might make him attractive to another. The therapist then coaches Richard's rehearsal of this new expectation.

In CBT: Richard explains that he is recently divorced, and he is very hurt and angry at his ex-wife. After probing for how Richard would like to vent his anger, the therapist works to help Richard find more appropriate behavioral expressions for his pain and anger.

In these examples, we see that the CT focus is more 'cognitive' while the CBT focus deals more with emotion and behavior. Exemplifying CT, Beck helps Richard to confront and challenge his hopeless expectations, and to imagine that his fear that others won't be interested in and attracted to him may be faulty. In essence, he helps Richard to shift his cognitive appraisals of reality from negative and depressing ones to hopeful ones.

The underlying assumption is that it is Richard's view of his world that dampens his mood and probably hinders more effective social/interpersonal action; with an altered cognitive scheme, he should be loosened to act more constructively. By contrast, Meichenbaum focuses not on altering Richard's view of reality, but instead on shaping his behavior in the hope of guiding Richard to more productive social interactions. Simplifying somewhat, we can imagine that had the cognitive-behavioral therapist been offered the description of Richard's intense loneliness and his fear of remaining lonely in the future, the CBT focus may have been to help the client think of activities that would lead to greater social interaction, and thus decreased loneliness, rather than helping Richard to see that his reality is in fact different than he perceives. Similarly, had the cognitive therapist been offered Richard's discussion of intense anger around the divorce, we can imagine that the discussion may have turned toward uncovering the belief system that results in his anger and hurt (that is, perhaps his belief that the rejection means he is worthless), and that the goal would have been to challenge this underlying belief about his wife leaving him, in order to alleviate his anger and hurt.

Along with these differences in therapeutic focus, many similarities were found. Virtually no patterns in Richard's intrapersonal functioning (that is, noting patterns in thought, affect or behavior across situations or time) were pointed out by either, and virtually no incongruities in intrapersonal functioning (that is, 'You say you are sad, yet you are smiling') were highlighted by either the cognitive or cognitive-behavioral therapists. Both, however, had a fairly strong focus on noting intrapersonal consequences (noting how one aspect of functioning leads to another, such as, 'That thought is causing your sadness' or 'Your anger makes you want to hit and scream'). Another similarity was that therapeutic questions and interventions in both types of therapy were largely focused on the following two time-frames: Richard's recent adult past and his future. These findings highlight a shared belief in these two treatments that it is useful for clients to gain a sense of the causal or lawful relationship between their various intrapersonal facets (how thoughts cause feelings, how feelings result in actions, how different behaviors will lead to altered feelings), and that, to be effective, therapy need largely concern itself with the immediate past and the future.

Psychodynamic therapy versus cognitive and cognitive-behavioral therapy
The ways in which CT and CBT are like one another but different from PDT is also an interesting comparison, and one we examined with the demonstration dataset as well. As noted, a focus on intrapersonal patterns was missing from both CT and CBT; by way of contrast, this focus was present in Strupp's demonstrations of PDT. For instance, it was pointed out to Richard in PDT that he had disappointments not only in his recent life, but also in his childhood. It was also pointed out that he feels the same way toward his wife as he does to his previous co-worker (both categorized

as 'bitches'). These highlighted patterns serve as mild confrontations; they tend to force a questioning of where the responsibility for problems lay. If it is pointed out that the same feelings or views keep surfacing despite differing situations, periods of time or people, it might cause the client to consider whether these feelings or views have more to do with him- or herself than with the people or situations.

PDT also differed from both CT and CBT in the time-frames employed, with PDT focusing more on the past (both childhood and the more recent past) and less on in-session and future time-frames. Such differences are consistent with PDT's theoretical premise that the roots of problems originate far in advance of adulthood, and thus should be understood in that context. Thus, they tend to have a greater focus on the past, and a lesser focus on the future. It is surprising, however, that CT and CBT had a greater in-session focus than did PDT, given PDT's strong emphasis on the here-and-now relationship with the therapist. It is probable that this has to do with the fact that the PDT session in this dataset was a demonstration first session between therapist and client. Minimal if any transferential material would likely be dealt with under such circumstances.

Differentiating between the two cognitively based therapies, and comparing each to PDT, offers still more information. In both the demonstration dataset and the comparative-outcome dataset, a greater CBT focus on present and future time-frames relative to PDT was found, while PDT displayed a greater focus than did CBT on the client's past (childhood and recent past) in both studies. Again, this points toward the cognitive-behavioral theory that change is facilitated through analysis of recent events, the present and the future, and the psychodynamic theory that change occurs following an explication of one's past. Similarly, in these two studies, CBT showed a stronger emphasis upon client actions than did PDT. As these findings were replicated across two very different datasets, we believe the differential focus on time-frame and attention to client behaviors to be a somewhat firm difference of focus in these two treatments, and we would expect to continue to find this in future investigations.

Less clear are findings that do not replicate across datasets. For instance, no differences were found for how much cognitive-behavioral and psychodynamic therapists focused on client expectations in the demonstration dataset, but PDT evidenced a significantly greater focus on client expectations in the comparative-outcome study. Similarly, in the demonstration dataset, PDT focused more on pointing out intrapersonal patterns to the client than did CBT, but this difference was not found in the comparative study outcome. Also, in the demonstration dataset, CBT had a stronger focus on client emotion than did PDT, but in the comparative-outcome dataset, PDT had a stronger focus on emotion than did CBT.

In the dataset of important change sessions in CBT and PDT, where depth of client emotional experiencing was studied (Wiser & Goldfried, 1993), it was determined that there was equivalence between these two forms of treatment in the depth of emotional experiencing that their clients were able to achieve in-session. What did differ between these two orientations was the view that the therapists held of these deeper emotional periods. Therapists pinpointed the most clinically significant portion of their sessions, and we found that in PDT these highlighted portions of sessions tended to contain those deep emotional periods for their clients, while, in CBT, clients' deeper affective explorations tended to lie *outside* of these highlighted portions. In other words, while the two therapies do not appear to facilitate differing degrees of affective depth in the session as a whole, psychodynamic therapists seem to place a higher value on the emergence of this material, while cognitive-behavioral therapists seem to think it less critically linked to change. It would be in keeping with CBT to value rational responding and behavioral discussion more highly than the elaboration of affect. A possible interpretation for the discrepant findings cited above between the demonstration and comparative-outcome datasets could be that the findings highlight the difference between how a therapy is practiced *prototypically* (the demonstration dataset being attempts at prototypic practice of each of the three forms of therapy), and how it is practiced *actually*. Also, as the demonstration dataset used only one client, it is unclear how much of the therapeutic foci were pulled by the particular type of client and his particular issues.

Along with these findings of differential focus between CBT and PDT, many aspects of client functioning were not demonstrated to be emphasized differently in these two treatments. For instance, no differences were found in either dataset concerning the degree to which these two types of therapists focused on:

(a)   clients' situations (that is, being in the hospital, getting promoted at work);
(b)   clients' ability to self-observe (that is, 'Are you aware of what things you are telling yourself?'; 'Now you realize that you become angry every time her name is mentioned');
(c)   the nature of clients' self-evaluation (that is, 'Do you think that makes you worthless?'; 'You feel that you are a moral and honest person');
(d)   clients' general thoughts (that is, 'What are your thoughts on that?');
(e)   clients' intentions (that is, hopes, desires, plans, goals, wishes);
(f)   clients' affective physiology (that is, feeling jittery, short of breath, nauseous);
(g)   choices or decisions faced by clients (that is, 'Each time he speaks to you like that you can either take it, or speak back');
(h)   clients' perceptions of reality (that is, 'You think there's no way out, but there actually is a way');
(i)   clients' imagined reactions of others (that is, 'You expect that she'll be terribly hurt if you say how you feel');
(j)   themes in clients' lives (that is, 'You feel rejected that he died, and you've felt rejected every time you've lost someone close to you');

(k) offering therapeutic support of clients' efforts (that is, 'You're making great progress');

(l) offering psychoeducational information (that is, 'Depression is quite common');

(m) changes in the client (that is, 'You are much more open with your feelings than you were when we began');

(n) intrapersonal consequences (that is, 'Thinking that you'll never feel better actually causes you to feel worse');

(o) incongruities in the client (that is, 'You say you're not angry, but you act as if you are').

Clearly, there were many therapeutic foci that, at least in these two studies, are not differentially used by these two schools of therapy. Actually, there seem to be fewer findings of difference here than there are failures to find difference, which may be surprising to many readers. It is the case also that the advanced graduate students who provided the coding for the demonstration dataset were able to easily determine which session was the CT session, but they were unable to distinguish between the CBT and the PDT sessions. What does this mean about these two forms of treatment? Certainly on a theoretical level, CBT and PDT are exceedingly disparate. PDT is sensitive to client unconscious motivation and the ways in which clients replay (with the therapist as well as others) early learned maladaptive ways of being and interrelating with others, while CBT is sensitive to the power of cognitive schemata, environmental reinforcers and punishers, and skill deficits. On this theoretical level, it seems that these therapists are dealing with two completely different realities. That may be true. Perhaps it also might be the case that cognitive-behavioral and psychodynamic therapists target a variety of similar areas for discussion, but toward different ends.

For instance, cognitive-behavioral therapists may highlight their clients' tentative wish to stand up for themself at work, while psychodynamic therapists might highlight their patients' wishes to be taken care of by the therapist. In both cases, we find a focus on clients' intentions. However, in the CBT case, this focus could lead to a program of behavioral assertion training, while in PDT, the focus might lead to a discussion of early parental neglect that resulted in persistent attempts by the client at obtaining caretaking from others. Or, failure to find differences may signify that cognitive-behavioral and psychodynamic therapists target similar areas that aim toward similar ends, but are understood theoretically in very different manners. For example, cognitive-behavioral therapists might help clients to examine their expectation that *others* will dislike or reject them, while psychodynamic therapists might discuss their clients' fear that the *therapist* dislikes or might reject them. Both are coded as a focus on clients' expected/imagined reactions of others. In both treatments, the goal of such a focus may be to help patients shed their fears of interpersonal relatedness and risk deeper relationships. Theoretical discussions, however, might couch these similar foci and similar goals very differently – one as challenging irrational and distorted cognitions, the other as dealing with transferential material.

Turning to a comparison between CT and PDT, we find that CT looks far more distinct from PDT than CBT did. In the demonstration study, CT displays a greater focus on Richard's self-evaluations, expectations, thoughts and affective physiology. The cognitive therapist offers significantly more challenges to his perceptions of reality, and draws more links concerning the intrapersonal consequences of his functioning. CT also was far more concerned with in-session responses, the recent past and the future. PDT, on the other hand, focused more than CT on the intrapersonal patterns in Richard's life (highlighting patterns of thinking, feeling or acting), and on Richard's past. The two therapies did not show differences in the extent to which they focused on emotion or behavior. Nor was there a difference in the degree that the therapists highlighted the expected reactions of others, pointed out themes, provided support, gave information and noted changes in the client.

As with the previous comparison, the overall summary picture comparing CT and PDT is complex. The two therapies clearly share less of a therapeutic focus with one another than did CBT with PDT or than did CBT with CT, but there are also many areas where differences did not arise. In examining a few of these more interesting areas where statistical differences were not found, we actually do find some clinical differences within the supposed commonalities that are informative. For instance, both types of therapists focused at times on the what the client imagined another's reaction to him was, or would be ('expected/imagined reaction of other'). The cognitive therapist highlighted Richard's fear that no one would ever want him as a mate, while the psychodynamic therapist highlighted Richard's belief that his ex-wife thought of him as incompetent and was displeased and dissatisfied with him. Examining the ways that these therapists turned the discussions, then, we find that these intrapersonal fantasies were highlighted for very different purposes. In CT, the therapist chose to help the client to perceive his negative fantasy as inaccurate, and to refute it (to make him feel more positively about himself and his future), while in PDT, the therapist encouraged the client to take responsibility for whatever he might have done to bring about the negative feelings in the others ('Were you asking yourself questions as to what you might have been contributing to this . . .?').

Turning to another focus, both therapists made some use of support in the sessions. Upon inspection, we see that CT uses support to reinforce more positive views of self (heartily agreeing with the client that he *can* be a whole person without a woman), while PDT uses support to encourage the client to seek out longer-term treatment ('. . . encourage you to find a competent therapist and stick with it. I have a sense you probably would'). Clinically, these foci are very different and reflect a major difference between the views in these two theories of treatment. We see CT's effort at replacing the client's current negative view of self, others and future with one that is more hopeful and positive, and at strongly reinforcing all positive views that emerge. If we had to provide a single statement to capture these therapeutic efforts, it might be: 'Just as you are, you and your future are far brighter than you presently appreciate; if you allow me to help you see this, you will feel much better.' By contrast, we see PDT's efforts at uncovering aspects of the client's functioning that are implicated in his problems (presumably these problem areas would be understood in the context of early learning with significant others in the client's life), and at encouraging the client to own his or her contribution while encouraging any efforts to take an active role in addressing these problem areas. Our summary statement here might be, 'You at least partially create your problems, and the best way for me to help you out of them (thereby feeling better) is to help you see what you do, how this came to be, and to encourage you to risk doing differently – with me, and then also with others.' As found by Levenson and Overstreet (1994), clients in interpersonally oriented PDT may need to get worse before they get better, especially with regard to making interpersonal changes.

Practical applications If any one school of therapy dealt with all emotional and psychological phenomena completely, the others would be superfluous. We know that this isn't the case. When we read theory, and now as we review empirical data, we see that each orientation organizes and intervenes in clients' psychosocial worlds in somewhat distinct ways. To be sure, there are both up and down sides to this stage of affairs. On the positive side, each orientation, as a result of its selective focus, has areas of relative expertise; on the negative side, this same selective focus results in other areas of relative neglect. We hope that if we turn our attention to other orientations' areas of expertise, our treatments will gain more depth and breadth and we will be of more benefit to our clients.

In the most general sense, we found that CT practitioners are most finely attuned to their clients' cognitions about self, world and future, CBT practitioners are most attuned to clients' behavior and emotions, and PDT practitioners are most attuned to patterns and the remote past. As an example, imagine that we are seeing a male client who relays the following story. He is very distressed about an incident that happened at work the previous week. His boss called him into her office and raised some questions about the work that he submitted to her. He felt quite panicked at the time, and only poorly expressed to her the rationale behind the way he had handled the work. He spent the following several days anxious and insecure at work, feeling that he was an unworthy employee and a general failure.

There are a multitude of ways to intervene therapeutically with this client. There are the 'irrational' feelings of failure and worthlessness, which can be addressed and modified; there are his fantasies of what the boss thought of him and where those fantasies originate; there is his own evaluation of the work that he had done; there is the client's inability to express himself to his boss, which may be practiced at; and there is the issue of why such a mild confrontation sent this client into a panic to begin with. All seem important areas to address.

We know that, in general, cognitive therapists would tend to follow up on the client's feelings of worthlessness and failure, aiming for the modification of his negative self-evaluations that are causing so much distress; cognitive-behavioral therapists would tend to follow up on the client's difficulty of expression, aiming to facilitate greater skill for the future; and psychodynamic therapists would tend to explore his extreme reaction to the questioning from authority, looking for patterns and for roots in early relationships.

Clinicians cannot address everything at once. We must constantly choose our responses to guide the in-session discussion to areas that we deem most beneficial for our clients. It is probably the case, however, that due to our training, experience and theoretical alignment, we often guide our clients into *our own* areas of competence, rather than into their most immediate or critical areas of need. It is our contention that all three lines of therapeutic work could prove quite useful to this client, and to the extent that we are aware of all three, we will be able to choose purposefully among them to best benefit our particular clients at their present positions.

Focusing now more specifically on the types of interventions made by therapists, we will highlight strategies that seem underutilized by practitioners in an effort to provoke thought about their potential appropriate use. We hope to call attention to areas that therapists of a given orientation may not typically traverse. We describe our understanding of the functions of these interventions so that therapists may examine whether they might make use of them more than they presently do.

Relative to PDT clinicians, cognitive and cognitive-behavioral therapists tended not to point out frequently intrapersonal patterns in their clients. In our example, such a statement might be: 'I remember you describing other instances of being questioned when you similarly felt a panic and then a worthlessness.' Pointing out such an intrapersonal pattern functions to: shift the client's focus from external situations, events and others (that is, what the boss did) to internal processes; convey the import of the client's emotional responses; and put one specific event into a broader context, helping the client to see how this event is just one instance of perhaps a root issue that needs to be explored and understood.

Cognitive and cognitive-behavioral therapists, again relative to PDT adherents, typically did not highlight observed incongruities such as: 'You are telling me that you felt panicky when she questioned you, but your tone is angry and your fist is clenched.' The function of such a statement is to confront the client with some aspect of his experience that he is either unaware of or denying to himself. Perhaps, in this example, he does not allow himself to become angry at superiors; perhaps be believes that he has no right to be angry; perhaps he fears retribution for feelings of anger;

perhaps he fears the therapist's negative judgment about his anger. There is likely some felt threat concerning his anger if his body expresses it but his words do not. Observing incongruities can be a way of inviting the client to explore an aspect of his experience that is threatening to him in some way.

And finally, in comparison to psychodynamic therapists, cognitive and cognitive-behavioral therapists tended to focus less on the client's past, with comments such as: 'The questioning and the panic – does that remind you of anything that went on when you were young?' The function of such a past focus is to evoke the early emotional material that perhaps is presently being replayed in the client's current life.

Psychodynamic therapists, relative to CT and CB practitioners, infrequently highlighted intrapersonal consequences for clients, such as 'Thinking that you are incompetent makes you feel even more anxious,' or 'Your anxiety causes your mind to go blank of thoughts.' Such comments serve to educate clients on how various internal processes are related to one another and provide the opportunity for clients to take responsibility for the chain of events that is taking place inside of them. It can give the control back to the client by conveying, 'This distressing chain goes on within you, and, therefore, you can intervene to circumvent the chain's completion.'

Compared to cognitive and cognitive-behavioral therapists, PDT clinicians focused far less on their client's future, such as: 'The next time you feel panicked like that, you can practice your breathing techniques and quiet yourself right down.' A focus on the future bolsters clients' own hope for change by conveying the therapist's confidence and expectation that change will occur; reminds clients that every day brings new chances and opportunities to act differently and thereby feel better about themselves; makes therapy feel immediately relevant as a method to improve their life situations; and provides a clear and specific direction for the future.

Relative to CBT, neither CT nor PDT focused greatly on clients' overtly expressed behaviors, such as: 'You weren't able to explain your work sufficiently to your boss.' A focus on client actions/inactions can serve a multitude of purposes. The behaviors that we engage or don't engage in feed our sense of ourselves, others' evaluations of us, and the impact of the environmental response that we receive. Discussions can serve to highlight consequences of our actions, reinforce appropriate behaviors, explore alternative courses of action, practice new behaviors, make known underlying motivations of what we do and examine personal costs of our behavior, just to name a few. We believe it important to foster responsibility for how one lives one's life by therapeutically attending to what clients do as carefully as we attend to what they feel.

Comparative process findings: Interpersonal aspects

Thus far, we have looked mainly at comparative research on the feedback that therapists give clients concerning their intrapersonal functioning. As we turn to research findings pertaining to the interpersonal functioning of clients, there are three separate domains that we have looked at: (1) feedback that the therapist gives to clients concerning their interpersonal functioning; (2) types of interpersonal issues that clients and therapists deal with; and (3) the relationship between the client and therapist, or the therapeutic relationship.

Feedback on interpersonal functioning   One way that therapists can provide clients with feedback about their relationships with others is by making links or drawing connections between an aspect of the client's functioning and an aspect of someone else's functioning. For example, when a therapist suggests that a client's wife became angry when he showed up late, the focus is on a link between the client's action and another's consequent emotion. When a therapist notes that a client tends to withdraw from others when others try to get close to her, the focus is on the effect of others' behavior on the client's behavior. Note that these interpersonal links can highlight two different aspects of the client's interpersonal functioning: (1) the effect that the client has on another and (2) the effect that another has on the client. Presumably, making these types of links or connections serves to increase clients' awareness and provide them with a better understanding of both how they affect and are affected by others.

Our research findings from the comparative-outcome dataset suggest that when we compare CBT and PDT there is no difference in the degree to which therapists use interpersonal links in general. This failure to find differences was not anticipated. We expected cognitive-behavioral therapists to provide fewer of these connections because CBT emphasizes the development of new behaviors and the effect of cognitive distortions on mood, rather than emphasizing relationships with others. Cognitive-behavioral therapists, however, often encourage clients to change certain patterns of behavior in order to make subsequent changes in their relationships with others, and cognitive distortions and maladaptive behavior often arise in interpersonal contexts. Perhaps this accounts for the equivalent use of interpersonal links provided to clients in both CBT and PDT.

In the demonstration dataset, where we compared PDT, CBT and CT, we similarly failed to find differences in therapist use of interpersonal links concerning the effect that others have on the client. However, both psychodynamic and cognitive-behavioral therapists used significantly more interpersonal links, relative to cognitive therapists, where they pointed out the effect that the client had on others. In other words, while therapists from the three orientations did not differ in their use of such statements as: 'How do you feel about what she did?' (the effect of another on the client), psychodynamic and cognitive-behavioral therapists were more likely than cognitive therapists to make statements such as: 'Is there something you might have done to make your wife feel that way?' (the effect of the client on another).

Another way that we have studied feedback from the therapist concerning the client's relationships with others has been to note the frequency with which therapists focus the client's attention on other people in their lives. Findings to date indicate a greater focus by PDT on the client's parents. This was found in the comparative-outcome dataset, but not the demonstration dataset, where this was not emphasized by any of the three therapists. In the demonstration, but not the comparative-outcome dataset, CT and CBT focused more on acquaintances or strangers in the client's life than did PDT. No difference among therapies in either dataset was found on a focus on the client's mate. The PDT focus on parents, combined with the previously mentioned greater focus on childhood time-frame, is consistent with a dynamic exploration of the origin of clients' patterns of functioning. In contrast, the previously mentioned greater emphasis by CT and CBT on current and future time-frames is consistent with the behavioral goal of relating more effectively with others, whether they be one's mate, an employer or a stranger.

Interpersonal issues in therapy   Although interpersonal issues relevant to progress in psychotherapy have been the focus of considerable research, often this occurs within a theoretical framework specific to one orientation of psychotherapy. Consistent with our goal of developing methodologies appropriate *across* orientations, we have examined interpersonal issues by drawing on both cognitive-behavioral and psychodynamic perspectives. We began by examining the types of issues that are actually discussed in sessions from the two orientations, and then we looked at how graduate students in clinical psychology programs emphasizing one of the two orientations conceptualized these issues. Thus we were able to study both the types of issues actually *present* in sessions as well as the ways that these issues are *categorized* by people trained in the two orientations.

After identifying the interpersonal issues in the change session dataset that were discussed in-session by either the client or the therapist, we found groups of issues that were either characteristic of one or both orientations. Both CBT and PDT placed a great emphasis on the client's excessive feelings of responsibility for her/his partner, the client's relationships with family members, the client's tendency either to yield to or to withdraw from others, and the ways the client was interacting effectively with others. Other types of issues were exclusively or predominantly associated with only one orientation. CBT sessions were more likely to deal with clients being excessively concerned with the actions of others toward them and the ways others evaluate them. PDT sessions, on the other hand, dealt with transference issues, as manifested by the clients' stated dissatisfaction with the therapist; this was not found in CBT sessions.

We also found that when graduate students in clinical psychology programs categorized the issues that were actually present in these sessions, they were able to make finer discriminations about issues that were consistent with their own orientations. That is, CBT judges were able to recognize a cluster of issues about the impact that others have on the client that is almost exclusively derived from CBT sessions, whereas PDT judges did not see this cluster as distinctly. Similarly, PDT judges separated transference issues from all other issues, while CBT judges combined these together with other issues pertaining to clients' dissatisfaction with persons other than the therapist.

The therapeutic relationship A last area of interest that falls in the interpersonal domain concerns the relationship between the client and therapist. The therapeutic relationship has been identified as a common strategy of change characteristic of all psychotherapies (Goldfried & Padawer, 1982), and thus we were interested in comparing the quality of the relationship in CBT and PDT. The scale that we chose to use in our comparative study, the Working Alliance Inventory (WAI; Horvath & Greenberg, 1989), complemented our intentions by being designed from a trans-theoretical perspective. It relies on Bordin's (1979) conceptualization of the alliance as consisting of three components: the development of a therapeutic bond (the mutual liking and attachment between the client and therapist); an agreement between the participants on the goals (objectives, or areas targeted for change); and an agreement on the tasks (global strategies and their associated techniques). We applied the observer form of the WAI to the change session dataset, where sessions were selected by the therapists as being particularly significant in terms of helping the client change.

Our findings revealed relatively high alliance scores for both therapy groups (that is, means of 6.39 for the CBT group and 5.82 for the PDT group on a seven-point scale), but significantly higher scores for the CBT group. A comparison of the standard deviations also indicated significantly higher variability in the PDT alliance scores. Our interpretation for this finding is that CBT puts a greater emphasis on providing structure within sessions, making the tasks and goals clearer and maintaining a collaborative relationship that can be used as a tool to enhance specific techniques. Most typically, the focus is on how change can take place in the client's life between sessions. PDT, on the other hand, focuses deliberately on the transference, using the relationship to address the client's problematic ways of dealing with others.

An informal inspection of lower alliance PDT sessions confirmed that there was a strong focus on the client's perception of the therapist and the therapeutic relationship (for example, being frustrated with the therapist's unhelpfulness; being defensive and not sharing emotion in and out of session; distrust of the therapist). This focus was notably absent in higher alliance PDT sessions. In lower alliance CBT sessions, the foci were on non-relationship issues (for example, the therapist highlighting past sexual abuse and its effect on the client while the client minimizes it; the therapist's focus on the client's contribution to interpersonal problems; the therapist's focus on his or her own experience at the expense of the client's).

Thus, in contrast to the PDT sessions, there was much less of a focus on the client's perception of the therapist and the therapeutic relationship.

In this same study, we also attempted to assess the relationship between alliance scores and client level of symptomatology, as measured after the selected session. Our findings indicated a negative correlation between client symptomatology and alliance scores across orientations, which was significant for PDT but not for CBT. This reflects either a greater difficulty for more symptomatic clients in PDT to engage in the work required in this type of therapy, or a tendency for low-alliance sessions to lead to an increase in client reports of symptomatology. Because the symptom measure was obtained after the session, statements of direction of impact are impossible.

Although there are some different possible interpretations to the above findings, the results are based on a unique dataset and raise many important questions relevant to the comparative nature of the alliance. Extensions of this line of research should focus on what factors contribute to a positive alliance in each of these therapies and whether strains on the alliance can have positive long-range therapeutic consequences.

As noted above, PDT in the change session dataset focused more on the client's dissatisfaction with the therapist than did CBT (Vakoch & Goldfried, 1994). But an examination of a broader range of sessions from the CT-outcome dataset shows that CT also draws clients' attention to issues involving the therapist (Vakoch, Goldfried, Castonguay & Raue, 1994). Sometimes this takes the form of therapists' comments that seem directed at repairing problems in the alliance, such as the therapist question: 'Is there anything about the way that we're talking about things, or the way that I'm approaching things, that bothers you?' At other times, the therapist raises issues that may cause a strain in the alliance, such as: 'You didn't do the thing that we had talked about at the end of our last session.' Regardless of whether the therapist addressed a pre-existing rupture in the alliance or created a strain, sessions in which CT focuses on the client–therapist relationship tended to have lower alliance ratings than sessions in which the therapist focused on interpersonal issues involving people other than the therapist.

The strength of the alliance was also related to the particular *way* that CT focused on issues involving clients and others. There was a definite trend toward all aspects of the alliance being lower in sessions focusing on the client–therapist relationship. These differences were significant for only some aspects of the alliance, however, and then only when comparing these sessions with sessions in which therapists focus on clients' interpersonal issues in certain ways. For example, although the *bond* was significantly lower for sessions focusing on the client–therapist relationship than for sessions dealing with the client's self-criticism, this difference was not significant for agreement on the *tasks* and *goals* of therapy. In contrast, sessions highlighting the client–therapist relationship were markedly lower on both *bond* and *goals* than sessions in which the therapist explored the client's relationships with others without challenging the accuracy of the client's beliefs. From these findings, it would seem that in CT a gentle exploration of issues is predictive of a strong alliance, that challenging a client – even by noting that the client is too self-critical – can cause some strain in the alliance, and that the alliance is lowest when the therapeutic relationship is a focus of discussion in-session.

Practical applications   As noted previously, despite the process of therapy often being intrinsically interpersonal in nature – even when clients explore their internal experience, this often arises in the context of an interpersonal trigger – there are times when therapists may focus more explicitly on this interpersonal context. For example, take the previous example of the male client who felt anxious, insecure and worthless after an encounter with his boss. Therapists may choose to focus on intrapersonal issues, such as mentioned in the earlier section (for example, fantasies, emotional reactions, interpretations or self-evaluations). Alternatively, they may choose to highlight the interpersonal trigger for these internal experiences, namely the actions of his boss, or they may choose to highlight the effect of the client on his boss. We define a focus by the therapist on interpersonal functioning when therapists call attention to the client's relationship with others by either (1) noting the effect of another on the client or (2) noting the effect of the client on another.

Staying with the above example, if therapists choose an interpersonal focus (whether exclusively or as a precursor to intrapersonal exploration), there are several ways they may do this. They may note any number of the boss's actions or emotions (for example, calling the client into her office and questioning his work; exhibiting a stern, businesslike manner) and their effect on the client (for example, interpretation or fantasies of these behaviors; feelings; self-evaluations; client acting flustered, defensive, inexpressive). Conversely, therapists may also note any number of the client's actions (for example, actual performance on the work in question; behavior towards his boss like submissiveness, defensiveness, aggression) and their effect on his boss (for example, her manner of delivering feedback; her evaluation/opinion of the client).

Based on our preliminary empirical findings, CBT and PDT did not differ in their use of either of the above types of interpersonal links (effect of other on client or effect of client on other). CT shares a similar proportionate focus on the effect of others on the client, but focuses significantly less on the effect the client has on others. These findings suggest that the three orientations may not differ in noting interpersonal triggers for intrapersonal functioning, whatever the type of functioning (for example, fantasies, emotions, interpretations, etc.). Thus, all three orientations may deem it fruitful to identify these types of links, even CBT and CT, where the emphasis on situational contexts of internal reactions seems to be very often interpersonal in nature. Similarly, CBT and PDT deem it useful to note the effect of the client on others. This similarity, however, might disguise content differences in these types of links. For example, CBT may analyze the client's effect on others in the context of communication of assertiveness training, where the goals are to change the client's behavior toward others to ensure optimal interactions and outcomes. PDT, on the other hand, may make these links by emphasizing the negative impact on others of dysfunctional personality styles. CT, in contrast to CBT and PDT, does not focus as much on these types of links. This is consistent with the goals of CT, where the focus is much more on the client's internal experience and the subjective evaluation of interpersonal events. This seems to be a relative area of neglect for CT, and although consistent with its goals, CT may benefit by broadening its scope to deal with real negative impacts that clients have on others rather than naïvely attempting to replace all negative thoughts and self-evaluations with positive ones. In other words, CT could benefit by becoming somewhat more attentive to real skill deficits or abrasive personality styles.

As we turn to the specific types of interpersonal issues in CBT and PDT, we recognize two considerations that therapists might take into account as they work with clients having interpersonal difficulties. As noted above, although there is no difference in the *amount* of interpersonal focus in the two orientations, this similarity may obscure differences in the specific *content* of this interpersonal focus. There are a number of interpersonal issues that are focused on by both CBT and PDT: clients feeling too responsible for their partners; clients' relationships with family; clients' submission to or distancing themselves from others; and effective inter-actions between clients and others. However, it is important also to recognize differences of the content of interpersonal focus that characterize the two orientations, for it is here that we can learn to expand our range of options when dealing with clients.

CBT focuses more than PDT on clients' concerns with how others evaluate them. To return to the example of the client who felt worthless after meeting with his boss, CBT might highlight the client's tendency to feel inadequate if others criticize him. Or it might emphasize the client's belief that if he is not perfect in the eyes of others, he is a completely inadequate person. By challenging these maladaptive beliefs, CBT provides an alternative viewpoint from which clients can evaluate the actions and attitudes of others. Therapists from other orientations might well profit from this CBT emphasis on clients' tendencies to be constrained by what they believe are negative reactions of others.

As we have seen, in particularly good sessions PDT sometimes thematizes the therapeutic relationship, whereas CBT tends to ignore it. In these good PDT sessions, the therapist will often draw out the client's dissatisfactions with the therapist. This can serve the purpose of providing a corrective experience for clients by letting them know that it is acceptable to talk openly about their disappointments with others. Rather than focusing on clients' interactions with others that occur outside the session,

PDT tends to make concrete clients' interpersonal issues by dealing with them in the therapeutic relationship. Just as PDT may profit from increased attention to between-session experiences, CBT could benefit by focusing on clients' problems in the immediacy of the client–therapist dyad.

In addition to differences in what therapists of different orientations actually do in-session, there are also differences in how therapists with different backgrounds categorize interpersonal issues. CBT not only focuses more on the client's concerns with the evaluations of others, but clinicians trained in this approach can more readily discern these issues. Similarly, PDT spends more time on dealing with transference issues in therapy, and therapists trained in PDT more clearly see these issues as being more unique to therapy than do CBT judges. Regardless of orientation, then, therapists should be aware that the range of interventions they *use* as well as their ability to *perceive* different types of issues may at times be constrained by their theoretical frameworks. Thus, expanding therapeutic repertoires becomes a matter of being open to alternative practices as well as different ways of conceptualizing clinical issues.

Concerning the therapeutic relationship, practical applications reflect how much therapists from each orientation use the relationship and what treatment goals they are attempting to accomplish. For PDT, a good relationship and attachment to the therapist could function either curatively or to allow the client to withstand interpretations, which may concern the transference relationship. Confrontation and the examination of defenses and resistance, however, cause inevitable strains or fluctuations in the therapeutic relationship. Optimally, these strains are only temporary, and client expression of negative affect may indicate significant progress (for example, greater comfort in expressing anger). It is an empirical question, however, whether being attentive to and encouraging of these client expressions leads to eventual positive outcomes, and whether this holds true in different therapies. For CBT, a good relationship facilitates the influence of therapists and their interventions, increases their value as models of adaptive and effective behavior, and promotes positive expectations and counteracts despair. Given the emphasis on a collaborative relationship within this orientation, strains may occur for a number of reasons, but the presence of these strains is not seen as necessary for the process of change. For example, if a client completes a homework assignment, but without much enthusiasm, instead of exploring possible negative client reactions toward the therapist, CBT would be more likely to reinforce the client for its completion and point out its benefits. Optimally, treatment goals can be reached without a focus on the relationship with the therapist, but quite likely there are times when CBT emphasizes support and collaboration at the expense of addressing negative feelings toward the therapist or therapy that might enhance treatment efficacy.

In spite of this possibility of CBT minimizing clients' negative reactions to the therapist in sessions that the therapist judged to be particularly good, there is evidence that in a wider range of sessions therapists do focus on these issues. As we have seen, CT does sometimes draw attention to the client's relationship with the therapist, and this occurs in sessions with a poor alliance. There are two interpretations of this finding, each with its own lesson. One is that the low alliance suggests that the work of therapy is impeded, and the source of the problem must be found for there to be progress. A possible cause of a client's dissatisfaction is something the therapist has done. If the therapist can directly address this issue, the obstacle might be overcome. An example of this would be when therapists raise the question of whether the way they are dealing with the client is creating a problem. In this case, the strain occurred before the therapist focused on his/her impact on the client. This example deals with clinicians' attempts to strengthen the alliance by probing for possible client dissatisfaction.

Alternatively, the alliance might start out sound, but the therapist may feel it is necessary to bring up issues that could strain the alliance. For example, in CT a central part of the treatment plan is often having clients complete homework assignments. Unless clients do this, their prospects for improvement may be limited. Thus, one can imagine a scenario in which the client comes into the session feeling quite satisfied with the therapist, but then hears the therapist comment on the client's failure to follow through on what was agreed upon in the previous session. In this instance, the therapist may have needed to confront the client directly about not complying with an earlier agreement. Clinicians should be aware, however, that this may make the working relationship with the client more tense, at least in the short run.

Process-outcome findings: Intrapersonal aspects

Our above review of comparative process findings suggest that (1) there are some shared therapeutic foci among all three orientations, although there appears to be the least overlap between CT and PDT; (2) there are some unique foci that seem to distinguish among the three orientations; and (3) some areas of client functioning that are emphasized to equivalent degrees among different schools may be emphasized for entirely different purposes. With all three of these observations in mind, we now turn to findings that relate specific focus areas in treatment to client post-treatment adjustment and functioning. In doing so, we will attempt to present the findings in the context of theory, and in the context of the information obtained from the comparative process work.

The CT-outcome study was conducted to determine the aspects of CT that were most associated with client improvement at the end of treatment. An expectation grounded in CT theory is that focusing on 'cognitive' elements should be linked to post-treatment gain (Beck, Rush, Shaw & Emery, 1979). As has been found elsewhere (Jones & Pulos, 1993), however, such a focus also was not demonstrated by our investigations to reliably predict treatment success, as none of the following was associated with reduced symptomatology; a focus on client expectations, self-evaluations, thoughts, self-observations, imagined reactions of others; challenges to clients' beliefs about reality; explication of intrapersonal patterns or intra-personal consequences.

Another theoretically unexpected finding was that a focus on clients' intrapersonal consequences, a key CT technique, was actually negatively associated with improvement in the CT-outcome dataset (Castonguay, Goldfried, Wiser, Raue & Hayes, in press). As noted earlier, a focus on intrapersonal consequences attempts to highlight how one aspect of intrapersonal functioning (thoughts, feelings, actions) causes or is associ-ated with another, and includes therapeutic statements such as: 'You see that when you think that way, it makes you feel depressed'; 'Telling yourself that you're worthless leads to the self-hatred'; 'Counter those thoughts of failure with a review of your successes, and then see how that makes you feel.' Interestingly, a qualitative analysis suggests that sessions high in this focus often involved clients who were feeling negatively toward the CT rationale and tasks. The therapists responded to this resistance by increasing their explanations of the cognitive route to change, highlighting the need for understanding intrapersonal consequences. Perhaps such a strict adherence to the application of treatment may be self-defeating, while a more moderate, appropriate use of such a focus, as well as a different exploration of client resistance, might be useful.

One process that was expected to result in treatment gains in CT that did hold up was how much therapists prescribed between-session *behavioral* assignments (Hayes, Castonguay & Goldfried, in press). Such behavioral assignments included tasks aimed at behavioral activation, practicing behavioral skills and behavioral coping strategies, and making changes in one's environment. In this CT study of depressed clients, these behavioral assignments were positively associated both with symptom reduction at post-therapy and with a longer time to relapse. Perhaps such assignments helped clients to learn new skills, new methods of coping and ways of stabilizing their environments that helped to relieve symptoms and prevent the return of depression. Surprisingly, however, the prescription of between-session *cognitive* assignments was not associated with any outcome measures in this study. Here again, we find that processes predicted to be efficacious by CT, at least in our limited number of investigations, do not seem to account for significant patient change.

A second process found to predict decreased symptomatology in CT was depth of in-session client emotional experiencing (Castonguay et al., in press). Thus, clients who achieved deeper levels of affective experience during their sessions of treatment had more symptom reduction at the conclusion of therapy. Although speculative, two interpretations are offered for the finding. First, it is possible that core 'irrational' beliefs are best modified in the context of high affective arousal (Mahoney, 1991). Thus, clients who had more access to their emotional experience, and expressed such experience in-session, might have been more able to deeply restructure the thinking that was thought to be associated with their depression. A second possibility is that allowing oneself to experience deeper emotional states leads to increased awareness about one's needs, which then in turn might facilitate behavioral changes (Greenberg & Safran, 1987). For instance, a passive client who allows herself to deeply experience her anger at her spouse's treatment of her may, following this affective experience, be more energized, inclined and motivated to make changes in how she responds to him.

Turning to CBT in the comparative-outcome dataset, we found a trend that demonstrated an association between a therapeutic focus on clients' intrapersonal links and decreased symptomatology at post-treatment for a sample of depressed patients (Kerr, Goldfried, Hayes, Castonguay & Goldsamt, 1992). Note that this contrasts with the finding from the CT-outcome study, also with depressed patients, that such a focus was unrelated to outcome. It is unclear at present why this discrepancy exists. It could be that the types of links drawn by cognitive and cognitive-behavioral therapists differ, such as with CT's links being more focused on the relationship between thoughts and emotions, while CBT's links are more focused on the relationship between affect and behaviors. Content analyses are warranted for such ambiguous findings.

We also found in the comparative-outcome study that therapists' challenges to clients' perceptions of reality were related to symptom relief at post-therapy. This finding of the possible positive impact of cognitive-behavioral therapists challenging their clients' views of reality was particularly interesting because in the same dataset the reverse was found for the psychodynamic therapists. Here, a negative association was demonstrated between a focus on challenging the clients' reality and symptom relief. As this finding was particularly intriguing, we followed it up with informal qualitative analyses in order to determine how it might be that one orientation's use of such challenges was associated with improvement, while the other's was not. Our content analysis helped to clarify our confusion. When cognitive-behavioral therapists encouraged clients to differentiate between reality and their distorted sense of reality, they seemed to be conveying the message that 'Things are not as *bad* as you think they are'. For example, challenges of this sort include: 'Do you really think there's no hope for you?', 'It wasn't your fault that she was unhappy with her life' and 'You're more courageous than you think'. By contrast, when psychodynamic therapists employed this intervention, they tended to communicate that 'Things are not as *good* as you think', as in 'You must have contributed to the breakup of your marriage too', 'Getting better is going to be more work than you seem to anticipate' and 'There was hostility in that message, not just facts'. What these findings may point to is a differential emphasis between therapies on either reframing circumstances in a positive light, on the one hand, or revealing the clients' own contribution to his or her present problems, on the other. This CBT finding is in keeping with CT's emphasis, discussed earlier, on helping the client to see his or her present reality for what it is presumed to be in actuality – more positive than he or she is able to appreciate.

Psychodynamic therapists, while also seeming invested in helping their clients perceive their present reality more accurately, see a more complex reality, of which the client has a greater part in creating than he or she presently imagines. And one potential effect of this type of challenge might be increased symptomatology. What we don't know is whether this indicates an unhelpful, or even hurtful, intervention, or whether perhaps it is simply the first phase of something that is ultimately useful. We can imagine that being challenged to see one's reality as more complicated, negative or more one's own responsibility might leave one feeling at least temporarily distressed. As suggested in the finding by Levenson and Overstreet (1994), if this ultimately leads one to take more responsibility for one's circumstances, then it might ultimately lead to decreased symptomatology. Perhaps in PDT one must feel worse before feeling better, while in CBT one simply must feel better.

Practical applications   Several therapeutic strategies appear to be related to treatment gains. First, designing inter-session assignments that encourage clients to experiment with new behaviors or consolidate new skills appears helpful to clients. There are likely two reasons for the usefulness of such homework assignments. First, any success experiences with new behaviors would tend to enhance mood, bolster self-confidence and heighten hope for further change. Second, new and appropriate skills and behaviors used by clients are likely to elicit positive feedback from people in their environment and/or result in more need satisfaction for them.

To date, assigning therapeutic homework has been associated more with behavior therapy than with psychodynamic interventions. We invite a shifting of this imbalance. Certainly, as external pressure for briefer courses of treatment increase, we believe that all types of therapists will of necessity look more to adjunctive help from inter-session therapeutic work. We also believe that encouraging clients to take risks with new behaviors conveys confidence in their abilities to change and grow, a supportive stance for any therapist to take.

Another process associated with change is heightened client affective experiencing. It seems that when our clients get emotional, deeper and perhaps more enduring shifts occur for them. The reason for this is probably varied. A heightened emotional state may make our clients' cognitions more susceptible to change, it may bring up suppressed or repressed historical material that can then be addressed and integrated, and/or it may result in the hoped for reduction of the affective experience. There is mounting evidence that facilitating clients' affective experience of their issues can lead to positive shifts for them. This means that a move away from 'talking about' their affective experience, to an in-the-moment 'experiencing of' affective experience is critical.

Methods to facilitate such in-the-moment emotional experiencing are then needed. A host of Gestalt techniques are often used for this purpose, and several will be discussed briefly. Attention to bodily cues is one vast area of intervention that is typically underutilized by cognitive, behavioral and psychodynamic therapists. This method is typically used to facilitate clients' awareness of emotional reactions that they are presently unaware of or to which they are not attending. By directing their awareness to the physical expression of affect, they are most likely to connect with the fuller emotional experience underlying it. Therapists may make observations of bodily signs ('I see tears in your eyes as you talk', 'I notice your body closes up when you bring that up', 'Are you aware that you are clenching your fist right now?') or prescribe the exaggeration of bodily cues ('Really exaggerate the tapping of your foot right now', 'Let yourself sigh like that some more, but even louder').

Another technique to move from 'talking about' an experience to 'having' an experience in-the-moment is to use the empty chair technique. If clients, for example, are discussing their spouse, they are likely to talk about what distresses them about the spouse, what they would like the spouse to really know about them, what they need from the spouse, how the spouse makes them feel, how they would like the spouse to make them feel, etc. Therapists can move the discussion from a low-level emotional discussion where the client talks 'about' these things, to a deeper emotional experience by directing the client to picture the spouse in an empty chair, and to say these same things to the spouse, as if the spouse were really there.

Still another method of facilitating emotional immediacy is to bring the discussion into the present with comments such as, 'What are you aware of feeling as you tell me about that?' or 'How does it feel to be here with me today?' Again, it seems that while the ultimate purpose of facilitating emotional immediacy may differ by orientation, its potential for efficacy does not.

A third important finding to note is that providing positive reframing of clients' experiences and their views of self may alleviate some depressive symptomatology, at least in the short-term. Challenges to clients' beliefs that are of the flavor 'Things are not as bad as you presently think' have been found to be associated with a reduction in symptomatology. Examples of such positive reframing are: 'You are more articulate than you give yourself credit for', 'You simply cannot hold yourself responsible for the happiness of everyone in your family' and 'It's not crazy to feel angry about that – in fact it seems quite reasonable'. Such reframing might nudge clients out of habitual ways of viewing something, and allow them to think about issues in new and more positive ways. Even though the statements are challenging clients' views, they tend to feel validating and supportive, which is often sorely needed. In sum, they offer at least a momentary step out of the maze of the depressive perspective.

A final practical point concerns the rigidity of treatment delivery. We found preliminary evidence to suggest that rigid adherence to treatment rationales and methods in the face of client disagreement were counter-productive. Although this finding was garnered from CT, it has face validity for all types of therapies. If our clients are telling us that our methods don't fit for them or seem inaccurate, we believe that it should give us pause. Certainly, such protestations may be due to resistance and fear, but just as certainly, clients may be giving us important and accurate information about how best to help them. Given our findings, it seems ill advised to continue to push our treatment rationale and methods if the client is resistant, for whatever reason. We believe that an exploration of the client's feelings and position is warranted, followed by a flexibility in treatment methods. Certainly, if we are at odds with our client with respect to the goals and methods of therapy – key aspects of the therapeutic alliance – progress cannot readily be made. Although it might be uncomfortable for us to put aside for the moment our 'tried and true' methods, we should remember that these same methods that worked so well with others are unlikely to be effective with clients who are resistant to them.

Process-outcome findings: Interpersonal aspects

In addition to studying those intrapersonal processes associated with positive outcome, we have also looked at those interpersonal factors that contributed to change. After controlling for clients' severity of symptomatology prior to receiving treatment, in the CT-outcome dataset, we found a good alliance in CT to be positively associated with improved depressive symptomatology. Similarly, the quality of alliance predicted clients' overall adjustment at the end of treatment, even after pre-treatment level of adjustment was controlled for (Castonguay et al., in press). These findings held true when the client was evaluated both at the middle and the end of therapy. In fact, in addition to the association between higher alliance and lower symptomatology as measured by an interviewer, the same relationship was found at the completion of therapy when the client completed the Beck Depression Inventory to provide a self-report of depressive symptoms. That is, the better the alliance was *during* CT, the lower the self-report of depressive symptomatology was *after* therapy was completed. The importance of the alliance in predicting outcome is understandable given the tendency of the alliance to be somewhat strained by the therapist's challenges of the client's irrational thoughts (Vakoch et al., 1994). It may be that when the alliance is very strong, the therapist is able to be more direct in pointing out the impact of the client's self-defeating cognitions. In therapeutic dyads with a low alliance, some of the client's most central problems may not get addressed adequately.

Examining these same sessions with an eye to other interpersonal relationships, we found that when cognitive therapists focused more on the client's parents, there was greater reduction of depressive symptoms from pre-treatment to post-treatment, as well as a longer time of recovery (Hayes et al., in press). This is consistent with the view that a major component of successful cognitive therapy involves changing the client's core assumptions (Beck et al., 1979). Since these assumptions were formed early in the client's life, in large part from his or her interactions with his or her parents, access to these assumptions might successfully be gained when the therapist focuses on the client's parents.

In contrast to the impact of focusing on the client's parents, however, a more general focus by cognitive therapists on trying to change clients' perceptions of other interpersonal issues was predictive of poor outcome (Hayes et al., in press). This is consistent with the finding in the comparative-outcome dataset that there was no change in the client's social adjustment or self-esteem when CBT highlighted the client's interpersonal functioning, but there was an improvement in both of these measures when PDT focused on interpersonal links between the client and others. This finding is also reflected in a broader pattern: when PDT focused on more 'transferential' aspects of the client, the clients improved more. Specifically, focusing on the therapist, the client's parent, self-observation and the expected or imagined reaction of others was predictive of better social adjustment, but only when PDT highlighted these aspects. This pattern does not hold for CBT, with the exception of the positive impact of focusing on parents that was noted above.

These findings may indicate that an interpersonal focus is effective in different situations for the orientations we examined. In PDT, a focus on a broad range of interpersonal interactions is effective. Clients in CT and CBT, however, seem to profit from an interpersonal focus in a much more narrow sense. Insofar as CT can address the client's core irrational beliefs through concentrating on the client's parents, an interpersonal focus may be effective.

Practical applications   The strength of the alliance in CT for depression is clearly important for a good outcome. As therapists consider exactly *how* to ensure a good alliance, it is useful to think about the three components of alliance that we have discussed. First, the *bond* between client and therapist should be nourished. Before a client will be willing to try new activities and re-evaluate ways of looking at things, a sense of trust and respect for the therapist is clearly needed. If therapists can convey their genuine liking and caring for the client, an environment has been developed for the other components of the alliance. Next, there should be agreement on *goals* of therapy. Unless client and therapist can reach a consensus about where their work together is headed, little can be accomplished. Finally, once they know what their joint objectives are, they must agree on the specific *tasks* that therapy will involve, for example completing homework assignments or discussing difficult experiences the client had as a child. By conceptualizing the alliance in terms of these three components, the therapist can begin to identify aspects of the therapeutic work that might be especially difficult for the client.

For example, clients may come to therapy with explicit goals that may seem secondary to the therapist. It is certainly not unusual to find that the stated purpose of the client for seeking treatment does not match the client's true motivation. As the therapist proceeds in trying to clarify the client's goals, the client may be resistant to seeing the true nature of his or her problem. In this case, therapists need to find a way that they and clients can work toward a commonly shared endpoint. If the goal is not or cannot be stated explicitly, the therapist should not be surprised to find the client dissatisfied with or confused by the uncertainty of the therapeutic process.

As to the particular persons who are an appropriate focus for therapy, across orientations it seems useful to focus on the client's parents. Whether the parent–child relationship is seen as important because it provided the basis for core beliefs or because it gave the client prototypical patterns for relating with others, in both CT and PDT this focus was related to good outcome. Although a focus on interpersonal issues in general was related to good outcome in PDT but poor outcome in CT, this does not mean that the broad range of interpersonal issues should be off-limits to CT. Rather, it may reflect a historical emphasis on intrapersonal functioning in CT. That is, CT sessions with a high interpersonal focus may have represented sessions in which the therapist was not doing effective CT. A possible solution is to make more explicit ways that CT can focus on the client's interpersonal issues with a broad range of individuals.

Similarly, as we noted above, PDT focused on clients' dissatisfaction with their therapists in sessions that the therapists deemed particularly good, while a focus on the therapist was not found in CBT in comparably selected sessions, but was found in CT when sessions were randomly sampled. While a focus on these transferential issues may not seem to play as central a role in CT and CBT as they do in PDT, this does not necessarily reflect anything that is intrinsically incompatible with CT and CBT. Again, the point may be that CT and CBT therapists could profit from a greater focus on themselves in session, but that their orientations do not currently have adequate formulations about how that could be done most effectively. Future work by researchers and clinicians alike might help provide such guidelines.

Conclusions

On the basis of the comparative process analyses conducted thus far, we have found some commonalities between the various orientations, which, upon closer inspection, also reveal important, subtle differences nested within them. For example, contrary to theoretical expectations, we have preliminary findings to indicate that cognitive-behavioral and psycho-dynamic-interpersonal therapists focus to an equivalent degree on increasing clients' awareness of both intrapersonal and interpersonal issues. However, beyond this common focus lie important differences between the orientations. Although there are similarities in the kinds of interpersonal issues on which both orientations focus (for example, clients' tendencies to withdraw, excessive feelings of responsibility for others), cognitive-behavior therapy is more likely to focus on clients' excessive concerns about the evaluation of others, and psychodynamic therapy more typically deals with clients' dissatisfaction with the therapist. Further, the cognitive-behavior therapy focus on intrapersonal consequences (provided it is presented within the context of a good therapeutic alliance) is positively related to clients' improvement in symptomatology, while this is not the case in the psychodynamic sessions. Conversely, the psychodynamic focus on interpersonal consequences is related to improvements in clients' level of self-esteem and social adjustment, while this is not found for the clients in cognitive behavior therapy.

A parallel preliminary finding was that of the common therapeutic focus of increasing clients' awareness as a means of challenging their distorted perception of reality. Used in both cognitive-behavioral and psychodynamic therapies, the therapist's attempt to correct a client's view of reality was found to be positively related to a decrease in symptomatology for clients undergoing cognitive-behavior therapy, while negatively relating to symptom reduction for clients receiving psychodynamic-interpersonal therapy. The reason for such a differential impact may lie in the different ways that therapists of these two orientations use this intervention. In cognitive-behavior therapy this challenge to distorted beliefs is used to show clients that things are better than they presently think, while in psycho-dynamic therapy it tends to be used to show clients that things are worse than they presently believe.

This finding of a commonality that, upon closer inspection, actually comprises an important difference, is found again with respect to clients' affective experiencing. Equivalent depths of experiencing were obtained in both types of therapy during important change sessions. However, the psychodynamic therapists perceived *higher* levels of client emotional exploration as reflective of clinical significance, whereas cognitive-behavior therapists found *lower* levels of emotional experiencing to be clinically important. Nonetheless, in another dataset, higher levels of clients' emotional experience facilitated symptom reduction in cognitive therapy for depression. A similar unexpected positive relationship was obtained between a cognitive therapy focus on clients' parents and a decrease in depression.

An analysis of the therapeutic alliance in cognitive therapy found that it was positively related to decrease in depression. When the therapeutic alliance was compared in good sessions of cognitive-behavior therapy and psychodynamic therapy, the alliance was found to be higher and less variable in the former. Moreover, an inverse relationship was found between client symptomatology and a good alliance for the psychodynamic, but not the cognitive-behavior therapists. It is possible that cognitive-behavior therapy seems to have less difficulty in maintaining a good alliance with symptomatic clients than does psychodynamic therapy.

Based on an analysis of a demonstration case in the treatment of depression, we have also found that cognitive therapy (that is, Beck) focused primarily on cognitive shifting as a means to bring about change, while both cognitive-behavioral (that is, Meichenbaum) and psychodynamic (that is, Strupp) therapies matched their focus on intrapersonal cognitive shifts with an additional focus on the interpersonal impact that the client had on others. With respect to the content of material focused on, analyses showed a pattern of in-session, current time-frame and future-oriented material in the cognitive and cognitive-behavioral sessions, contrasted with a focus on material from the clients' childhood and adult past in the psychodynamic session.

Our findings in general seem to indicate that differences across orientations with regard to common change processes likely reflect unique higher order conceptualizations of client issues, and implicit assumptions of routes to therapeutic change. As noted earlier, uncovering common factors between orientations has a dual purpose: sometimes we might find that one orientation indeed walks their clients over the same bridge as another orientation, while at other times we might find that the same type of bridge can be used by different orientations to cross very different types of terrain. Both kinds of information are useful, as they both inform us regarding what therapists do, for what reason, and with what result.

Taken together, our results indicate that cognitive-behavioral sessions seem to be relatively optimistic, collaborative and both present- and future-oriented, while psychodynamic sessions, which deal with problematic interpersonal patterns, are more pessimistic and conflictual, highlighting past difficulties. Given the preliminary findings that associate therapist focus with client outcome, it seems that the former may be better designed for client symptom reduction, while the latter is more impactful on clients' problematic patterns of interpersonal relations. Such findings, if they hold up under further scrutiny, have clear implications for ultimately combining and integrating aspects of these two orientations.

References

Alexander, F., & French, T.M. (1946). *Psychoanalytic therapy*. New York: Ronald.

Beck, A.T., Rush, A.J., Shaw, B.F., & Emery, G. (1979). *Cognitive therapy of depression*. New York: Guilford.

Bordin, E. (1979) The generalizability of the psychoanalytic concept of the working alliance. *Psychotherapy, 16,* 252–260.

Castonguay, L.G., Goldfried, M.R., Wiser, S.L., Raue, P.J., & Hayes, A.M. (in press). Predicting the effect of cognitive therapy for depression: A study of unique and common factors. *Journal of Consulting and Clinical Psychology*.

Dahl, H., Kaechele, H., & Thoma, H. (Eds.). (1988). *Psychoanalytic process research strategies*. Heidelberg: Springer.

Frank, J.D. (1961). *Persuasion and healing*. Baltimore, MD: Johns Hopkins University Press.

Freedheim, D.K. (Ed.). (1992). *History of psychotherapy: A century of change*. Washington, DC: American Psychological Association.

Goldfried, M.R., & Padawer, W. (1982). Current status and future directions in psychotherapy. In M.R. Goldfried (Ed.), *Converging themes in psychotherapy* (pp. 3–49). New York: Springer.

Greenberg, L.S., & Pinsof, W.M. (Eds.). (1986). *The psychotherapeutic process: A research handbook*. New York: Guilford.

Greenberg, L.S., & Safran, J.D. (1987). *Emotion in psychotherapy*. New York: Guilford.

Guidano, V.W., & Liotti, G. (1983). *Cognitive processes and emotional disorders: A structural approach to psychotherapy*. New York: Guilford.

Hayes, A.M., Castonguay, L.G., & Goldfried, M.R. (in press). The effectiveness of targeting vulnerability factors for depression in cognitive therapy. *Journal of Consulting and Clinical Psychology*.

Hollon, S.D., DeRubeis, R.J., Evans, M.D., Wiemer, M.J., Garvey, M.J., Grove, W., & Tuason, V.B. (1992). Cognitive therapy and pharmacotherapy for depression: Singly and in combination. *Archives of General Psychiatry, 49*, 774–781.

Horvath, A.O., & Greenberg, L.S. (1989). Development and validation of the Working Alliance Inventory. *Journal of Counseling Psychology, 36*, 223–233.

Jones, E.E., & Pulos, S.M. (1993). Comparing the process of psychodynamic and cognitive-behavioral therapies. *Journal of Consulting and Clinical Psychology, 61*, 306–316.

Kerr, S., Goldfried, M.R., Hayes, A.M., Castonguay, L.G., & Goldsamt, L.A. (1992). Interpersonal and intrapersonal focus in cognitive-behavioral and psychodynamic-interpersonal therapies: A preliminary analysis of the Sheffield Project. *Psychotherapy Research, 2*, 266–276.

Levenson, H., & Overstreet, D. (1994). *Stages of meaningful change and clinical significance in time-limited dynamic psychotherapy*. Unpublished manuscript.

Mahoney, M.J. (1991). *Human change processes: Theoretical bases for psychotherapy*. New York: Basic Books.

Shapiro, D.A., & Firth, J. (1987). Prescriptive v. exploratory psychotherapy: Outcome of the Sheffield Psychotherapy Project. *British Journal of Psychiatry, 151*, 790–799.

Shostrom, E.L. (Producer) (1986). Three approaches to psychotherapy: III [Film]. Corona del Mar, CA: Psychological & Educational Films, Inc.

Vakoch, D.A., & Goldfried, M.R. (1994, June–July). *Psychodynamic-interpersonal and cognitive-behavioral views of interpersonal issues*. Paper presented at the meeting of the Society for Psychotherapy Research, York, England.

Vakoch, D.A., Goldfried, M.R., Castonguay, L.G., & Raue, P.J. (1994, June–July). *Interpersonal therapeutic focus and the working alliance*. Paper presented at the meeting of the Society for Psychotherapy Research, York, England.

Wiser, S.L., & Goldfried, M.R. (1993). A comparative study of emotional experiencing in psychodynamic-interpersonal and cognitive-behavioral therapies. *Journal of Consulting and Clinical Psychology, 61*, 892–895.

6

A Cognitive-Behavioral Approach to Couples' Problems: A Program of Research and Its Clinical Applications

Norman Epstein and Donald H. Baucom

Research on cognitive and behavioral factors in couple relationships

In the early 1980s, we became aware of each other's research on cognitive and behavioral factors influencing marital adjustment, through reading each other's journal publications and attending each other's presentations at the annual conventions of the Association for Advancement of Behavior Therapy (AABT). Initially, one of us (Baucom) tended to focus more on the traditional components of behavioral marital therapy (contracting, communication training and problem-solving training) (cf. Jacobson & Margolin, 1979), while the other (Epstein) placed an emphasis on applying a cognitive mediation model typical of the cognitive therapies of Beck, Ellis and Meichenbaum (cf. Beck, 1976; Beck, Rush, Shaw & Emery, 1979; Ellis, 1962, 1976; Meichenbaum, 1977) to the conflicts and distress that often arise in couple relationships. However, each of us generally conceptualized marital interaction in an integrative manner that took into account the interplay of the behavioral interactions, cognitions and affective responses of two individuals in an intimate relationship. This integrative view was in keeping with the basic behavioral contingency and cognitive mediation principles of social learning theory (cf. Bandura, 1977) that have been the organizing concepts of behavioral marital therapy, from its roots in the work of writers such as Stuart (1969, 1980). In each of our individual research programs, we investigated both behavioral and cognitive factors associated with marital distress. Given the considerable overlap in our ways of conceptualizing the processes involved in satisfying versus distressed relationships, as well as the complementarity of our empirical work, we formed a collaborative research program that has continued to the present. The major goals of our individual and joint research have been: (1) to increase knowledge about cognitive, behavioral and affective factors that influence conflict and subjective satisfaction in marriage and similar intimate relationships; (2) to develop new methods for assessing spouses' cognitions concerning their relationships; and (3) to develop and evaluate treatments for marital problems.

The following is a review of our individual and collaborative empirical studies that have examined couple relationships within a cognitive-behavioral theoretical framework. Because each of us is engaged in the teaching and practice of couples therapy on a regular basis, there are significant links between our research and clinical work. On the one hand, experiences with our clients have shaped our thinking about constructive and dysfunctional processes in close relationships, and, on the other hand, the results of our studies and those of colleagues in the couples research area have influenced how we assess and treat relationship problems.

Initial studies of cognitive factors in marital distress

As described above, one of the major goals of our research has been to increase knowledge about specific cognitive, behavioral and affective variables that are associated with levels of satisfaction versus distress in couples' relationships. There is a substantial body of empirical evidence that members of distressed couples are more likely than non-distressed partners to engage in exchanges of negative behavior and to exhibit deficits in problem-solving skills (for reviews, see Baucom & Epstein, 1990, and Weiss & Heyman, 1990). These findings have supported the systematic use of behavioral marital therapy procedures such as communication training and problem-solving training in the treatment of relationship problems. However, until recently there has been little research testing observations in the theoretical and clinical literature that partners' behaviors toward each other are influenced by their cognitions about themselves, each other and their relationship. For example, Epstein (1982) described the use of cognitive therapy procedures to (1) modify partners' unrealistic beliefs about intimate relationships, (2) challenge their negative attributions about the causes of each other's negative (as well as positive) behaviors, and (3) improve their skill at using self-instruction to decrease destructive responses toward each other (for example, verbal attacks) and to increase constructive problem-solving. Given the need for empirical evidence to support such cognitive interventions, which have become increasing popular among couple therapists, one component of our research has been focused on the question of whether cognitions such as beliefs and attributions about relationships are indeed related to marital distress and conflict. This section describes the initial studies that each of us conducted concerning marital cognition prior to our collaborative efforts. These studies are reviewed in the context of current theory and research by other marital investigators.

Epstein and Eidelson developed the Relationship Belief Inventory (RBI; Eidelson & Epstein, 1982; Epstein & Eidelson, 1981), a questionnaire that assesses the degree to which an individual adheres to potentially unrealistic beliefs concerning intimate relationships. Epstein and Eidelson's intent was to assess beliefs that most likely had formed over the course of an individual's life, shaped by his or her idiosyncratic experiences, such as observations of parental and other couple relationships. Theoretically, when an individual's beliefs are unrealistic (that is, when they involve standards that are unlikely to be met in most real-life relationships), the individual may become distressed when the characteristics of his or her current relationship do not match the beliefs. This way of conceptualizing one source of marital distress and conflict is consistent with the concepts of irrational and dysfunctional beliefs in the cognitive psychotherapy literature (for example, Beck et al., 1979; Ellis, 1962), as well as with theory and research on how relatively stable cognitive schemata serve as 'templates' by which individuals evaluate their daily experiences (cf. Fiske & Taylor, 1991).

Based on a survey of marital therapists and an examination of clinical literature, RBI scales were constructed to assess the beliefs that (1) disagreement is destructive, (2) partners should be able to 'mindread' each other's thoughts and emotions, (3) partners cannot change themselves and their relationship, (4) one should be a perfect sexual partner, and (5) marital problems are due to innate differences in needs and personalities between men and women. A number of research studies have indicated that spouses who score higher on the RBI report lower marital satisfaction, less commitment to working on relationship problems, more pessimism about potential progress in marital therapy and more negative communication between partners, and they actually exhibit more negative behavior toward each other when instructed to discuss their relationship problems in a laboratory setting (Bradbury & Fincham, 1993; Eidelson & Epstein, 1982; Epstein & Eidelson, 1981; Epstein, Pretzer & Fleming, 1987; Fincham & Bradbury, 1987; Gaelick, Bodenhausen & Wyer, 1985). In addition, in marital therapy outcome studies (for example, Baucom & Lester, 1986; Baucom, Sayers & Sher, 1990; Epstein, Pretzer & Fleming, 1982; Huber & Milstein, 1985), the RBI has been found to be a sensitive measure of cognitive change. Thus, research with the RBI has supported theoretical views that adherence to potentially unrealistic beliefs about intimate relationships is related to partners' negative emotional and behavioral responses toward each other. However, the studies have been correlational and have not answered the question of whether partners' beliefs actually cause the problematic emotional and behavioral responses.

It is also noteworthy that Epstein and Eidelson (1981) found that the unrealistic relationship beliefs assessed by the RBI were more strongly associated with couples' marital distress than were the more individually oriented beliefs tapped by the Irrational Beliefs Test (IBT; Jones, 1968), a scale based on the irrational beliefs described by Ellis (1962). This finding appears to reflect 'cognitive specificity', in which relationship distress is linked with beliefs that have specific relationship themes. It is a basic premise of cognitive therapy (cf. Beck et al., 1979) that therapeutic interventions need to be focused on altering the specific content themes that elicit clients' distress, and in the case of marital problems, our research suggests that the more salient themes are dyadic (for example, viewing disagreement as destructive; expecting mindreading) rather than individual (for example, perfectionism; low frustration tolerance).

In the early 1980s, marital theoreticians and researchers also were influenced by the increasing focus on attributional processes in the social psychology and psychopathology literatures. For example, Doherty (1981) drew upon Abramson, Seligman and Teasdale's (1978) attributional learned helplessness model of depression, as he proposed that marital and family conflict is influenced by the attributions that the parties make about events in their relationships. Doherty predicted that when an individual attributes another family member's negative behavior to causes that are voluntary versus involuntary, global versus specific, stable versus unstable, and based on negative versus positive intent, the individual is more likely to exhibit blaming attitudes and behavior toward the other person. Doherty also proposed that the family member who makes global, stable, negative attributions about other members' negative behavior also is likely to have low efficacy expectancies (that is, believes that he or she cannot act in ways that will solve the relationship problems) and will engage in learned helplessness responses such as giving up attempts at problem-solving. Baucom (1987) described a number of functions that can be served when spouses make attributions about each other's behavior, including: (1) increasing the individual's perception that he or she understands the partner; (2) giving the individual a sense of control over his or her life, either by planning ways to alter causes of a partner's behavior or by communicating the attributions to the partner and inducing the partner to change; (3) reducing one's disappointment within the marriage by making stable, global attributions about the partner and thus lowering one's expectancies concerning change; (4) enhancing the individual's self-esteem by blaming the partner for relationship problems; and (5) enhancing positive views of one's partner or marriage by attributing negative partner behavior to external causes (for example, job stress rather than a lack of caring).

Theoretical predictions that particular types of attributions would be associated with spouses' marital distress and negative behavioral approaches to solving their problems have led to a large number of empirical studies, focused both on developing measures of couples' attributions and on testing the predictions about correlates of attributions. Our own individual and joint research on marital cognition has addressed both of these issues. The following is a summary of our efforts to investigate the roles of attributions in marital relationships and to develop measures of attributions that can be used in research and clinical practice.

The large majority of studies of couples' attributions have assessed the dimensions of causal attributions (stable–unstable; global–specific; self, partner or other external locus) derived from learned helplessness theory, and they have provided support for the prediction that distressed spouses would be more likely than non-distressed spouses to attribute their partners' negative behavior to stable, global sources within their partners (see Baucom & Epstein, 1990, and Bradbury & Fincham, 1990, for reviews). In contrast, non-distressed spouses are more likely to attribute positive partner behaviors to global and stable causes. In some studies (for example, Baucom, Bell & Duhe, 1982) spouses were asked to report attributions for hypothetical partner behaviors, whereas other investigations (for example, Fincham, Beach & Baucom, 1987) asked spouses to make attributions about behaviors that actually occurred in their marriages. Overall, the findings from these studies of causal attribution dimensions indicate that in clinical practice it is important to assess partners' attributional inferences about relationship problems and examine whether particular types of attributions are contributing to distress and negative approaches to resolving marital conflicts.

Baucom, Sayers & Duhe (1989) investigated another important question concerning marital attributions; namely, whether individuals have stable attributional *styles*, in which they make similar types of attributions for their partners' behaviors across various situations. Using their Dyadic Attribution Inventory, which was developed to assess couples' attributions about hypothetical relationship events, Baucom et al. examined variability in individuals' ratings of positive and negative relationship events on causal dimensions (self, partner, outside circumstances, stable–unstable and global–specific) from one situation to another. For both men and women, there was considerable variation in the number of types of attribution used to explain causes of both positive and negative partner behavior. The individuals who used few different types of attributions across situations appear to be employing an attributional style, in contrast to individuals whose attributions varied more from one situation to another. Baucom, Sayers and Duhe (1989) also found that spouses who showed a more restricted attributional style reported higher levels of marital distress. Because these results were correlational, it is not possible to determine whether using an attributional style produces distress (for example, rigidity in interpreting relationship events contributes to rigid behavioral inter-actions and discord) or whether marital distress leads spouses to focus on particular explanations for their partners' behaviors. In the absence of more information about causality between attributions and marital distress, it seems prudent for the clinician to consider both possible causal processes when evaluating the extent to which their clients make particular types of attributions about each other's behavior.

Although earlier studies of couples' attributions focused on the causal dimensions derived from learned helplessness theory, there has been an increasing emphasis on investigating particular aspects of attributional *content* that may be associated with distress. Epstein et al. (1987) found that greater marital distress was associated with spouses' tendencies to attribute relationship problems to a lack of love and malicious intent on their partner's part, as well as to their partner's behavior and personality (as opposed to their own). These content aspects of spouses' attributions were assessed with the Marital Attitude Survey (MAS; Pretzer, Epstein &

Fleming, 1991), which asks respondents to report the degrees to which they believe that problems in their relationship are associated with the characteristics noted above (for example, 'It seems as though my partner deliberately provokes me.'). Similarly, Fincham and his colleagues (Fincham, Beach & Nelson, 1987; Fincham & Bradbury, 1987) found that attributions concerning partner motives (positive versus negative intent; selfish motivation; blameworthiness) were equally or more strongly correlated with marital distress than were attributions concerning causal dimensions. These initial findings contributed to the development of our current conceptualization and research on the content of couples' attributions and other cognitions concerning their relationships, which are described later.

Thus, before we began our collaboration, each of us had focused increasingly on assessing particular types of cognitive factors that theoretically affect spouses' affective and behavioral responses to each other, and on conducting studies to examine such roles of marital cognition. In addition, each of us had conducted outcome research evaluating the impact of cognitive restructuring on marital maladjustment. The following section describes these treatment studies.

Investigations of cognitive restructuring for marital problems

Baucom (1982, 1984) initially conducted treatment outcome studies that compared the effectiveness of the major components of traditional behavioral marital therapy (BMT): contingency contracting and problem-solving/communication training. Consistent with the overall pattern of findings by other researchers, he found that the components were equally effective in reducing marital discord. Baucom's studies (Baucom, 1982; Baucom & Lester, 1986) also indicated that behavioral marital therapy was superior to waiting-list conditions in reducing behavioral presenting complaints and self-reported marital distress. Epstein and his colleagues (Epstein, DeGiovanni & Jayne-Lazarus, 1978; Epstein & Jackson, 1978) conducted studies that compared the effectiveness of assertiveness communication training with insight-oriented and minimal-attention couples' treatments that lacked behavioral interventions. The findings indicated that the behaviorally oriented treatment had greater impact on the specific assertive and non-assertive behaviors that had been the targets of the interventions, but the impact on overall marital satisfaction was minimal. Although our research demonstrated that behavioral interventions are effective in altering behavioral interactions of distressed couples, both of us saw a need to investigate the potential for improving the effectiveness of behavioral treatments by adding a focus on spouses' cognitions concerning their relationships. Consequently, in each of our research programs, a cognitive restructuring component was added to treatment outcome studies.

Epstein et al. (1982) randomly assigned distressed couples to two marital group treatments: (1) eight weeks of cognitive therapy that integrated the procedures of individual cognitive therapy (cf. Beck et al., 1979) with Epstein's (1982) focus on addressing partners' unrealistic beliefs and negative attributions concerning their relationships; or (2) eight weeks of communication training, which included four weeks of Guerney's (1977) relationship enhancement (RE) training and four weeks of couples' assertion training (Epstein, 1981; Epstein et al., 1978). They found that the cognitive restructuring intervention was more effective than the communication training in reducing spouses' adherence to unrealistic relationship beliefs and negative attributions, and in increasing perceived empathy between partners. The study did not include an assessment of change in couples' positive and negative behavior exchanges.

Baucom and Lester (1986) randomly assigned distressed couples to three conjoint treatments: (1) 12 weeks of behavioral marital therapy (BMT), including 6 weeks of communication and problem-solving training followed by 6 weeks of training in the use of quid pro quo contingency contracts; (2) 6 weeks of cognitive-behavioral therapy (CBT), focused on attributions and the expectations (potentially unrealistic beliefs) that spouses held for themselves and their partners, followed by 6 weeks of BMT (3 weeks on communication and problem-solving and 3 weeks on contracting); and (3) a 12-week waiting-list condition, followed by 12 weeks of treatment. The interventions were provided in a module format; for example, each of three CBT sessions focused on one attributional dimension (internal–external, global–specific or stable–unstable), with the therapist providing a didactic explanation of what is known about the impact of such attributions on marital discord, and then coaching the couple in applying the concepts to their own relationship. Baucom and Lester (1986) found that couples in both the BMT and CBT/BMT conditions improved significantly from pre-test to post-test in self-reported marital adjustment. Couples receiving only BMT improved on problem-solving, positive, and negative behaviors coded from their taped problem-solving discussions of relationship issues, but they exhibited little change on measures of marital cognitions. Husbands in the combined CBT/BMT condition showed both positive cognitive and behavioral changes, whereas wives exhibited cognitive change but only a behavioral change in the problem-solving category. Waiting-list couples showed minimal change.

Baucom, Sayers and Sher (1990) compared five treatment conditions: (1) 12 sessions of BMT; (2) six sessions of cognitive restructuring (CR) plus six sessions of BMT; (3) six sessions of BMT plus six of emotional expressiveness training (EET); three sessions of CR, six of BMT and three of EET; and waiting-list. The EET treatment focused on the communication skills of expressing emotions and responding empathically, as taught in Guerney's (1977) relationship enhancement approach. Although it had been hypothesized that supplementing BMT with CR and/or EET would increase its effectiveness, all four active treatments were virtually equally effective and superior to the waiting-list condition, on measures of behavioral, cognitive and affective improvement. The equivalence of the four groups was maintained when a more limited self-report follow-up assessment of marital satisfaction and requests for behavior change from the partner was conducted six months later. Although the findings were that adding cognitive restructuring and emotional expressiveness training to traditional BMT did not produce greater overall effectiveness compared to pure BMT, these results must be interpreted with caution. In particular, because the total number of therapy sessions was restricted to 12 due to research design considerations (that is, to keep clients' exposure to treatment equivalent across conditions), adding one type of intervention necessarily meant providing less of another. For example, in the treatment that included all three components, there were only three sessions of cognitive restructuring and three of emotional expressiveness training, and Baucom, Sayers and Sher (1990) noted that couples in this group were given fewer opportunities to practice applying the principles from didactic presentations to issues in their own relationships. This is an instance in which the requirements of research rigor did not allow therapists to provide each couple with as much of each treatment component as they needed. The equivalent effects of the four treatments does suggest that the three components had similar impact on marital adjustment, because substituting one for another did not decrease efficacy. Thus, providing less BMT and substituting some cognitive restructuring and/or emotional expressiveness training, in a 'module' format, did not result in more effective treatment, but neither did it result in reduced effectiveness. It remains for future studies to operationalize and evaluate marital therapy that integrates behavioral, cognitive and affective interventions.

Collaborative research on cognitive factors in marital maladjustment

Our collaborative work has included efforts to (1) develop more comprehensive models of marital interaction and dysfunction that take into account the interplay of behavior, cognition and emotion; (2) conduct research on the development of measures to tap the range of cognitive factors that may influence the quality of couples' relationships; and (3) present a systematic therapeutic approach for working with distressed couples. Initially, based on a review of theory and research on marital cognition, we proposed a taxonomy of five major classes of cognition that have been implicated in the development and maintenance of marital problems (Baucom & Epstein, 1990; Baucom, Epstein, Sayers and Sher, 1989). These include (a) *selective perception* (what each partner notices, out of the array of stimuli that occur during any interaction the couple have), (b) *attributions* (inferences about the determinants of events in their relationship), (c) *expectancies* (inferences about future events in the relationship), (d) *assumptions* (beliefs about the characteristics of individuals and intimate relationships) and (e) *standards* (beliefs about the characteristics that partners and their intimate relationships 'should' have.

Although varying degrees of research had been conducted on each of these forms of cognition, including our own studies of attributions and unrealistic beliefs (which included both assumptions and standards), we argued that progress in the field had been constrained by insufficient attention to some of these cognitive factors, as well as limited work on integrating them into a model of marital interaction. Through the late 1980s, the large majority of studies had focused on attributions, with a modest number of investigations of assumptions and standards (which in fact were not distinguished on Epstein and Eidelson's RBI), and few studies of selective perception and expectancies. Consequently, we developed a joint research program focused on constructing inventories to measure each of the five types of cognition in our taxonomy.

In constructing a model to describe the interrelationships among perceptions, attributions, expectancies, assumptions and standards, as well as their relations to partners' behavioral interactions and affective responses to each other (Epstein & Baucom, 1993), we were guided by the literatures on social cognition (cf. Fiske & Taylor, 1991), cognitive psychotherapies (cf. Beck et al., 1979; Ellis, 1962, 1976) and marital research (cf. Baucom & Epstein, 1990; Fincham & Bradbury, 1990). In addition, we believed that it was important to organize the assessment of all five types of cognition around a common set of content areas that have been identified in the marital literature as major issues that couples deal with in their relationships. Three include (1) the *boundaries* that partners consider appropriate between them (that is, how much autonomy versus sharing of time, activities, information), (2) how *control/power* is distributed between partners when making decisions about relationship issues, and (3) the degree of *investment* (various kinds of contributions) that partners make to their relationship. Thus, our goal has been to develop measures of selective perception, attributions, expectancies, assumptions and standards that all tap these common relationship content areas.

We began by constructing the Inventory of Specific Relationship Standards (ISRS; Baucom, Epstein, Rankin & Burnett, in press; Epstein, Baucom, Rankin & Burnett, 1991), writing items to tap individuals' personal standards about boundaries, power/control and investment in their relationships. Two subscales were constructed for the control/power dimension, focused on the *process* by which partners make decisions (for example, the degree to which one attempts to exert control during decision-making) and the *outcome* of decisions (the degree to which decisions represent compromises or one person's preferences). Similarly, two investment subscales were constructed, one concerning *instrumental investment* (efforts expended to accomplish tasks, such as household chores, for the relationship) and *expressive investment* (efforts to increase one's partner's happiness through acts of caring and concern). The ISRS addresses relationship content issues further by assessing each of the five content dimensions in each of 12 domains of relationship functioning: finances, affection, household tasks, relations with family, relations with friends, religion, sexual interaction, career issues, parenting, communicating negative thoughts and feelings, communicating positive thoughts and feelings, and leisure. Thus, the ISRS consists of 60 items.

Each ISRS item has three parts. First, the respondent is asked how often the behaviors described in the standard should occur in his or her relationship, on a five-point Likert scale ranging from 'never' to 'always'. Second, the respondent indicates whether or not he or she is satisfied with the way in which the standard is being met in the relationship, answering either 'yes' or 'no'. Finally, the respondent indicates how upsetting he or she finds it when the standard is not met, using a three-point scale, from 'not at all upsetting' to 'very upsetting'. It seemed important to include all three aspects of partners' standards because it was not clear a priori what aspect(s) would be associated with relationship distress.

We administered the ISRS and several other marital assessment instruments (for example, measures of marital satisfaction, communication patterns and desire that the partner make particular types of behavior changes) to a sample of 386 married couples recruited from a mailing list company's random sampling of couples in the areas surrounding Chapel Hill, North Carolina, and in Maryland suburbs near Washington, DC. Using US census data, we attempted to match the proportions of married couples nationally in terms of age, education and ethnic status. The results of the study were complex, but overall they demonstrated that the ISRS taps standards that are related to the quality of couples' relationships. The following is a summary of representative findings.

A factor analysis of the ISRS indicated clear factors for the intended boundary, control/power and investment dimensions of relationship standards; partners indeed conceptualize standards along these dimensions. Although we had hypothesized that differences between two partners' standards would be associated with distress, that correlation was weak. In addition, consistent with literature on unrealistic and irrational beliefs, as well as the clinical concept of dysfunctional 'enmeshment' in family relationships, we expected that partners who held extreme levels of standards would be more distressed. However, we found that the more that couples reported wanting fewer boundaries (that is, a lot of sharing), equal division of power and high relationship investment, the higher was their marital satisfaction. At least in our sample of community couples, the ISRS appeared to tap relationship-focused standards that enhance marital functioning. Furthermore, there were non-significant or trivial level gender differences in the standards assessed by the ISRS.

Knowing the degree to which an individual holds a relationship standard and knowing whether the individual is satisfied with how the standard is being met in his or her relationship (the first two questions asked about each standard) each accounted for unique variance in the statistical prediction of marital satisfaction scores. Responses to the third question, concerning how upsetting it is when standards are not met, did not add to the prediction of marital distress scores once the first two questions were taken into account. Beyond global satisfaction versus marital distress, there was overall support for our hypotheses that the three relationship-focused standards would be associated with couples' self-reports of mutual constructive communication, and with lower levels of communication patterns in which partners exhibit mutual avoidance or in which one partner makes demands and the other withdraws. (Coop, Baucom, Epstein, Rankin & Burnett, 1994). This was especially so for satisfaction with how standards were being met, and for the boundaries and control-outcome standards (those concerning how the partners work together).

The couples in our community sample also were administered another instrument that we developed within our framework of assessing relationship cognitions along the central content dimensions of boundaries, control/power and investment: the Relationship Attribution Questionnaire (RAQ: Baucom, Epstein, Carels & Daiuto, 1991). The RAQ asks the respondent to rate the degree to which each of the same 12 content domains tapped by the ISRS (finances, affection, household tasks, etc.) currently is a problem in the couple's relationship, on a 100-point scale. For each of the six domains with the highest problem ratings, the respondent uses Likert scales to report his or her attributions concerning the problem. First, the degrees to which the problem is caused by the self, the partner, the relationship and outside circumstances are rated; then the extent to which the respondent assigns blame to each of the same four sources is rated. The next items ask about the extent to which the problem is caused by boundary, control/power and investment thematic content issues. Then, the respondent is asked to rate the problem in terms of the dimensions of stability and globality. Next, the respondent reports the degree to which the problem makes him or her feel each of four negative (depressed, angry, tense, guilty) and one positive (hopeful) emotions. Finally, four items ask the individual to report how often he or she responds to the problem with active/constructive, active/destructive, passive/ constructive and passive/destructive behaviors. More detailed description of the RAQ is precluded by space limitations, but, overall, its construction was based on the goals of (1) assessing both the traditionally studied causal attributional dimensions and attributions focused on the same core relationship content areas (boundaries, power/control, investment) tapped by the ISRS, (2) surveying attributions made for particular relationship domains (for example, finances, affection, household tasks), and (3) assessing affective and behavioral responses associated with attributions concerning relationship problems.

In our sample of community couples, we investigated affective and behavioral correlates of each type of attribution assessed on the RAQ, as well as the relationship between attributions and the standards assessed by the ISRS. We found that partners who reported greater marital distress were more likely to attribute their relationship problems to their partner (seeing the partner as the cause, and blaming him or her), to global and stable causes, and to content issues concerning boundaries, control/power and investment. Causal attributions had only low to moderate correlations with attributions to content issues, indicating that these tend to be different kinds of cognitions. The content attributions were more strongly associated with negative affective responses to relationship problems, as well as with active and passive destructive behavioral responses to the problems, than were causal attributions. Thus, the results were consistent with previous research indicating that partners' attributions are an important component of their cognitions concerning their relationship, associated with both their emotional and behavioral responses to marital problems. Furthermore, the results underscore the importance of assessing specific thematic content of couples' attributions.

Although we had hypothesized that partners would make more attributions concerning relationship issues (for example, boundaries) for which they held stronger standards, this was not the case within our community sample. However, for all three categories of relationship standards assessed by the ISRS (boundaries, control/power, investment), the number of standards that partners reported as being unmet was associated, for both genders, with greater tendencies to attribute relationship problems to (a) the partner and relationship, (b) boundary, control/power and investment issues, and (c) global and stable causes. Having more unmet standards also was associated with reporting more negative affect regarding top problem areas in one's relationship (as assessed by the RAQ), and more active-destructive behavioral responses (that is, doing hurtful things to create distance from one's partner) to those relationship problems (Baucom, Epstein, Daiuto, Carels, Rankin & Burnett, in press). Not only do these results provide additional support for theoretical models linking cognitions, emotions and behavior in couples' problems (cf. Epstein & Baucom, 1993), but they identify particular types of cognitions (for example, the degree to which standards are unmet, rather than the degree to which they are extreme) that are especially salient in couples' subjective experiences of their intimate relationships.

Clinical implications

The foregoing was a summary of a fairly complex set of studies that we have conducted both individually and collaboratively, with an emphasis on our assessment of cognitive factors that interact with behavior and emotional responses in determining the quality of couples' relationships. We believe that it was important to trace the development of the research program, because it reflects the close interaction that has occurred between our research and clinical practice over the years. Repeated observations of partners becoming distressed and escalating their conflicts when their core relationship standards were unmet, and when they attributed each other's negative behaviors to factors involving core relationship themes (for example, a partner's lack of investment in their relationship), shaped our conceptualization of the kinds of cognitions that should be studied. Our conclusion that there were no existing instruments for assessing these important cognitive factors led directly to the design and development of content-oriented measures such as the ISRS and RAQ. In turn, the empirical findings from our studies have had significant impact on our clinical practice with distressed couples.

Clinical implications of treatment outcome studies

As described above, our studies investigated the impact of cognitive restructuring interventions for distressed couples, either in comparison to or in combination with behavioral interventions. Taken together, the studies indicated that the cognitive interventions had positive impacts on couples' relationships that were at least comparable to those found with the behavioral interventions, and there was some evidence that cognitive restructuring was the more effective way of modifying partners' negative cognitions concerning their marriages. The designs of the studies did not clarify whether adding cognitive interventions to behavioral marital therapy, in either a modular or integrated way, can enhance treatment efficacy. The results of the Baucom, Sayers and Sher (1990) study suggest that if one combines cognitive, behavioral and affective interventions, it is important that the addition of one component not be at the expense of clients' getting adequate amounts of another component.

In clinical practice, we attempt to assess each couple's needs for each type of intervention, both at intake and on an ongoing basis, with the focus of therapy shifting from one component to another as the assessment indicates this is needed (Baucom & Epstein, 1990). For example, in one couple who presented for treatment of chronic conflict marked by both escalating verbal arguments and periods in which the husband withdrew while the wife pursued him, the initial assessment indicated that modification of the partners' negative behavioral interaction patterns, negative affect and negative cognitions could be beneficial. Given the couple's tendency to escalate their arguments quickly, to the point where their anger precluded reasoned problem-solving, the therapist decided to emphasize behavioral change initially, to decrease the aversive exchanges and promote constructive communication.

During the initial sessions, the therapist periodically asked the couple to discuss the problems that were of concern to them, observed their interaction pattern and gave them feedback about those patterns. For example, it was common for the partners to alternate making critical statements about each other's approaches to finances, childrearing and other aspects of family life. Most often, the husband would reciprocate the wife's criticisms for a short time, then defend his actions, and then withdraw from her (for example, by avoiding eye contact with her and making comments that it was impossible to talk to her). It soon became clear that the negative exchanges had become 'automatic' over time. Even though each member of the couple exhibited good communication skills with the therapist, and reported constructive communication with friends and co-workers, even a minor negative response from one partner quickly elicited a reciprocal negative response from the other partner. Consequently, the therapist spent a considerable amount of time modeling and coaching the couple in the use of more constructive communication with each other. Because their anger toward each other tended to elicit negative behaviors such as criticisms, the therapist also emphasized the importance of their managing the intensity of emotion and making a concerted effort to avoid problem-solving discussions when they were emotionally aroused. The partners were coached in noticing the verbal and non-verbal cues of increasing anger and the use of 'time-out' periods, in which they would agree to separate (for example, go into different rooms; one of them go out for a walk) and 'cool down' before resuming their discussion.

At the same time, an assessment of the couple's cognitions concerning their relationship revealed that they commonly made negative attributions about the determinants of each other's negative actions, and that these attributions appeared to increase their anger and adversarial behavior. For example, when the wife expressed disagreement with her husband, he attributed her behavior to both a lack of respect for his ideas and a desire on her part to control their finances, childrearing, etc. In return, she attributed his expressions of anger, attempts to 'fight back' and withdrawal as due to a lack of investment in their relationship, as well as a desire to dominate their relationship. Unfortunately, as long as their negative attributions about each other's motives contributed to more negative affect and behavior, the cycle of conflictual interaction continued. Therefore, it was important for the therapist to integrate cognitive interventions with the behavioral strategies for reducing verbal attacks and withdrawal. Based on our own and others' research on attributions, the therapist guided each partner in disclosing the themes in his or her attributions about the other person (for example, control/power, investment) and discussed with the couple how each person's negative emotions and behaviors made sense in light of their attributions about the other's behavior. Each partner was given opportunities to provide alternative explanations (that is, re-attributions) for his or her actions, and the therapist emphasized how important it was for members of a close relationship to feel that their partner respected them, cared, was invested in the relationship and wanted to share control/power. As the partners were more able to consider more benign motives for each other and at least partly accepted the validity of the therapist's position that it was constructive to create an atmosphere of respect, caring, etc., in their relationship, the therapist was able to introduce more practice of positive communication in sessions. Increasingly, the couple were able to spend time in sessions engaged in problem-solving concerning their areas of conflict.

Clinical implications of research on standards, assumptions and attributions

As described earlier, our research also has demonstrated that partners' standards and assumptions about their relationships are associated with their degrees of satisfaction with the relationship, their attributions about each other's behavior, and their behavioral patterns when communicating about areas of conflict. Therefore, it is important to conduct an assessment of these cognitions when a couple present with complaints of marital problems.

During initial therapy sessions, it is common for partners to describe their complaints about each other's behavior, sometimes in global terms (for example, 'She doesn't treat me like I'm important to her'), and sometimes with reference to specific actions that do or do not occur with satisfactory frequencies (for example, 'She rarely takes time away from her work to sit down and talk with me'). These behavioral problem descriptions provide an opportunity for the clinician to probe for each individual's standards about how his or her relationship 'should' be. In other words, our research suggests that each partner is making comparisons (not necessarily in an intentional, conscious manner) between the events that occur in the current relationship and an internal set of standards. Furthermore, the research results indicate that the individual's satisfaction with the relationship is not so much a matter of how extreme the standards are, but rather a function of whether he or she perceives that the standards are being met satisfactorily in the relationship. Consequently, when a member of a couple describes a complaint about the partner, it is important to inquire about (a) the specific behaviors that the partner currently exhibits, (b) the behaviors that the person believes the partner should exhibit (that is, the standard), and (c) what changes the person would find to be acceptable ways of meeting the standard. Although at first glance it might seem that the third of these points is simply a shift of the partner's behavior toward matching the behavioral standard, this is not the only therapeutic alternative. In our studies, it has become clear that many couples achieve satisfaction in their relationships in spite of their awareness that their partners' behaviors are not matching the standards that they would most want in an intimate relationship. Whether this reflects a willingness to compromise in certain areas of the relationship in exchange for getting what one wants in other areas, or a general philosophical acceptance of relationships as imperfect yet potentially satisfying, it is important to assess the degree to which each partner can accept discrepancies from his or her personal standards.

In addition, the therapist can explore whether an individual has considered alternative ways in which his or her partner could behave in order to address an unmet standard. It is our experience that members of a couple often have different idiosyncratic definitions of what behaviors constitute 'investment' in one's relationship, and how much they emphasize instrumental or expressive investment. These definitions can be influenced by the attributions that each person makes about the causes of the other's behaviors. For example, in one couple the wife perceived the husband as investing little in their marriage, in either an instrumental or expressive manner, whereas the husband saw himself as investing a great deal of himself in both areas. As a prime example of his instrumental investment, the husband emphasized the many hours that he spent at work, earning money for the family. Concerning expressive investment, he noted that he complimented his wife on her appearance, spent leisure time with her (for example, going out to dinner) and was physically affectionate. However, the wife attributed the husband's long hours at work as motivated primarily by his own ambition to succeed, and she viewed his expressive behaviors as focused on relatively superficial levels of relating. She interpreted his compliments as a reflection of his attention to her physical appearance rather than her ideas and feelings, his interest in dining out as reflecting his enjoyment of good food, and his physical affection as correlated with his desire for sex. Thus, the same behaviors that the husband defined as expressions of his investment in the marriage were discounted as such by the wife, based on her attributions concerning the meanings of the behaviors. When the therapist inquired about behaviors that the wife considered more appropriate expressions of investment, she noted that her husband rarely initiated work on household chores (that is, she usually had the responsibility of organizing what had to be done and had to request his assistance), and that his choices of joint leisure activities involved being spectators (for example, sporting events, movies) rather than talking together. The husband replied that his wife failed to appreciate his efforts and his enjoyment of their time together.

The therapist's tasks at this point were to help the partners understand the conflict between their behavioral standards concerning investment in their relationship, consider the subjectivity of standards and the absence of one 'right' way to invest oneself in a relationship, and devise ways of taking each other's preferences into account. The therapist emphasized that when partners blame each other for not meeting standards and invalidate each other's standards, the chances that each person will become defensive about his or her own ideas and behavior increase. Because standards for intimate relationships are part of an individual's long-standing world view, it is important for members of a couple to communicate empathy and respect for each other's views, as well as a willingness to restructure their inter-actions in a manner that is acceptable to both parties. It is unlikely that partners in most relationships will have exactly the same standards about core relationship concerns such as investment, boundaries and the distri-bution of control/power, but our research indicates that many couples successfully integrate their personal standards with the realities of living with another person. Consequently, a central task of couples therapy is to assist partners in experimenting with ways of reconciling their different relationship standards.

Although some of a couple's standards for their relationships may be revealed through their descriptions of the changes that they would like to see in their behavioral interactions, a thorough assessment of standards usually requires that the therapist initiate an inquiry about what each person wants in the core relationship content dimensions of boundaries, control/power and investment. As described earlier, the Inventory of Specific Relationship Standards (ISRS) was designed to tap these beliefs across 12 important areas of relationship functioning (for example, finances, affection, household tasks). Our factor analysis and construct validity findings for the ISRS indicate that these content dimensions are indeed important to couples and are related to indices of marital adjustment versus discord. Thus, whether or not one chooses to assess partners' standards with a self-report questionnaire such as the ISRS or through systematic interviewing, eliciting their views about boundaries, control/ power and investment is likely to be helpful in developing a conceptualization of the cognitive factors influencing the couple's functioning.

The results of our research on the ISRS indicate that the subscales assessing standards for the major relationship dimensions of boundaries, control/power and investment tend to have moderate levels of internal consistency when Cronbach's alpha coefficients are computed for respondents' ratings of their standards across the 12 relationship areas (finances, affection, children, etc.). Although it usually is desirable to have questionnaires with very high internal consistency, it may not be reasonable to expect that degree of homogeneity in people's standards across different areas of their relationships. Our results indicate that an individual's standards for boundaries, control/power and investment may vary, depending on the area of the relationship that he or she is considering. For example, although an individual may generally tend to favor minimal boundaries between himself or herself and a partner, this preference might be stronger in some areas (for example, sharing feelings, expressing affection) than in others (for example, finances, career issues). In terms of clinical assessment, this underscores the importance of a careful assessment of each partner's standards in each area of their relationship that has been a source of conflict or satisfaction.

A clinician may be tempted to describe or label a couple based on their standards in one or two areas of their relationship, when in fact their standards vary considerably. Thus, a therapist might hear both members of the above couple describing their strong desires for minimal boundaries in the areas of sharing feelings and expressing affection, and may conclude that the couple even borders on being 'enmeshed'. However, if the clinician has failed to identify other areas in which one or both partners desires at least moderate boundaries (for example, concerning finances and career issues), labeling the couple as enmeshed may interfere with achieving a clear conceptualization of the couple's sources of conflict and distress. In fact, the members of this couple may have been attracted to each other initially because the boundary standards that they shared regarding sharing feelings and expressing affection were evident in the early stages of their relationship. Because they felt a mutual desire to spend time together, had long conversations about their lives and personal interests, and expressed affection for each other both verbally and physically, it is likely that each person inferred that the other valued closeness as much as he or she did. However, the areas in which the partners' boundary standards differ only became evident after they established a committed relationship and faced decisions regarding finances and careers. It is our experience that members of couples often make generalizations about each other's relationship standards, assuming that each person's views about some key issues also hold for other issues, and that the validity of such generalizations varies considerably. Thus, it may have been only after this couple began living together that it became clear that they had different standards about sharing the financial and career areas of their lives. For example, when they finally discussed how they would organize their finances, perhaps one partner expressed the belief (standard) that they should merge all of their individual assets into joint bank accounts, whereas the other partner stated a strong desire to maintain individual accounts, except for a joint checking account where equal contributions from the partners would be used to pay bills. Similarly, when one partner's opportunities for advancement in his or her job began to increase, perhaps that individual began to spend more time working, both at the office and at home, and believed that he or she should be able to spend as much time on work tasks as was needed for him or her to feel comfortable. Furthermore, this individual held a standard that self-actualization requires that people pursue some work activities that are not shared (or even discussed in detail) with their partners. In contrast, the other partner believed that work tasks should impinge minimally on a couple's life together, beyond a 40-hour per week schedule, and that members of a couple should discuss their work experiences with each other in detail, as part of their shared life. Consequently, this couple discovered that they had significant areas of their relationship where their standards concerning boundaries were different. Furthermore, when it came to discussing possible solutions to their conflict, and when decisions were faced concerning changes in work schedules, or even a possible relocation due to a job transfer, it became apparent that the partners had different standards concerning the distribution of control/power in making decisions about career issues. The partner who believed in at least a moderate degree of boundaries in the area of work also expected that each person should have most of the power in decisions affecting his or her career, whereas the other person believed that all career decisions should be made through negotiation between the two of them.

This couple, who initially had experienced a comfortable, rewarding sense of togetherness, and a sense of shared standards concerning boundaries in their relationship, now argued and increasingly perceived their bond as threatened. On the one hand, the partner whose standards concerning finances and career focused on minimal boundaries within the couple began to question the other partner's commitment to a close relationship, finding it difficult to reconcile the other's boundary setting for finances and work with the couple's sharing of feelings and affection. On the other hand, the partner who desired greater independence in the finance and work areas experienced the other person as imposing uncomfortable constraints on his/her freedom. In fact, at this point, the partner whose standards favored more clear boundaries developed a new attribution about the other partner's affiliative and affectionate behaviors, viewing them more as attempts to foster an unhealthy dependent attachment between the two people than as expressions of healthy attraction and caring. Thus, the initial overlap of the two partners' standards within particular areas of their relationship masked the existence of some differences in their standards in other areas, and the uncovering of the differences during developmental changes in the relationship (that is, when financial and career issues became more relevant) led each person to reassess the extent of their shared standards and to reinterpret each other's motives.

If this couple lack skills for constructive communication to clarify their standards, motives, etc., and are ineffective in applying problem-solving skills to resolve their differences, the conflict that they have discovered in their standards may become a source of alienation in their relationship. In such circumstances, a therapist can help the partners see whether a discrepancy in their standards in one area of their relationship necessarily invalidates what appeared to be consensus in another area, addressing any negative attributions that have developed about each other's motives (as in the above example). Furthermore, the therapist can help the couple in applying problem-solving skills (for example, defining the relationship problem in clear behavioral terms, brainstorming alternative solutions) to identify and initiate solutions to the conflicts in their standards within certain areas of their relationship. In the above case example, the partners may come to see that their apparent similarity in standards for sharing feelings and expressing affection was valid, and that the difference in their standards for boundaries concerning finances and work was fairly independent of the other aspects of sharing in their relationship. If the conflict about boundaries indeed is compartmentalized in the areas of finances and work, the therapist then can help the couple examine exactly how far apart their views are, communicate with each other clearly about their personal rationales concerning their desired degrees of boundaries in those areas, and explore whether there is a negotiable pattern of behavior that can bridge their individual standards. For example, regarding finances, the partner who held a standard for minimal boundaries may have grown up seeing his/her parents and other couples sharing all their financial assets, and thus views the other's desire for separate bank accounts as 'abnormal'. This may be especially troubling if the former individual attributes the latter's reluctance to share all bank accounts to a lack of commitment to their relationship (for example, 'He/She wants to be able to develop a personal "nest egg" to make it easy to leave me and live alone'). If in fact there is some truth in this attribution (for example, if the partner suffered financial hardship when an earlier relationship that involved shared finances ended), it would be important for the therapist to help the couple discuss the self-protective motives involved in the partner's standard about independent finances. Especially if the other partner can be coached in empathizing with the self-protective motives, the couple may then be able to brainstorm ideas about ways in which they could interact that would address the fears based on the partner's past experiences. It may be important for the partner who seeks minimal boundaries concerning finances to become aware that his or her attempts to coerce the other person into merging their finances may increase the other's fears and resistance to modifying the standard about independent finances.

Thus, efforts to help a couple reconcile differences in their standards in particular areas of their relationship often will be aided if the therapist conducts a systematic assessment of how each person's standards may have been shaped by experiences in various past relationships, including his or her family of origin and past romantic relationships. Not only can this reduce overt conflict by increasing each partner's empathy for the forces that have shaped the other's standards, but it may open each individual to the possibility of modifying his or her own standards, by highlighting how standards relevant to past relationships may not hold in the same manner in the present relationship. For example, in the above case example, the person whose standard was for clear boundaries in the area of finances may be able to see evidence that the current relationship is considerably safer than past ones, and may be willing to experiment with taking gradual steps toward sharing finances, as long as his or her partner communicates empathic support and cooperates with the experiments.

A clinical issue that has not been addressed directly by our research but is important to consider in the assessment and modification of standards concerns instances in which an individual's standard requires not only that the partner behaves in particular ways but also that he or she *wants to* behave in that manner. For many individuals, it is not sufficient for their partners to change their behavior in prescribed ways; it is important that the partners be motivated by their own desire to change rather than by the other person's requests for change. For example, when the husband in the case example described earlier, where the spouses had different definitions of what constitutes expressive investment in their relationship, agreed to spend more time talking with his wife about personal matters, her response was mixed. In part she was pleased by his behavior change, but she also was upset that he did not appear to have the motivation to seek her out for such conversations without her asking. The therapist first attempted to address her concern by noting that the husband's taking the time to talk when it did not seem to come naturally to him may reflect investment in the marriage, even if it was not the same type of behavior (that is, initiating conversations) that the wife tended to think of as reflecting investment. In the cognitive therapy tradition of Socratic questioning, the therapist engaged the couple in listing as many different behaviors as possible that could represent a person's investment in an intimate relationship. Second, the therapist noted that even though it had required initiative on the wife's part (an external cause) to motivate the husband to start conversations, the couple might find that if he had some enjoyable talks with his wife, he would then look forward to more talks (an internal cause) and initiate more of them.

Our research did not differentiate clearly between investing time, energy, etc., in one's relationship and the source or kind of motivation behind those behaviors, but for many clients that distinction is a very important one. Couples often need assistance in removing themselves from the paradoxical trap of requesting changes in each other's motives, because any compliance can be seen as externally motivated; for example, 'If you change because I tell you to, then you haven't done it because *you* want to.' It is important for the therapist to acknowledge how good it feels when one's partner spontaneously initiates positive behavior, but also to coach the couple in exploring the traps of standards that require specific positive motives and to encourage them to experiment with mutual behavior changes that can develop *new* positive motivation.

Thus, the case example described above also illustrates the impact that attributions have on partners' emotional and behavioral responses to each other. As the therapist explored the partners' attributions about determinants of each other's and their own behaviors further, evidence of significant discrepancies in their views surfaced. Although the husband viewed his compliments and affectionate behavior as due to his love for his wife, her alternative attributions for those behaviors were far less positive. Consistent with our research and that of others who have studied attributions (cf. Bradbury & Fincham, 1990), the wife's distress was associated with her attributing her spouse's actions to selfish motivation (desires for good food and sex). In return the husband described his attempts to plan social activities for them as a couple (for example, going out to dinner with friends, attending plays and movies) and discussed how he viewed her voicing disinterest in many of the plans as reflecting a lack of caring and respect for him.

As is often the case in the escalation of conflict in a relationship, each partner's tendency to attribute the other's behaviors to stable, global negative characteristics (motives and attitudes) contributed to negative emotions such as hurt and anger, as well as negative behaviors such as criticism. In order to interrupt and alter the escalating cycle of negative cognitions, emotions and behavior, the therapist spent part of each therapy session focusing on substituting constructive behavior change requests for the couple's aversive criticism (using communication training procedures), part of each session on coaching the partners to consider alternative attributions for each other's behavior, and part of each session on techniques for moderating high levels of anger in each other's presence. As yet our treatment studies have not determined how much of each type of intervention may be needed, or what order may be optimal for the behavioral, cognitive and affective interventions. Given that the answers to these questions are likely to vary according to the characteristics of each client couple, further construction of measures such as the ISRS for assessing partners' cognitions should contribute to the development of an assessment battery covering the behavioral, cognitive and affective domains of couple interaction.

Research on couples has indicated that individuals' marital distress is influenced more by negative partner behaviors than by positive ones, and that distressed partners' responses to conflict tend to involve reciprocal exchanges of negative behavior rather than positive problem-solving responses (cf. Baucom & Epstein, 1990; Gottman, 1993; Weiss & Heyman, 1990). As noted earlier, we found that partners' tendencies to attribute their relationship problems to boundary, control/power and investment issues were associated with active and passive destructive behavioral responses but not with constructive behavioral responses. Our findings are consistent with Gottman's (1993) hypothesis that distressed couples' escalation of negative behavior exchanges is influenced by the partners making stable negative attributions about each other, which are difficult to disconfirm. We suggest that one of the reasons why they are difficult to modify is because they involve core relationship themes (for example, boundaries, control/power, investment) that are very important to people in intimate relationships where partners are potentially highly vulnerable to the effects of each other's behavior. Thus, once an individual has seriously considered the possibility that his or her partner has negative motives or attitudes concerning a core relationship theme (for example, cares little about investing time and energy into the relationship), the potential costs that the individual will perceive in being vulnerable to such a partner are likely to be high. Consequently, the individual is likely to be vigilant concerning additional signs of danger and reluctant to accept instances of positive partner behavior as sufficient evidence that the partner's motives etc. are benign. Our hypotheses about the impact of attributions concerning core relationship themes remain speculative at this point, and we must await the results of future studies to support or refute them.

In clinical practice, we have found that it is important to acknowledge to our client couples the risks that partners perceive in allowing themselves to be vulnerable with each other, based on their past painful experiences in the relationship and their tendencies to attribute the causes of those experiences to stable, global negative traits in each other. This is especially the case when one partner has broken the other's trust through an affair, physical or psychological abuse, substance abuse or some other negative behavior. Although it is common for the person who has broken the trust to pressure his or her partner to 'put it in the past' and focus on positive change in the present (which to some extent would be part of a couple therapist's agenda as well), the partner typically has much difficulty doing so, for compelling reasons. First, the hurt, anger and anxiety associated with being treated in a very negative manner by one's partner are vivid experiences that are likely to produce strong, recurrent memories. Second, the inequities inherent in the breaking of trust in a close relationship (that is, the perpetrator has greater control and has taken advantage of the other person in some way) are likely to motivate the recipient to desire and perhaps seek retribution. Third, the breaking of trust tends to violate basic assumptions and standards that people commonly hold about close relationships, in a sense turning the person's world upside-down. Janoff-Bulman (1992) has provided an excellent description of the traumatic nature of the experience when one's basic assumptions about the world are violated by life events, as well as the tendency that people have to seek explanations for such disturbing experiences, often by assigning blame. As noted earlier, marital researchers also have found that members of couples tend to assign blame, to themselves and to each other, for relationship problems, and it becomes a crucial task for marital therapists to help each person make a careful assessment of his or her attributions. In the case of broken trust, the perpetrator may be likely to focus on unstable, external causes of the events (for example, 'I had just been passed over for a promotion at work, my best friend moved away, and I was in a weakened state when the other woman showed interest in me and made me feel important. Things are going better at work now, and I have been making new friends.'), whereas the victim may attribute the events to negative traits within the partner (for example, 'I had thought that he was committed to me, but he's selfish and only thinks of himself'). On the one hand, the husband's attribution minimizes his personal responsibility for his affair, and it suggests that the restoration of trust is at least partly dependent on better external circumstances in the future (which should hardly be reassuring to his wife). On the other hand, the wife's attribution holds the husband responsible, but it focuses on characteristics that can be viewed as unchangeable. The husband, in turn, may feel frustrated that his spouse's attribution discounts any attempts that be makes to behave in a more trustworthy manner. Thus, from either partner's perspective, there may be little that they can do in a proactive way as individuals or as a couple to reduce the chance of another affair in the future.

As described earlier, some of our earlier research has shown that individuals vary in the extent to which their attributions about relationship events vary across situations versus following a set pattern or attributional style. In the above case example, the factors that contributed to the husband's marital affair may be more complex than either one of the spouses' attributional explanations. For example, the husband's attribution that the stressors in his life were influential may have some validity; however, not all people who experience such stressors engage in affairs, and it would be important to identify his own characteristics that may have interacted with the stressors to increase the risk of extramarital involvement. Thus, his comment about being in a 'weakened state' could be pursued, with a systematic inquiry about his self-esteem, his past use of particular coping styles when faced with various life stressors, his standards concerning boundaries and investment in close relationships, etc. A therapist might challenge his external attributions (and focus on internal responsibility) by asking him to devise plans for monitoring his level of vulnerability when under stress in the future and for engaging in other coping strategies that will not threaten his marriage.

Likewise, the wife's attributing the affair to her husband's selfishness may be an oversimplification of the processes involved. First, a therapist might encourage her to review the couple's relationship, looking for both patterns and variations in how her husband has related to her, with an emphasis on boundary, investment and commitment themes. It is important that this review be conducted with an understanding that the wife's present anger may make it difficult for her to acknowledge positive past behavior on her husband's part. The therapist may need to stress that identifying some positive behaviors does not relieve her husband of responsibility for his affair; rather, it is important to identify variations in a person's behavior and the circumstances associated with the variations. Of course, even if the wife concludes that her husband has exhibited behaviors that seemed to reflect investment and commitment to their relationship most of the time, except when he was faced with life stressors that diminished his self-esteem, this perspective still may be consistent with her view that he has a trait of selfishness. However, her attribution now takes into account the qualifying condition of 'selfish when under stress'. If in turn the husband is willing to acknowledge that he has not coped well under stress and if he begins to make efforts to improve his coping skills, his wife may decide that she is willing to work toward improving their relationship. In addition, if the therapist also conducts a review of the relationship history with the husband, and he reports difficulty communicating his vulnerable feelings to his wife when he is under stress, the therapist can introduce the idea that another factor that can help prevent future affairs would be improved communication between the partners. Again, the spouses may have different attributions for the communication problem (for example, he may attribute it to his wife responding in an unsympathetic manner when he does disclose vulnerability; she may attribute it to her husband being an inhibited person), and it is the therapist's responsibility to help the couple avoid overly simplistic (and blaming) explanations, focusing instead on considering any possible factor influencing a problem and planning interventions to minimize all of them.

Implications of findings concerning gender and relationship cognitions

We found minimal gender differences in partners' adherence to relationship-focused standards concerning boundaries, control/power and investment. Similarly, there were minimal gender differences in the degree to which members of couples attributed relationship problems to boundary, control/

power and investment issues, or to levels of causal factors (stability, globality and locus). These findings are notable in the context of research literature suggesting that women are more relationship-focused than men (Baucom, Notarius, Burnett & Haefner, 1990). At least through their self-reports on the ISRS, men and women endorse comparable degrees of boundaries, sharing of control/power and investment in their intimate relationships. Furthermore, for both genders, standards for fewer bound-aries (that is, more sharing), more egalitarian distribution of control/power and greater instrumental and affective investment in one's relationship are associated with higher levels of marital satisfaction and more constructive communication. Although men may be more likely than women to exhibit defensiveness and 'stonewalling' (withdrawal from interaction) during conflictual discussions (Gottman, 1993), this may not necessarily reflect greater autonomy and lower investment in their intimate relationships. In fact, Gottman's research suggests that men's defensive and withdrawn behavior may result from greater emotional distress when their partners criticize them compared to the distress experienced by women who are criticized. For the clinician, our results indicate that themes of boundaries, control/power and investment are important to both genders, and standards concerning these themes should be assessed carefully with both members of any couple.

As illustrated by the case examples presented earlier, the members of a couple may value investment in their relationship equally but have different definitions for what behaviors reflect investment. In one of the couples whom we described, the husband pointed to his hours spent at work earning his paychecks, the leisure activities shared with his wife and his physical affection as expressions of his investment in their relationship. In contrast, the wife viewed efforts to take the initiative with household tasks and to spend time communicating about personal feelings as hallmarks of investment. Although these differences may be idiosyncratic to this couple, they may reflect some systematic differences between men and women concerning the forms rather than the amount of investment desired in a close relationship. Thus, we must interpret the overall lack of gender differences on our measures of standards and attributions with caution, because the ISRS and RAQ do not provide assessments of different ways of expressing either instrumental or expressive investment in a relationship. At present, the clinician must rely on careful interviewing in order to determine whether gender plays a role in a particular couple's conflicts.

Conclusion

Our research has been designed to address clinical issues in the assessment and treatment of marital problems, and the findings have had direct implications for clinical practice. As couple therapists increasingly have used cognitive-behavioral approaches to address their clients' relationship problems, there has been a clear need for research in two major areas. First, it has been important to test whether the cognitive, behavioral and affective factors described in the theoretical and clinical literature indeed play significant roles in marital conflict and distress. Closely tied to this question is the need for research focused on the development of standardized ways of assessing these factors. Our past and current studies have resulted in the development of questionnaires designed to assess types of cognition (especially standards and attributions), and we have demonstrated their relationships to partners' marital satisfaction, communication patterns and other indices of relationship functioning. Although the research in this area is still in an early stage, the measures that we and other marital researchers have developed appear to have considerable utility as parts of a relationship assessment battery. The validity evidence for scales such as the Inventory of Specific Relationship Standards and the Relationship Attribution Questionnaire also has demonstrated that clinicians should attend to particular content themes (boundaries, control/power, investment) in partners' cognitions. Even though it is likely that some of the cognitions that affect individuals' levels of distress about their relationships are beyond awareness, there is ample evidence that the cognitions that partners can identify and report on questionnaires such as the ISRS and RAQ are important parts of the subjective experience in a close relationship.

Our initial studies on behavioral and cognitive interventions have demonstrated that these treatments have positive impacts on distressed couples. Whereas there are important unanswered questions about the optimal amounts and sequencing of behavioral and cognitive interventions, especially depending on variations in couples' presenting problems, it appears that existing approaches to cognitive-behavioral treatment do address processes in negative couple interaction. Because this is another area of marital research that is at an early stage of development, we believe that it is important to interpret the findings with caution and to design future studies to extend our knowledge about the impacts of cognitive-behavioral marital therapy further.

Integrating research and clinical practice has been a stimulating and productive process for each of us. In the empirical tradition of cognitive-behavioral therapy, we attempt to select particular therapeutic interventions on the basis of an assessment of each couple's areas of strength and difficulty, and to continue to modify the treatment according to an ongoing assessment of its impact on presenting problems. Similarly, we have devised hypotheses about the roles of cognitive, behavioral and affective factors in intimate relationships (often on the basis of our clinical experience), worked to refine measurement of these factors and tested our hypotheses in a series of studies. As some hypotheses are supported and others not, we refine our conceptualization of marital interaction, as well as our clinical assessment and treatment of relationship problems. This is a continually evolving process, and a rewarding one.

References

Abramson, L.Y., Seligman, M.E.P., & Teasdale, J. (1978). Learned helplessness in humans: Critique and reformulation. *Journal of Abnormal Psychology, 87,* 49–94.

Bandura, A. (1977). *Social learning theory.* Englewood Cliffs, NJ: Prentice-Hall.

Baucom, D.H. (1982). A comparison of behavioral contracting and problem solving/ communications training in behavioral marital therapy. *Behavior Therapy, 13,* 162–174.

Baucom, D.H. (1984). The active ingredients of behavioral marital therapy: The effectiveness of communication/problem solving training, contingency contracting, and their combination. In K. Hahlweg & N.S. Jacobson (Eds.), *Marital interaction: Analysis and modification* (pp. 73–88). New York: Guilford.

Baucom, D.H. (1987). Attributions in distressed relations: How can we explain them? In S. Duck & D. Perlman (Eds.), *Heterosexual relations, marriage and divorce* (pp. 177–206). London: Sage.

Baucom, D.H., Bell, W.G., & Duhe, A. (1982, November). *The measurement of couples' attributions for positive and negative dyadic interactions.* Paper presented at the annual meeting of the Association for Advancement of Behavior Therapy, Los Angeles.

Baucom, D.H., & Epstein, N. (1990). *Cognitive-behavioral marital therapy.* New York: Brunner/Mazel.

Baucom, D.H., Epstein, N., Carels, R.A., & Daiuto, A.D. (1991, November). *The Relationship Attribution Questionnaire: A new instrument for assessing relationship attributions and their impact.* Paper presented at the annual meeting of the Association for Advancement of Behavior Therapy, New York.

Baucom, D.H., Epstein, N., Daiuto, A.D., Carels, R.A., Rankin, L.A., & Burnett, C.K. (in press). Cognitions in marriage: The relationship between standards and attributions. *Journal of Family Psychology.*

Baucom, D.H., Epstein, N., Rankin, L.A., & Burnett, C.K. (in press). Assessing relationship standards: The Inventory of Specific Relationship Standards. *Journal of Family Psychology.*

Baucom, D.H., Epstein, N., Sayers, S., & Sher, T.G. (1989). The role of cognitions in marital relationships: Definitional, methodological, and conceptual issues. *Journal of Consulting and Clinical Psychology, 57,* 31–38.

Baucom, D.H., & Lester, G.W. (1986). The usefulness of cognitive restructuring as an adjunct to behavioral marital therapy. *Behavior Therapy, 17,* 385–403.

Baucom, D.H., Notarius, C.I., Burnett, C.K., & Haefner, P. (1990). Gender differences and sex-role identity in marriage. In F.D. Fincham & T.N. Bradbury (Eds.), *The psychology of marriage: Basic issues and applications* (pp. 150–171). New York: Guilford.

Baucom, D.H., Sayers, S.L., & Duhe, A. (1989). Attributional style and attributional patterns among married couples. *Journal of Personality and Social Psychology, 56,* 596–607.

Baucom, D.H., Sayers, S.L., & Sher, T.G. (1990). Supplementing behavioral marital therapy with cognitive restructuring and emotional expressiveness training: An outcome investigation. *Journal of Consulting and Clinical Psychology, 58,* 636–645.

Beck, A.T. (1976). *Cognitive therapy and the emotional disorders.* New York: International Universities Press.

Beck, A.T., Rush, A.J., Shaw, B.F., & Emery, G. (1979). *Cognitive therapy of depression.* New York: Guilford.

Bradbury, T.N., & Fincham, F.D. (1990). Attributions in marriage: Review and critique. *Psychological Bulletin, 107,* 3–33.

Bradbury, T.N., & Fincham, F.D. (1993). Assessing dysfunctional cognition in marriage: A reconsideration of the Relationship Belief Inventory. *Psychological Assessment, 5,* 92–101.

Coop, K.L., Baucom, D.H., Epstein, N., Rankin, L.A., & Burnett, C.K. (1994). *An exploration of the relationship between marital standards and communication patterns.* Unpublished manuscript.

Doherty, W.J. (1981). Cognitive processes in intimate conflict: I. Extending attribution theory. *American Journal of Family Therapy, 9*(1), 5–13.

Eidelson, R.J., & Epstein, N. (1982). Cognition and relationship maladjustment: Development of a measure of dysfunctional relationship beliefs. *Journal of Consulting and Clinical Psychology, 50*, 715–720.

Ellis, A. (1962). *Reason and emotion in psychotherapy.* New York: Lyle Stuart.

Ellis, A. (1976). Techniques of handling anger in marriage. *Journal of Marriage and Family Counseling, 2*, 305–316.

Epstein, N. (1981). Assertiveness training in marital treatment. In G.P. Sholevar (Ed.), *The handbook of marriage and marital therapy* (pp. 287–302). New York: Spectrum.

Epstein, N. (1982). Cognitive therapy with couples. *American Journal of Family Therapy, 10*(1), 5–16.

Epstein, N., & Baucom, D.H. (1993). Cognitive factors in marital disturbance. In K.S. Dobson & P.C. Kendall (Eds.), *Psychopathology and cognition* (pp. 351–385). San Diego, CA: Academic Press.

Epstein, N., Baucom, D.H., Rankin, L.A., & Burnett, C.K. (1991, November). *Relationship standards in marriage: Development of a new measure of content-specific cognitions.* Paper presented at the annual meeting of the Association for Advancement of Behavior Therapy, New York.

Epstein, N., DeGiovanni, I.S., & Jayne-Lazarus, C. (1978). Assertion training for couples. *Journal of Behavior Therapy and Experimental Psychiatry, 9*, 146–156.

Epstein, N., & Eidelson, R.J. (1981). Unrealistic beliefs of clinical couples: Their relationship to expectations, goals and satisfaction. *American Journal of Family Therapy, 9*(4), 13–22.

Epstein, N., & Jackson, E. (1978). An outcome study of short-term communication training with married couples. *Journal of Consulting and Clinical Psychology, 46*, 207–212.

Epstein, N., Pretzer, J.L., & Fleming, B. (1982, November). *Cognitive therapy and communication training: Comparisons of effects with distressed couples.* Paper presented at the annual meeting of the Association for Advancement of Behavior Therapy, Los Angeles.

Epstein, N., Pretzer, J.L., & Fleming, B. (1987). The role of cognitive appraisal in self-reports of marital communication. *Behavior Therapy, 18*, 51–69.

Fincham, F.D., Beach, S.R.H., & Baucom, D.H. (1987). Attribution processes in distressed and nondistressed couples: 4. Self–partner attribution differences. *Journal of Personality and Social Psychology, 52*, 739–748.

Fincham, F.D., Beach, S.R.H., & Nelson, G. (1987). Attribution processes in distressed and nondistressed couples: 3. Causal and responsibility attributions for spouse behavior. *Cognitive Therapy and Research, 11*, 71–86.

Fincham, F.D., & Bradbury, T.N. (1987). The impact of attributions in marriage: A longitudinal analysis. *Journal of Personality and Social Psychology, 53*, 510–517.

Fincham, F.D., & Bradbury, T.N. (Eds.). (1990). *The psychology of marriage: Basic issues and applications.* New York: Guilford.

Fiske, S.T., & Taylor, S.E. (1991). *Social cognition* (2nd ed.). New York: McGraw-Hill.

Gaelick, L., Bodenhausen, G.V., & Wyer, R.S. (1985). Emotional communication in relationships. *Journal of Personality and Social Psychology, 49*, 1246–1265.

Gottman, J.M. (1993). A theory of marital dissolution and stability. *Journal of Family Psychology, 7*, 57–75.

Guerney, B.G., Jr. (1977). *Relationship enhancement.* San Francisco: Jossey-Bass.

Huber, C.H., & Milstein, B. (1985). Cognitive restructuring and a collaborative set in couples' work. *American Journal of Family Therapy, 13*(2), 17–27.

Jacobson, N.S., & Margolin, G. (1979). *Marital therapy: Strategies based on social learning and behavior exchange principles.* New York: Brunner/Mazel.

Janoff-Bulman, R. (1992). *Shattered assumptions: Towards a new psychology of trauma.* New York: Free Press.

Jones, R.G. (1968). *A factored measure of Ellis' irrational belief system, with personality and maladjustment correlates.* Unpublished doctoral dissertation, Texas Technical College.

Meichenbaum, D. (1977). *Cognitive-behavior modification.* New York: Plenum Press.

Pretzer, J.L., Epstein, N., & Fleming, B. (1991). The Marital Attitude Survey: A measure of dysfunctional attributions and expectancies. *The Journal of Cognitive Psychotherapy: An International Quarterly, 5,* 131–148.

Stuart, R.B. (1969). Operant interpersonal treatment for marital discord. *Journal of Consulting and Clinical Psychology, 33,* 675–682.

Stuart, R.B. (1980). *Helping couples change: A social learning approach to marital therapy.* New York: Guilford.

Weiss, R.L., & Heyman, R.E. (1990). Observation of marital interaction. In F.D. Fincham & T.N. Bradbury (Eds.), *The psychology of marriage: Basic issues and applications* (pp. 87–117). New York: Guilford.

7

Modifying Irrational Control and Certainty Beliefs: Clinical Recommendations Based Upon Research

Frank W. Bond and Windy Dryden

Western society places great importance on people's ability to control and be certain about what occurs in their lives. Medical doctors should *control* illness, airline pilots should *control* their planes, stockbrokers should be *certain* that stocks will go a particular way, and members of a jury should be *certain* that the witnesses are telling the truth. Since beliefs surrounding control and certainty are hypothesised to be one of the primary causes of anxiety (for example, Barlow, 1988; Beck & Emery, 1985; Seligman, 1975), it may not be surprising that anxiety is the most prevalent psychological disorder (Barlow, 1988). After all, if a society emphasises control and certainty to a great extent, then it encourages the ubiquitous development of anxiety.

People in every type of helping profession from medical doctors to psychologists and social workers encounter people with anxiety, and, thus, people who demand that they must have control over and certainty about their lives. From the theoretical perspective of rational emotive behaviour therapy (REBT), the effective treatment of these people will require the modification of irrational, or dysfunctional, beliefs about control and certainty, since these beliefs are seen to be at the root of their emotional problem. This chapter describes five experiments that can inform clinicians about how to modify unhelpful control and certainty beliefs, so that their clients can be helped to overcome their anxiety problems.

This chapter begins by discussing three concepts (rational and irrational beliefs, ego and discomfort themes, and control and certainty themes) that are examined in these five experiments. It then describes in brief, four experiments by Bond and Dryden (in preparation). These experiments examined how rational and irrational beliefs and their various contents (such as control and certainty) affected the functionality of inferences that people formed about situations. The results of these four experiments are briefly mentioned, and then their psychotherapeutic implications are discussed. Lastly, findings from an experiment by Bond (in preparation) are described, in order to show how the results of Bond and Dryden (in preparation) may be clinically implemented most effectively.

Rational and irrational beliefs

REBT states that dysfunctional emotions (such as depression, anxiety and guilt) stem largely from beliefs that contain demanding evaluations (Ellis & Whiteley, 1979). These types of evaluations often take the form of 'musts' in people's beliefs (Dryden & Ellis, 1987); for example, 'People must respect me.' In REBT, these 'must' beliefs are called irrational beliefs (Ellis, 1962) because they are illogical, dogmatic, inconsistent with reality, destructive, and they tend to thwart goal attainment and maximise emotional disturbance.

Unlike irrational beliefs, rational beliefs aid and abet human happiness, are flexible, consistent with reality, logical, and tend to minimise emotional disturbance (Dryden & Ellis, 1987). When people use rational beliefs, they evaluate themselves, others, and situations using a flexible, preferential philosophy; for example, 'I would prefer that other people respect me, but they don't have to do so.' With this preferential philosophy, people evaluate the world according to their own desires, or preferences; they do not, however, transmute these preferences into demands (or irrational beliefs) that the world must be a particular way.

Beliefs and inferences

An important hypothesis of REBT states that irrational beliefs lead to more dysfunctional, or unhelpful, inferences than do rational beliefs. REBT states that inferences are people's conclusions about events which go beyond the data at hand (Dryden & Ellis, 1987). Inferences are very important in REBT theory because some may trigger rational or irrational beliefs which then lead to either functional or dysfunctional emotions, respectively; therefore, identifying which type of beliefs lead to the most functional and dysfunctional inferences poses important implications for REBT theory, other cognitive-behavioural theories, psychological interventions and social cognition.

Dryden and colleagues (Dryden, Ferguson & Clark, 1989; Dryden, Ferguson & Hylton, 1989; Dryden, Ferguson & McTeague, 1989) conducted three experiments to examine whether rational or irrational beliefs lead to more dysfunctional inferences. The results from all three of their experiments supported REBT's hypothesis that irrational beliefs lead to more dysfunctional inferences than do rational beliefs (Ellis, 1977).

Ego and discomfort beliefs

REBT states that the thematic content of both rational and irrational beliefs fall into one of two universal categories, or themes (Ellis, 1979,

1980). The first category, called ego beliefs, describes how people view themselves. For example, people can accept themselves as fallible human beings (which is a rational ego belief), or they can consider themselves awful or wonderful (both of which are irrational ego beliefs). The second category of beliefs is called discomfort beliefs, and these describe the extent to which people can tolerate or bear frustration (Ellis, 1979, 1980). People with irrational discomfort beliefs often evaluate situations as too hard, too uncomfortable or too dangerous, and people with rational discomfort beliefs often evaluate situations as being tolerable, but not always comfortable or easy (Ellis, 1979).

Despite the theoretical importance that ego and discomfort categories have in REBT theory, no experiment has examined how these different thematic belief contents compare in their ability to produce dysfunctional inferences. Whilst Dryden et al. (Dryden, Ferguson & Clark, 1989; Dryden, Ferguson & Hylton, 1989; Dryden, Ferguson & McTeague, 1989) demonstrated that irrational beliefs lead to more dysfunctional inferences than do rational beliefs, neither they, nor anyone else, have determined whether ego or discomfort thematic contents interact with rational and irrational beliefs to affect the functionality of inferences.

DiGiuseppe and Leaf (1990) and Burgess (1990), however, have studied the relationship of ego and discomfort beliefs to emotional disturbance, using the Attitudes and Beliefs Inventory (ABI). DiGiuseppe and Leaf (1990) demonstrated that a general clinical population endorsed success beliefs more strongly than comfort beliefs. Since success beliefs are ego-related, and comfort beliefs are discomfort-related (Burgess, 1990), this suggests that ego beliefs were more associated with emotional disturbance than were discomfort beliefs. This result suggests that ego beliefs may lead to more dysfunctional inferences than will discomfort beliefs. It should be noted, however, that approval beliefs (which are ego-related) and comfort beliefs (which are discomfort-related) were endorsed to the same extent by DiGiuseppe and Leaf's (1990) clinical population. In addition, in Burgess's (1990) study, his more limited clinical population endorsed discomfort (comfort) beliefs and both types of ego beliefs (success and approval) to the same extent. Based upon the results of Burgess (1990) and DiGiuseppe and Leaf (1990), it appears that no firm conclusion can be reached as to whether ego or discomfort beliefs will lead to more dysfunctional inferences.

Control and certainty

According to several cognitive-behavioural therapy theorists (for example, Barlow, 1988; Beck & Emery, 1985; Lazarus, 1991), irrational beliefs that have thematic contents of control and certainty are important in producing dysfunctional negative emotions, particularly anxiety. These theorists do not agree, however, as to whether control or certainty themes are more important in producing these dysfunctional emotions. For example, Beck and Emery (1985) and Barlow (1988) hypothesise that beliefs with control themes are more important than beliefs with certainty themes in producing anxiety, and Lazarus (1991) hypothesises the opposite. No cognitive-behavioural therapy theorist has made explicit hypotheses about the relative effects of control and certainty beliefs on inferences; however, several cognitive-behavioural therapy theories (for example, Beck, 1976; Ellis, 1962) would suggest that if a belief content leads to dysfunctional emotions, it will also lead to dysfunctional inferences.

No experiment has compared the relative effects of control and certainty *belief* themes on inferences or emotions; however, experiments using animal and human subjects have been conducted which compared the relative effects of controllable and certain *situations* on emotions (Burger & Arkin, 1980; Geer & Maisel, 1972; Maier & Warren, 1988; Mineka, Cook & Miller, 1984; Rosellini, DeCola & Warren, 1986; Rosellini, Warren & DeCola, 1987; Schulz, 1987). Results from these very well-controlled animal-learning experiments indicate that control over an aversive situation prevents anxiety and behavioural deficits better than certainty about a situation (Maier & Warren, 1988; Rosellini et al., 1986). These results suggest that control is more important than certainty in determining anxiety, at least in animals. If this also holds for humans, it can be hypothesised that a rational belief will lead to more functional inferences if its theme is control than if its theme is certainty. In addition, it can be hypothesised that an irrational belief will produce more dysfunctional inferences if its theme is control rather than certainty.

With regards to control and certainty experiments that employed human subjects, two of these experiments indicated that a controllable and certain situation prevents negative emotions and behavioural problems equally well (Burger & Arkin, 1980; Schulz, 1976), One experiment, however, demonstrated that a controllable situation prevents anxiety better than a certain one (Geer & Maisel, 1972). Although equivocal, these results might indicate that certainty and control are equally effective in preventing negative emotions.

When developing the hypothesis for the present experiments regarding the effect of control and certainty on the functionality of inferences, conclusions from the animal subjects experiments were used, rather than the contradictory, yet equivocal, conclusions from the human subjects' data. The reasons for this decision were: (1) there are fewer experiments with human subjects than there are with animal ones that compare control and certainty; and (2) the human subjects experiments are not as well controlled, nor are the control and certainty situations as systematically varied, as they are in the animal experiments. In summary, then, it was hypothesised that, for the present experiments: (1) rational beliefs will lead to more functional inferences if their theme is control than if their theme is certainty; and (2) irrational beliefs will produce more dysfunctional inferences if their theme is control rather than certainty.

The four experiments

Four experiments by Bond and Dryden (in preparation) attempted to determine how control, certainty, ego and discomfort contents (which will be referred to as the contents) interacted with rational and irrational beliefs to affect the functionality of inferences (FI) that people formed. (In this chapter, for simplicity's sake, the term 'beliefs × contents' is used to refer to the interaction of rational and irrational beliefs and their contents.) The effect of 'beliefs × contents' on the FI was examined in four experiments that varied in terms of: (1) whether 'beliefs × contents' referred to the self (for example, 'I must control *my* anxiety') or others (for example, 'I must control *other people*'s opinion of me'); and (2) whether 'beliefs × contents' referred to the self or others in a social context (for example, going to talk to a person in a bar) or a personal context (for example, trying to fall asleep, alone). (When the beliefs about self or others are referenced, these will be called belief objects.) Since 'beliefs × contents' referred to distinct belief objects and contexts, these experiments could determine whether or not 'belief × contents' affected FI patterns similarly, regardless of type of belief, type of context and their interaction.

Method

The methodology employed in each of Bond and Dryden's (in preparation) four experiments was the same, and it is briefly discussed below. Only two differences existed between each experiment, and these were: (a) type of belief objects employed, that is, whether 'beliefs × contents' referred to the self or others; and (b) type of content employed, that is, whether 'beliefs × contents' referred to the self or others in a personal or a social context.

Subjects

Ninety-six male ($N = 48$) and female ($N = 48$) students between the ages of 18 and 28 years served as subjects in each of the Bond and Dryden (in preparation) experiments.

Design

The design of each study was a 2×2×2 factorial design in which there were three independent variables, each having two levels. These three independent variables were: (a) rationality: whether the subject held a rational or an irrational belief; (b) category: whether their belief content was in the discomfort or ego category; and (c) whether their belief content was control or certainty.

The three independent variables, with two levels each, formed eight 'beliefs × contents' conditions into one of which subjects were randomly assigned. As will be recalled, these conditions were the same in all four experiments. The only difference in the various 'beliefs × contents' conditions existed between experiments; and this difference was whether the 'beliefs × contents' referred to the subjects, or to other people. Examples of 'beliefs × contents' that referred to one's self (that is, the subjects) are as follows:

1   *An irrational discomfort disturbance control belief.* I must absolutely control my anxiety; not having such control would be unbearable.

2   *A rational discomfort disturbance control belief.* I would prefer to control my anxiety, but it is not essential; not having such control would be difficult to tolerate, but not unbearable.

3   *An irrational ego control belief.* I must absolutely control my anxiety; not having such control would make me an inadequate individual.

4   *A rational ego control belief.* I would prefer to control my anxiety, but it is not essential; not having such control would make me a fallible person, not an inadequate individual.

Examples of beliefs that referred to other people are as follows:

5   *An irrational discomfort disturbance certainty belief.* I must be absolutely certain of people's opinion of me; not having such certainty would be unbearable.

6   *A rational discomfort disturbance certainty belief.* I would prefer to be certain of people's opinion of me, but it is not essential; not having such certainty would be difficult to tolerate, but not unbearable.

7   *An irrational ego certainty belief.* I must be absolutely certain of people's opinion of me; not having such certainty would make me an inadequate individual.

8   *A rational ego certainty belief.* I would prefer to be certain of people's opinion of me, but it is not essential; not having such certainty would make me a fallible person, not an inadequate individual.

Subjects in each 'beliefs × contents' condition were asked to imagine themselves in a context that was either social or personal. The social context was: you are sitting in the Union bar and notice a person whom you find attractive. You decide to talk to that person so you get up to do so. As you're walking over, you notice yourself getting fairly anxious. Unlike the scenario for the social context, there were two scenarios for the personal context. Specifically, there was one scenario for subjects who held a self-related belief in a personal context (You are currently preparing to go to sleep. You notice yourself getting fairly anxious because you have had difficulty falling asleep for the past few nights, and tonight, you do not wish to have this problem); and there was another scenario for subjects who held a belief that related to other people in a personal context (You are currently sitting in your bedroom revising for an exam. You begin to wonder whether or not people think that you can succeed in your chosen career, and you notice yourself getting fairly anxious). The reason that the personal context differs between belief objects (self and other people) and the social context does not is that the authors thought that two different personal contexts were necessary if the belief objects were to relate realistically with the personal contexts. It was thought, however, that both belief objects could relate very realistically to the same social context.

In summary, in each experiment, 'beliefs × contents' referred to the self or other people in either a social or a personal context. Specifically, in the first experiment, the beliefs referred to the self (for example, 'I must absolutely control my anxiety . . .'), in a stressful context that was *social* (becoming anxious about going over to talk with an attractive person in a bar). In the second experiment, the beliefs referred to other people (for example, I must absolutely control people's opinion of me . . .'), in a stressful context that was also *social* (becoming anxious about going over to talk with an attractive person in a bar). In the third experiment, the beliefs, again, referred to the self (for example, 'I must absolutely control my anxiety . . .'), but in a stressful context that was *personal* (going to sleep alone, and becoming anxious about not being able to fall asleep). Finally, in the fourth experiment, the beliefs referred to other people (for example, 'I must absolutely control people's opinion of me . . .'), in a stressful context that was *personal* (becoming anxious whilst revising for an exam and wondering whether or not people think that they [the subject] can succeed in their chosen field). Thus, Bond and Dryden's (in preparation) experiments ensured that 'beliefs × contents' referred to the self and other people in a *social* and a *personal* context; and by doing this, it could be determined whether or not 'beliefs × contents' produced different FI patterns when they referred to different belief objects and contexts.

Measure

In each Bond and Dryden (in preparation) experiment, subjects rated the extent of their agreement to 14 dysfunctional inferences, all of which were on a nine-point Likert-type scale (1 = not at all agree; 9 = agree to a great extent). Subjects who rated an inference with a 9 created a very dysfunctional inference. Those who rated an inference with a 1 formed a very functional inference. In the four experiments, two different measures were used: one of them assessed inferences that related to the social situation; and the other assessed inferences that related to the personal situation. Inferences on both measures were developed by the authors.

Procedure

Space limitations preclude a detailed presentation of the procedure used in the Bond and Dryden (in preparation) experiments; however, in summary, subjects were first given a rationale for each experiment that sought to decrease the demand characteristics associated with this role-playing paradigm; and they were then handed a card with one of the eight belief conditions mentioned above. The experimenter then said, 'This is a belief which I would like you to imagine having during this study. As you can see, it reads . . . Now, if you will please take a minute and imagine yourself holding this belief.'

Subjects were then told, 'I am going to read you a scenario, and I would like you to imagine yourself in this situation while holding your belief.' The experimenter then read the scenario that was appropriate to the subjects' condition.

Subjects were then told: 'Take a minute to imagine yourself in this situation while holding your belief.' Subjects were then asked, 'On a scale from one to nine, to what extent can you picture yourself in this situation, while holding your belief? One means that to no extent can you picture yourself in this situation. Nine means that you can picture yourself in this situation to a great extent.' If the answer was less than seven to this question, they were thanked for volunteering but took no further part in the study. The authors considered that subjects who answered the question with less than a seven could not imagine their role well enough to manipulate the independent variable; therefore, in order to maximise the external validity and reliability of the experimental results, these subjects were dismissed for the experiment. It should be noted that there did not appear to be a differential loss of subjects between the eight comparison conditions in any of the four experiments.

Subjects who answered seven or above to this question were given a card with the relevant scenario on it. They were then asked to complete the rating scale, referring to both cards before completing each question. The last statement on the questionnaire was another manipulation check, and if subjects' ratings on this last item fell below seven, their data were excluded from the study; they were excluded, as subjects were at the first exclusion point, in order to maximise the external validity and reliability of the experimental results.

A post-experimental manipulation check was conducted after the subjects had been debriefed.

Results

Results from the four Bond and Dryden (in preparation) experiments indicated similar FI patterns across type of belief object and context. First, in each experiment, there was a main effect for the rationality factor, such that subjects who held irrational beliefs formed significantly more dysfunctional inferences than did subjects who held rational beliefs (these particular results replicated earlier findings by Dryden et al.: Dryden, Ferguson & Clark, 1989; Dryden, Ferguson & Hylton, 1989; Dryden, Ferguson & McTeague, 1989). In addition, ego and discomfort contents did not interact with rational and irrational beliefs to affect the FI in any of the experiments. Control and certainty contents, however, always interacted with rational and irrational beliefs to affect the FI. These interactions resulted from certainty contents producing different inference functionalities for rational and irrational beliefs. Specifically, in each of the four experiments, subjects who held a certainty content formed significantly more functional inferences if they held a rational, rather than an irrational, belief. With a control content, however, subjects who held a rational belief and those who held an irrational belief formed inference functionalities that were not statistically different.

Therapeutic suggestions for people with dysfunctional inferences: Focus on irrational beliefs

The findings from Bond and Dryden's (in preparation) experiments, like the results from the Dryden et al. experiments (Dryden, Ferguson & Clark, 1989; Dryden, Ferguson & Hylton, 1989; Dryden, Ferguson & McTeague, 1989), supported REBT's (for example, Ellis, 1994, Walen, DiGiuseppe & Dryden, 1992) recommendation that clients challenge their core irrational beliefs from the outset of therapy. After all, Bond and Dryden's (in preparation) experiments demonstrated that rational and irrational beliefs greatly affect the way that people perceive and interpret their environment. Knowing this, REBT's recommendation that irrational beliefs should be challenged from the beginning of therapy makes sense. For, by challenging irrational beliefs, clients address a major determinant of their negatively distorted inferences and emotional disturbances; and thus avoid the much less effective strategy of identifying and correcting distorted inferences before challenging irrational beliefs.

In addition, if clients were to focus their attention on correcting each individual dysfunctional inference, there is no guarantee that this corrective process would change irrational beliefs into rational ones; and this change is necessary in order to stem the flow of dysfunctional inferences. In the worst case, then, clients who focus on correcting unhelpful inferences are trying to prevent their kitchen from flooding by bailing water, instead of by fixing the broken pipe which is producing the flow; in this case, no matter how much water these clients bail out, there is still more water flowing in with which they will need to deal. It should be noted that dysfunctional inferences can be challenged after clients' irrational beliefs have been modified to rational ones; however, as Dryden and Ellis (1987) indicate, if people adopt rational beliefs, then their inferences are unlikely to be dysfunctional.

An example of why rational and irrational beliefs should be challenged before dysfunctional inferences

For an example of the ineffective therapy that can result if clinicians only correct inferences, consider John, who is a 30-year-old married man (with no children) who commutes 30 minutes into London each day. From the railway station, John travels the Underground for approximately 15 minutes (changing once), until he arrives at his advertising job. Upon arriving, he is usually exhausted from the journey, but greatly relieved that he has not met with harm during his travel. John is very worried (or has dysfunctional inferences) that his train and tube carriages will meet with disaster whilst he is riding in them. He is particularly afraid that the tube will be bombed, and then his carriage will be stuck, alight, in between two stations. Whether he imagines himself on a train or on a tube carriage, John's primary worry is that he will not be able to escape a disaster. He attempts to prevent himself from worrying but finds himself unable to do so successfully. As a result, John considers his worries to be 'out of control', which makes him even more anxious. (It should be noted that John's perception of his worries being 'out of control' is noted in many people who have these distressing inferences. For example, research by Tallis, Davey and Capuzzo (1994) has shown that people with worries often feel that their negative thoughts are uncontrollable.)

John sought psychotherapy for his worries, and his therapist showed him how the inferences that he formed about various aspects of his journey were distorted. He was asked to keep thought records of his inferences and then indicate how each one was distorted. For example, John identified one of his dysfunctional inferences as: 'When the tube train stops between stations for a period of time, then something is dreadfully wrong.' After writing down this inference, John decided which type of distortion it reflected; and he concluded that it represented a 'jumping to conclusions', or 'arbitrary inference' distortion. After John mastered this task, he was asked to indicate the evidence for this distorted thought, and, upon failure to do so, he created a new thought that was more reflective of the actual situation: 'When the tube train stops between stations for a period of time, this does not mean that something is dreadfully wrong.' John continued to identify his many distorted inferences for about two months, but he still did not feel sufficiently relieved from his inferences (worries) whilst commuting. According to REBT and cognitive therapy (CT), this is not surprising, because during those two months of therapy, John was not addressing a primary determinant of his distorted inferences: his irrational beliefs.

As Bond and Dryden (in preparation) and Dryden et al.'s (Dryden, Ferguson & Clark, 1989; Dryden, Ferguson & Hylton, 1989; Dryden, Ferguson & McTeague, 1989) experiments indicated, the dysfunctional inferences from which John was suffering resulted, at least in part, from his irrational beliefs. Therefore, identifying and correcting John's distorted inferences was not preventing other ones from arising, or the same ones from returning frequently. After all, correcting distorted inferences does not correct the irrational beliefs that lead to the dysfunctional inferences. John's therapist would have been more helpful if he or she had taught him to change his irrational beliefs into rational ones; because then John's dysfunctional inferences and emotions would have probably become more functional more quickly, or at least he could have challenged them more effectively.

The role of external events in emotions, inferences and psychotherapy

When discussing Bond and Dryden's (in preparation) experiments, and John's problem, it is easy to overemphasise the effect of irrational beliefs on the production of dysfunctional inferences. Whilst this effect is hypothesised to be the most significant determinant of inferences and emotions, REBT and CT purport that the environment is also an important contributor (Beck, 1976; Ellis, 1962, 1994; Hollon, 1993). In fact, the hypothesis that environment is an important element in producing emotions and inferences has been demonstrated in experiments by cognitive-behavioural psychologists. For example, experiments have shown that severe situations can contribute to the production of dysfunctional emotions (Försterling, 1985) and dysfunctional inferences (Dryden, Ferguson & Clark, 1989; Dryden, Ferguson & Hylton, 1989; Dryden, Ferguson & McTeague, 1989).

Whilst it may be tempting for therapists to identify and change dysfunctional external stressors, REBT (Ellis, 1994) argues that irrational beliefs should be the main focus of psychological intervention. In fact, Ellis (1994) suggests that changes in people's environment should be forestalled until their irrational beliefs about it have been changed to rational ones. The rationale for this suggestion is that when people possess rational beliefs, their inferences about external situations are more realistic; and changes that they might have made when they had irrational beliefs would not necessarily be made whilst they hold rational ones.

In summary, research by Bond and Dryden (in preparation) and Dryden et al. (Dryden, Ferguson & Clark, 1989; Dryden, Ferguson & Hylton, 1989; Dryden, Ferguson & McTeague, 1989) indicated that rational beliefs lead to functional inferences and irrational beliefs lead to dysfunctional inferences; therefore, clinicians would do well to avoid altering their clients' dysfunctional inferences until they have helped them change their irrational beliefs to rational ones. For, by concentrating therapy at the rational and irrational beliefs level, clinicians intervene at the root of an emotional problem and therefore minimise the time that clients have to endure dysfunctional inferences and unhealthy negative emotions.

Intervening with people who have irrational control and certainty beliefs

The experiments by Bond and Dryden (in preparation) showed that rational and irrational beliefs interacted with control and certainty contents to affect significantly the functionality of inferences. Specifically, in each of the four experiments, subjects who held a certainty belief formed more functional inferences if they held that belief rationally rather than irrationally. Interestingly, subjects who held control beliefs formed inferences that were functionally similar, regardless of whether they held a rational or an irrational belief about control.

These results indicated that the functionality of inferences produced by a certainty content is influenced by the rationality of the certainty belief; but the functionality of inferences produced by a control content is unaffected by the rationality of the control belief. These findings suggest, therefore, that clients who have an irrational certainty belief can be effectively helped by cognitive interventions that attempt to change that belief to a rational one. Interestingly, clients who hold an irrational control belief may have to be helped using interventions that do not involve changing their irrational control belief to a rational one.

Bond and Dryden's (in preparation) results also indicated that rational certainty beliefs produced inferences that were more functional than those that were produced by rational control beliefs, in three out of the four experiments. Only when rational beliefs referred to another person in a social situation (other-social) did having a control or a certainty content lead to inferences of equal functionality. Thus, it appears that, in most cases, having rational certainty beliefs may help clients produce inferences that are the most functional; and even when rational beliefs refer to another person in a social context, holding a rational certainty belief will not produce inferences of the situation that are less functional than those that are produced by a rational control belief.

Therapeutic recommendations for clients with control beliefs

It was noted that Bond and Dryden's (in preparation) experiments suggested that people who held a rational control belief formed inferences that were as dysfunctional as those who held an irrational control belief. Thus, it appears that people who have a demand for control should not be encouraged to adopt a desire for control. Instead, it is recommended that clinicians attempt to help their clients who have a demand for control adopt a strategy that Wells and Matthews (1994, p. 305) call 'disconnected mindfulness' or passively 'letting go' of thoughts. Wells and Matthews propose the therapeutic strategy of disconnected mindfulness as a result of their cognitive model of emotional disorders. Their model is not discussed here, but, instead, their therapeutic strategy of passively letting go is described, and it is shown how this technique can be applied in a clinical context.

Adopting a strategy of disconnected mindfulness

When a therapist encounters clients with irrational control beliefs, Bond and Dryden's (in preparation) research indicates that challenging these beliefs would be ineffective in making their inferences (and perhaps their emotions) more functional. Instead, it is recommended that therapists attempt to teach their clients how to adopt a strategy of disconnected mindfulness with regards to their control beliefs. To appropriate this strategy, clients should be taught to detach themselves emotionally from their beliefs and observe them objectively, as if they were words that were being displayed on a cinema or television screen. By employing this objective observation or disconnected mindfulness strategy, Wells and Matthews (1994) hypothesise that clients with anxiety can increase the probability that their control beliefs will not produce a full-blown emotional and physiological reaction; and without these strong reactions, clients may be able to remain in anxiety-provoking situations long enough to disconfirm their beliefs that they must have control over their emotions and/or external environment.

Adopting a strategy of disconnected mindfulness: An example

As noted previously, John, who is fearful of travelling by train or by the Underground, is particularly disturbed that his worries are 'out of control', which, according to REBT, result from his demand that he control his thoughts. As the research of Bond and Dryden (in preparation) indicates, it is probably not helpful to challenge John's irrational belief that he must control his thinking. Instead, John's therapist should encourage him to observe objectively his control belief whilst he is riding the tube. Specifically, John can be told only to observe the control beliefs that develop in his mind when he rides the tube, without trying to affect (or control) them in any way. John's therapist can propose to him that by watching and passively letting go of his control beliefs he can decrease their frequency and magnitude, and by decreasing their frequency and magnitude John's behaviour of disconnected mindfulness can be negatively reinforced. Eventually, John can disconfirm his belief that he must try to control his thoughts lest they get out of control.

To teach John how to adopt a strategy of disconnected mindfulness, his therapist can encourage him to watch the thoughts that enter into his consciousness as if they were on a cinema or television screen. Whilst watching these thoughts from an objective vantage-point, or an emotional distance, he can, with practice, note that his thoughts are merely words that materialise on a screen, and that they are not accurate heralds of impending doom. Eventually, it is hoped, John will notice that his thoughts begin to occupy less time and space on his cinema or television screen.

After John is taught this disconnected mindfulness strategy, he and his therapist can set up experiments where John is instructed to test two hypotheses: (1) if I try to control and regulate my distressing thoughts, then I will become more relaxed and my worries will decrease in frequency; alternatively, (2) if I do not try to control my worries, but just watch and note them, then I will become more relaxed and my worries will decrease in frequency. To test these two hypotheses, John can be asked to implement the strategies that are implied by them. That is, on six journeys he can attempt to control his worries, and on another six he can try only to observe them objectively. After each journey, John can note his anxiety level and the percentage of time that he engaged in worrisome thoughts.

With his therapist, John can then decide which of the two strategies led to the least worries and the smallest percentage of time engaged in worrying. John can then be able to decide for himself which hypothesis and strategy fit the 'data' best.

Following the implementation of this disconnected mindfulness strategy, a clinician can ensure that rational certainty beliefs are promoted, which, as Bond and Dryden (in preparation) showed, have the ability to provide very functional inferences.

Therapeutic recommendations for clients with irrational certainty beliefs: An example of how to change an irrational certainty belief into a rational one

It is possible that John's inference about dying in an inescapable disaster will be made more functional by learning techniques to minimise his desire for control. This possibility might be likely if John holds a rational certainty belief about successfully escaping disasters. Thus, if John were to believe: 'I would like to be certain that I will not die in a train or tube disaster; but if I cannot have such certainty, I will be able to tolerate not knowing', he will probably produce functional inferences.

If John does not hold a rational certainty belief, but, instead, holds an irrational one, the Bond and Dryden (in preparation) experiments indicated that he would probably form very dysfunctional inferences, which would require psychological intervention. In this case, John's irrational certainty belief can be challenged directly, in order to change it into a rational belief that would lead to very functional inferences. After all, Bond and Dryden's experiments showed that people formed inferences that were significantly more functional if they held a rational belief about certainty rather than an irrational one.

Should John have an irrational certainty belief that requires challenging, the normal REBT methods of doing so can be employed (for example, Ellis, 1994; Walen et al., 1992). This chapter will examine below, however, some evidence by Bond (in preparation) that suggests that the normal REBT challenging methods may not lead to the most functional inferences in people with irrational certainty beliefs. Challenging methods that do lead to functional inferences in people who hold irrational certainty beliefs will be discussed in the next section.

In summary, the experiments by Bond and Dryden (in preparation) indicate that changing irrational control beliefs to rational control ones does not produce inferences that are more functional; however, changing irrational certainty beliefs to rational certainty ones does result in inferences that are significantly more functional. In therapy, it is recommended that irrational certainty beliefs be challenged with the multitude of techniques available in the REBT armamentarium. With irrational control beliefs, challenging the need for control is not recommended. Instead, it is recommended that clinicians attempt to help their clients adopt a strategy of disconnected mindfulness towards their control beliefs.

Challenging an irrational certainty belief: Recommendations based upon research

An experiment by Bond (in preparation) indicates an effective way to challenge irrational certainty beliefs; however, before this experiment and its recommendations are discussed, it will be helpful to define two concepts that are referred to frequently in this discussion. These concepts are 'necessary' and 'sufficient', and they are defined in the context of how factors (for example, beliefs) relate to the FI.

Defining the terms 'necessary' and 'sufficient'

If a factor is *necessary* to affect the FI, then this factor must be present in order for the FI to be affected. Thus, if the presence of a factor (F) is necessary in order for the FI to be affected, then in terms of formal logic this means: if FI then F, or, in mathematical terms, probability (F/FI) = 1.00 (Abramson, Alloy & Metalsky, 1988). Furthermore, if a factor is necessary for the FI to be affected, then this means that the FI cannot be affected if the factor (F) is not present. So, in terms of formal logic, this means if $\overline{F}$ then $\overline{FI}$, and in mathematical terms it means probability (FI/$\overline{F}$) = .00. (It should be noted that a bar, ‾, over a term such as FI or F indicates the absence of what that term represents; thus, in the above example, $\overline{F}$ indicates that a necessary factor is not present, and $\overline{FI}$ indicates that the FI is not affected.) It should be noted that if a factor is present that is necessary to affect the FI, it does follow that the FI will actually be affected. For, if the FI is to be affected, then both a (a) necessary and a (b) sufficient factor need to be present.

If a factor is *sufficient* to affect the FI, then this factor guarantees that the FI will be affected. Thus, if the presence of a factor (F) is sufficient to affect the FI, then in terms of formal logic this means if F then FI, or, in mathematical terms, probability (FI/F) = 1.00 (Abramson et al., 1988). In addition, if a factor (F) is sufficient to affect the FI, then if the FI is not affected, the factor (F) cannot be present; thus, in terms of formal logic, this means if $\overline{FI}$ then $\overline{F}$, and, in mathematical terms, this means probability (F/$\overline{FI}$) = .00. It should be noted that if a factor is sufficient to affect the FI, this factor does not have to be present in order for the FI to be affected (because another sufficient factor can be present); thus, a sufficient factor is not, by definition, a necessary one. It is possible, of course, that a sufficient factor can also be a necessary one, but this need not be the case. In addition, a factor can be necessary but not sufficient to affect the FI. In summary, then, the FI will be affected under the following conditions: (1) if there is a sufficient factor present, or (2) if there is a necessary and sufficient factor present; however, the FI will not be affected if there is a necessary (but not a sufficient) factor present.

In applying the concepts 'necessary' and 'sufficient' to the relationship of beliefs to the FI, it can be said that REBT, as well as other cognitive-behavioural therapies, such as CT, view beliefs as sufficient but not necessary to affect the FI (Abramson et al., 1988). For, whilst REBT (Ellis, 1994) and CT (Beck, 1976) maintain that beliefs are sufficient to affect the FI, they maintain that it is possible that the FI can be affected as a result of factors that do not involve beliefs (for example, biological factors and environmental stimuli).

Necessary and sufficient: How these terms relate to the experiment by Bond

The four experiments by Bond and Dryden (in preparation) demonstrated that rational and irrational beliefs (which will be referred to as beliefs) affect the FI; and these beliefs also interact with control and certainty contents to affect the FI. The experiment by Bond (in preparation) examined the rational and irrational beliefs that produced these effects in the Bond and Dryden experiments; and it attempted to determine whether or not it is necessary for these beliefs to refer to musts and preferences, if they are to affect the FI. It should be made clear that the previous sentence means that the Bond experiment examined whether or not it is *necessary* for beliefs to refer to the terms 'must' and 'prefer' (which represent demands and preferences) if those beliefs are to affect the FI. Stated another way, the following two beliefs comprised the rationality variable that had a significant main effect on the FI in the Bond and Dryden experiments: 'I must be absolutely certain of other people's opinions of me; not having such certainty would make me an inadequate individual'; and 'I would prefer to be certain of other people's opinions of me, but it is not essential; not having such certainty would make me a fallible person, but not an inadequate individual.' This experiment examines whether or not it is *necessary* for these beliefs to refer to the terms 'must' and 'prefer' if the rationality variable is to affect the FI; after all, it may be sufficient for these beliefs to refer to the terms 'inadequate' and 'not inadequate' (which are, respectively, the dysfunctional and functional contents of these beliefs) if the rationality variable is to affect the FI (and, in fact, this hypothesis is consistent with CT theory). Stated yet another way, the Bond experiment examines whether or not beliefs can affect the FI if the beliefs make no explicit references to demands and preferences, but only refer to functional and dysfunctional contents.

As suggested above, in contrast to REBT, CT posits that beliefs do not have to refer to demands and preferences if those beliefs are to affect the FI. Rather, CT hypothesises that it is necessary and sufficient for beliefs to refer to functional and dysfunctional contents if those beliefs are to affect the FI. As can be seen, and will be made more clear below, the experiment by Bond (in preparation) compared the effects of REBT- and CT-related beliefs on the FI; and in so doing, it showed what type of belief structure (CT- or REBT-related) would be most helpful in producing functional inferences.

The functionality of inferences produced by REBT and CT core beliefs: Bond's experiment

As indicated above, a belief with a REBT-related structure explicitly refers to an evaluation that is represented by either a demand (that is, the term 'must') or a preference (that is, the term 'prefer'). In contrast, a CT-related belief structure does not explicitly refer to an evaluation, rather, it only refers to either a functional content (for example, 'I am *adequate*') or a dysfunctional concept (for example, 'I am *inadequate*'). Bond's (in preparation) experiment fully crossed functional and dysfunctional beliefs with REBT- and CT-related belief structures. This resulted in four conditions into which subjects were randomly assigned:

1 *A dysfunctional belief with an REBT structure.* I must be absolutely certain of people's opinion of me; not having such certainty would make me an inadequate individual.
2 *A dysfunctional belief with a CT structure.* If I am not certain of people's opinion of me, then I am an inadequate individual.
3 *A functional belief with an REBT structure.* I would prefer to be certain of people's opinion of me, but it is not essential; not having such certainty would make me a fallible person, not an inadequate individual.
4 *A functional belief with a CT structure.* If I am not certain of people's opinion of me, then I am a fallible person, not an inadequate individual.

The methodology of this experiment is exactly the same as that used in the four experiments by Bond and Dryden (in preparation), which were discussed above. In this experiment by Bond (in preparation), subjects were asked to imagine themselves in the social situation that was described above, namely: you are sitting in the Union bar and notice a person whom you find attractive. You decide to talk to that person so you get up to do so. As you're walking over, you notice yourself getting fairly anxious.

Results

Results indicated a main effect for the functionality factor, such that subjects who held dysfunctional beliefs formed inferences that were significantly more dysfunctional than those formed by subjects who held functional beliefs. In addition, the CT and REBT belief structures factor interacted with the functionality factor to affect the FI. Specifically, subjects who held a belief with a CT structure formed inferences that were significantly more functional if the belief was functional rather than dysfunctional. Subjects who held a belief with an REBT structure formed similarly functional inferences, regardless of whether the REBT belief structure was functional or dysfunctional. Furthermore, subjects who held a functional belief formed more functional inferences if the belief had a CT structure than if it had an REBT structure.

It should be noted that these results were unexpected, in light of the Bond and Dryden (in preparation) experiments. For, in these latter experiments, there was a significant difference in the FI between rational certainty and irrational certainty beliefs. This significant difference did not occur in the Bond (in preparation) experiment, and no explanations can be offered as to why this was so. It should be noted, however, that the alpha for every simple effects comparison was set at .025 in the Bond and Dryden and Bond experiments; and this was done in order to comply with statistical recommendations by authors such as Pedhazur and Schmelkin (1991) and Maxwell and Delaney (1990). However, not all researchers comply with this conservative attempt to avoid a Type I error. For those researchers who do not, it is noted that subjects who held functional and dysfunctional beliefs with an REBT structure produced inference functionalities that differed at the $p = .036$ level.

Clinical implications

The results from Bond's (in preparation) experiment indicated that clients would do well to hold functional beliefs with a CT structure rather than with an REBT one. After all, subjects who held a functional belief formed more functional inferences with a CT structure than with an REBT structure. The reason for these results may be twofold. First, REBT may be incorrect in its assertion that beliefs need to refer to demands and preferences, if those beliefs are to affect the functionality of inferences and emotions. Rather, these results appear to indicate that CT may be correct when it posits that it is sufficient for beliefs to refer to functional and dysfunctional contents if those beliefs are to affect the FI.

The second reason for Bond's (in preparation) results may be that the REBT functional belief structure is more cumbersome than the CT functional belief structure; therefore, the CT structure may be easier than the REBT one to employ when disputing dysfunctional beliefs. For example, it may be easier to learn and utilise this functional CT belief: 'If I am not certain of people's opinion of me, then I am a fallible person, not an inadequate individual', than this functional REBT belief: 'I would prefer to be certain of people's opinion of me, but it is not essential; not having such certainty would make me a fallible person, not an inadequate individual.' It should be noted that just because the CT belief structure may be easier to use and understand than is the REBT belief structure, it does not follow that people's core beliefs are actually represented in a CT structure.

Despite the reasons for Bond's (in preparation) results, the clinical implication remains the same: clients would do well to hold functional beliefs with a CT structure rather than an REBT one. When discussing the clinical implications of this experiment, it should be noted that the contents used in these beliefs were ego and certainty. It is, of course, possible that if other contents were used, the FI pattern observed in this experiment would not be replicated. Future research will have to determine this possibility.

When talking with clients, discuss their rational and irrational beliefs with a CT structure

The experiment by Bond (in preparation) suggested that clinicians might consider discussing rational and irrational beliefs with a CT structure with their clients. Thus, with John, who is phobic about travelling by train and tube and has an irrational belief concerning his journeys, a clinician might wish to construct John's irrational belief with a CT structure; for example, 'If I am not certain that my journey will be safe, then that uncertainty would be intolerable.' In addition, John's therapist might wish to have him hold, eventually, a rational belief with a CT structure, such as, 'If I am not certain that my journey will be safe, then I will be able to tolerate this uncertainty.'

These CT-related rational and irrational belief structures will probably be easier for John to understand and employ than ones which use an REBT structure. In particular, note the potential difficulty that John may have in learning and utilising the following rational belief with an REBT structure: 'I would prefer to be certain that my journey will be safe, but I do not need such certainty; not having such certainty would be difficult to endure, but it would not be intolerable.' As can be seen, this rational belief is very cumbersome to say, much less to learn. Moreover, this REBT statement also requires knowledge regarding the putative role of musts in psychological disturbance; a role about which John would probably not come to therapy knowing.

Thus, John would have to be taught a concept which is not (at least immediately) congruent with his perception about how he thinks. Teaching this demandingness theory, then, runs the risk of confusing John and making therapy less effective than it could be. So, if only due to the relative ease involved in teaching beliefs with a CT structure rather than an REBT one, clients may do well to hold functional beliefs with a structure that reflects the former rather than the latter.

In summary, it is unknown whether the results of Bond's (in preparation) experiment reflect (1) the fact that CT is correct in hypothesising that it is not necessary for beliefs to refer to musts and preferences if those beliefs are to affect the FI; (2) the fact that CT-structured beliefs are just more easy to conceptualise than REBT-structured beliefs; or (3) some other reason not mentioned here. Nevertheless, it remains that functional CT-structured beliefs produced inferences that were significantly more functional than those that were produced by rational REBT-structured beliefs; therefore, it is recommended, until empirically demonstrated otherwise, that John and other clients adapt functional CT-structured beliefs and then test out the efficacy of these beliefs in ways described by CT and REBT.

Summary

The experiments by Bond and Dryden (in preparation) indicated that changing irrational control beliefs to rational control ones does not produce inferences that are more functional; however, changing irrational certainty beliefs to rational certainty ones does result in inferences that are significantly more functional. In therapy, it is recommended that irrational certainty beliefs be challenged with the multitude of techniques available in the CT and REBT armamentaria. However, according to Bond's (in preparation) experiment, clients' rational and irrational certainty beliefs should be composed in a way that reflects a CT structure, at least when discussing them with clients. This means that core beliefs should be conveyed to clients without mention of musts and preferences; thus, clients should be encouraged to adopt a belief with the following structure: 'If I am not certain that my journey will be safe, then I can tolerate the anxiety.' For clients who have irrational control beliefs, changing their need for control to a preference is not recommended. Instead, it is recommended that clinicians attempt to help their clients adopt a strategy of disconnected mindfulness toward their irrational control beliefs.

References

Abramson, L.Y., Alloy, L.B., & Metalsky, G.L. (1988). The cognitive diathesis-stress theories of depression: Toward an adequate evaluation of the theories' validities. In L.B. Alloy (Ed.), *Cognitive processes in depression* (pp. 3–30). New York: Guilford.

Barlow, D.H. (1988). *Anxiety and its disorders*. New York: Guilford.

Beck, A.T. (1976). *Cognitive therapy and the emotional disorders*. New York: Meridian.

Beck, A.T., & Emery, G. (1985). *Anxiety disorders and phobias: A cognitive perspective*. New York: Basic Books.

Bond, F.W. (in preparation) Is it necessary for beliefs to refer to musts and preferences, if those beliefs are to affect the functionality of inferences?

Bond, F.W., & Dryden, W. (in preparation) Testing an REBT theory: the effects of rational beliefs, irrational beliefs, and their control or certainty contents on the functionality of inferences 1. in a social context 2. in a personal context.

Burger, J.M., & Arkin, R.M. (1980). Prediction, control, and learned helplessness. *Journal of Personality and Social Psychology, 38*(3), 482–491.

Burgess, P.M. (1990). Toward resolution of conceptual issues in the assessment of belief systems in rational-emotive therapy. *Journal of Cognitive Psychotherapy, 4*(2), 171–183.

DiGiuseppe, R., & Leaf, R.C. (1990). The endorsement of irrational beliefs in a general clinical population. *Journal of Rational-Emotive and Cognitive-Behavior Therapy, 8*(4), 235–247.

Dryden, W., & Ellis, A. (1987). Rational-emotive therapy. In K.S. Dobson (Ed.), *Handbook of cognitive-behavioral therapies* (pp. 214–272). New York: Guilford.

Dryden, W., Ferguson, J., & Clark, T. (1989). Beliefs and inferences: A test of rational-emotive hypothesis: 1. Performing in an academic seminar. *Journal of Rational-Emotive and Cognitive-Behavior Therapy, 7*(3), 119–129.

Dryden, W., Ferguson, J., & Hylton, B. (1989). Beliefs and inferences: A test of rational-emotive hypothesis: 3. On expectations about enjoying a party. *British Journal of Guidance and Counselling, 17*(1), 68–75.

Dryden, W., Ferguson, J., & McTeague, S. (1989). Beliefs and inferences: A test of a rational-emotive hypothesis: 2. On the prospect of seeing a spider. *Psychological Reports, 64*, 115–123.

Ellis, A. (1962). *Reason and emotion in psychotherapy*. New York: Lyle Stuart.

Ellis, A. (1977). The basic clinical theory of rational-emotive therapy. In A. Ellis & R. Grieger (Eds.), *Handbook of rational-emotive therapy* (pp. 3–34). New York: Springer.

Ellis, A. (1979). Discomfort anxiety: A new cognitive behavioral construct. Part 1. *Rational Living, 14*(2), 3–8.

Ellis, A. (1980). Discomfort anxiety: A new cognitive behavioral construct, Part 2. *Rational Living, 15*(1), 25–30.

Ellis, A. (1994). *Reason and emotion in psychotherapy* (rev. and expanded ed.). New York: Birch Lane Press.

Ellis, A., & Whiteley, J.M. (Eds.). (1979). *Theoretical and empirical foundations of rational-emotive therapy*. Monterey, CA: Brooks/Cole.

Försterling, F. (1985). Rational-emotive therapy and attribution theory: An investigation of the cognitive determinants of emotions. *British Journal of Cognitive Psychotherapy, 3*(1), 12–25.

Geer, J.H., & Maisel, E. (1972). Evaluating the effects of the prediction–control confound. *Journal of Personality and Social Psychology, 23*, 314–319.

Hollon, S.D. (1993). Controversies in cognitive therapy: A dialogue with Aaron T. Beck and Steve Hollon. *Journal of Cognitive Psychotherapy, 7*(2), 79–93.

Lazarus, R.S. (1991). *Emotion and adaptation*. New York: Oxford.

Maier, S.F., & Warren, D.A. (1988). Controllability and safety signals exert dissimilar proactive effects on nociception and escape performance. *Journal of Experimental Psychology: Animal Behavior Processes, 14*, 18–25.

Maxwell, S.E., & Delaney, H.D. (1990). *Designing experiments and analyzing data*. Belmont, CA: Wadsworth.

Mineka, S., Cook, M., & Miller, S. (1984). Fear conditioned with escapable and inescapable shock: Effects of a feedback stimulus. *Journal of Experimental Psychology: Animal Behavior Processes, 10*, 307–324.

Pedhazur, E.J., & Schmelkin, L.P. (1991). *Measurement, design and analysis: An integrated approach*. Hillsdale, NJ: Erlbaum.

Rosellini, R.A., DeCola, J.P., & Warren, D.A. (1986). The effect of feedback stimuli on contextual fear depends upon the length of the minimum ITI. *Learning and Motivation, 17*, 229–242.

Rosellini, R.A., Warren, D.A., & DeCola, J.P. (1987). Predictability and controllability: Differential effects upon contextual fear. *Learning and Motivation, 18*, 51–58.

Schulz, R. (1976). Effects of control and predictability on the physical and psychological well-being of the institutionalized aged. *Journal of Personality and Social Psychology, 33*, 563–573.

Seligman, M.E.P. (1975). *Helplessness: On depression, development and death*. San Francisco: W.H. Freeman.

Tallis, F., Davey, G.C.L., & Capuzzo, N. (1994). The phenomenology of non-pathological worry: A preliminary investigation. In G. Davey & F. Tallis (Eds.), *Worrying: Perspectives on theory, assessment and treatment*. Chichester: Wiley.

Walen, S.R., DiGiuseppe, R., & Dryden, W. (1992). *A practitioner's guide to rational-emotive therapy* (2nd ed.). New York: Oxford.

Wells, A., & Matthews, G. (1994). *Attention and emotion: A clinical perspective*. Hove: Erlbaum.

8

Clients' Perceptual Processing: An Integration of Research and Practice

Shaké G. Toukmanian

In the last two decades, there has been an unprecedented growth in the sophistication of research concerned with the evaluation and understanding of the processes and outcomes of psychotherapy. Recent reviews of this literature (for example,Goldfried, Greenberg & Marmar, 1990; Lambert & Bergin, 1992; Strupp & Howard, 1992) show that diverse research paradigms and quantitative and qualitative research methods and strategies are now being used to examine the efficacy of various systems of psychotherapy for particular kinds of disorders, to discern the unique and common therapeutic ingredients in various therapies, to analyze the processes that mediate client change, and to relate aspects of this change process to therapy outcome. This literature has produced a host of important findings of varying degrees of relevance to practicing psychotherapists. Yet the relationship between knowledge gained through this research and clinical practice still remains elusive to most practitioners.

Surveys of clinical psychologists continue to show that, by and large, therapists do not consider psychotherapy research findings helpful to their practice and that they judge sources such as descriptive accounts of therapy (Morrow-Bradley & Elliott, 1986), discussions of cases with colleagues and workshops on clinical practice (Cohen, Sargent & Sechrest, 1986) as being among the most useful aids to their work as therapists. A typical criticism voiced by all therapists is that psychotherapy research tends to be over-simplified and hence irrelevant because it does not mirror the complexities of the therapeutic endeavor. Most practitioners also share the impression that researchers are concerned mainly with methodology and only secondarily with the practical implications of their findings for therapists (Cohen et al., 1986). These views clearly suggest that if psychotherapy research is to have more of an impact on the actual conduct of therapy it must become relevant to clinical practice. It is my contention that one way to achieve such relevance would be to elucidate the processes through which therapeutic change occurs and transmit this information in a way that would be useful in guiding the work of psychotherapists.

The presentation in this chapter focuses on the practical applications of my program of psychotherapy process research. It begins with a brief overview of my approach to conceptualizing and studying the processes of client change, followed by a description of a series of investigations and the results that have emerged from this perspective. In the final section of the chapter, I discuss and demonstrate the implications of these findings for psychotherapy supervision and practice.

Background and conceptual framework

As therapists, we are aware of the complexities of the therapeutic endeavor. We are aware that each client and each therapy encounter is unique, that each therapy participant has his or her unique experiential history, that transactions have multiple meanings, that some sessions progress better than others, that some events within sessions are more important than others, and that often therapy is only one of the many possible client experiences contributing to positive outcome. But we are also aware that, despite this apparent diversity, therapy is not necessarily chaotic, that there are some clinically perceived regularities in the process, and that whatever it is that we do in therapy is often guided not only by our moment-to-moment responsiveness to what is unique in our clients but also by our 'clinical sensitivity' to what is less unique in our transactions with them.

In view of this complexity, how can the phenomenon of psychotherapeutic change be studied and understood from an ecologically valid perspective? Or more to the point, how can psychotherapy research address the observed regularities in this process across clients without losing sight of the idiosyncrasies in individual clients?

I have attempted to deal with this issue by advancing a framework for psychotherapy research that recognizes the centrality of clients' perceptions and conceptualizes change from the vantage-point of their cognitive–affective processes and structures. This approach is based on the belief that, while the *experience* of change is unique to each client, there are common or core processes underlying this phenomenon for all clients, and that without an understanding of the nature of these processes there can be neither a satisfactory explanation of how psychotherapy brings about change nor a fruitful search for the therapeutic ingredients that account for change in diverse treatments.

Theoretical framework

I have conducted my research within the framework of a model of client perceptual organization and change wherein the phenomenon of change is viewed from a constructive information processing perspective. This model, which has been elaborated upon elsewhere (Toukmanian, 1990, 1992), proposes that psychological dysfunctions are, by and large, difficulties associated with people's inability to process the elements of their experiences more fully and in ways that would help them generate more functional perspectives on self and on self-relevant events in everyday life situations. This view is based on three fundamental propositions. It is postulated that (1) perceiving is the dynamic act of construing and representing one's own view of reality, that (2) individuals are capable of engaging in a variety of mental activities and ways of perceiving that are learned through experience (Neisser, 1967), and that (3) people's perceptions play a significant role in how they act and interact with their environment.

Thus, perception in this model is conceptualized as a schema-driven and experientially based process involving the anticipation, organization and interpretation of information on the basis of past transactions with the world (Mahoney, 1985; Neisser, 1976). The perceptual processing system is viewed as consisting of two interactive components: a *structural* component, which consists of the perceiver's network of schemata relevant to the event being perceived (for example, Anderson, 1981; Fiske & Dyer, 1985; Ingram & Kendall, 1986; Rumelhart, 1984) and an *operational* component entailing the particular mode of information processing used during the event's construction. Schemata pertaining to the event range along a simplicity–complexity dimension, while the mode of processing is either automated or controlled (Shiffrin & Schneider, 1977). The automated mode is pre-reflective and efficient but undiscriminating because it hampers schematic development. The controlled mode, on the other hand, is seen as involving the deliberate and careful enactment of qualitatively different mental operations (scanning, elaborating, differentiating and integrating) on the elements of the event. The model contends that this mode of processing leads to an increasing complexity of schematic structures resulting in fundamental changes in the client's perception of a given experience.

Based on this schematic developmental view of perception, the model maintains that difficulties experienced by clients are the function of construals (particularly those of self and of self-in-relation to others in everyday life situations) that are formulated through a predominantly automated mode of processing applied to simple or undiscriminating schemata. The model contends that when people are repeatedly exposed to situations that contain redundant or highly familiar information (for example, interpersonal encounters, subjective reactions, certain characteristics of familiar environments, etc.) they learn, for the sake of efficiency, to process this kind of information automatically or non-reflectively. Environments may contain familiar information and appear similar, but they are almost never identical. Thus, in order to perceive a situation more fully, people also need to process the 'new' or less familiar aspects of the situation in a slow and controlled manner. When they fail to do so, or when they base their perceptions mainly on the automated processing of a narrow range of readily detectable information, their construal of that situation becomes rigid, stereotypical and/or incomplete. This is because automatization in processing impedes the enactment of different mental operations and hampers schematic development. When such construals occur out of context, they generally are dysfunctional or inappropriate because they have neither the breadth nor the flexibility to accommodate the exigencies of different life circumstances. Thus, having limited generalizability and functional value, they led to experiences that are vague, discomforting, devoid of personal meaning and hence troubling for the individual.

According to this conceptualization, therapeutic change occurs through the elaboration and development of the structural and operational components of the client's perceptual processing system (cf. Kelly, 1955). Thus, the central process of therapy is to help clients *learn* to modify, in response to interventions that stimulate their enactment of different kinds of perceptual processing operations, the way in which they construe their experiences of problematic life events (Toukmanian, 1990). Engaging clients in an in-depth exploration of information surrounding such events is seen to be crucial to the development of more complex and differentiated networks of schematic structures and the enhancement of their ability to generate alternative and potentially more functional perspectives that lead to greater flexibility and adjustment.

Research framework

How does one go about investigating the processes that mediate change in clients' perceptions? Are there research strategies and methods that are sufficiently sensitive to the complexities of this process to allow for a more comprehensive understanding of the psychotherapeutic phenomenon?

Currently, there are two basic strategies and their associated methods represented in psychotherapy process research. The majority of studies follow the paradigmatic or positivist tradition of scientific inquiry which prizes objectivity. Research conducted within this framework is deductive, theory-guided and quantitative (Rennie & Toukmanian, 1992). Its focus is on hypothesis testing and on the verification of expected regularities in the occurrence of specific client and therapist performances during therapy. In this approach, change is conceptualized from the standpoint of the researcher in terms of a preferred theory and studied through the application of objectivistic research methods and procedures. Although therapy participants may be called upon to provide information about their experience of therapy, usually such information is solicited indirectly, through self-report measures (for example, rating scales, inventories, etc.) that draw on the researcher's own understanding of the nature of change in psychotherapy (Rennie & Toukmanian, 1992). Thus, a major drawback of the paradigmatic research strategy is that it abrogates the role of the client as a valid source of information about the therapy process, and, in doing so, it limits the possibility of developing a richer and hence a more comprehensive perspective on the phenomenon.

An alternative strategy now available to psychotherapy researchers is the narrative approach to scientific inquiry. Narrative research is atheoretical and qualitative. It is concerned with the exploration of therapy participants' experience of therapy. It is guided by the assumptions of 'human science' (Rennie, 1994), which emphasizes the primacy of human experience, self-awareness and reflexivity and views behavior as the expression of people's intentionality (Rennie, 1992; Rennie & Toukmanian, 1992). Psychotherapy, like any other social interaction, is conceived of as a co-constructive process that can be studied and understood only from the vantage-point of the client's and/or therapist's experience of it. Thus, studies conducted within this framework 'characteristically use natural language both as data and in representation of results; all embrace reports on subjective experience as legitimate data; all typically work with a small number of selected data sources; all emphasize discovery more than verification; all recursively combine inquiry and analysis; and all are interpretive at root' (Rennie, 1994, pp. 237–238). However, as this research strategy aims ostensibly at gaining an understanding of the client's experience of therapy, it runs the risk of being oblivious to the kinds of change processes that occur out of awareness and that may account for some of the regularities observed in clients' performances during therapy.

To the extent that each of these two research strategies offers a unique perspective on the process of therapy, both are important in furthering our understanding of how change occurs in psychotherapy. My earlier attempts at instantiating the paradigmatic strategy and its associated methods in my research proved to be fruitful but insufficient for addressing the complexities of this phenomenon and consequently for improving the conception of therapeutic change advanced in the perceptual processing model. With the advent of the qualitative research methods of the narrative approach as complements to those of the paradigmatic strategy, it has been possible to develop a more effective research strategy constituted of methodological pluralism. As Feyerabend suggests, an investigator 'who wishes to maximize the empirical content of the view he [she] holds and who wants to understand them as clearly as he [she] possibly can must therefore introduce other views; that is he [she] must adopt a pluralistic methodology' (1975, pp. 29–30). This is the perspective taken in my more recent research.

Description of research

The main objective of our program of psychotherapy process research has been to see whether the perceptual processing model is valid as a conceptualization of the processes mediating change in clients' perceptions. The studies described below share this common objective. They differ, however, in terms of research design and methodology, with each study adopting a particular set of research methods for the investigation of this phenomenon.

Changes in self-schemata

One of our earlier attempts at testing the model's hypothesized processes of schematic change was an analogue study by Sander (1990) conducted on a group of undergraduate university students. The study was guided by recent information processing formulations and research concerning the role of self-schemata in the processing and interpretation of self- and other-relevant information. The primary purpose of this investigation was to evaluate the impact of an experimental manipulation, which was derived from the model, on the content and processing efficiency of non-depressed and mildly depressed participants' self-schemata. This involved having participants engage in the guided recall (that is, controlled processing) of personal experiences that were known to be discrepant with their self-perceptions. The prediction based on the model was that having participants engage in the deliberate search for and in-depth analysis of information surrounding experiences that did not fit with their self-conceptions would increase the positive content and enhance the processing efficiency of their self-schemata (for example, Markus & Kunda, 1986; Ross, Lepper & Hubbard, 1975; Toukmanian, 1985). It was also expected that engaging in the guided recall of self-discrepant experiences would have a differential impact on the content and processing efficiency of non-depressed and mildly depressed participants (for example, Kuiper & Derry, 1981; Kuiper, Derry & MacDonald, 1982).

The research design consisted of a positive self-discrepant recall condition, a negative self-discrepant recall condition and a no recall condition for each of the non-depressed and mildly depressed groups. The 120 participants, who were tested for level of depression on the Beck Depression Inventory (BDI; Beck, Rush, Shaw & Emery, 1979), were randomly assigned to these three experimental conditions, each consisting of 20 non-depressed and 20 mildly depressed participants. The content and processing efficiency of each participant's self-schemata were assessed prior to the experimental manipulation and again five days later, using research methods adapted from the social-cognitive literature.

Specifically, participants were asked in the first session to make self-referential judgments on 30 positive and 30 negative personal trait adjectives randomly presented on a personal computer which was pro-grammed to record the respondent's yes/no decision and reaction time for each adjective. This procedure yielded three scores: a score indicating the frequency of positive self-referent judgments ('yes' responses to positive content adjectives and 'no' responses to negative content adjectives) and an average reaction time calculated separately for the positive and negative self-referent decisions. Following this task, the experimenter examined the participant's responses to positive and negative content adjectives. Four responses to adjectives reflecting negative self-referent decisions were selected randomly for each participant in the positive self-discrepant recall condition. For example, the adjective 'self-assured' was presented to a participant in the positive recall condition who had indicated that the adjective 'confident' did not describe her. Conversely, items reflecting positive self-referent decisions were selected for participants in the negative self-discrepant recall condition. Participants were then asked to recall and describe a specific personal experience associated with each of the four adjectives. They were given time to think about each experience and were allowed five minutes to write down their descriptions. The content and processing efficiency of self-schemata were reassessed for all participants in a second session five days later using the same computerized procedure described earlier.

Our findings indicated that, regardless of level of depression, participants who recalled and described positive self-discrepant experiences subsequently displayed greater increases in both the frequency of positive self-referential judgments and the efficiency with which these judgments were made than those in the no recall condition. However, we found that the experimental manipulation did not have an influence on either the content or processing efficiency of participants in the negative self-discrepant recall condition. As well, the expectation based on prior research that mildly depressed participants would engage in an active or controlled mode of processing and hence would be more receptive to self-discrepant information than non-depressed participants was not borne out by the results of our study. In other words, the presence or absence of mild depression was not a factor influencing change in either the content or the processing efficiency of participants' self-schemata.

Overall, the results of this analogue study provided partial support to the basic tenets of the perceptual processing model of therapy (Toukmanian, 1992). However, the finding that participants in the positive but not the negative self-discrepant recall condition responded to the experimental manipulation in the expected direction raised the possibility that the demands put on the perceptual processing system by these two types of experiences, in terms of amount of time and energy required to accommodate self-discrepant information, may differ. Such differences in processing may not be apparent in actual therapy, where a considerable amount of time is devoted to exploring clients' problematic experiences. Thus, the contrived experimental manipulation and the arbitrary time limit imposed on the recall of participants employed in this study may well have precluded the possibility of their attaining a satisfactory resolution of negative experiences.

To illustrate, in response to the adjective 'non-judgmental', a young woman in the positive self-discrepant recall condition remembered an incident when an unmarried friend had expressed the fear that she was pregnant. She recalled that arranging a pregnancy test for her friend, accompanying her to the clinic and being supportive of her during this crisis made her feel quite good about herself. By contrast, in response to the adjective 'non-achieving', a young man in the negative self-discrepant recall condition described his discouraging experiences in elementary school when he was told that he would not be allowed to continue his program and would have to attend a basic level school. He recalled being angry but accepting the situation, believing deep down that he was not intelligent enough to succeed in school. Although his negative feelings were partially alleviated when he subsequently completed high school and was admitted to university, this young man had to contend with a host of enduring negative self-perceptions, including his anger and self-doubt about his intellectual ability, which were not possible to deal with under laboratory conditions. If he were in therapy, he possibly would have benefited from being repeatedly exposed to interventions that, over time, would have stimulated a controlled and more thorough exploration of his negative experiences, leading him to resolve inconsistent self-perceptions and achieve a more positive or accepting view of self. In fact, the results from several of our investigations (for example, Toukmanian, 1988; Toukmanian and Roese, 1989) conducted on actual clients treated by the perceptual processing method of experiential therapy (Toukmanian, 1990) support this contention, which is also substantiated by the findings of Day's (1994) study described below.

Operational changes in clients' processing

We have sought to test our model's basic proposition that therapeutic improvement is associated with changes occurring on the level of clients' perceptual processing operations. In this line of research, we typically have employed the pre-test–treatment–post-test control group design and used external judges to evaluate clients' in-therapy discourse on the Levels of Client Perceptual Processing (LCPP) measure (Toukmanian, 1986). In this coding system, the model's postulated interaction between the structural and operational components of the perceptual processing system is operationalized in terms of seven mutually exclusive categories. Each category depicts a particular pattern of processing which is inferred from the differential quality of clients' verbalizations in therapy. Good processing is characterized by client discourse reflecting construals that are formulated through internally differentiating, re-evaluating and integrating types of mental operations applied to complex schemata (that is, by the upper levels of the taxonomy).

We used this paradigmatic research strategy in one of our recent studies undertaken by Day (1994) to investigate the relationship between clients' level of in-therapy perceptual functioning and treatment outcome. We hypothesized that clients receiving therapy in the perceptual processing method would have greater pre- to post-treatment gains in self-concept and complexity of self-schemata than individuals in a self-help training program serving as the control group. We also predicted that clients with greater improvement in processing ability during therapy would display significantly higher gains in level of self-concept and complexity of self-schemata than those showing less improvement.

The study involved 40 self-referred clients, 20 in each of the treatment and control groups, who were recruited from the population of clients seen at the counseling center of a large urban university. A client's suitability for this research was established in terms of three criteria: (1) absence of thought disorder, suicidal ideation and history of psychiatric hospitalization; (2) a presenting problem that was of an interpersonal nature; and (3) having no prior individual or group therapy experience.

Participants in the treatment group received 10 to 12 hours of individual therapy over a period of 10 weeks, while those in the control group had an equivalent number of contact hours in a self-help skills training group program. Pre- to post-treatment gains were assessed on the Tennessee Self-Concept Scale (TSCS; Fitts, 1965) and on a measure of perceptual congruence (PC) which was used to evaluate structural changes in clients' self-schemata (Toukmanian, 1992). These measures were administered to all participants prior to and shortly after their involvement in the study. All therapy sessions of clients in the treatment group were audio-taped. Two sessions per client were involved in the analyses.

The first session served as a baseline measure of clients' initial level of perceptual functioning. The remaining sessions were examined by the researcher and the session in which the client was judged to have engaged in high levels of processing was identified. From this latter session, a segment reflecting good processing was isolated. As well, a segment of equivalent duration and topic, where possible, was extracted from the first session. The two segments selected in this manner were then transcribed and rated on the LCPP.

We used participants' pre- to post-treatment difference scores on the TSCS and the PC to test the first hypothesis. Consistent with our prediction, results indicated that clients receiving the perceptual processing method of therapy had significantly higher TSCS and PC scores than those in the control group. This evidence in support of the efficacy of the therapeutic approach was particularly meaningful in view of the fact that the control group participants showed some gains as a result of being exposed to a form of group treatment.

To test the second hypothesis, we first determined the proportion of each client's responses that were classified in the upper levels of the LCPP taxonomy for the two therapy segments separately. We then calculated a difference score for each client. A difference score of over 1.5 standard deviations of the group's initial level of processing was used to separate the highly improved from the less improved clients. Similarly, a difference score greater than 0.6 standard deviation of the groups pre-treatment scores on the TSCS and the PC was used to identify the high and low performers on these measures. Our prediction that there would be a significant association between in-treatment improvement in processing ability and gains in level of self-concept and complexity of self-schemata was supported by the result. The findings were consistent with our model's postulation that learning to engage in more complex mental operations (as depicted by the upper levels of the LCPP taxonomy) is crucial for the modification of clients' self-schematic structures, for the enhancement of their self-perceptions and for therapeutic improvement.

The results emerging from this and similar other studies (Toukmanian & Grech, 1991; Toukmanian & Jackson, 1994; Zink, 1990) have been encouraging. However, being based on aggregate research designs, these studies have provided us with probabilistic estimates of the kinds of processes that mediate client change over the course of therapy but with very little information regarding the specific context(s) or the conditions under which these processes occur (Greenberg, 1986). Nor have we been able to ascertain whether these processes are in fact associated with clients' own experience and/or awareness of change at such moments in therapy.

We have attempted to address these issues, at least in part, by using the 'events paradigm' (Rice & Greenberg, 1984) and studying the processes entailed in client change through both qualitative and quantitative research methods. This approach has given us the flexibility with which to study these processes more intensively with a small number of clients, from multiple perspectives and in the context of specific kinds of clinically relevant therapeutic episodes.

To illustrate, in a study undertaken by Sinclair (1990), we attempted to see whether or not and in what way clients' perceptual processing shifted as a function of the introduction into the therapeutic dialogue of a metaphor by either the client or therapist. The study was guided by Angus's (1986) qualitative research on metaphors in psychotherapy wherein two types of metaphorical communications were distinguished. When a communication involving a metaphor led to a deepened understanding between client and therapist through the articulation of the meaning context symbolized by the metaphor, it was termed conjunctive. Conversely, a meaning-disjunctive metaphorical communication was seen as one that led to a mutual mis-understanding (Angus, 1986; Angus & Rennie, 1988, 1989). This classifi-cation based on the facilitative function of the 'metaphor event' taken as a whole was used in our study to determine whether clients differed in the way they processed their experiences before, during and after conjunctive and disjunctive metaphoric episodes.

Consistent with Angus's (1986) findings, our investigation was based on two assumptions. First, we assumed that a metaphoric interaction could be categorized as conjunctive or disjunctive only by gaining access to each therapy participant's implicit meanings associated with such an interaction. Second, we contended that metaphoric communications within a given therapy session would be either conjunctive or disjunctive, depending upon the collaborative or non-collaborative nature of the therapeutic relation-ship. Thus, our study entailed the use of a combination of qualitative and quantitative research methods. The former were used in the selection and specification of metaphoric events as conjunctive or disjunctive, while the latter were used for assessing clients' manner of processing within these events as well as for evaluating the strength of the therapeutic relationship in the sessions in which they occurred.

Six female therapy dyads were recruited from our ongoing programme of psychotherapy research in which clients underwent 10 sessions of perceptual processing experiential therapy. Twelve metaphor events were selected from one of the middle therapy sessions, one therapist- and one client-generated per case. The selection procedure entailed two steps. We first identified a target session for each dyad in which the interactions appeared to reflect, on the basis of clinical judgment, a collaborative or non-collaborative exploration of the client's interpersonal issues. We then identified, within these interactions, a metaphor that captured the issues being explored plus enough of the interaction preceding and following the metaphor to make the sequence a comprehensible unit. Clients' responses in each of these 12 metaphoric events were rated on the LCPP by two external judges. Responses in the two minutes immediately preceding and immediately following an event were also rated and used as control segments. Furthermore, we used Horvath's (1981) Working Alliance Inventory (WAI) with both clients and therapists to obtain information on the strength of the therapeutic relationship in these sessions.

The specification of an event as conjunctive or disjunctive was accomplished by means of an open-ended interview, conducted with each participant, within 24 hours of the target therapy session. In this interview, the audio-tape recordings of both client- and therapist-generated metaphoric events were replayed for each participant separately and in chronological order as they had occurred in the therapy session. After each event was replayed, the participant was asked to recall, in response to a series of open-ended questions, her experience (that is, thoughts, images, feelings, etc.) at that moment in the therapy session. Our descriptive analyses of participants' subjective accounts revealed that six metaphoric events were experienced as being conjunctive and six as being disjunctive. In four of the dyads, both metaphor events were either conjunctive or disjunctive, while in the remaining two, only one of the events was experienced as conjunctive and the other as disjunctive.

Our results also revealed that, by and large, clients exhibited the same pattern of processing regardless of whether the metaphor was generated by the client or the therapist. It was found that in dyads where *both* metaphor events were meaning-*disjunctive* clients' level of perceptual functioning before, during and after the event was predominantly low, involving simple recognition and scanning types of mental operations that were external or factual in their focus. Similarly, in dyads with *mixed* types of metaphors, clients' processing tended to be predominantly low regardless of type of metaphor. However, in dyads where *both* metaphoric events were meaning-*conjunctive*, the pattern was characterized by a shift from a predominantly low mode of processing before the event to an ostensibly high processing *during* the event. In other words, results indicated that during a conjunctive metaphoric event clients typically engaged in the exploration of a given experience through the enactment of internally focused differentiating, re-evaluating and integrating types of mental operations, and that there was a carry-over of this higher level of perceptual processing *after* the event. Furthermore, we found that participants' perception of the strength of the therapeutic relationship tended to be somewhat different, with meaning-conjunctive dyads rating it highly, disjunctive dyads less highly, while those in the conjunctive/disjunctive dyads were mixed in their evaluation. These findings suggest, albeit tentatively, that metaphors may be useful in facilitating a shift from a less productive to a more productive mode of client processing but only when they are meaning-conjunctive and occur within conjunctive-only dyads. More telling perhaps was our finding that, regardless of the direction of change, the subtleties in processing observed by an external judge on the LCPP were verifiable by the clients' own subjective reports of the experience of conjunction and disjunction.

Another illustration of methodological pluralism comes from a pilot study conducted in conjunction with Day's (1994) research described above. Here, instead of selecting a 'change event' in terms of an external source (that is, metaphor events), we used an event or an episode of therapy which was identified by a client as being significant. The main purpose of this exploration was (1) to see whether or not the course of the client's processing in this event was consistent with the kinds of processing operations that are specified by the perceptual processing model as being crucial to therapeutic improvement, and (2) to determine whether the client was aware of her processing strategies when exploring her experiences during the event.

The client was one of the 20 participants involved in Day's (1994) treatment group described earlier. A session from the late phase of therapy was targeted for study. Within 24 hours of this session, a judge located on the audio-tape of this session a segment of the client's dialogue that reflected high levels of processing according to the LCPP taxonomy. Shortly after, an interview was conducted with the client consisting of two phases.

First, the client was asked to think back and consider whether anything significant had occurred at any particular point in the therapy session. The interviewer played the therapy tape and the client identified an event and where the event began and ended on the tape. A non-directive inquiry was then made into the client's recollection of the self-identified most significant event in the session.

In the second phase, the interviewer played the segment of therapy tape that had been previously rated on the LCPP as high level of processing and a non-directive inquiry was made into the client's experience of this event. The purpose of this latter inquiry was to see whether or not the client could spontaneously describe the cognitive strategies that she was engaged in during this segment of therapy. Given that the client was not expected to talk in terms of the constructs of the perceptual processing model, we instituted a 'testing of the limits' component during the last half of this phase of inquiry. At this point, the client was given a broad description of the model and was asked to step outside of herself and look at what she was doing cognitively when talking about her experiences during this segment of therapy. The segment was then replayed and a directed inquiry was made into the client's awareness of cognitive processes or strategies. Both phases of the interview were tape-recorded and submitted to descriptive analysis.

The comparison between the client's initial, spontaneous account of her experience in the self-identified most meaningful segment of therapy and the segment rated independently on the LCPP as high processing were found to be almost identical. The client characterized her experience at that moment in therapy as one of being engaged in an internal dialogue with herself and of coming to a tentative 'realization' that nobody was there for her, that her experience was one of fear and loneliness, that she was afraid of being assertive for fear of rejection, and that she realized that she was not to blame for the interpersonal difficulties she was experiencing with her boyfriend. The pattern of LCPP ratings of the same segment entailed a large percentage of client's responses evaluated as internally differentiating, re-evaluating and integrating, which was compatible with the model's description of the nature and progression of productive processing.

The descriptive analysis of the second phase of the interview concerning the client's awareness of her processing strategies revealed that, initially, the client was unable to grasp the nature of the task when the inquiry was conducted non-directively. However, after she was briefed on some of the underlying assumptions of the perceptual processing model and was asked directly to evaluate what she was doing cognitively in the therapy segment, she was able to become more reflective and to describe, in her own language, the processes involved in her attempts to make sense of her experiences, which, for the most part, were consistent with the LCPP ratings of her responses in the therapy segment under study. However, given that this was a pilot study involving only one client who required a considerable amount of prompting to become aware of her internal processes, this interpretive analysis must be regarded as providing only tentative support for the contention that, on some level at least, clients are aware of the cognitive strategies with which they explore their experiences in therapy.

In summary, to the extent that there is an inferred relationship between our model's postulated processes of client change and those depicted by the LCPP taxonomy, the evidence from the studies described above suggests that changes to clients' manner of communicating in therapy are indicative of changes to the component processes and structures of their perceptual processing system. Our evidence further suggests that these change processes are common or generic across clients and that they are centrally involved in therapy episodes that are reported by clients as being significant and characterized as such by the LCPP ratings of external observers.

Practical implications

The main thrust of the research described above has been the belief that in order to understand how psychotherapy works we need first to delineate the kinds of inferential processes that mediate change in clients' perceptions and then to study these processes in various contexts and from the standpoint of multiple perspectives by means of both quantitative and qualitative research methods. The interplay between these two investigative strategies has allowed us to confirm the general parameters of our model and draw some tentative conclusions concerning the practical implications of our findings for psychotherapy supervision and practice.

Implications for psychotherapy

Client process-oriented approach to therapy If, as our findings suggest, there is a relationship between the manner in which clients process their experiences in therapy and treatment outcome (Day's study above), then it would be useful for practitioners to recognize the importance of not only *what* clients are actually saying but also *how* they are saying what they are saying in therapy. Let me elaborate.

It is safe to say that, as clinicians trained in the methods of mainstream theories of counseling and psychotherapy, most of us attempt to understand the nature of our clients' difficulties by focusing on their accounts (that is, images, thoughts, expressed affect, views, impressions, etc.) or recollections of problematic experiences and circumstances in their life. From an information processing perspective, these accounts are the *end products* (for example, Ingram & Kendall, 1986; Toukmanian, 1992) of our clients' experientially learned ways of representing self in relation to others and events in their environment. Thus, when we listen to them in therapy, what we often do is piece these varying products together and, depending on the particular therapeutic orientation from which we work, draw a global impression or a diagnostic formulation concerning the nature of their intra- and interpersonal difficulties without, however, paying much attention to the *way* in which these products (that is, perceptions of events) are constructed. We may, for example, develop an impression that the client is defensive, clinically depressed or highly anxious, or that he/she is not in touch with feelings, lacks in self-confidence or has a great deal of suppressed anger.

While these theory-based formulations about the client's psychological state *are* important to our work as therapists, they are not sufficiently *specific* to inform us of the kinds of interventions that we need to generate, on a moment-to-moment basis, to facilitate change in the client. After all, therapy is not a social interaction but a therapeutic one, which implies that whatever it is that we say or do in therapy should gradually lead the client to develop a sense of ability to resolve issues and perceive self and others in ways that are not only functional but also personally meaningful and satisfying for him/her.

As conceptualized by the perceptual processing model and supported by our research conducted to date, change appears to take place on the level of clients' information processing operations. If this indeed is the case, then the strategies with which clients construe their experiences at any given moment in therapy can serve as diagnostic guides for the formulation of therapeutic interventions that are specific to each client's dysfunctional *ways* of perceiving. In such an approach, the therapist's actions would be guided by the client's moment-to-moment manner of responding rather than by assumptions or expectations of what needs to be talked about in therapy. Thus, by focusing on specific 'process markers' (Rice & Greenberg, 1984), the therapist's task would be to engage clients in the exploration of their experiences through a controlled mode of processing so that they can differentiate facets of implied meanings in the information being processed and develop new and potentially more functional ways of 'seeing' and interpreting events in everyday life situations (Toukmanian, 1990).

The following excerpt illustrates how a process-oriented approach to therapy actually works. This segment, which was identified as being a significant change episode by both the client and the LCPP ratings of an external judge, is from the seventh therapy session of a young woman in her late twenties whose marriage to her ex-husband had been physically abusive. She had sought counseling immediately after her divorce for help to 'get back to normal life'. However, her subsequent attempts at heterosexual relationships had been 'disastrous'. At the time of therapy, the client was mildly depressed, had difficulties concentrating on her work, complained of being highly anxious, and, even though she was in a caring and supportive relationship with a man, she was extremely ambivalent about it.

C1: There is a real give and take . . . I can be *strong* with him . . . I can be *vulnerable* . . . he supports me and I support him . . . there is a real balance . . . something I have never had before . . . [*Connotative expressions rich in subjective meaning not easily understandable to the therapist serve as markers.*]

T1: You say I can be vulnerable . . . what does that mean to you? [*Therapist focuses client's attention on one of the markers.*]

C2: I guess . . . it is almost ironic for me . . . I guess it means I am not going to be rejected [*laugh*] . . . that he knows there is also that *strong* part . . . [*Client is engaged in differentiating implied meanings; the manner of processing is somewhat detached and analytical.*]

T2: It seems that it is necessary to have a strong part to keep that relationship . . . [*The second marker re-emerges; therapist follows it up and focuses client's attention onto it.*]

C3: I guess I have difficulty being vulnerable . . . I guess I see it as a weakness . . . as something I have difficulty with a lot of times with people . . . but I admire it in people . . . I think vulnerability is a strength . . . I think it is important . . . when I can be vulnerable . . . it is because I'm comfortable that there is an inner strength that's going to come back . . . [*Client continues to be engaged in an analytically differentiating and reflective manner of processing in search of personal meaning.*]

T3: It seems that there is something in you that when you need it you can dig in and pull it out . . . something deep down . . . [*Intervention serves to maintain client's focus and possibly deepen the process.*]

C4: [*Pause*] . . . Maybe it's the feeling that there is nothing that people can shove at me that I cannot handle . . . I guess it's sort of *determined fight* . . . [*Client is engaged in the process of internal differentiation, producing a highly personalized and idiosyncratic response that seems to capture the essence of vulnerability as both a weakness and a strength.*]

T4: There is something in there . . . something so precious that when the punch comes you'll do anything to protect it . . . you can take it . . . and take it . . . until it reaches *that* boundary . . . and then you say, 'No way . . . I am not going to lose it . . . it's time to draw the battle lines.' What is it that you're fighting for? It must be something very worthwhile! [*Therapist uses the client's unique expression 'determined fight' as a marker and generates a metaphor to capture the experience and help her concretize and further her internally focused differentiations.*]

C5: [*Pause*] . . . I don't know . . . I only know that I thrive during crises . . . I sort of go into the battle with all the strength but then . . . after the fact I sort of feel vulnerable . . . I sort of click into this superperson mode [*laugh*] and I just fight and fight . . . I don't know where it comes from . . . that certainly has been a problem . . . it may have started when I got out of my marriage . . . I was a bloody mess . . . I was so weak in that relationship but as I got my strength back . . . and I got angry, *a resolve came back* and I said 'No way anybody will ever do that to me again . . . .' [*Client is engaged in identifying and re-evaluating past experiences; a tentative suggestion that her experience of strength and vulnerability are merging into a perspective that accommodates both.*]

T5: When you say a 'resolve came back' I guess I get the sense that what your husband did to you was chipping away at something inside you . . . that previous something that you are ready to fight for . . . [*Therapist uses the marker in C5 to enhance client's processing toward an integrated view of self.*]

C6: [*Pause*] . . . I don't know what it is. . . . It may be . . . I guess it is ME that I'm fighting for. . . . I guess I AM worthwhile. . . . [*laugh*] . . . I have never been able to say that before. . . . It feels kind of strange . . . but . . . yes I am worthwhile . . . I AM worth fighting for . . . [*Client arrives at a new perspective with an acknowledgment of her own self-worth and agency.*]

In the above example, the presence of an automated pattern of schematic processing was suggested by the client's use of connotative expressions which, although rich in subjective meaning, represented condensed portrayals of a complex inner experience not readily understandable to the therapist. In T1 and T2 the therapist used the expressions 'vulnerable' and 'strong' as markers, to get the client to differentiate and clarify her own experiential meaning of these qualifiers. As the client struggled with these bids for clarification, she was able to 'see' her vulnerability not as a weakness but rather as a crucial aspect of her sense of survival as an individual, which was captured in her expression of 'determined fight'. An interpretation to this effect would probably have been accurate with respect to the content of what the client was saying but it would have hindered her from recognizing how she came to construe herself as a fighter. Instead, the therapist used the 'battle' metaphor (T4) to concretize the client's experience in an attempt to 'cue' her processing to some of the 'hidden' aspects of her inner struggle as a fighter. In response, the client (C5) was able to recall subjective reactions of 'resolve' in past experiences. And when she was encouraged to maintain her focus on and explore this felt sense of 'resolve' (T5), she was able to recognize quite spontaneously that what she was fighting for was her worth and agency as a person (C6).

The therapeutic value of metaphors   There appears to be a general consensus among psychotherapists that metaphors serve an important function in facilitating the process of therapy. This broad-brush acceptance of their usefulness, however, may be misleading. Indeed, based on the results of her study and those of others (Angus, 1986; Angus & Rennie, 1988; Black, 1979) Sinclair (1990) suggests that the facilitative power of a metaphoric communication does not reside in the metaphor per se but rather in what the therapy participants do with it once it is generated.

Metaphor has the unique capacity to encapsulate many levels of experiential meaning, particularly those not fully in awareness (Rohovit, 1960). Thus, in order to be functional, a metaphorical communication must not only capture and symbolize the client's experience but also be elaborated in such a way that it leads to a deepened mutual understanding of the 'hidden' meanings associated with the client's inner world of experience (Angus & Rennie, 1988). From the vantage-point of the perceptual processing model, these hidden meanings entail the inaccessible or undetected information that needs to be processed in a controlled manner for a fuller representation of problematic experiences to occur. Thus, when a client- or therapist-generated metaphor is attended to and explored collaboratively, this facilitates a shift to a controlled mode of processing wherein the metaphor provides access to previously inaccessible components of the client's experience. It is this mutual elaboration of the metaphor that potentiates a shift to higher levels of processing. It is also at these levels that more idiosyncratic language is employed to express uniquely personal meanings and qualities of experience (Toukmanian, 1990, 1992). An example may help clarify this point.

In the above transaction, the therapist generated the 'battle' metaphor (T4), in response to the client's idiosyncratic qualifier 'determined fight', to capture her implied meaning of what appeared to be an internal struggle for an acceptance of her vulnerability as a condition for self-acceptance. Using the metaphor in her subsequent response, the client was able to elaborate on her experience by recalling other circumstances of clicking into a 'superperson mode' and having the 'resolve' to fight in the past. In this instance, the introduction of the metaphor helped the client to identify and reappraise past experiences by shifting from an internally differentiating to a higher level, re-evaluating manner of processing (from a level V to a level VI on the LCPP) that gave her the flexibility with which to construe self differently. And when the client was encouraged to have a closer look at herself in relation to past experiences, she was able to redefine and perceive self from a new perspective.

It is important to recognize that most clients do not spontaneously elaborate their own metaphors nor those supplied by their therapist. Thus, when the therapist fails to address the client's metaphor as a marker by assuming that he/she understands what the metaphor means, then there is no exploration around the metaphor. Under these circumstances, meaning-disjunctive communications are more likely to occur, with the likelihood of observing no shifts to higher levels of processing in the client. A similar process may be expected to be set in motion when the therapist generates a metaphor but fails to invite the client's participation in modifying it to fit the client's experience. In other words, if metaphors are to perform a useful function in therapy, they need to be elaborated and explored by *both* therapy participants.

The therapeutic value of positive experiences   In Sander's (1990) study, we found that the guided recall and the processing of self-discrepant aspects of positive experiences in a controlled manner can potentiate structural changes in self-schemata. Although this finding emerged from an analogue study and its generalizability to real therapeutic situations is yet to be established, we believe that it deserves some attention as it relates to an aspect of therapy practice rarely talked about in the literature.

By definition, psychotherapy implies working with people who are dysfunctional, troubled and unhappy with difficulties of varying degrees of intensity. Thus, our work as psychotherapists demands that our attention, particularly in the early stages of therapy, be focused primarily on prob-lematic or negative aspects of our clients' actions, thoughts and feelings (that is, negative self-perceptions, inadequacies, failures, pain, hopelessness, etc.) and only secondarily on what appears to be positive and functional in their life. Such experiences are often elusive and, consequently, they either remain unnoticed or are deemed incidental to what is being talked about in therapy. In other words, because of our propensity to respond to the negative content of our clients' disclosure, we may overlook instances of spontaneously uttered positive qualifiers or expressions (for example, 'I am a giving person . . .', 'I feel confident . . .', 'I have the patience of Job . . .'), the experiential meaning of which may not be readily apparent or accessible to either the client or the therapist.

As noted earlier, the perceptual processing model maintains that the controlled exploration and in-depth analysis of either positive or negative experiences results in the development of more differentiated and complex schematic structures that in turn mediate change in clients' perceptions leading to greater behavioral flexibility and adjustment. Given that this is a desirable goal of most psychotherapeutic orientations, a recognition by therapists of the value of exploring clients' positive experiences, particularly in the early phases of therapy, could contribute to the therapeutic endeavor. The following excerpt from the second therapy session of a young woman illustrates this point.

The client was a 21-year-old university student who sought therapy to lift 'the fog of depression' which she perceived as being the cause of her poor academic performance. She complained of being highly anxious, often depressed, having 'unpleasant thoughts' about her future, suffering from severe headaches, having difficulties concentrating on her work and being in a general state of malaise.

C1: I just don't understand . . . I never used to be this way before . . . I have the support of my parents . . . my friends . . . I am sort of a *decent* person . . . I like people, I like socializing with them . . . but I feel that . . . lately I am withdrawing . . . and I don't know why . . .

T1: I am not sure what you mean when you say 'I am sort of a decent person' [*Therapist focuses on client's own positive self-description in C1 as the marker for further exploration.*]

C2: What I mean is . . . I have a small circle of friends . . . I have known them for sometime . . . we do things together and . . . I am . . . dependable . . . they can count on me to be there . . . for them . . . kind of helpful . . . giving of my time . . . when they want to talk about problems . . . mostly about their boyfriends . . . kind of like a *big sister* . . . I guess I am used to this . . . even with my family . . . my mother and sisters . . . I seem to be THE person they turn to when in need of something [*Client responds to the intervention by attempting to differentiate the implied meaning of being 'a decent person' from an external framework, using referents external to self to identify different facets of her self-perception.*]

T2: I get the impression . . . and correct me if I am wrong . . . that you have some mixed feelings about your role as a 'big sister' . . . [*Therapist's intervention captures the newly emerged marker in a tentative way to allow for further elaboration.*]

C3: [*Pause*] . . . well . . . not really . . . it kind of makes me feel useful . . . you know kind of good . . . like what people should do with friends and family . . . as much as they can to help each other . . . make allowances for their shortcomings . . . as human beings . . . be accepting . . . considerate [*Client continues her externally focused differentiation in search of personal meaning.*]

T3: Being accepting of people as they are, being helpful to them and giving them as much as you possibly can is something that you value highly in you. [*Therapist attempts to shift client's focus of differentiation from an external to an internal framework.*]

C4: Yeah . . . that's really important . . . it's important for me to be that kind of a person . . . caring . . . giving . . .

T4: And when you are not . . . [*Attempts to engage client in the deliberate search for self-discrepant experiences to promote her internally focused differentiation.*]

C5: [*Pause*] . . . I can't think of a time when I wasn't . . . [*long pause*] . . . but I see that in my friends . . . my family . . . I know they care in their own funny way . . . but I feel I give more . . . much more than I receive . . . [*sigh*] . . . I guess they think that I've got it all together . . . that I am strong . . . but you see I am not . . . I can't even handle my own problems . . . [*Client is engaged in identifying inconsistencies between self- and other-relevant experiences; a tentative suggestion of source of conflict emerging.*]

In this transaction, the client's positive self-portrayal in C1 (that is, 'I am sort of a decent person') was a passing remark, couched in a string of other positive statements, which could have been ignored quite easily as being tangential to what the client was concerned about at that moment in therapy (that is, her withdrawal from interpersonal contacts). However, to the discerning ear of the therapist, the expression was more than a simple qualifier. It was a self-descriptive statement, packed with subjective meanings, that offered only a glimpse into the client's perception of herself in relation to others. In other words, its telegraphic quality suggested a construal based on a complex network of internal representations that needed to be accessed and reprocessed in a controlled manner. Recognizing its immediate therapeutic value, the therapist singled out the expression as a 'marker' for an intervention that potentiated the client's subsequent search for and differentiation of various facets of meanings implied in her self-characterization as 'a decent person', thus moving her closer to developing a broader perspective on her conflictual experiences with others.

Implications for supervision

As the therapeutic goals and strategies advocated by the perceptual processing method of therapy stem directly from the same model that has provided the framework for our research, most of what has been said regarding the implications of the studies described in this chapter for practicing therapists may be applied also to the supervision of students in counseling and psychotherapy. Let me elaborate.

Psychotherapy supervision and practice have a number of features in common. In both contexts, the therapist/supervisor is an agent of change; both entail a dyadic interaction; both require the active involvement of their respective participants; both are discovery-oriented and experiential in nature; both are carried out over an extended period of time; and both embrace the view that an open, trusting and collaborative relationship between participants is essential for the success of their respective endeavors. However, supervision is not psychotherapy in disguise, as some have suggested it to be (for example, Mueller & Kell, 1972; Truax, Carkhuff & Douds, 1964). The processes underlying the two may be similar, but they are not identical. Moreover, the purpose of each function is different (Blocher, 1983). While psychotherapy aims at helping clients achieve greater self-understanding and develop more functional ways of dealing with problematic experiences, the primary goal of supervisory practice is to ensure that trainees learn and develop professionally.

Supervision concerned mainly with skills training is a didactic endeavor. It is guided by the assumption that there are 'desirable' counselor or therapist behaviors and that once trainees have sharpened their skills along these prescribed dimensions they will be able to formulate therapeutically appropriate interventions and function effectively as therapists. In this approach there is no explicit recognition of the transactional nature of therapy encounters nor a clear delineation of the conditions for which the skills targeted for acquisition may be of maximum benefit to the clients. Furthermore, as the emphasis in skills training is on *teaching* trainees how to *perform* in the role of therapists, supervision guided by this approach runs the risk of overlooking the unique ways in which each trainee experiences the supervisory process and learns from it.

As therapy supervisors, we need to acknowledge that trainees enter supervision with different beliefs, views and conceptions about human interactions and psychotherapy practice. It is also important for us to recognize that, because of their unique experiential histories, trainees perceive and respond to the exigencies of supervision differently. Most approach this task with a great deal of trepidation and anxiety. They are unsure of themselves; they do not know what to anticipate from their supervisors; and, although they have their own perceptions and expectations of themselves as therapists, they often are uncertain about their capabilities and fearful of engaging in a process that may threaten their self-identity. When such experiences are not recognized and addressed, they remain dormant, put a strain on the supervisory relationship and, consequently, curtail the possibilities for learning. In other words, a supervisor who is not responsive to the way in which trainees construe their supervisory experience and who fails to provide them with opportunities to explore and become aware of the meaning that the experience has for them is likely to inhibit their receptivity to information and limit their personal as well as professional growth and development.

In fact, we have learned from a recent study (Lawless, 1990) conducted within our programme of research that the major impact of supervision on interns' learning is reflected not in skills acquisition per se but rather in the gradual, and sometimes dramatic, changes that they themselves observe in the way they construe themselves and their work in the role of therapists. The qualitative analyses of trainees' accounts of their supervisory experience, obtained through individual interviews during early, middle and late supervision, revealed that the personal significance of trainees' expectations of the therapeutic process and their preconceptions about their role as therapists had to be explored and re-evaluated before they were free to accept new ideas and attend more fully to their clients. Furthermore, when these accounts were rated on the LCPP, our findings indicated that change in interns' perspectives, mediated through self reflection and the re-evaluation of held beliefs and preconceptions, was associated mainly with explorations that were characterized by internally differentiating, re-evaluating and integrating types of information processing operations.

Thus, with the view that learning to become a psychotherapist is an experientially based developmental process, the main thrust of my supervisory practice has been the belief that the fundamental goal of supervision is to help trainees learn to develop, through their transactions with the supervisor, an increased self-understanding and a broader perspective on issues related to their work as psychotherapists. The emphasis here is on the process of trainee learning and what facilitates it rather than on skills training. In this sense, each supervisory encounter is unique and tailor-made to meet the developmental needs of individual trainees.

Furthermore, to the extent that this approach is concerned with helping trainees process their experiences more fully, it requires that the supervisor function in ways that would potentiate the development of their perceptual processing capabilities.

Within this framework, the supervisor's most critical function is to provide trainees with a 'safe' learning environment, an environment that is characterized not only by mutual trust, openness and collaboration but also by the supervisor's ability to understand and be attuned to the way in which trainees construe themselves and their experiences in the role of student-therapists. As noted earlier, trainees have their own personal issues to contend with in their quest for learning to become psychotherapists. The struggle with such issues is often ongoing and not confined necessarily to the early phases of supervision. Different experiences with different clients may trigger different concerns that need to be addressed whenever they arise during the course of supervision. This is of crucial importance for it is only by being responsive to trainees at this level that a supervisor can increase the likelihood of creating a truly safe supervisory relationship wherein learning can occur.

Helping trainees gain a meaningful understanding of the therapist's role as a change agent is the second important function performed by a supervisor working from a perceptual processing perspective. It may be argued that this function is indeed the raison d'être of most of the activities undertaken by all therapy supervisors, irrespective of orientation. All supervisors engage in some form of skills training and most, if not all, in helping would-be therapists learn about the symptomatologies of various psychological disorders and acquire knowledge of specific therapeutic processes and interventions. Obviously, these are the necessary ingredients in the education and training of therapists and counselors. However, supervision is more than a collage of activities. It is first and foremost an interpersonal process that, in order to be productive, must be a personally meaningful experience for the trainee. And it is precisely for this reason that I believe the perceptual processing perspective, with its focus on experiential learning, can be a useful framework for supervisory practice.

In this approach, the primary medium of supervision are the audio-taped recordings of trainees' actual therapy sessions with clients. This material is crucial as it provides the grist that runs the supervisory mill. Without it supervision would be based on the presentation and discussion of 'cases', leading to didactic as opposed to experiential learning. These sessions typically revolve around three major themes or areas of trainee learning: awareness of self and self-in-the-role-of therapist, knowledge of concepts and issues related to psychotherapy practice, and the acquisition of therapeutic skills. These themes may best be thought of as overlapping dimensions or processes, occurring throughout the course of supervision, rather than as mutually exclusive tasks or units of learning.

In my experience, I have found that one of the most effective ways of facilitating trainees' process of learning across these dimensions is through modeling, in my interactions with them, the therapeutic procedures advocated by the perceptual processing method of experiential therapy (Toukmanian, 1990). In this sense, the way I conduct my supervisory sessions has a number of features in common with the way I interact with my clients. I monitor and attempt to stay attuned to the manner in which trainees formulate their thoughts, interpret events, raise questions, talk about clients, express their views and evaluate their work as therapists. Much like in psychotherapy, I also attempt to help trainees explore, elaborate and re-evaluate the personal meaning of their experiences, examine their held beliefs and opinions, generate alternative views and experiment with new ways of perceiving, thinking and behaving in the role of therapists.

Thus, to the extent that it is possible, I try to refrain from teaching, instructing, correcting and providing trainees with directives as to how to formulate their views and behave accordingly. Instead, I attempt to facilitate their learning by leading them to do their own processing. I use reflections, bids for clarification and open-ended inquiries to encourage them to question and challenge their own views and assumptions, be more differentiating and less rigid in their construals and develop more flexible processing strategies to accommodate different ideas and opinions. I believe one of the main advantages of using this approach in supervisory practice is that it provides trainees with the opportunity to see the supervisor 'in action' as a change agent and learn about ways of relating and communicating directly from experience.

It is important to emphasize, however, that students often need and indeed want to receive some form of systematic training in therapeutic methods and techniques. For this reason, I would like to provide a brief description of some of the structured activities that I have found to be useful in helping students acquire process-oriented diagnostic and intervention skills – the two most fundamental dimensions of the perceptual processing method of experiential therapy.

With regards to the former, training entails providing students with opportunities to develop habits of 'listening' and attending to clients' manner of communicating. Thus, when segments of actual therapy session(s) are replayed in supervision, I ask students to identify, on a response-by-response basis, client expressions that they think are significant and to provide a rationale for their choice(s). This sets the stage for a free discussion of opinions wherein I encourage them to describe, by drawing on their theoretical knowledge of the perceptual processing model, the processing strategies entailed in these construals. The intent here is to get them to shift their attention away from the content and onto the quality of clients' discourse, to think in 'process' terms and to see if they can recognize 'markers' indicative of an automated mode of perceptual activity. Procedurally, this involves focusing students' attention on a given expression and 'teaching' them to adopt a questioning stance (that is, 'What is this person trying to tell me?', 'Do I really understand the meaning of this expression?') as a way of helping them develop more discerning habits of listening for ambiguities of meaning in clients' verbalizations. Often this is accomplished by using open-ended questions that encourage them to examine the assumptions underlying their own perceptions of the client in light of their understanding of the client's communication, to explore other interpretations, and, in the process, to recognize the expression as a possible marker for intervention.

Once trainees receive a thorough grounding in listening for 'client markers', attention is turned to developing their skills for interventions that serve to facilitate clients' progressive engagement in more complex information processing operations. Here the procedure is similar to that described above. When listening to the replay of segments of actual therapy sessions, interventions for any given client response containing an identifiable marker are first identified and then discussed in terms of their subsequent impact on clients' processing.

Initially, the discussion centres on whether or not a given intervention has served to deploy the client's attention to the marker expression and led the client to its elaboration. This procedure is repeated for several client–therapist transactions, after which the focus moves on to discussing the quality of the client's elaborations subsequent to the 'marker intervention'. Trainees are guided to listen closely to the client's response and are asked to indicate whether the source of information contributing to his/her construals following the intervention is predominantly internal or external to the client. For any given client response with an external focus, trainees are encouraged to practice generating alternative interventions to the one discussed. At this stage, attention is directed particularly to helping students make systematic use of open-ended questions, focused probes, reflections of perceived affect and metaphoric language as aids to engaging clients in an in-depth exploration of perceived meanings and meaning associations. Supervision proceeds by discussing the quality of each of these interventions in terms of its anticipated effects and its likelihood of contributing to the enhancement of the client's capabilities to process and perceive experiences more fully. In short, my approach may best be characterized as process-directed, interactive and collaborative, and my function as a supervisor as that of a catalyst in that I am there to facilitate the process, but not to interfere with the course, of trainee learning.

In conclusion, it would seem that an approach to psychotherapy research that recognizes the centrality of clients' perceptions and addresses the phenomenon of change at the level of their cognitive processes and structures can have a number of important implications for practicing psychotherapists and therapy supervisors. The finding of a consistent pattern of processing operations associated with client change and therapeutic improvement is of particular importance in this regard as it suggests the existence of some core or common client change processes that may cut across different therapeutic orientations. Furthermore, as was demonstrated in this chapter, it would seem that a methodologically pluralistic approach to studying clients' experientially based constructions offers a perspective that accommodates rather than rejects individual differences in clients and, in doing so, holds forth the promise of generating more relevant and useful findings to guide the work of psychotherapy practitioners.

References

Anderson, J.R. (1981). Concepts, propositions, and schemata: What are the cognitive units? *Nebraska Symposium on Motivation* (Vol. 28, pp. 121–162). Lincoln: University of Nebraska Press.

Angus, L.E. (1986). Metaphoric expressiveness within the psychotherapeutic relationship: A qualitative analysis. *Dissertation Abstracts International, 47*, 3507A.

Angus, L.E., & Rennie, D.L. (1988). Therapist participation in metaphor generation: Collaborative and non-collaborative styles. *Psychotherapy, 25*, 552–560.

Angus, L., & Rennie, D. (1989). Envisioning the representational world: The client's experience of metaphoric expression in psychotherapy. *Psychotherapy, 26*, 362–379.

Beck, A.T., Rush, A.J., Shaw, B.F., & Emery, G. (1979). *Cognitive therapy of depression*. New York: Guilford.

Black, M. (1979). More about metaphor. In A. Ortony (Ed.), *Metaphor and thought* (pp. 19–43). New York: Cambridge University Press.

Blocher, D. (1983). Towards a cognitive developmental approach to counseling supervision. *Counseling Psychologist, 11*, 27–34.

Cohen, L.H., Sargent, M.M., & Sechrest, L.B. (1986). Use of psychotherapy research by professional psychologists. *American Psychologist, 41*, 198–206.

Day, S.M. (1994). *Self-concept, schematic processing and change in perceptual processing experiential therapy*. Unpublished master's thesis, York University, North York, Ont.

Feyerabend, P. (1975). *Against method*. London: Verso.

Fiske, S.T., & Dyer, L.M. (1985). Structure and development of social schemata: Evidence from positive and negative transfer effects. *Journal of Personality and Social Psychology, 48*, 839–852.

Fitts, W.H. (1965). *Manual: Tennessee self-concept scale*. Nashville, Tennessee: Counselor Recordings and Tests.

Goldfried, M.R., Greenberg, L.S., & Marmar, C. (1990). Individual psychotherapy: Process and outcome. *Annual Review of Psychology, 41*, 659–688.

Greenberg, L.S. (1986). Change process research. *Journal of Consulting and Clinical Psychology, 54*, 4–9.

Horvath, A.O. (1981). An exploratory study of the working alliance: Its measurement and relationship to therapy outcome. *Dissertation Abstracts International, 42*, 2503A.

Ingram, R.E., & Kendall, P.C. (1986). Cognitive clinical psychology: Implications of an information processing perspective. In R.E. Ingram (Ed.), *Information processing approaches to clinical psychology* (pp. 3–21). New York: Academic Press.

Kelly, G. (1955). *The psychology of personal constructs*. New York: Norton.

Kuiper, N.A., & Derry, P.A. (1981). Depressed and nondepressed content self-reference in mild depressives. *Journal of Personality, 50*, 67–80.

Kuiper, N.A., Derry, P.A., & McDonald, M.R. (1982). Self-reference in person perception in depression: A social cognition perspective. In G. Weary & H.L. Mirels (Eds.), *Integrations of clinical and social psychology* (pp. 79–103). New York: Oxford University Press.

Lambert, M.J., & Bergin, A.E. (1992). Achievements and limitations of psychotherapy research. In D.K. Freedheim (Ed.), *History of psychotherapy: A century of change* (pp. 360–390). Washington, DC: American Psychological Association.

Lawless, D. (1990). *Interns' experience of learning psychotherapy: A process description*. Unpublished master's thesis, York University, North York, Ont.

Mahoney, M.J. (1985). Psychotherapy and human change processes. In M.J. Mahoney & A. Freeman (Eds.), *Cognition and psychotherapy* (pp. 3–48). New York: Plenum.

Markus, H., & Kunda, E. (1986). Stability and malleability of the self-concept. *Journal of Personality and Social Psychology, 51,* 858–866.

Morrow-Bradley, C., & Elliott, R. (1986). Utilization of psychotherapy research by practising psychotherapists. *American Psychologist, 41,* 188–197.

Mueller, W.J., & Kell, B.L. (1972). *Coping with conflict: Supervising counselors and psychotherapists.* Englewood Cliffs, NJ: Prentice Hall.

Neisser, U. (1967). *Cognitive psychology.* New York: Appleton-Century-Crofts.

Neisser, U. (1976). *Cognition and reality: Principles and implications of cognitive psychology.* San Francisco: Freeman.

Rennie, D.L. (1992). Qualitative analysis of the clients' experience of psychotherapy: The unfolding of reflexivity. In S.G. Toukmanian & D.L. Rennie (Eds.), *Psychotherapy process research: Paradigmatic and narrative approaches* (pp. 211–233). Newbury Park, CA: Sage.

Rennie, D.L. (1994). Human science and counselling psychology: Closing the gap between research and practice. *Counselling Psychology Quarterly, 1,* 235–250.

Rennie, D.L., & Toukmanian, S.G. (1992). Explanation in psychotherapy process research. In S.G. Toukmanian & D.L. Rennie (Eds.), *Psychotherapy process research: Paradigmatic and narrative approaches* (pp. 234–251). Newbury Park, CA: Sage.

Rice, L.N., & Greenberg, L.S. (Eds.). (1984). *Patterns of change: Intensive analysis of psychotherapy process.* New York: Guilford.

Rohovit, D. (1960). Metaphor and mind: A re-evaluation of metaphor theory. *American Image, 17,* 289–309.

Ross, L., Lepper, M.R., & Hubbard, M. (1975). Perseverance in self-perception: Biased attributional processes in the debriefing paradigm. *Journal of Personality and Social Psychology, 32,* 880–892.

Rumelhart, D.E. (1984). Schemata and the cognitive system. In S.R. Wyer & T.K. Srull (Eds.), *Handbook of social cognition* (Vol. 1, pp. 161–168). Hillsdale, NJ: Erlbaum.

Sander, H.D. (1990). The self-schemata of nondepressed and mildly depressed individuals: Induced changes in content and processing efficiency. *Dissertation Abstracts International, 51,* 1560B.

Shiffrin, R.M., & Schneider, W. (1977). Controlled and automated human informative processing: II. Perceptual learning, automatic attending, and a general theory. *Psychological Review, 84,* 127–150.

Sinclair, L.M. (1990). Metaphor and client perceptual processing. *Dissertation Abstracts International, 51,* 4608B.

Strupp, H.H., & Howard, K.I. (1992). A brief history of psychotherapy research. In D.K. Freedheim (Ed.), *History of psychotherapy: A century of change* (pp. 309–334). Washington, DC: American Psychological Association.

Toukmanian, S.G. (1985, June). Preliminary findings from an experimental approach to evaluating self-schema change following short-term experiential psychotherapy. In S. Toukmanian (Chair), *Paradigms for the assessment of self-schema change in psychotherapy research.* Workshop conducted at the Annual Meeting of the Society for Psychotherapy Research, Evanston, IL.

Toukmanian, S.G. (1986). A measure of client perceptual processing. In L.S. Greenberg & W.M. Pinsof (Eds.), *The psychotherapeutic process: A research handbook* (pp. 107–130). New York: Guilford.

Toukmanian, S.G. (1988, June). The development and evaluation of self-schema change following short-term experiential therapy. In J. Martin (Chair), *The client's developing of meaning structure: Cognitive and metacognitive considerations.* Symposium conducted at the 1st International Conference on Developmental Counseling Psychology, Porto, Portugal.

Toukmanian, S.G. (1990). A schema-based information processing perspective on client change in experiential psychotherapy. In G. Lietaer, J. Rombauts & R. Van Balen (Eds.), *Client-centred and experiential psychotherapy in the nineties* (pp. 309–326). Leuven: Leuven University Press.

Toukmanian, S.G. (1992). Studying the client's perceptual processes and their outcomes in psychotherapy. In S.G. Toukmanian & D.L. Rennie (Eds.), *Psychotherapy process research: Paradigmatic and narrative approaches* (pp. 77–107). Newbury Park, CA: Sage.

Toukmanian, S.G., & Grech, T. (1991). *Changes in cognitive complexity in the context of perceptual-processing experiential therapy* (Tech. Rep. No. 193). North York, Ont.: York University, Department of Psychology.

Toukmanian, S.G., & Jackson, S. (1994, September). *An analysis of clients' self-narratives in brief experiential psychotherapy*. Paper presentation at the IIIrd International Conference on Client-Centered and Experiential Psychotherapy, Gmunden, Austria.

Toukmanian, S.G., & Roese, R. (1989, June). *Self-schema change: Its assessment and relationship to therapeutic outcome*. Poster presentation at the annual meeting of the Canadian Psychological Association, Halifax, NS.

Truax, C.B., Carkhuff, R.R., & Douds, J. (1964). Toward an integration of the didactic and experiential approaches to training in counseling and psychotherapy. *Journal of Counseling Psychology, 11*, 240–247.

Zink, D. (1990). *Change in anxiety in the context of perceptual-processing experiential therapy: Process and outcome research*. Unpublished master's thesis, York University, North York, Ont.

9

Resolving Unfinished Business: A Program of Study

Shelley McMain, Rhonda Goldman and Leslie Greenberg

We have long lamented the lack of integration between research and practice. In our view they are inextricably linked and each is inherently necessary for the continuing growth and development of the other. In this chapter, we will describe how our research perspective and program of study are implicitly intertwined with therapy practice.

What follows is a description of a program of psychotherapy research that focused on the processes of client change related to the resolution of a particular client problematic emotional state. According to a process-experiential theory of therapy (Greenberg, Rice & Elliott 1993), client presenting problems, including traditionally defined clinical syndromes such as anxiety and depression, can be linked to various underlying cognitive–affective processing difficulties (Greenberg, Rice & Elliott, 1993; Greenberg & Safran, 1987; Rice & Greenberg, 1984). The identification and understanding of particular types of processing difficulties presented by a client at a given moment in therapy guide the implementation of specific therapeutic interventions designed to deal with the particular processing difficulty.

The program of research to be described involved a series of studies directed at understanding how clients resolve a specific type of processing difficulty referred to as 'unfinished business'. Psychotherapy clients frequently present with unresolved emotional experiences that involve significant others. This difficulty, which is often revealed by statements of lingering bad feelings toward a significant other, is typically related to the frustration of salient needs. For example, many clients describe bad feelings toward a parent, feelings that are tied to struggles for independence or issues of trust or nurturance. One client, who struggled for acceptance from her mother, whom she experienced as rejecting, made the following statement early in therapy: 'I never felt that I could be good enough for my mother. . . . ' Unresolved issues with a significant other can be triggered by a variety of cues in current relationships that are re-evoked by underlying unmet needs. In this regard, unresolved feelings can interfere with a person's ability to be fully present in new situations (Daldrup, Beutler, Engle & Greenberg, 1988). From a process-experiential perspective, issues of unfinished business are most efficiently resolved with the therapeutic intervention of the Gestalt empty chair.

The following program of research on unfinished business developed according to a task analytic model of the study of change (Greenberg, 1984). From this perspective, the research focus is on the identification, description and explanation of the types of changes that are promoted by specific interventions (for example, Gestalt empty chair intervention) as applied to specific in-session problematic client states (unfinished business). Before discussing the specific studies which comprised this research program, we will outline more fully the research and theoretical perspectives that informed our program of research.

A change process research perspective

In this approach, recurring patterns of in-session client and therapist behaviors, related to the resolution of particular cognitive–affective problems, are identified as potent change events that merit further study. There are two fundamental assumptions that guide a change process research perspective (Greenberg 1986, 1991; Greenberg & Pinsof, 1986; Rice & Greenberg, 1984). The first is that the therapeutic encounter is a complex performance that can be broken down into a set of events that need to be viewed on multiple levels and analyzed from many different perspectives. The complexities of the therapeutic context are dealt with by intensively analyzing the participants' moment-by-moment performance, taking the relevant event and relationship context into account. Thus clients' moment-by-moment performance is studied in the context of an unfinished business event, which itself is embedded in a therapeutic relationship characterized both as empathic and as having a good working alliance.

The second central assumption of this perspective is that not all psychotherapy processes have equal significance or similar meaning, and that meaning depends on the context. For example, the moments in therapy during which a client breaks down into intense sobbing over a lost relationship are very different from the moments early in a session when the client struggles to decide upon a focus for discussion. Some moments are therefore more important than others, and, similarly, behaviors have different meanings, depending on their context. Thus, sobbing about a lost relationship is different from sobbing about being violated. Certain therapeutic occurrences, such as particular types of weeping events, can be viewed as critical or potent therapeutic change events, and, depending on when they occur, will differ in their change process and in the type of interventions that facilitate these processes (Greenberg, 1994; Greenberg & Korman, 1993; Rice & Greenberg, 1984).

A therapeutic event is distinguishable by four salient features: a patient problem marker (for example, clients' statement of unfinished business indicated by lingering anger toward a parent), a therapeutic operation (for example, introduction of the Gestalt empty chair dialogue when indicators of unfinished business are present), client performance (clients' anger is heightened, underlying feelings of sadness and loss emerge and unmet needs are expressed) and the immediate in-session outcome (for example, resolving resentment and letting go of the anger and unmet need) (Greenberg, 1986; Rice & Greenberg, 1984). Some examples of key change events that have been identified include the resolution of self-evaluative conflicts using the Gestalt two-chair dialogue, systematic evocative unfolding at a problematic reaction point and the working through of 'unfinished business' through the Gestalt empty chair intervention (Greenberg, Rice & Elliott, 1993; Greenberg & Safran, 1987).

A task analytic methodological approach

The specific research methodology which guided the study of the resolution of unfinished business was a rational-empirical task analytic strategy (Greenberg, 1977, 1984, 1991). This method has two major phases: (1) a discovery phase, which involves a rational-empirical task analysis of the change event; and (2) the verification phase, in which the model of change is validated.

The rational aspect of the analysis refers to the process of explicating one's clinical notions about what is important. Rational conjecture involves using the clinician's tacit knowledge as relevant data for study. The empirical aspect of the task analysis entails the observation of actual in-session therapy process and a comparison of the clinically and theoretically driven model to the actual client performance.

The development of the rational-empirical model of client change involves a number of subsidiary steps. First, the specific task or problem is selected and described, the components of the client marker identified and the therapist interventions specified. The next steps involve constructing a rational model of resolution and cycling between observation of actual data (that is, examples of client change episodes) and the rational model to produce a more refined description of actual in-situation client performance. The final refined description culminates in the construction of a rational-empirical model.

The second major phase of a rational-empirical task analysis involves verifying the rational-empirical performance. There are two steps in this phase, which include validating the components of the model and relating the in-session change components to change assessed at treatment outcome. To validate the client performance model, a comparison of task resolvers to non-resolvers is conducted in order to determine whether each group can be distinguished by the presence or absence of the resolution components suggested by the model. The relationship between in-session and out of session client behaviour is assessed by determining whether the specified resolution components predict treatment success measured at outcome. Throughout this chapter, we will describe how the task analytic strategy and methodological approach to research promoted increased understanding and specification of key client processes involved in the resolution of unfinished business. Research findings continually revealed which processes were in need of further specification and clarification. Ultimately this research informed clinicians as to the nature and sequence of client processes involved in the resolution of unfinished business and what therapist operations were necessary to facilitate this process.

Explication of the theory of unfinished business

Our perspective on the development of lingering bad feelings toward significant others and the resolution of these feelings is understood within an experiential perspective informed by Gestalt and client-centered theory and research on cognition and emotion.

According to Gestalt theory (Perls, Hefferline & Goodman, 1951), unfinished business refers to bad feelings which linger in response to previously frustrating situations with people. Individuals who are troubled by unfinished business commonly manifest unresolved grief, separation and loss, or persistent anger, resentment, frustration and resignation which interferes with their ability to fully attend to current life situations.

Gestalt theory posits that experiences of unfinished business stem from a disruption to the organism's self-regulatory cycle (Perls et al., 1951). From an emotion theory perspective (Greenberg & Safran, 1987), unfinished business arises from a failure to completely process emotional experience and needs. Emotions are thought to be linked to action tendencies that are motivational in nature and adaptive. Chronic experiences of unfinished business arise because unmet needs interfere with the individual's ability to respond adaptively. Unmet needs have heightened salience to the individual and become easily triggered by cues in new situations (Greenberg & Safran, 1987). This results in the reactivation of associated feelings of anger, frustration and hurt that may be inappropriate to the new situation.

Clinical observation and writings from Gestalt literature suggest that an effective therapeutic environment for addressing unfinished business is Perls' empty chair dialogue (Perls et al., 1951). In Gestalt theory, the empty chair dialogue is utilized to access suppressed unresolved emotions. This intervention is an evocative technique for enhancing emotional arousal and the expression of associated needs by means of a behavioral engagement in an imaginary dialogue with a significant other (Daldrup et al., 1988; Greenberg et al., 1993; Perls et al., 1951). The client engages in a dialogue between self and imagined other. As Perls et al. (1951) suggested, re-experiencing situations in fantasy can be effective for helping clients become aware of their blocks to awareness and gain access to interrupted experiences.

Research on the description of the client task

The first task was to specify the components of the client marker that identified the problem to be resolved. An intensive analytic approach was employed to help discern the distinguishing features of unfinished business. It was important to determine whether markers of unfinished business could be differentiated from other cognitive–affective processing problems.

Clinical theory and practice guided the selection of segments of unfinished business. These segments were given to raters who were blind to the purpose of the research. Raters were asked to describe the salient features of the client's process.

Research findings

This research yielded the production of a number of visible indicators of experiences of unfinished business. As noted earlier, unfinished business was reliably marked by the following four indices: (1) experience of a feeling of anger, sadness, hurt or grief; (2) feeling related to a significant other; (3) interruption or failure to fully express the feeling, for example the client may clench his or her jaw to hold back his or her anger; (4) the feeling of interruption is problematic for the client (Greenberg et al., 1993; Greenberg & Safran, 1987). Raters were found to be able to identify these performance patterns with very high reliability (Greenberg & Rice, 1990).

Practical implications

This research was important because it showed that within clients' discussions of their life experience and past relationships clear indicators of the presence of unfinished business are observable. Other research revealed that markers of unfinished business could be reliably discriminated from two other types of processing difficulties: splits and problematic reactions (Greenberg & Rice, 1990).

This research suggests that diagnosing client problems in terms of currently operating processing difficulties is an alternative to simply applying traditional diagnostic taxonomies. Identifying markers of various processing difficulties is valuable because it enables a more differentiated perspective on client problems. First, the presence of a marker of a particular processing difficulty points to the fact that a client is currently amenable to intervention, as indicated by the client's manner and current level of distress. Further, defining client problems in terms of cognitive–affective processing difficulties that occur in-session enables a differentiated assessment of problems and interventions. Thus, two clients who present with overt symptoms of major depression may experience very different processing difficulties. For example, some clients may reveal indications of internal harsh critics that make them feel small and powerless. With clients who show markers of splits, it would be appropriate for a therapist to engage the client in a two-chair dialogue that would enable the client to be more aware of and deal with their internal critic. For other clients, experiences of depression may be related to lingering anger and disappointment toward a critical parent. At these markers of unfinished business, it may be most helpful for the therapist to engage the client in an empty chair dialogue. Hence, a process diagnostic approach enables the utilization of differential interventions in response to specific processing difficulties.

Specifying the therapist operations: The task environment

Another important phase of the research program was to specify the intervention for facilitating change. From a process-experiential perspective, the therapeutic goal of an unfinished business dialogue is to promote sufficient arousal so as to facilitate emotional relief and recovery and bring about cognitive reorganization in the form of change in one's view of self, other and the relationship. To develop a manual that would outline the therapeutic techniques involved in performing an unfinished business task, a task analytic research strategy (Greenberg & Minden, 1988; Greenberg et al., 1993) was employed. This method of inquiry has a number of advantages: (1) the therapist's behavior is studied in the natural context of the therapeutic sessions, allowing for a fuller understanding of the behavior observed; (2) rational conjecture permits the clinician's tacit knowledge to be considered relevant for study; (3) the investigator describes the actual flow of the therapist's performance, and then organizes these observations into sequences of actions.

Research findings

The task analysis revealed the following three phases of therapeutic intervention when implementing an unfinished business task: arousal, expression and completion, in addition to a pre- and post-dialogue stage. With each phase the specific therapist operations were specified. A presentation of the specific therapist operations is briefly summarized in Table 9.1.

In the pre-dialogue stage, the therapist responds to a marker of unfinished business by suggesting that the client focus on the issue. Upon obtaining the client's agreement, the therapist structures the dialogue by moving over a chair and beginning the dialogue.

During the arousal stage, the therapist helps the client to evoke the significant other's presence. The therapist attempts to establish contact between the self and significant other by instructing the client to react to the imagined presence of the other and directing statements to the other in the empty chair. Therapists discourage clients from hurling accusations at the other and help clients identify with their own experience. The therapist then attempts to heighten the figural negative, verbal and non-verbal expression of the significant other through repetition, exaggeration and enactment. Often clients recall a specific episodic memory that is particularly painful.

Table 9.1   *Therapist operations*

Pre-dialogue stage

  1   Establish collaboration.
  2   Structure the experiment.

Arousal stage

  3   Evoke the sensed presence of the significant other.
  4   Establish contact between self and significant other.
  5   Facilitate the taking of responsibility.
  6   Access client's initial feelings in response to the significant other.
  7   Facilitate enactment of the significant other and intensify the stimulus value of the significant other.
  8   Evoke a specifically recalled event or episodic memory.

Expression stage

  9   Differentiate feelings toward significant other.
 10   Promote full expression to significant other of differentiated primary/adaptive emotion by graded experiments of expression.
 11   Help client maintain a balance between expression and contact with inner referent.
 12   Facilitate expression to significant other of unfulfilled needs and expectation in regard to significant other.

Completion stage

 13   Identify with other and support emerging new representations of other.
 14   Support emerging new understanding of other and of relationship with other.
 15   Empower the client.
 16   Close contact with the other appropriately.

Post-dialogue stage

 17   Create meaning/perspective.

In the expression stage, the therapist facilitates the client's full expression of emotion in relation to the other by focusing the client's attention on micro-signals of emotion and expressive signs of interruptions to emotional experiencing and expression. In fostering full expression of the unfinished emotion, the therapist starts small (for example, 'point your finger again') and builds in a step-by-step fashion to larger and more comprehensive expressive actions (for example, 'pushing the other away'). In doing this, the therapist looks for congruence between client's experience and client's expression. At this point, the therapist directs the client to tell the imagined other what he or she needs or wants from the other.

In the completion stage, the therapist supports and promotes the 'letting go' of the unfulfilled expectation in relation to the significant other. Letting go often follows naturally from the full expression of anger or sadness, or lingering resentment, hurt or disappointment. The therapist supports the new, emerging, more positive, or less controlling, representation of the other. In the event that the client cannot let go of an unfulfilled expectation of the other and holds onto an unmet need, the client is encouraged to restate the unmet need. At the end of a session, the therapist assesses the extent to which the client has resolved the unmet need.

In the final, post-dialogue stage, the therapist helps the client integrate the new view of self and significant other (if achieved) into his or her current life experiences, which may include the other. This helps the client close the issue or take some action with the other, if desirable.

Practical implications

Generally speaking, manuals can be useful tools to help ensure quality control of clinical services. Therapist adherence to particular interventions can be evaluated and the efficacy of particular treatment approaches for specific problems can be assessed. The manual developed for the implementation of the empty chair dialogue provides specific guidelines about how to respond to particular momentary client states. Grounded in concrete therapist actions, this manual offers clinicians clarity and a practical aid in dealing with unfinished business issues (Greenberg & Minden, 1988). In addition, the manual allows for the training of therapists in specific operations necessary to facilitate the empty chair dialogue. The model outlines how to assess particular momentary client states and facilitate the necessary steps in working toward a resolution of the unfinished business issue. For example, if a client describes feeling misunderstood and unrecognized by his father in the therapy session, the therapist would recognize this as a marker of unfinished business and direct the client to evoke the father's imaginary presence in the empty chair and express feelings toward him. At another point in the dialogue, when the client has expressed both intense feelings of sadness and anger toward his father, the therapist might facilitate a statement of need to the father in the empty chair.

Preliminary steps toward empirical verification of the efficacy of the empty chair intervention

Before engaging in an intensive investigation of the resolution of unfinished business it was important to assess the potency of the empty chair intervention to effect resolution of unfinished business issues. A study by King (1988) was designed to assess the efficacy of the empty chair technique for helping clients resolve issues of unfinished business. Using university students as subjects, King conducted a two-session analogue study to compare the effects of empathy plus the empty chair intervention to empathic reflection alone for resolving issues of unfinished business.

Research findings

Results, based on outcome measures administered one week following the sessions, revealed that people in the empathy plus empty chair treatment group were significantly more tolerant of the significant other and more confident in relation to the significant other than those who received the empathy alone treatment. In the empty chair therapy group the critical change process seemed to involve a shift in self–other schematic structures from hostile dependence to affiliative autonomy. An adjunctive study by Maslove (1989) also revealed that at markers of unfinished business the empty chair dialogue facilitated significantly greater depth of experiencing than empathic reflection.

Practical implications

These studies confirmed that when presenting client problems are expressed as unresolved feelings related to past relationships it is more fruitful for the therapist to work through the unfinished business by encouraging clients to re-experience and express aroused emotions to the significant other rather than to respond to clients with empathic reflection. Therapists who direct clients to engage in an empty chair dialogue with a significant other and encourage them to vividly describe specific aspects of a troublesome memory help clients achieve greater expression of feelings and greater self-understanding. Further, encouraging clients to fully access relevant emotional schemata and reprocess the associated emotions and beliefs results in the reorganization of self–other schematic structures. This treatment approach facilitates the development of a more positive and healthy perspective on a troubling interpersonal relationship.

Developing a preliminary model of the resolution of unfinished business

After the specific client problem of unfinished business had been reliably identified, the development of a model of resolution could proceed. The first step involved constructing a rational model of the process of resolution of unfinished business (Greenberg & Safran, 1987). This entailed imaging the various ways in which the task could be resolved and then comparing this rational model to observations of actual client performances. In the rational model, depicted in Figure 9.1, a number of elements were deemed integral to the resolution process. First, the client begins by describing an unfinished feeling such as disappointment, anger, hurt or sadness in relation to a significant other. The client acknowledges that these feelings interfere with his or her functioning. Next the recollection of a specific episodic memory concerning the significant other is crucial. In other words, the client moves from a generalized feeling to vividly reliving and describing the idiosyncratic features associated with a particular situation. For example, a client may recall the tone of voice of his or her mother, a look of disappointment or a feeling of constriction and tension in his or her body. In the next step, the specific components of the schematic memory are clarified and explored. For example, the client may attend to the feeling

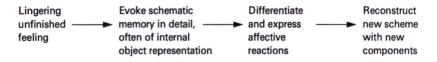

Figure 9.1   *Rational model of unfinished business*

of tension in his or her body and express these feelings to the imagined other. In doing so, the reaction to the other becomes less automatic and the associated emotions are less reactive. In the final step, some new inner experience is symbolized in awareness. The new schema that is constructed contains less traumatic elements associated with the representation of the other. In addition, the representation of the other often includes new elements, such as a recognition of the positive aspects of the other.

Once a rational model had been constructed, the next step was to inspect actual performances to determine whether the rational model accurately captured the complexity of the therapeutic interaction. In this case, two transcripts of successful unfinished business work were used as a basis for the comparison with the rational model (Greenberg & Safran, 1987). The comparison involved intensively observing the resolution performances of these two clients and looking for places where there was a match or mismatch with the rational model. In addition, methods for empirically measuring the important components of resolution were explored. The information generated by this intensive analysis was then used to refine the original model. The initial rational model was elaborated upon by moving in circular fashion between the observations of actual client performances and the simple model.

Research findings

The result of this intensive analysis was the development of a preliminary empirical model ((Figure 9.2). This empirical model expanded upon the components of the rational model in a number of ways. First, intensive analyses revealed that a critical component of the resolution process was the arousal, differentiation and expression of emotion. Vividly imagining the other seemed to help to intensify the expression of emotion. Further, the intensified expression of emotion helped the client access the schematic emotional memory and led to the differentiation of hurt from anger, which in turn led to the full expression of these feelings.

Another important aspect of the resolution performance, which followed from the intense expression of hurt and anger, was a restructuring of schematic memories of the significant other. After the previously inter-rupted emotions were fully expressed, a positive representation of the other emerged. The positive other reflected a new appreciation of the other's situation, for example the difficulties that limited the other.

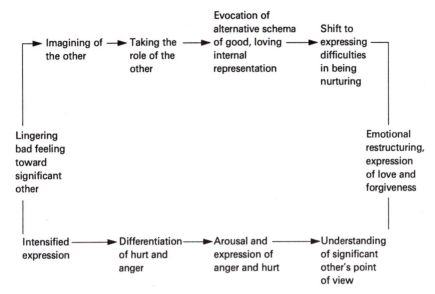

Figure 9.2 *Preliminary empirical model*

The following clinical example illustrates the salient components of resolution. One young man presented in therapy with unresolved feelings toward his father, who had abandoned him when he was age 11. Early in therapy, the client's anger toward his father was so intense that he had difficulty making contact with his father in an imaginary dialogue. This tendency to avoid contact related to his long-standing efforts to try not to think about his father. He had always been told by others to forget about his father and move on. After he identified this difficulty, he was able to begin to express his feelings of anger toward his father. 'I completely trusted you and you abandoned me. I can't forgive you.' The client allowed himself to express the full intensity of his anger toward his father. Following this expression he stated, 'I needed a father, I needed you to be there for me.' The primary anger that was expressed had likely never been previously accessed by the client nor had the unmet need been clearly articulated. After this, a new, more compassionate, loving and remorseful representation of the father emerged. The client shifted toward a more compassionate view of his father.

This new view of the other was revealed in the following statement: 'I understand. You did what you did for your reasons, you had a lot of pressures on you. I forgive you ... I want you to know that I missed you ...'

Practical implications

While this model still needed empirical verification, it gave researchers and clinicians a refined understanding of the client processes involved in the exploration and resolution of unfinished business. Such models help to clarify the specific nature and sequence of steps involved in the resolution process. They truly inform clinical practice. It is this model-building aspect of the research that is most relevant to practice. The model remains close to the level of practice and serves to specify what clients (and therapists) actually do in therapy to effect change. Thus, steps such as differentiating complaint or blame into primary anger or sadness highlight the importance of the arousal of emotion as a precursor to a shift in the representation of the other.

Development and testing of the model of the resolution of unfinished business

The rational-empirical model of the resolution of unfinished business was a preliminary effort toward modelling the change process. An intensive examination of additional unfinished business events was undertaken to develop a more refined empirical model of resolution. It was important to determine whether the components of resolution could be identified and measured in a reliable and empirical manner. A number of dialogues were rigorously described in a performance diagram using a variety of process descriptors in order to more clearly discriminate crucial processes (see Figure 9.3). As shown, this performance diagram depicts the interactional states in the dialogue on a measure of affiliation and autonomy (SASB – Structural Analysis of Social Behavior; Benjamin, 1988) as well as depth of experiencing (Experiencing Scale; Klein, Mathieu, Kiesler & Gendlin, 1969) and vocal quality (Vocal Quality Scale; Rice & Kerr, 1986). Time flows from left to right and top to bottom. In this diagram we see the self in state 1 rated on SASB as blaming in an external voice and lecturing quality with experiencing level 3 (reaction to external events) and low emotional arousal; in state 2 the self attacks in an emotional voice with both high emotional arousal and high experiencing levels (focused inwards in a descriptive and associative manner); in state 3 the self whines and complains in an external voice with low experiencing and arousal. The other chair in state 4 responds by walling off (ignoring) in a limited voice (tense, low energy quality) and low experiencing and emotional arousal; followed, in state 5, by separating (going own separate way), an external voice and low experiencing and low emotional arousal; in state 6, the other repeats the ignoring stance but now uses an external voice. In state 7, the self repeats the complaints. A shift occurs in state 8 in which the client discloses in a focused (inner directed and exploratory quality) and emotional voice with higher experiencing and high emotional arousal (sobs). The other, in state 9, responds by disclosing and revealing in a focused voice with high experiencing (offering a proposition about the self) and moderate emotional arousal. The transaction ends in state 13 with the self rated on SASB as actively expressing love in a focused voice. This type

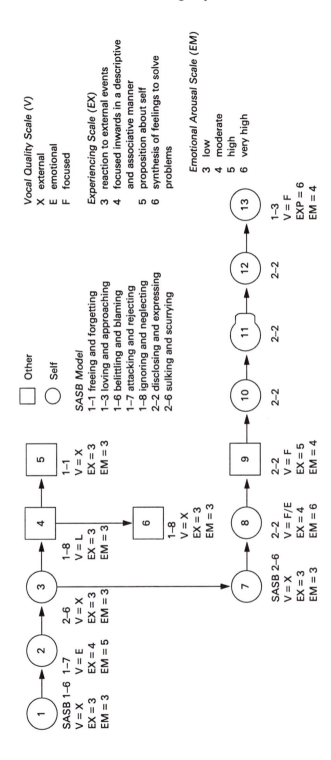

Figure 9.3 *Client performance diagram of the resolution of unfinished business*

of fine-grained process analysis revealed more closely what the process of change involved and how the different states could be measured.

A study by Foerester (1990) finalized the development of a more refined understanding of how change occurs in the resolution of unfinished business and provided the first empirical verification of the model of resolution. The preliminary rational-empirical model (Figure 9.2) served as the basis upon which a more refined rational-empirical model of resolution was developed. In the preliminary, discovery-oriented phase of the study, three resolution and three non-resolution performances were selected for further intensive observation.

Research findings

A refined rational-empirical model (Figure 9.4) was articulated and yielded three advances over the earlier rational-empirical model. The first place of revision was identified at the start of the dialogue, tracking the client in the self chair. It was apparent that not all clients began the dialogue by expressing feelings of blame or complaint, as previously thought. Instead some clients began by expressing feelings of hurt. For example, in the clinical example described earlier, the client initially spent a lot of time expressing his feelings of pain about being alone in the world without his father.

A second area of refinement from the earlier model was the observation that the expression of needs was a necessary step in the resolution process. In comparison with non-resolution events, the resolution of unfinished business was characterized by the expression of personal, intimate needs. For example, a state of non-resolution could be characterized by the following statements, 'I need you to get off my back', and 'I don't want your criticism'. Resolved cases contain statements of needs that are more elaborate and personal and directly convey a basic need for autonomy, such as 'I need you to see all of me and not just the bad'.

A final point of revision in the model involved differentiating between two forms of resolution. Not all clients came to a place of understanding the other in the resolution process. For some clients, resolution involved assuming a more assertive self posture and holding the other accountable. For clients, particularly those resolving issues of abuse and violation, an adaptive response could involve assuming a position of power in the relationship and holding the other accountable. For example, one woman addressing the man who had repeatedly molested her as a child stated, in the empty chair dialogue, 'I feel good about having the tables turned. I feel good about being where I am. You know who I am and what I've accomplished in comparison to you. I'm glad that I put you behind bars.'

To verify empirically the revised model of resolution, 22 unfinished business events were selected. Of these 22 events, half were judged to be resolved and half were judged to be unresolved on the basis of specific criteria of resolution. Four therapy process measures were selected to

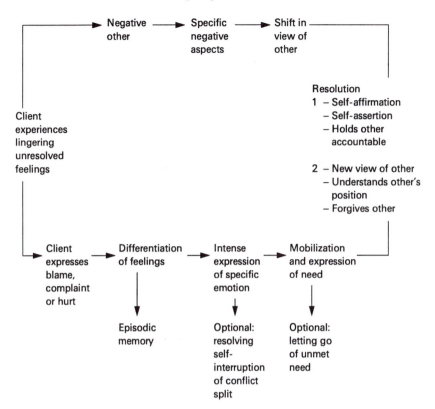

Figure 9.4 *Refined model of the resolution of unfinished business*

describe more fully the features of the components of resolution. Resolution components were assessed in terms of clients' involvement in the session Experiencing Scale (EX), an assessment of the nature of the interaction between the two chairs (SASB), the expression of primary emotions (the client's Emotional Arousal Scale, EM; Daldrup et al., 1988) and a need measure devised for this study based on Murray's (1938) list of needs. The presence or absence of resolution components were verified based on specific configurations of scores on these process measures.

Practical implications

The results of this study provided empirical support for the refined model of the resolution of unfinished business. Clients who resolve experiences of unfinished business are more likely than those who do not to engage in the following processes: 'intense expression of emotion', 'expression of need', 'change to new and positive view of other' and 'self-affirmation, self-assertion or understanding of the other'. These components were predicted by the model and supported by ratings on the four therapy process measures. The refined resolution model is presented as a linear sequence of steps in Figure 9.4. Clients, however, typically move in a back and forward fashion between the steps. Having once attained a stage, they are able to move on to the next stage. Furthermore, clients, over the course of treatment, may repeatedly return to work on the unfinished business issue until it is resolved.

Consider the following example of a woman who resolved her feelings of anger about being neglected by her mother. She began, over the course of a 12-session treatment, with a non-specific expression of her unresolved feelings: 'I have a lot of anger towards you.' The therapist directed the client to address the mother with these feelings and the client responded by becoming more specific and intense in her expression: '. . . you were absolutely impossible. . . . God damn it you were stubborn.' The therapist then guided the client to speak from the position of the mother. The client, as mother, defending her position stated, 'I always did my best for you. I always cared for you.' In a later session following the enactment of the mother, the client intensified her emotional expression and in doing so, identified her personal unmet need: 'I'm pissed off . . . I needed you and you weren't there . . . I needed you to defend me . . . I felt so alone I wanted more from you . . . .' After the expression of the need to the imagined other, a positive and more vulnerable mother emerged: 'If I were to give you what you wanted, I would have to open up . . . I would unleash my demons. I've shut the lid on my demons.' Finally, in a later session the client revealed her new perspective of her mother and their relationship in the following statement: 'At least now I look at you in a different light. . . . Maybe I look at you as a mother that knew she was doing wrong, didn't know any other way. . . . You know maybe we can go on from here.'

Practical applications

The empirically validated task analytically generated model further clarified our understanding of the key processes necessary in the resolution of unfinished business. Describing and verifying the process of change helped to establish the specific mechanisms of change. Work with unfinished business through the empty chair method appears to enable clients to return to earlier situations and relive situations in the present in order to find new solutions to troubling feelings. The intense expression of primary emotion, such as pure sadness and pure anger, appears to be particularly important in allowing the differentiated emotional processing that leads to an articulation of unmet needs. The differentiated expression of personal needs appears to be critical to enabling clients to make more realistic and adaptive adjustments to the environment. The emotional processing plus mobilization of an unmet need in turn leads to a cognitive reorganization, expanding clients rigid, constricted and negative views of other and self. Therapists must allow the particular idiosyncratic resolution to emerge from the dialogue. The resolution of an unfinished business issue may even take the form of either forgiveness or holding the other accountable, depending on the nature of the unfinished business. The development and testing of this model of resolution resulted in the mounting of a treatment program for the resolution of unfinished business with a significant other. A program of therapy for unfinished business was advertised in Toronto and received 300 inquiries within five days. This indicated that this problem tapped a highly recognizable concern for people.

An empirical assessment of the efficacy of the empty chair intervention for resolving unfinished business experiences

Three verification-oriented studies were conducted in conjunction with the treatment program. These studies involved: (1) establishing the effectiveness of a manual-guided method of treatment intervention developed on the basis of a task analysis; (2) developing and testing a measure of unfinished business resolution; and (3) empirically assessing whether the specified change components related to outcome. The first study assessed whether a process-diagnostic treatment of unfinished business was more effective than a psychoeducational treatment (Paivio & Greenberg, 1995). Thirty-four clients were randomly assigned to an empty chair therapy or a psycho-educational control group ($N = 17$ per group). The process-experiential therapy, in which empty chair was the primary method of intervention, was 12–15 weeks in duration.

Research findings

Results confirmed that the empty chair therapy was a highly successful approach for resolving unfinished business experiences. The empty chair therapy group showed superior efficacy over the psychoeducational group, revealing a significantly greater reduction in symptom distress, decrease in interpersonal distress and a greater sense of resolution of the unfinished business problem. In addition, clients indicated changes in their perceptions of self and significant other in the relationship. As a group, empty chair therapy clients became increasingly friendly and less hostile in their attitudes about the relationship. Therapy clients also reported greater self-love and self-acceptance. Importantly, these therapeutic gains were maintained by four months post-therapy.

Practical applications

The results of this study are significant for a number of reasons. First, they demonstrate that emotional disturbances can be meaningfully identified in terms of an emotion processing difficulty related to unresolved feelings toward another. For the first time, a population of individuals for whom unfinished business was a predominant problematic state was readily identified. In addition, the empty chair dialogue was found to be an effective intervention in short-term therapy for helping people overcome unresolved negative feelings toward another. This therapeutic intervention could also be utilized as a potentially powerful component of a more comprehensive treatment program.

We believe that a more differentiated process-diagnostic perspective, in which the therapist identifies specific client processing problems and targets these difficulties for differential therapeutic interventions, is a viable alternative to traditional diagnostic approaches and less differentiated treatment approaches. This method is invaluable to process assessment and treatment. Furthermore, this approach is highly compatible with the current move toward psychotherapy integration. Many clinicians are beginning to recognize the utility of applying different therapeutic interventions arising from different orientations to address varying clients' problems. This research confirms the efficacy of such approaches and outlines a viable framework for integrating therapeutic interventions.

Specifying the post-session change process

An advantage of studying specific therapeutic processes for particular types of client problems is that measures of change specific to these particular phenomena can be developed. Within many clinical and research programs 'change' is assessed using global measures of symptom reduction that do not provide as much differentiated information as does an investigation of change in terms of the unique aspects of specific problems. In this regard, Singh (1994) developed a self-report instrument to measure the resolution of unfinished business. This instrument allows investigators to track the status of unfinished business over the course of therapy. Although the scale was developed within the framework of process-experiential therapy, the scale might be applicable for measuring the resolution of unfinished business with a significant other within other treatment approaches.

The scale consists of 11 items that fall into the following four subcategories: (a) 'perceptions of the self'; (b) 'perception of the other'; (c) 'degree of distress associated with lingering feelings'; and (d) 'not having needs met'. For example, an item that measures 'perceptions of the self' is 'I feel worthwhile in relation to this person'. An item that measures 'perception of the other' is 'I have a deep appreciation of this person's own personal difficulties'. The scale items were factor analyzed in order to determine the dimensionality of the scale and the acceptability of the instrument as a measure of change. Three factors were identifiable. The factors corresponded to the subcategories of the scale, with the exception of subcategories three and four, which collapsed into one component, identified as 'degree of distress associated with lingering feelings and unmet needs'.

Singh (1994) used the scale to track the resolution of unfinished business in clients who went through the process-experiential therapy that focused on resolving unfinished business with significant others. Results showed that, by the sixth session, the post-session resolution was predictive of decreases in symptoms and interpersonal problems as well as an increase in self-acceptance. By termination, the report of resolution was also predictive of changes in the perception of self as well as the degree of affiliation toward the significant other. In addition, Singh found that prolonged session change, one week after a high change session, was the best predictor of final improvement.

Practical implications

Clients who report significant changes by post-session in terms of their degree of resolution of unfinished business were more likely to show enduring session changes. This example is consistent with our view that change in therapy occurs cumulatively over a number of sessions, and that resolution must be sustained over time, and sometimes reworked and reintegrated to form a new view of self. These findings suggest that it is necessary to identify and focus upon unresolved feelings toward a significant other early enough in the therapy sequence to allow the process to be reworked sufficiently often (approx. three to eight times). In-session problem resolution that endures over a week appears to be a good index of lasting change. Furthermore, clients who attain a sense of resolution by the end of therapy are likely to sustain this change long after therapy ends.

An empirical test to relate client change processes to treatment outcome

An important step in the process of verifying the model is to determine whether the posited mechanisms of change in the resolution of unfinished business can account for treatment success. A study by McMain (1995) is the first to link unfinished business therapy process to treatment outcome. The specific aim of this study was to evaluate whether the predicted changes in perceptions about self and other were associated with treatment success. It was predicted that if clients moved from a position of hostility toward the other in early therapy dialogues, to greater friendliness and/or greater self-affirmation in late therapy dialogues, then this change would be reflected by improved outcome as measured by the reduction of symptom distress, an increase in the level of interpersonal functioning, and change in attitudes about the relationship and about oneself.

A subgroup of 27 clients was drawn for study from the unfinished business therapy program. To assess the change in perceptions of self and other in therapy, an early and late dialogue were selected from each therapy. Two process measures were applied to therapy transcripts in order to quantify information about clients' representations of self and other. One measure assessed the changes in components of the conflictual relationship theme with the significant other (Core Conflictual Relationship Theme, CCRT; Luborsky & Crits-Christoph, 1990) and the other measure assessed dimensions of the interpersonal interaction between the two chairs (SASB; Benjamin, 1981, 1988).

Research findings

The result of this study confirmed that the emotionally focused therapy which relied upon the Gestalt empty chair intervention to resolve experiences of unfinished business worked by changing views of the self. The critical components of change involved more autonomous, affiliative and positive representations of the self in relation to the significant other. The development of independent behavior by the self in relation to the other appeared to be particularly important in that increased self-autonomy not only predicted a change in the attitude about the targeted relationship, but also predicted a reduction in symptom distress and interpersonal problems.

Practical implications

Success hinges on changes in the perceptions of self in relation to the other. Just as Foerester's (1990) study indicated that encouraging the expression of needs is a specific therapeutic technique which helped to empower the client, McMain's (1995) study revealed that therapeutic interventions which emphasize the development of more autonomous, independent stances in the self, across early and late empty chair dialogues, are particularly important in terms of reducing symptom distress and interpersonal functioning. Another observation made previously that was further substantiated in this study was that expecting changes in the representation of the other may not always be an appropriate treatment goal or index of improvement for all clients, particularly in abuse cases, where forgiveness of the other is not necessarily an indication of healthy development. Finally, this study indicated that therapists need not promote a decline in degree of negative perceptions of self or other, as these factors were not associated with a successful outcome. Rather, the curative process of therapy appears to involve the incorporation of more positive ways of responding.

Conclusion

In this chapter, we have described a change process research program that continually informs our clinical understanding and practice. Our research questions were born out of gaps in our clinical knowledge. The research methods that were employed to address these questions attempted to be sensitive to the complexities of the clinical encounter. Modeling the specific components of client change relevant to particular cognitive–affective processing difficulties, in this instance unfinished business, advanced our knowledge of the complex issues inherent in this affective information processing task. This enabled a richer description of the processes that underlie the various components of change, thereby allowing us to determine the most appropriate therapeutic interventions to facilitate each change step.

References

Benjamin, L. (1981). *Manual for coding social interaction in terms of structural analysis of social behavior (SASB)*. Madison: University of Wisconsin Press.

Benjamin, L. (1988). *SASB Short Form user's manual*. Salt Lake City, UT: Intrex Interpersonal Institute Inc.

Daldrup, R.J., Beutler, L.E., Engle, D., & Greenberg, L.S. (1988). *Focused expressive psychotherapy: Freeing the overcontrolled patient*. New York: Guilford.

Foerester, F.S. (1990). *Refinement and verification of a model of the resolution of unfinished business*. Unpublished master's thesis, York University, Toronto.

Greenberg, L.S. (1977). A task analytic approach to the study of psychotherapeutic events (Doctoral dissertation, York University, Toronto, 1975). *Dissertation Abstracts International, 37*, 4647B.

Greenberg, L.S. (1984). A task analysis of intrapersonal conflict resolution. In L.N. Rice & L.S. Greenberg (Eds.), *Patterns of change: Intensive analysis of psychotherapy process* (pp. 67–123). New York: Guilford.

Greenberg, L.S. (1986). Change process research. *Journal of Consulting and Clinical Psychology, 54*, 4–9.

Greenberg, L.S. (1991). Research on the process of change. *Psychotherapy Research, 1*, 14–24.

Greenberg, L.S. (1994). A task analysis of intrapersonal conflict resolution. In L.N. Rice & L.S. Greenberg (Eds.), *Patterns of change: Intensive analysis of psychotherapy process* (pp. 67–123). New York: Guilford.

Greenberg, L., & Korman, L. (1993). Assimilating emotion into psychotherapy integration. *Journal of Integrative Psychotherapy, 3*, 249–266.

Greenberg, L.S., & Minden, R. (1988). *Gestalt therapy experiments: A manual and adherence measure*. Unpublished manuscript, York University, Toronto.

Greenberg, L.S., & Pinsof, W.M. (1986). Process research: Current trends and future perspectives. In L.S. Greenberg & W.M. Pinsof (Eds.), *The psychotherapeutic process: A research handbook*. New York: Guilford.

Greenberg, L.S., & Rice, L.N. (1990). *Experiential change processes in depression*. NIMH Grant #RO1MH450403, Washington, DC.

Greenberg, L.S., Rice, L.N., & Elliot, R. (1993). *Facilitating emotional change: The moment by moment process*. New York: Guilford.

Greenberg, L.S., & Safran, J.D. (1987). *Emotion in psychotherapy: Affect, cognition, and the process of change*. New York: Guilford.

King, S. (1988). *The differential effects of empty-chair dialogue and empathic reflection on unfinished business*. Unpublished master's thesis, University of British Columbia, Vancouver.

Klein, M., Mathieu, P., Kiesler, D., & Gendlin, E. (1969). *The experiencing scale*. Wisconsin: Wisconsin Psychiatric Institute.

Luborsky, L. (1977). Measuring a pervasive psychic structure in psychotherapy: The core conflictual relationship theme. In N. Freedman & S. Grand (Eds.), *Communicative structures and psychic structures* (pp. 367–395). New York: Plenum Press.

Luborsky, L., & Crits-Christoph, P. (1990). *Understanding transference: The core conflictual relationship theme method*. New York: Basic Books.

Maslove, V.J. (1989). *The differential effects of empathic reflection and the gestalt empty-chair dialogue on depth of experiencing when used with an issue of unfinished business.* Unpublished master's thesis, Department of Counselling Psychology, University of British Columbia, Vancouver.

McMain, S. (1995). *Relating changes in self–other schemas to psychotherapy outcome.* Doctoral dissertation, York University, Toronto.

Murray, H.A. (1938). *Explorations in personality.* New York: Oxford University Press.

Paivio, S., & Greenberg, L. (1995). Resolving unfinished business: Experiential therapy using empty chair dialogue. *Journal of Consulting & Clinical Psychology, 63*(3), 419–425.

Perls, F., Hefferline, R., & Goodman, P. (1951). *Gestalt therapy.* New York: Delta.

Rice, L.N., & Greenberg, L.S. (1984). *Patterns of Change: Intensive analysis of psychotherapy process.* New York: Guilford.

Rice, L., & Kerr, G. (1986). Measures of client and therapist vocal quality. In L.S. Greenberg & W. Pinsof (Eds.), *The psychotherapeutic process: A research handbook* (pp. 73–105). New York: Guilford.

Singh, M. (1994). *Validation of a measure of session outcome in the resolution of unfinished business.* Unpublished doctoral dissertation, York University, Toronto.

10

Discovery-Oriented Research on How to Do Psychotherapy

Alvin R. Mahrer

I am trying to answer two questions. The first one is: How can we do research to help discover how to do psychotherapy? If this way of wording the question is not clear, here are some other ways: How can we discover the secrets of psychotherapy? How can we do research so that what is discovered helps contribute to a science of psychotherapeutic practice (Mahrer, 1985)? How can we do research so that the pay-off makes a difference in what psychotherapists can do in their sessions?

The first part of the chapter is an attempt to answer this question. However, the answer will be more of an overview than a detailed mapping of how to do psychotherapy research in this way. Most of the chapter is an attempt to answer the second question: What has this research told us about how to do psychotherapy? Other ways of wording this question are: What has this research discovered about the secrets of how to do psychotherapy? What do the findings of this research have to say to practitioners that might help them in their sessions? On the basis of these findings, what is it that practitioners can do, and how can they do it, to accomplish what kinds of things in their actual sessions? What has this research perhaps contributed to the science of psychotherapeutic practice?

How can we do research to discover how to do psychotherapy?

From about 1954 to 1978, I spent a great deal of time trying to coax fine psychotherapists to let me listen to audio-tapes of their sessions. My main aim was to learn how to do psychotherapy. I was fortunate to be able to study hundreds of tapes from many gracious therapists, representing many approaches. Some of these therapists were well known. Many were not. From about 1978, I continued trying to add to my library of taped sessions. I also continued to try to discover how to do psychotherapy. However, now I studied the tapes more carefully and rigorously with a group of colleagues, a psychotherapy research team, and we published our findings. Here are the broad outlines of what we did, and continue to do, in our efforts to try to discover how to do psychotherapy.

What is discovery-oriented psychotherapy research? It is research aimed at discovering how to do psychotherapy

Our purpose is to try to learn how to do psychotherapy, to discover its secrets, to help develop a science of psychotherapy practice (Mahrer, 1988a). Even more personally, the purpose is to enable me to become a better psychotherapist. In line with the spirit of this book, each piece of our research should have direct consequences for how to do psychotherapy. We are practitioners who are doing research to help us become better practitioners, to discover how to do psychotherapy (Mahrer, 1985, 1988a; Mahrer & Gagnon, 1991).

Why do researchers do research on psychotherapy? What is the purpose or aim of doing the research?   It is easy to think of general reasons for doing research, and then simply apply them to the study of psychotherapy. So you can say that the reason for doing research is to increase knowledge, and therefore researchers do research on psychotherapy to increase knowledge about psychotherapy. But suppose we take a somewhat closer look into just why researchers actually do research on aspects of psychotherapy. What are they after?

There are many ways of setting forth and organizing the reasons, the purposes and aims of doing research on this or that aspect of psychotherapy. What follows is one example. It enables us to get somewhat closer to what discovery-oriented research may be, and how it takes form and shape, by contrasting it with other reasons, purposes and aims of doing research in this field of psychotherapy.

1   Research is done to confirm that psychotherapy works, that it is effective. Usually the researcher believes that psychotherapy does work, but it is helpful to show that it is effective, is useful, does something constructive, especially in comparison with not doing psychotherapy, or, for example, with employing a medical or social treatment approach.

2   Research is done to confirm that my psychotherapy is better than competing psychotherapies. Usually the reason is to show that my psychotherapy is at least as good as, and hopefully better than, some other psychotherapies for the treatment of some kind of problem or mental disorder.

3   Research is done to confirm that using this in-session technique, method or procedure is as good as or better than using this other one. Research can lend credence or some justification to what the researcher believes is a workable, useful, effective in-session intervention, technique, method or procedure.

4   Research is done to confirm my theory. The purpose of the study is to lend credence, to justify, to show that my way of thinking, my conceptualization, my theory, is good, sound, right. Typically, the researcher tries to deduce some hypothesis from the theory, test the hypothesis and show that the findings justify that the theory is good, sound, right, or at least not refuted or undermined (Mahrer, 1988a).

5   Research is done to confirm that what the researcher believes is a general truth about psychotherapy really qualifies as such. These researchers usually believe in a body of universal truths about psychotherapy. This is often called a cumulative body of psychotherapeutic knowledge. It includes general truths that have been stamped as such by researchers. Research is supposed to be the gatekeeper of what is admitted into the cumulative body of knowledge.

6   Research is done to discover how to do psychotherapy. The aim is to improve what the practitioner actually does in the session. The aim is to study the nuts and bolts, the working operations, what the practitioner actually does, in order to make it better. The aim is to discover how the in-session practice of psychotherapy can be helped to become a practical science.

These six reasons for doing psychotherapy research may touch on one another, and there may be other reasons, but there are some big differences in what they try to accomplish, in their working pay-offs. I want to learn more about how to do psychotherapy, about how to do fine in-session work. I want to help develop a science of psychotherapeutic practice. For these reasons or purposes, it is far more useful to do discovery-oriented psychotherapy research. If you want to do research to discover how to do psychotherapy, then the other reasons for doing research, the other aims and purposes, won't be of much use to you.

What are some research questions that are meaningful to many practitioners, and for which discovery-oriented psychotherapy research is probably the most useful way to try to answer them?   There are a few questions that are meaningful to many practitioners, and are also central for discovery-oriented psychotherapy researchers. The first, and probably most important, question may be phrased as follows: What are the kinds of in-session events that impress you, that are important to you, that you would like to achieve? What is it that you truly want to accomplish in the session?

The second question may be phrased as follows: What seemed to help bring about this impressive change? What did the therapist and patient seem to do that may account for this important change? What did the therapist do, under what patient condition, or when the patient was apparently being like this or that, that seemed to help bring about the in-session change that impressed you?

The third question may be phrased as follows: Once this impressive change occurred, how did the therapist seem to use it? What did the therapist seem to do to help bring about further or subsequent kinds of impressive changes? What did the therapist do once this impressive change occurred?

These questions are important to some practitioners. They are the kinds of questions that both justify and define discovery-oriented psychotherapy research. That is, discovery-oriented psychotherapy research is designed to try to answer these kinds of questions.

How can you determine which reason, purpose or aim for doing research is better, more 'scientific'? It is very hard to determine which reason or purpose or aim for doing psychotherapy research is somehow better or more scientific. Suppose that one reason is to try to discover how to do psychotherapy, to help make the actual practice more of a science. It seems very hard to decide that this reason is more or less scientific, or better, than trying to see which brand of psychotherapy is more effective to treat some given mental disorder.

It also seems hard to compare the actual designs or methodologies or ways of doing the research when one study is aimed at discovering more about how to do psychotherapy and another study is aimed at confirming that, say, my theory of psychopathology is a good one. Depending on the reason or purpose or aim for doing the research, the way you carry out the studies would probably be quite different. Because the way you carry out the study would likely differ, it is hard to say that one is better or more scientific.

Regardless of the reason, purpose or aim, it seems that the particular way of carrying out a study may be somewhat loose, sloppy, hard to duplicate, or may be careful, rigorous, systematic, justifying confidence in the findings, scientific.

I cannot agree that any particular reason, purpose or aim for doing psychotherapy research is somehow better or more scientific than the others. Nor can I agree that any specific way of doing research is universally better or more scientific than the others. I do not agree that it is universally better or more scientific to use pre–post comparisons, control groups and most of the methods generally associated with doing 'experiments'. One of the risks in doing research to try to discover more about how to do psychotherapy is that we do not usually rely on the methods used in doing psychotherapy research for other reasons, purposes or aims. I prefer relying on methods that are useful, appropriate, careful, rigorous and systematic from the point of view of doing discovery-oriented research, rather than using whatever research methods are regarded as being scientific for other reasons, purposes and aims.

Discovery-oriented research is done to discover how to do psychotherapy, to help build a science of psychotherapeutic practice. But how is this kind of research done? What do you do to discover the secrets of the actual practice of psychotherapy?

We collect many tapes from many therapists

We are trying to assemble our own library of psychotherapy tapes. Should they be audio-tapes or video-tapes? It would be nice if we had a library full of video-tapes, but that is usually hard to obtain. Most practitioners are not in a position to video-tape their sessions. Audio-tapes are very useful, much easier to obtain than video-tapes, and worlds better than nothing at all.

We try to get tapes of actual sessions with actual patients. These usually have higher pay-off than tapes with actors as patients, or demonstration tapes with someone from the audience as a volunteer patient.

Because our research is designed to discover more about how to do psychotherapy, we usually do not need anything on the tape that can identify the patient, or even the therapist. Accordingly, there are technical ways of deleting any such identifying signs and of altering voices to make them less recognizable. This safeguarding of anonymity is preferable from the point of view of legal-professional considerations, while still allowing careful study of the tape.

We try to get as many tapes as we can. It is nice to have a number of sessions of work with the same patient, but even one or two tapes are valuable. We have about four hundred and fifty tapes.

We try to get tapes from as many therapists as we can. Fortunately, we have tapes from a large variety of therapists, kinds of approaches and psychotherapy-related professions. Our data pool includes some sessions of my experiential psychotherapy. With these as minor exceptions, the therapists represent as wide a variety of therapists as we can get. Typically, we plead with a large number of colleagues to send us tapes. We also ask them whom they respect as fine practitioners in their communities, and then ask these practitioners if we may have a tape or tapes of their sessions. We ask for any tapes at all, perhaps an initial session, just an ordinary session, or ones that they are reasonably proud of, or tapes with impressive changes for a particular patient, or ones that are somehow representative or interesting.

We treasure tapes of special sessions containing significant, impressive patient changes

We do our best to get tapes of special sessions containing significant, impressive patient changes. We ask therapists to let us study any of their sessions that they are proud of, where they accomplished what they wanted to accomplish, where something very fine happened even though they may not have expected it. Therapists may feel that this tape is a fine example of their work. Or it may be an exceptional session, one they rarely attain. Some therapists send us such tapes because they know we are single-minded about trying to see what might have led to that impressive change. These tapes are precious. One way to get tapes that may contain impressive changes is to ask for them straightforwardly from other therapists, or to go through our present tape library to find these special sessions.

Another way we get tapes like this is to pick them out from our own work. I tape most of my own sessions. Usually I rerecord sessions using the same tape. But then there are those special sessions. Something went very well. Something unusual happened. Those are the special tapes that I treasure. Those are the tapes that I study. Sometimes the significant, impressive change is one that I have been trying to get, and here is an exceptional instance of its actual occurrence. Sometimes the significant, impressive change is something that seems beyond or different from what I expected.

Our research team is dedicated to discovering how to do psychotherapy

Our psychotherapy research team has a fluctuating membership of from 8 to 12 or more (Mahrer, Paterson, Theriault, Roessler & Quenneville, 1986). The team can include psychologists, psychiatrists, social workers, students, trainees, therapists of all kinds. Perhaps the main characteristic is that we are dedicated to helping to discover how to do psychotherapy by careful study of tapes of actual practitioners. Almost everyone stays on the team for at least a year; most usually stay for two or three years. We meet every week to carry out our studies (Mahrer & Gagnon, 1991).

How do we pick out the impressive changes that we will study?

We listen to tapes. The guiding question is: Do you think this tape contains any significant, impressive changes that you would be interested in studying? Whatever we study comes from this ongoing, continuous tape-listening to try to find patient changes that we might wish to study. It is exciting to look for these impressive changes.

Having a large team looking for all kinds of impressive changes keeps me honest, and enables us to find impressive changes that a single shared orientation would probably miss. On the other hand, if all the team members share a single orientation, you can concentrate on the kinds of patient changes that are especially relevant for that approach.

We rely on the team members' own clinical judgment in picking out the impressive change that we may study. However, it can be helpful to give them various lists and category systems of significant in-session changes, representative of various therapeutic approaches (for example, Mahrer, 1985, 1988b; Mahrer, Gagnon, Fairweather & Cote, 1992; Mahrer & Nadler, 1986; Mahrer et al., 1992). Make sure these are merely helpful guides to assist the judges' own determination of what should be studied.

There are some different ways of selecting impressive changes to study:

The patient seems to be impressively different in the opening of this session, as compared with the prior session In experiential sessions, at the beginning of the session, the therapist especially looks for at least three kinds of impressive changes (Mahrer, 1996):

1   Does the person seem to be a qualitatively new person? The prior session gave the patient a chance to be a qualitatively new person. Is the patient this whole new person in this session?

2   Did the patient do his or her homework? That is, does it seem that he or she was able to be and to behave as this new person in the way and in the situational context that were determined in the prior session?

3   Is the person free of the scene filled with bad feelings that was upper-
    most in and central to the last session? Hopefully, this will be the case.

Regardless of the approach, the impressive change can be found by
looking at the way the person is in this session as compared with the
previous session.

Listen for whatever seems to be an impressive change   Start out by letting
judges be on the look-out for any changes that seem significant and
impressive. At this preliminary stage, it can be helpful to have a reasonably
helpful description of what you mean by significant and impressive
changes. The definition helps. But let the judges do their work by flagging
anything that seems to strike them as impressive. They do not even have to
name the change. It is enough for the judges to say that some kind of
impressive change seemed to occur right about here.

The impressive change would be if the patient were free of that bad thing   In
the session, look for something that could or should go away, that the
patient could or should be free of. If the patient can be free of that
particular thing, the change would be impressive. For example, suppose
that the patient is crying, scared, hopeless, frightened, and seems to be
attending mainly to the way her husband yells at her. You reason that if
she is no longer feeling that awful way, in that scene filled with those kinds
of bad feelings, the change would be impressive, significant, valuable. So
you keep that in mind as you listen to the rest of the session. Suppose that,
later on, she is happy, tough, sure of herself in relation to her husband.
That can be seen as an impressive change.

In a similar·way, it might be judged as an impressive change if, in the
session, the person no longer stutters, is free of the constant headache he
says he has, is no longer so gloomy and ready to die, is eager to be with the
son he had been hating so much. If these changes occur within the session,
they may qualify as impressive.

*The impressive change would be the occurrence of what the therapist seems to
be trying to accomplish*   Sometimes it is rather clear what the therapist is
trying to accomplish, and the judge determines that if this is actually
accomplished, the change might indeed be significant and impressive. In
each experiential session, for example, the therapist tries to enable the
patient to attain four sequential steps (Mahrer, 1996). One is to be in a
moment of strong feeling and to access the deeper experiencing. A second is
for the patient to welcome and appreciate that accessed deeper experiencing. A third is for the patient actually to undergo the qualitative change
into being this deeper experiencing. The final step is for the person to be
and to behave as this new person in the prospective extra-therapy world.
High-grade instances of this four-step sequence would probably qualify as
significantly impressive changes.

In a similar way, knowledgeable judges can tell that this therapist is trying to get the patient to have a significant insight, or to be able to scream and yell at his father, or to be able to touch the snake without being tense, or to enter into a hypnogogic state of being a baby. If any of these are accomplished, it may be judged as an impressive change.

Once we select a significant, impressive change, we look for other fine examples of that change Each of the above ways will help to pick out a change that is impressive to us. Now we have something to guide us in looking through other tapes. This means that we can be a little more rigorous in trying to identify just what constitutes the kind of significant, impressive change that we are looking for. We try to find as many instances of it as we can.

Once we have found the impressive changes, what research questions do we want to ask? What do we want to discover?

Picture that we have found one or 10 or 60 instances of some kind of significant patient change. What kinds of research questions do we want to ask? What do we want to discover? In our studies, there are two main kinds of research questions, two things we want to discover.

How did the therapist do that? What did the therapist do to help bring about that impressive change? Perhaps a more careful way of framing the research question is: When the patient seems to be like this, is in this state or condition, what do therapists do so that there is a reasonable likelihood of achieving that particular kind of significant, impressive, consequent change in the patient? The purpose of our research is to try to answer this question (Mahrer, 1985, 1988a).

If we are fortunate and careful in answering this question, then we may frame a proposition that when the patient is being like this, is in this state or condition, if the therapist does this and that, then there is a reasonable likelihood of achieving that particular kind of significant, impressive, consequent patient change.

How did the therapist use that? In other words, what did the therapist do once the impressive change occurred? Essentially, we are asking the same research question: When the patient seems to have undergone this significant, impressive change, what do therapists do so that there is a reasonable likelihood of achieving what kinds of subsequent, consequent changes in the patient?

The therapist might not use the impressive change in any way that we can tell. Or maybe the therapist did use that impressive change to move on to some further impressive change, or for some other use. Answering this question shows us what to do once we are fortunate enough to have attained that impressive change.

*We try to be reasonably rigorous in seeking to discover answers to
our research questions*

Once we have selected the kind of impressive change we want to study, we
get as many tapes as possible containing that kind of impressive change.
The aim is to answer the research questions in a way that is rigorous,
careful, duplicatable and precise enough for us to have confidence, certainty
and trust in our findings.

We concentrate on one tape at a time. One group of judges studies the
tape to identify the location of whatever we are looking for, where
the impressive change seems to be on the tape. Once we find where the
impressive change seems to be, the large team of judges studies the tape to
answer the questions for this study. For example, each judge independently
tries to answer questions such as:

1   How would you describe what is happening right here? Is there a
     change happening? How would you describe the change?
2   What do the therapist and patient seem to do to help bring about the
     occurrence of this change?
3   Once this change has occurred, how does the therapist seem to use this
     change?

Each question is studied one at a time. The judges independently write
their answers to the question, and a second group of judges collates the
independent answers into a single composite which is accepted, modified or
fails to meet criterion approval of the large team of judges. These composite
answers to the research questions are the working data for each study.

Typically, we start with the impressive change and work carefully backward and forward. The purpose of looking backward is to try to discover
how the therapist helped to bring about that change. Looking forward
allows us to discover how that impressive patient change may be used once
it occurs.

We try to be rigorous if we only have a few instances of some impressive
change. If we have enough instances, being rigorous means being able to
apply statistical tests to our data. With a fair number of instances, we can
complement statistical findings by a rigorous examination of variations in
how each instance was brought about and then used.

Whatever kind of impressive change we study, we examine one instance
at a time. As we study each instance, we can see if we find what we found
from discovering previous instances. This allows us to confirm what we had
already found. However, we also are looking for whatever might be new.
Accordingly, with each instance, the question is whether we will confirm
what we have found and whether we will discover something new. In other
words, we discover what is new, and we confirm what we have discovered.
The two go together.

Gradually, carefully, we discover more and more about how to help
bring about particular impressive changes, and what to do with them when

they do occur. When these findings seem to make a difference in our own work, we try out what our findings have suggested to us. We also encourage others to use whatever findings seem to appeal to them. The circle is complete when we include tapes of these new sessions in our data pool. By a rigorous process of trying to discover how psychotherapy works, trying to use our own findings, and further trying to discover how psychotherapy works, we are continuously answering our research questions. Our aim is to do this as rigorously as we can, to enable continued discovery of the secrets of psychotherapy.

This is an overview of what the discovery-oriented approach means when it is applied to psychotherapy research. It is our answer to how we can do research to discover how to do psychotherapy.

What has this research told us about how to do psychotherapy?

In trying to answer this question, I read over each of our studies to see what answer each study offered, and then tried to organize the answers in ways that seemed reasonably sensible. My eye was on trying to see what these studies had to say to practitioners, since that was the reason for doing the studies in the first place. Accordingly, I am not going to present the more or less formal results and findings. Anyone who is interested in the formal findings can go directly to the studies themselves.

Instead, this section is organized into suggestions for how to do psychotherapy, with each suggestion based more or less directly on what we found. If you are drawn toward these suggestions, then I hope that you try them out and see if they work for you.

Try to find your own distinctive, singular, all-purpose small package
of things that you do, and things that you seek to achieve in the
session

Most therapists tend to think of what they do as a rather complicated combination of theory and methods. They describe their work as psycho-analytic or cognitive-behavioral. They talk about being integrative or flexible, as varying with the client, taking into account the client's problem, mental disorder, stage of treatment, developing a working alliance, using supportive methods, providing insight and understanding, using this or that kind of behavioral program, being empathic.

That may be a nice way of talking about what you do. But that is not especially the picture we get if we set aside all this professional-scientific vocabulary. If we simply take a close look at what practitioners actually do, it seems that most of those we studied relied mainly on their own small package of around three to six specific and concrete activities for most of the session. However, it seems that just about each of our practitioners had his or her own small package. There is plenty of variation from practitioner to practitioner, but the package for each was quite small.

Furthermore, the practitioner seems to use much the same small package in most sessions with the same client, and also with most clients. It is as if each practitioner relies on his or her own core of things that they do. For example, one therapist may rely heavily on (1) getting more information about what the patient is talking about, (2) giving interpretations about what the patient is like, and (3) suggesting what the patient might have done or should have done.

This small package includes both what you actually do in the session and what it is you try to accomplish. For example, what you do includes giving interpretations, and what you try to accomplish is to try to help the patient to accept the interpretation, to have a better way of understanding whatever the interpretation is about.

Accordingly, the suggestion is that you listen to some tapes of your own sessions, either by yourself or with one or two helpful colleagues, and see if you can identify the relatively small number of things that you seem to do and try to achieve in many of your sessions and with many of your patients (Mahrer, Nadler, Stalikas, Schachter & Sterner, 1988; Mahrer, Nadler, Sterner & White, 1989; Mahrer, Nifakis, Abhukara & Sterner, 1984; Mahrer, Sterner, Lawson & Dessaulles, 1986).

See if you want to stay with your own small package, or modify the package in some way or other Now that you might have some idea of the distinctive small package of things you tend to do and try to achieve in your sessions, you are free to keep it or to modify it. Remember that this is only a package of the relatively high-frequency things that you do and try to achieve. It is not an exhaustive profile. Yet this small package is relatively characteristic of your way of doing your therapy. If you are satisfied with your distinctive package, then keep it. But the opportunity is always here for you to modify your own package, to adopt two or three packages, to make slight refinements or major changes in the package or packages that are characteristic of your own work. I suggest that you keep modifying the package or packages until you are well and truly satisfied.

If you want to achieve that good, impressive change in the session,
first achieve this good, impressive change

The aim of some studies was to start with what seemed to be good, impressive changes in the session, and then to look at whatever good, impressive changes happened before and happened after, within the same session. We found that a good, impressive change usually did not just happen by itself. Instead, we found that such changes often seemed to be preceded and followed by other good, impressive changes in the session (Mahrer, Nadler, Dessaulles, Gervaize & Sterner, 1987; Mahrer, Nadler, Gervaize & Markow, 1986; Mahrer, White, Howard, Gagnon & MacPhee, 1992; Mahrer, White, Souliere, MacPhee & Boulet, 1991).

Occasionally there was only one significant change in the session. But it was much more common to have impressive changes occurring in sequence, first this one and then that one and then a third. Aside from the actual content of the significant changes, the important finding here was that so many impressive changes were preceded and followed by other impressive changes.

Here are some suggestions that arise from these findings:

1   Listen to tapes of sessions and pick out the kind of in-session change that is good and impressive for you.
2   Look for other impressive changes that occur earlier in the session. Whether these are more or perhaps less impressive, think of these as possibly steps that lead to or feed the subsequent impressive change that you started with.
3   Be on the look-out for a relatively small number of these earlier impressive changes or steps. Look for at least one or more.
4   Be alert to finding several different kinds of impressive changes or steps that regularly come before the good, impressive change that you started with in the first place.

Once you seem to discover whatever impressive changes preceded the one that compelled you in the first place, then you may have something you can do to get that impressive change in the session.

Here are the changes that impress me, and here are the in-session steps that seem to help achieve these changes in each session

Our studies included a few experiential sessions, but the heavy preponderance of tapes were of other therapists doing lots of other kinds of therapies. What seemed to be occurring in study after study was that impressive changes apparently were preceded and followed by other kinds of impressive changes, in the very same session. Of all these sequences or patterns of somewhat regular relationships, some especially appealed to me in my own work. Indeed, the studies yielded a series of four steps that became the four impressive changes I wanted to achieve in every session, and the studies connected these with two impressive changes in the next session when this preceding session successfully and effectively attained these four steps (Mahrer, in press).

Here are the kinds of changes that impress me as the 'outcome' of a successful and effective session, and here are the four steps that I have adopted in order to have a successful and effective session (Mahrer, 1996). If any or all of these are attractive or appealing to you, then the invitation is for you to use them.

At the opening of the next session, the person is free of the scenes filled with bad feelings that were uppermost in and central to the previous session   In this immediate session, the remarkable change is that the person seems to be free of the scenes and situations filled with bad feelings that were uppermost in and central to the previous session. In that session, she was bothered and troubled by painful and troublesome scenes and situations in her life. Now, in this subsequent session, these are no longer a part of her life. She is relatively free of them.

At the opening of the next session, the person is a qualitatively new person The opening of the next session reveals a new person compared to the one who was present at the opening of the previous session. There is a qualitative change in who the person is. The deeper potential that was discovered in the previous session is now a core part of this substantially new person. This can be a magnificent change, an emergence of a qualitatively new person, wound around the deeper potential that had been accessed in the previous session.

Here are the four in-session steps that seemed to help achieve becoming a qualitatively new person and being free of the scenes filled with bad feelings There were several patterns and sequences of in-session changes that were opened up by our studies. Of these, one patterned sequence of four steps seemed especially compelling to me (Mahrer, in press). What seemed so impressive was that the person was virtually transformed into a qualitatively new person who was, in addition, relatively free of the troubling scenes and situations filled with bad feelings that had been uppermost in and central to him or her. Here are the four steps in each of the sessions of experiential psychotherapy.

The first step is being in a moment of strong feeling, and accessing the inner experiencing. This step enables the person to access, to be in touch with, sense, a deeper inner experiencing. Accessing a deeper potential, an inner experiencing, starts with the person's identifying some scene of strong feeling, some scene or attentional center that is accompanied with strong feelings. The feelings may be good, pleasant, or bad, unpleasant. Then the person is shown how to enter into this scene, to live and be in this scene. Once this scene is alive and real, the work is to discover the exact moment of strong feeling, and through this precise moment the therapist and person can access the deeper, inner potential for experiencing.

The second step is attaining integrative good relationships with the deeper potential, the inner experiencing. Once the inner experiencing is accessed, the second step enables the person to welcome and appreciate it, to have integrative good relationships toward it, to love and accept it, to enjoy and receive the accessed inner experiencing. It is an impressive achievement to have integrative good relationships with what had been deeper inside the person.

The third step is 'being' the deeper potential, the inner experiencing. This step enables the person to undergo a qualitative, radical change out of the ordinary, continuing person and into the qualitatively new person who is the deeper potential or inner experiencing. Being the inner experiencing is to occur within the context of scenes and situations from earlier in the person's life.

The fourth and final step is being the new person in the present. This step enables the person to be the qualitatively new person, in the present and prospective future, and to be free of the scene(s) filled with bad feelings of step 1. The inner experiencing is now an integral part of the new person that the person is, with new ways of behaving, thinking, feeling and being, in a new world. When the session is over: (a) the person is being the new person, including the deeper potential or inner experiencing as a new part of the new person; (b) the new person is ready and committed to being and behaving in some defined way that comes from and provides for the new inner experiencing; and (c) the new person is relatively free of the scene(s) filled with bad feelings that was/were uppermost in and central to step 1.

If it is important for you to enable the person to become a qualitatively new person, based upon the discovered deeper potential or inner experiencing, and if it is important for the person to be free of the scenes filled with bad feelings, then some of the studies suggest that you might adopt the four steps as helpful means of accomplishing these changes. If these changes are not especially compelling, then our studies suggest that most other in-session changes are also likely to occur in packages or sequences.

What are some of the research-generated soft impressions on how to help bring about impressive, in-session changes?

There was a bonus from having a research team of therapy-wise clinicians studying many sessions containing many different kinds of impressive changes. In addition to the hard findings, the judges also had some relatively soft impressions of how these fine therapists did such impressive work. Here are the fruits of our discussions, over many years, on this matter.

Be quite skilled in the operations   The judges were continually impressed by the therapists' consummate skill as they carried out the actual working operations, techniques, methods. These therapists were masters of their craft, exceedingly competent, at a high plateau of working expertise. What seemed clear was that the ordinary level of simply doing the operations or methods was just not enough. There was a qualitative difference between just doing the operation, carrying out the method, and doing it at this much higher plateau of competence, skill and expertise. It became clear that there was a level at which most therapists ordinarily function, and at which impressive changes happened only rarely. But there was also a higher plateau, a master level of skill far above the ordinary level, and it was here that these changes seemed to occur.

Be exquisitely sensitive and finely attuned to the way the patient seems to be at each fluctuating moment   Most therapists are probably somewhat aware of the patient's general state. However, when we examined our master therapists' behavior when in the close vicinity of the impressive changes, it seemed that they gauged what they did, and when they did it, as if they had a keenly tuned sensitivity to what was occurring in their patients from tiny moment to tiny moment. They could refine or modify what they did in accord with the sensitively fluctuating changes in the patient. These therapists seemed careful to know and to make use of the immediate condition of the patient, the way the patient was being right now, and to fine-tune what they did on that basis.

Keep at it; stay with it   These therapists seemed to have a remarkable degree of persistence and perseverance in working toward a particular change, and then in opening up or carrying forward the change that was achieved. At the actual working level of concretely specific activities, they seemed to stay with them, doing them over and over again, perhaps refining and modifying them. They persisted until they got the change they seemed to be working toward. Once the change occurred, these therapists seemed to stay with it, helping it to luxuriate, to stay around, to further develop, to sustain and grow (Mahrer, Howard, Gagnon & MacPhee, 1992; Mahrer, Nadler, Dessaulles, Gervaize & Sterner, 1987; Mahrer, Nadler, Gervaize & Markow, 1986; Mahrer, White, Howard, Gagnon & MacPhee, 1992).

It seemed relatively clear what the therapists were doing, trying to accomplish. Their lesson was that once the change had occurred, the point at which most therapists would stop, they would stay with the change, open it up further, sustain and develop it.

Be programmed toward the working step or substep   It seemed relatively easy for the judges to have an idea of where the therapists were heading. The therapists seemed to be programmed toward this or that direction. The important consideration was how far ahead the therapists seemed to be directed, or headed, or working toward. According to the judges, it seemed relatively clear what the immediate goal was, what the therapists seemed to be trying to accomplish right now, as well as the approximate working direction in which the therapists were going. In other words, these therapists seemed to have some relatively immediate working goal or aim, a direction, a functional substep or step they were working to accomplish or attain.

Use a package of methods to try to attain your goal   The therapists almost universally used a package of methods when trying to achieve some immediate goal. Sometimes the package of methods was used almost simultaneously. Sometimes the therapists first did this and then tried doing that and then attempted some third or fourth thing, all aimed at attaining the same goal or relatively immediate target. It seemed that the therapists had an arsenal of methods to attain their goal.

Rely on, respect, honor and use the patient's readiness, willingness and ability to do what the therapist invites the patient to do   Therapists seemed to elicit, to count on and to honor the patient's readiness and willingness to do what they invited him or her to do. It was impressive how explicitly the therapists seemed to respect the patient's immediate state of readiness and willingness. If the patient were not especially ready or willing, the therapists usually did not seem to push or somehow try to get him or her to go ahead and do it.

The patient's readiness and willingness were especially emphasized when the therapist seemed to be guiding or showing the patient what to do, and even proceeded to accompany the patient in doing it (Mahrer, Nadler, Dessaulles, Gervaize & Sterner, 1987; Mahrer, Nadler, Gervaize & Markow, 1986; Mahrer, White, Souliere, MacPhee & Boulet, 1991). The one exception was when the therapist seemed instead to be applying 'interventions' with regard to the patient.

Once the change is achieved, sustain it, develop it, further it, carry it forward   Once the change occurs, stay with it for a while. Let it be present. Sustain the change. Let it remain. Instead of rushing off to something else, to move on to the next thing, just relish the change. Remain in this state for a while. Enjoy it. These therapists took their time, once the change occurred, and they were thereby able to let the change develop, grow, flourish (Mahrer, Nadler, Dessaulles, Gervaize & Sterner, 1987; Mahrer, Nadler, Gervaize & Markow, 1986; Mahrer, White, Howard, Gagnon & MacPhee, 1992).

In initial sessions, when the patient is in a state of at least moderate feeling, how do you decide whether to get standard intake information or to accommodate to the feeling state?

In experiential psychotherapy and in some other therapies, the initial session is used for straightforward therapeutic work (Mahrer, 1996). The therapist does not try to get standard intake information. Suppose that we exclude these therapies that use the initial session, much like every session, for straightforward therapeutic change. Suppose that we also exclude times, in initial sessions, when the patient is so overcome with powerful feeling that she is sobbing hard, in a state of absolute fury, so drowned in depression that she barely is there with the therapist, or perhaps howling in sheer terror. Instead suppose that the concern is with most therapists, for whom a standard intake session is important, geared to get standard information from a patient who is in a state of moderate feeling. Picture the patient who is crying, or who is somewhat shaking and trembling, or who is rather fearful, or who is in a moderate state of irritation. The therapist has a choice of trying to return to getting standard intake information, or to work with the immediately present feeling state rather than to continue trying to get the intake information. How did our therapists deal with this choice?

When the therapist is seeking standard intake information, and when the patient enters into a state of moderate or stronger feeling, a useful indicator is the apparent extent to which the patient seems inclined to provide the requested information. If the patient seems inclined to do so, these therapists stay with such information gathering, but if the patient is clearly disinclined to do so, then this seems to be used as a sign to abandon the attempt to acquire this information, and instead to switch over to using this session to accommodate to the feeling state (Mahrer, Edwards, Durak & Sterner, 1985).

How can you enable the person to direct most of his or her attention onto something that is especially feeling-laden?

Some therapists, under some conditions, may find it useful for the client to direct most of his or her attention onto something that is fraught with feelings. The therapist may find it especially important for the person to focus most of her attention on the cancer, on that feeling-connected look on her mother's face, on that time she was in the elevator and so scared by what the stranger said, on the recent occasion when she slipped on the ice and broke her leg, on her being at the restaurant when her husband screams at her for not listening to him. The aim is for the person to attend mainly to these focal centers, to live and be in these scenes, to undergo the accompanying feelings. If this is something you want to achieve, what helps you to do so?

One study yielded a number of suggestions (Mahrer, Nadler, Gervaize & Markow, 1986):

1   It helps if you possess the useful skills to enable the person to focus attention on a feeling-laden center, and for you to be quite clear in showing the person how to carry it out. For example, show her how to close her eyes and to look directly at her mother's face. Show her how to say words in the present tense, and to say these words directly to her mother. Once you know these helpful skills, be clear in showing the person what to do and how to do it.

2   Rather than trying to 'get' the person to be in the elevator, invite her to do so if she is willing and ready. Allow her to be truly cooperative and, symmetrically, if the person is not especially willing and ready, or perhaps unwilling, then honor this state and do not try to push. Say, 'Is this all right? Are you ready and willing to do this, or not especially so?'

3   Join with the person in directing all your attention onto the cancer. Do this with feeling and with wholesale involvement. You may do this before the person does, as a kind of modeling. You may join with and accompany the person in directing most of the attention onto the cancer, and doing so with feeling.

For what kinds of in-session goals, aims, purposes and changes is a relatively weak level of feeling useful, and for what kinds is a relatively strong level of feeling called for?

By 'relatively strong level of feeling', I mean that the person is actually undergoing bodily sensations that are at least moderate in strength, that are exceedingly present in or on the body, and that may include tingling, warmth, coldness, heaviness in the legs, tension and butterflies in the stomach, lightness in the head, shakiness and trembling, sexual excitement in the groin. I mean that the person is laughing hard, crying, swearing in anger, moaning or groaning in heartfelt relief, yelling in sheer joy. I mean that the person is mostly caught up in the sheer feeling, giving in to the sheer feeling, whether or not the feeling is loud or quietly saturating.

Are there some kinds of in-session goals, aims, purposes, changes, that seem to call for a relatively strong level of feeling, and are there others that seem to call for a relatively weak level of feeling? If so, what are they (Mahrer, Lawson, Stalikas & Schachter, 1990; Mahrer, Nadler, Dessaulles, Gervaize & Sterner, 1987; Mahrer, Stalikas, Fairweather & Scott, 1989)?

These studies suggested that you may use a relatively weak or even neutral level of feeling when you are seeking to attain a good, helpful therapist–patient relationship, when you are trying to achieve insight and understanding, and when you are seeking to obtain straightforward clinical information, data and material from the patient. On the other hand, it seems that the person should be in a state of relatively strong feelings if you are seeking to obtain goals and changes such as the following: (1) the person is to move from one kind of feeling state into a substantially different kind of feeling state; (2) therapist and patient are to engage in an encounter or confrontation with one another; (3) the person is to enter into, to live and be in a defined scene or situational context; (4) the person is to open up, to be in touch with, to access, to sense and resonate with some inner deeper quality, potential for experiencing or way of being; or (5) the person is to disengage from or let go of being the person that he or she is, and to enter into actually being a qualitatively new and different person.

The suggestion is that the usefulness of the level of feeling strength depends on the kinds of goals, changes, aims and purposes you are working toward accomplishing.

What can you do to help enable the person to move from a relatively weak to a relatively strong level of feeling . . .

If you want to help the person move from a relatively weak level of feeling to a relatively strong level, what methods seem to be useful?

. . . when the person is mainly attending to and engaging with the therapist? Suppose that the person is mainly attending to and engaging with the therapist, and the feeling level is relatively weak. What can the therapist do to enable the person to have relatively strong feeling? A

number of studies have aimed toward answering this question (Mahrer, White, Howard, Gagnon & MacPhee, 1992; Mahrer, White, Howard & Lee, 1991; Mahrer, White, Souliere, MacPhee & Boulet, 1991).

These studies suggest that the following methods are helpful:

1   When the patient is trying to get the therapist to accept that the therapist is the kind of person the patient insists the therapist is, if the therapist wholly accedes and actually enjoys acknowledging that he is that way, the consequence may well be that the patient undergoes strong feeling.
2   The therapist can help bring about strong feelings in the person by deliberately shifting, switching and diverting the person's attention away from whatever he or she is attending to, concerned with, talking about.
3   The therapist may help bring about strong feeling by interpreting how the person is behaving with the therapist, and doing so in a way that is persistent, unwavering, unrelenting, confrontational and challenging.
4   The person may be directed to pay close attention to bodily felt feelings, and then be challenged to show and express these feelings.
5   When the person indicates a readiness to have a given feeling, the therapist can encourage the person to have that feeling, to enact, show, express or 'be' that feeling.

Once the relatively strong feeling occurs, these same methods appear to be effective in maintaining and sustaining it.

. . . when the person is mainly attending to and engaging with a focal center or scene, rather than mainly attending to and engaging with the therapist? In addition to the above studies, a few others help to answer this question (Mahrer, Nadler, Dessaulles, Gervaize & Sterner, 1987; Mahrer, Nadler, Gervaize & Markow, 1986).

These studies suggest that the person can be helped to move from a relatively low level of feeling to a relatively strong level of feeling by using a package of working methods:

1   Show the person how to identify a focal center or scene that is feeling-laden, accompanied with relatively strong feeling.
2   Elicit the person's readiness, willingness and cooperation in more fully attending to and engaging with the identified focal center or scene, in living and being fully in the scene.
3   Both therapist and person are to fully enter into, live and be in, the alive, real, immediate, ongoing scene of strong feeling, preferably with eyes closed.
4   Both therapist and person are to allow themselves to show, have, undergo, strong feelings, directly and completely within the context of the feeling-laden scene.

As a footnote, we are currently completing a study (Mahrer, Fairweather, Passey, Gingras & Boulet, in preparation) that is explicitly designed to find methods that therapists use to help bring about different kinds of strong feeling, and also to find the various ways that therapists use these strong feelings once they are brought about.

How can you help enable the person to access, open up and undergo
a deeper potential, inner way of being or deeper personality quality?

Some therapists understand patients in terms of deeper potentials for experiencing, ways in which the person is capable of experiencing, inner ways of being, deeper personality qualities. For example, these may be described as a potential for experiencing sensitivity, letting oneself be reached, vulnerability; or a deeper capacity for toughness, firmness, strength; or a deeper potential for being warm, accepting, close. These deeper potentials are thought of as further inside the person, not a part of the way the person typically acts, thinks, behaves.

Some therapists seek to show the person how to access these deeper potentials, to be reached by them, to sense them, to discover what they are, to undergo them. How can the therapist help accomplish this? This was the question fueling some studies in which such changes were found (Mahrer, Markow & Gervaize, 1992; Mahrer, Nadler, Dessaulles, Gervaize & Sterner, 1987; Mahrer, White, Howard, Gagnon & MacPhee, 1992). These studies suggested that one way of accessing a deeper potential is by following a series of steps:

1   Find a scene or situation that seems to be accompanied with relatively strong feeling.
2   Both therapist and patient enter into this scene of strong feeling. The aim is actually to be living and being in this scene.
3   The patient is to feel the feeling, to have and undergo the feeling even more fully, more intensely, more powerfully. The consequence is that the person is now in closer touch with what is deeper, the deeper potential for experiencing is now more accessible, what lies inside and deeper in the person is now closer to the surface, able to be sensed, reached, undergone.

A special condition is when the person explodes into hard laughter that is rather sudden and abrupt, strong and saturating. It appears that the person is probably in the momentary grip of a deeper potential that is impulsive, explosive, energetic, and that the person's immediate ongoing reaction to this deeper potential is one of riskiness, wickedness, devilishness, taboo and heightened excitement (Gervaize, Mahrer & Markow, 1985; Mahrer, Markow & Gervaize, 1992; Mahrer, Markow, Gervaize & Boulet, 1987). Under this condition of sudden hard laughter, the deeper potential may be accessed by living and being in a scene in which this immediate inner deeper potential is allowed to occur.

How can you help bring about a welcomed change in the way the
person relates to the therapist or to a part of one's self . . .

Some studies found ways in which therapists were successful in helping to
bring about certain kinds of changes in the ways in which the person
related to the therapist or to parts of one's self.

. . . so that the patient is less critical and negative toward the therapist?
There are times when the patient is directly and straightforwardly attacking
the therapist, critical and highly negative toward him or her. What can the
therapist do to ameliorate this? One answer is that the therapist can achieve
this change by being personally disclosing about his or her own life,
especially with regard to the specific content of the patient's attack,
criticism and negativity toward him or her (Mahrer, Fellers, Durak,
Gervaize & Brown, 1981).

. . . so that the patient is more accepting/welcoming and less bothered/
troubled by this part of one's self? The therapist's aim is to enable the
patient to be more accepting and welcoming toward some personality
aspect, dimension, quality or part that the patient is bothered by, troubled
by, pushes away, is threatened by, seals off, keeps distant. How can this be
accomplished? There are two combined methods that the therapist may use
(Mahrer, White, Howard, Gagnon & MacPhee, 1992; Mahrer, White,
Souliere, MacPhee & Boulet, 1991).

1   The patient is to attend directly and with vivid focused concentration
    to that manifest, alive, real personality aspect, dimension, quality or
    part.
2   The patient is to show all the feelings toward that part, to have feelings
    fully and intensely, in an alive and real interaction with it. The
    direction of change is toward a greater sense of acceptance and
    welcoming of that part.

How can you help promote insight, understanding, a new and better
way of seeing things?

Some studies seem to suggest that a substantive change in the core person is
often followed by a change in the person's perspective on things. The
guideline seems to be that if the person becomes a qualitatively new person,
there is a consequent change in the way this new person sees him- or herself
and the world; s/he has a different insight, a different way of understanding
things, a new and better perspective. In other words, insight and understanding follow a qualitative change in the person, rather than the
traditional clinical axiom that holds that insight and understanding lead to
therapeutic change.

There is another way that we found. When the patient seems to
have nicely pleasant feelings toward the therapist, the effective method

involves forcefully attacking the patient's problematic, problem-supporting, problem-related thoughts, ideas and beliefs. A consequence may include further insight, understanding and a new and better way of seeing things (Mahrer, Nadler, Gervaize & Markow, 1986; Mahrer, Gervaize, Nadler, Sterner & Talitman, 1988).

How can you enable the person's experiencing to be fuller, stronger, more pleasant and accompanied with good feelings?

The in-session condition or state is that the person is undergoing some kind of experiencing, which is mild or perhaps moderate, and the accompanying feelings are unpleasant, neutral or only mildly pleasant. What can the therapist do to help enable this low or mild experiencing to be fuller, stronger and also accompanied with much better feelings? According to one study (Mahrer, White, Souliere, MacPhee & Boulet, 1991), this change can be helped to occur when (1) the person is actually living and being in some scene that is highly appropriate for this particular experiencing; (2) the person actually tries out specific behaviors that come from and provide for this experiencing; and (3) the person refines, alters and modifies both the situational context and the behaviors until the experiencing is strong and full, and the accompanying feelings are wonderful. The key is progressively alternating, trying it out and refining both the behavior and the situational context to achieve the desired goal.

How can you enable the person to get a sense, a taste or sample, of what it can be like to be this new person in the extra-therapy world?

Here in the session, the person may be a qualitatively new person, behaving in whole new ways, free of the hurts and pains. The therapist may want the person to be able to see what it can be like to be and to behave as this new person in the extra-therapy world. How can the person have a sense, a taste, a sample of being and of behaving in this new way? A few studies have offered some answers to this question (Mahrer, Nadler, Dessaulles, Gervaize & Sterner, 1987; Mahrer, Nadler, Gervaize & Markow, 1986; Mahrer, Gervaize, Nadler, Sterner & Talitman, 1988; Mahrer, White, Souliere, MacPhee & Boulet, 1991). Here is a package of methods for achieving this aim:

1   Locate some prospective situational context, scene, imminent time or place in which the person might possibly be and behave as this new person. If the person is hesitant about a particular situational context or this particular behavior, honor this hesitancy and find some more acceptable situational context and behavior.
2   Instead of the overall tone being realistic, emphasize wholesale unreality, being and behaving this new way in sheer playfulness, slapstick, burlesque, silliness, fun, fantasy.

3   Do it right along with the person. Both of you are to join together in being and behaving as this new person in the prospective scene.
4   Once the person is doing it, invite him or her to do it again and again, with stronger and more enjoyable feelings.

What can you do to help ensure that the person is ready, willing, determined and committed to being this new person and carrying out this new behavior in the post-session extra-therapy world?

Typically, a point is reached, well into a session or toward the end of a session, when the question is whether or not the person is actually quite ready, willing, determined and committed to being this new person and carrying out this new behavior in the post-session extra-therapy world. Sometimes the person is eager and exceedingly ready to be and to behave as this new person in this particular scene or situation from tomorrow or in the near future. What can be done if the person is not especially eager, ready or committed? Here are some answers yielded by studies of therapists dealing directly with these issues and with attaining these specific aims (Mahrer, Gagnon, Fairweather, Boulet & Herring, 1994; Mahrer, Nordin & Miller, in press).

1   *Seeing the client as new person.* The therapist literally regards, or can picture, the client as a qualitatively new person who carries out the new post-session behavior.
2   *Client initiation.* The client is mainly the one who initiates what the post-session behavior is to be.
3   *Client readiness and control.* There is a heavy emphasis on the client's immediate readiness and determination to carry out the post-session behavior.
4   *Contingent conditions.* The therapist makes provision of other parts of the treatment program explicitly contingent on the client's agreement to carry out the post-session behaviors.
5   *Concrete specificity.* The post-session behaviors and situational contexts are identified in explicit, concrete specificity.
6   *Behavior–context clarification.* The post-session behavior and situational context are progressively clarified, refined and modified until therapist and client are satisfied.
7   *Negotiation and custom-fitting.* Therapist and client negotiate the number, nature, content and level of difficulty of the post-session behaviors.
8   *Justifying rationales.* The therapist provides justifying reasons, arguments and rationales for how and why the post-session behaviors are important and desirable.
9   *Reluctance-countering rationales.* If the client is reluctant, hesitant, resistant or negative, the therapist uses additional justifying reasons, arguments and rationales for undertaking the post-session behaviors.

10 *Encouragement/pressure.* The therapist encourages, pushes and presses the client to carry out the post-session behaviors.
11 *Acknowledgment of failure.* The therapist candidly acknowledges failure in obtaining client commitment to carrying out the post-session behavior.
12 *Assignment of homework.* The client is simply requested, told or instructed to carry out the post-session behavior as homework.
13 *Clarification and reassignment of homework.* If the client is unclear or not agreeable, clarify the assigned post-session behavior, emphasize commitment and reassign the homework.
14 *In-session try-out, rehearsal and refinement/elaboration.* The therapist has the client try out the post-session behavior in the session, and enables the client to see how it feels to repeat, refine and elaborate it.
15 *Therapist accompaniment.* The therapist joins with the client in trying out and carrying out the prospective post-session behavior in the session.
16 *Contractual agreement/commitment.* The therapist and client arrive at a contractual agreement that the post-session behavior will indeed be carried out.

If you want the person to be quite committed to carrying out the post-session behavior, to indicate that he or she is determined to do it, is quite eager to be this new way, then select from these 16 methods. Do you use just one or two? The answer seems to be to use a package of approximately five methods, perhaps somewhere between three and seven.

Is there a preferred package of methods? It seems that two methods were commonly used, almost regardless of the kind of post-session commitment you seek to attain. One is method 5, in which the therapist is concretely specific in defining the post-session behavior and the situational context, and method 16, in which the therapist and client arrive at a contractual understanding and agreement that the client will carry out the post-session behavior. The studies also suggested that some of the methods (that is, methods 8, 10 and 12) were helpful when the post-session behaviors were for reducing some problem, and other methods (that is, 1, 2, 3, 6, 14 and 15) were favored when the post-session behaviors were to enable whole new ways of being and behaving.

Conclusion

In conclusion, the continuing purpose of my psychotherapy research is to discover the secrets of all kinds of master therapists doing impressive work in their sessions. The purpose is to find out how to help bring about these impressive changes, how to do psychotherapy better and better. This chapter has given you a fair number of invitations on what you might do to help bring about this or that kind of impressive change, some minor and some major. The key consideration is whether or not a particular change is appealing to you. If the answer is yes, then I hope that at least some of these suggestions may be helpful in your own psychotherapeutic work. If they are, or especially if you have sessions of impressive changes, please send me tapes of your sessions.

References

Gervaize, P.A., Mahrer, A.R., & Markow, R. (1985). Therapeutic laughter: What therapists do to promote strong laughter in patients. *Psychotherapy in Private Practice, 3*, 65–74.

Mahrer, A.R. (1985) *Psychotherapeutic change: An alternative approach to meaning and measurement.* New York: Norton.

Mahrer, A.R. (1988a). Discovery-oriented psychotherapy research: Rationale, aims, and methods. *American Psychologist, 43*, 694–702.

Mahrer, A.R. (1988b). Research and clinical applications of 'good moments' in psychotherapy. *Journal of Integrative and Eclectic Psychotherapy, 7*, 81–93.

Mahrer, A.R. (1996). *The complete guide to experiential psychotherapy.* New York: Wiley.

Mahrer, A.R. (in press). Studying distinguished practitioners: A humanistic approach to discovering how to do psychotherapy. *Journal of Humanistic Psychology.*

Mahrer, A.R., Edwards, H.P., Durak, G.M., & Sterner, I. (1985). The psychotherapy patient and the initial session: What to do with the emotional state. *The Psychotherapy Patient, 1*, 39–48.

Mahrer, A.R., Fairweather, D.R., Passey, S., Gingras, N., & Boulet, D.B. (in preparation). *Strong feeling in psychotherapy: Therapist methods of promoting and using strong feelings.*

Mahrer, A.R., Fellers, G.L., Durak, G.M., Gervaize, P.A., & Brown, S.D. (1981). When does the counsellor self-disclose, and what are the in-counselling consequences? *Canadian Counsellor, 15*, 175–179.

Mahrer, A.R., & Gagnon, R. (1991). The care and feeding of a psychotherapy research team. *Journal of Psychiatry and Neuroscience, 16*, 188–192.

Mahrer, A.R., Gagnon, R., Fairweather, D.R., Boulet, D.B., & Herring, C.B. (1994). Client commitment to carry out post-session behaviors. *Journal of Counseling Psychology, 41*, 407–414.

Mahrer, A.R., Gagnon, R., Fairweather, D.R., & Cote, P. (1992). How to determine if a session is a very good one. *Journal of Integrative and Eclectic Psychotherapy, 11*, 8–23.

Mahrer, A.R., Gervaize, P.A., Nadler, W.P., Sterner, I., & Talitman, E.A. (1988). Good moments in rational-emotive therapy: Some unique features of this approach. *Journal of Rational-Emotive and Cognitive-Behavior Therapy, 6*, 146–161.

Mahrer, A.R., Lawson, K.C., Stalikas, A., & Schachter, H. (1990). Relationships between strength of feeling, type of therapy, and occurrence of in-session good moments. *Psychotherapy, 27*, 531–541.

Mahrer, A.R., Markow, R., & Gervaize, P.A. (1992). Promiscuity, psychotherapy, and strong laughter. *The Psychotherapy Patient, 8*, 157–170.

Mahrer, A.R., Markow, R., Gervaize, P.A., & Boulet, D.B. (1987). Strong laughter in psychotherapy: Concomitant patient verbal behavior and implications for therapeutic use. *Voices: The Art and Science of Psychotherapy, 23*, 80–88.

Mahrer, A.R., & Nadler, W.P. (1986). Good moments in psychotherapy: A preliminary review, a list, and some promising research avenues. *Journal of Consulting and Clinical Psychology, 54*, 10–15.

Mahrer, A.R., Nadler, W.P., Dessaulles, A., Gervaize, P.A., & Sterner, I. (1987). Good and very good moments in psychotherapy: Content, distribution, and facilitation. *Psychotherapy, 24*, 7–14.

Mahrer, A.R., Nadler, W.P., Gervaize, P.A., & Markow, R. (1986). Discovering how one therapist obtains some very good moments in psychotherapy. *Voices: The Art and Science of Psychotherapy, 22*, 72–83.

Mahrer, A.R., Nadler, W.P., Stalikas, A., Schachter, H.M., & Sterner, I. (1988). Common and distinctive therapeutic change processes in client-centered, rational-emotive, and experiential psychotherapies. *Psychological Reports, 62,* 972–974.

Mahrer, A.R., Nadler, W.P., Sterner, I., & White, M.V. (1989). Patterns of organization and sequencing of 'good moments' in psychotherapy sessions. *Journal of Integrative and Eclectic Psychotherapy, 8,* 125–139.

Mahrer, A.R., Nifakis, D.J., Abhukara, L., & Sterner, I. (1984). Microstrategies in psychotherapy: The patterning of sequential therapist statements. *Psychotherapy, 21,* 465–472.

Mahrer, A.R., Nordin, S., & Miller, L.M. (in press). If a client has this kind of problem, prescribe that kind of post-session behavior. *Psychotherapy.*

Mahrer, A.R., Paterson, W.E., Theriault, A.T., Roessler, C., & Quenneville, A. (1986). How and why to use a large number of clinically sophisticated judges in psychotherapy research. *Voices: The Art and Science of Psychotherapy, 22,* 57–66.

Mahrer, A.R., Stalikas, A., Fairweather, D.R., & Scott, J.M. (1989). Is there a relationship between client feeling level and categories of 'good moments' in counselling sessions? *Canadian Journal of Counselling, 23,* 219–227.

Mahrer, A.R., Sterner, I., Lawson, K.C., & Dessaulles, A. (1986). Microstrategies: Distinctively patterned sequences of therapist statements. *Psychotherapy, 23,* 50–56.

Mahrer, A.R., White, M.V., Howard, M.T., Gagnon, R., & MacPhee, D.C. (1992). How to bring about some very good moments in psychotherapy sessions. *Psychotherapy Research, 2,* 252–265.

Mahrer, A.R., White, M.V., Howard, M.T., & Lee, A.C. (1991). Practitioner methods for heightening feeling expression and confrontational strength. *Psychotherapy in Private Practice, 9,* 11–25.

Mahrer, A.R., White, M.V., Souliere, M.D., MacPhee, D.C., & Boulet, D.B. (1991). Intensive process analysis of significant in-session client change events and antecedent therapist methods. *Journal of Integrative and Eclectic Psychotherapy, 10,* 38–55.

Index

The following abbreviations have been used in the index:

CBT cognitive-behavioural therapy
CT cognitive therapy
GAD generalized anxiety disorder
PDT psychodynamic therapy
STS systematic treatment selection